Scottish Literacy and the
Scottish Identity

*Cambridge Studies in Population, Economy and
Society in Past Time 4*

Series Editors:

PETER LASLETT, ROGER SCHOFIELD and
E. A. WRIGLEY

*ESRC Cambridge Group for the History of Population and
Social Structure*

and DANIEL SCOTT SMITH

University of Illinois at Chicago

Recent work in social, economic and demographic history has revealed much that was previously obscure about societal stability and change in the past. It has also suggested that crossing the conventional boundaries between these branches of history can be very rewarding.

This series will exemplify the value of interdisciplinary work of this kind, and will include books on topics such as family, kinship and neighbourhood; welfare provision and social control; work and leisure; migration; urban growth; and legal structures and procedures, as well as more familiar matters. It will demonstrate that, for example, anthropology and economics have become as close intellectual neighbours to history as have political philosophy or biography.

Scottish Literacy and the Scottish Identity

Illiteracy, and Society in Scotland and Northern England 1600–1800

R. A. HOUSTON

Lecturer in Modern History
University of St Andrews

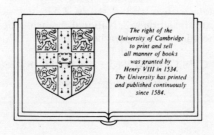

CAMBRIDGE UNIVERSITY PRESS

Cambridge
London   New York   New Rochelle
Melbourne   Sydney

Published by the Press Syndicate of the University of Cambridge
The Pitt Building, Trumpington Street, Cambridge CB2 1RP
32 East 57th Street, New York, NY 10022, USA
10 Stamford Road, Oakleigh, Melbourne 3166, Australia

First published 1985

Printed at The Bath Press, Avon

British Library Cataloguing in Publication Data
Houston, R. A.
Scottish literacy and the Scottish identity:
illiteracy and society in Scotland and Northern
England 1600–1800. – (Cambridge studies in
population, economy and society in past time; 4)
1. Literacy – Great Britain – History – 17th
century. 2. Literacy – Great Britain – History
– 18th century
I. Title
302.2'0941   LC156.G7

Library of Congress Cataloguing in Publication Data
Houston, R. A. (Robert Allan), 1954 –
Scottish literacy and the Scottish identity,
illiteracy and society in Scotland and Northern
England, 1600–1800.
(Cambridge studies in population, economy, and
society in past time; 4)
Bibliography: p. 304
Includes index.
1. Literacy – Scotland – History. 2. Literacy – Cross-
cultural studies. 3. National characteristics,
Scottish. 4. Comparative education. I. Title.
II. Series.
LC156.G72S354 1985   305'.09411   85–7800

ISBN 0 521 26598 3

Contents

Tables

vi

Abbreviations

BM	British Museum
DPDD	Department of Palaeography and Diplomatic, Durham
GRO	General Register Office
NCL	New College Library
NCRO	Northumberland County Record Office
NLS	National Library of Scotland
NSA	*New Statistical Account of Scotland*
OSA	*[Old] Statistical Account of Scotland*
PRO	Public Record Office
SAUL	St Andrews University Library
SRO	Scottish Record Office

For my parents

Preface

I should like to express my thanks to a number of individuals and institutions who have provided advice and facilities. In particular I am grateful to those who read earlier drafts of this book and helped me to think more deeply about its subject: Keith Wrightson, Bob Scribner, Peter Burke, Peter Laslett and Roger Schofield. The doctoral dissertation which provided the foundation for the present volume was supervised in turn by Donald Coleman, Christopher Smout and Tony Wrigley. I have also benefited from conversations with my colleagues at Clare College, Cambridge, where I held a research fellowship between 1981 and 1983, and with staff and students in the Department of Modern History at the University of St Andrews where I lectured in the academic year 1983–4. The facilities provided by the Cambridge Group for the History of Population and Social Structure were invaluable and I should also like to express my thanks to those departments in the Universities of St Andrews and Cambridge which (unwittingly) provided resources for my work. Assistance afforded by the staff of the following record offices is also acknowledged: Scottish Record Office, British Museum, National Library of Scotland, Public Record Office, Department of Palaeography and Diplomatic (Durham University), Northumberland County Record Office and St Andrews University Library.

Dates have been modernized to begin the year on 1 January. In the case of bound volumes of documents, especially in the Scottish Record Office, the use of numbering conventions for the pages is not consistent: some are paginated, some foliated. The reader's attention is drawn to this problem when searching manuscript sources referred to in the footnotes.

R.A.H.

1

The ideal of Scottish literacy

Two decades ago the study of education and literacy suffered from a set of assumptions about social history as a whole. The story of kings and queens, parliaments and churches, diplomacy and warfare were seen as the only important subjects for scholarly work. The lives of the mass of the population in the past were largely obscure. They were a topic to be treated anecdotally as a necessary but fundamentally unimportant backdrop to more academically respectable subjects. Except for the great R. H. Tawney, the Hammonds and some first-rate work by women historians such as Alice Clark and Mildred Campbell, social history was dominated by Trevelyan and by a style of analysis which concentrated on the upper classes, atypical individuals or curiosities. Of the characteristic patterns of everyday life little had been revealed.

One of the most significant historical developments of the 1960s and 1970s has been the breakthrough in our understanding of the lives of ordinary people in the past. We now know much more about the texture of their experiences. We have glimpses of relations between husbands and wives, parents and children; we understand the complexity of kinship relations and the way economic and demographic forces interacted; conflict and co-operation, power and authority in village communities have provided a fascinating focus for research. The mental world and cultural horizons of men and women dead for centuries are no longer a complete mystery.

The analysis of education and literacy offers a paradigm of these developments. In 1965 Peter Laslett affirmed: 'The discovery of how great a proportion of the population could read and write at any point in time is one of the most urgent of the tasks which face the historian of social structure.'[1] We now have a great deal of statistical information on

[1] P. Laslett, *The world we have lost* (1971): 207.

1

who among the population of sixteenth-, seventeenth- and eighteenth-century Europe and colonial North America could sign their names on a document. This period saw the beginnings of a transition from restricted to mass literacy, but many of the structures of literacy remained the same. Men were more literate on average than women, towns had lower illiteracy than rural areas and there were clear differences between different social classes. We know how these structures fit into the framework of society as a whole. There were significant differences between regions of Europe in literacy achievements, and nowhere in the early modern period was the progress of literacy other than hesitant and irregular. People's reading tastes are much clearer than before and the ways in which they used literacy are better understood. Vigorous historical debates exist on the importance of printing, the relationship between spoken and written forms and the importance of schooling to literacy. Indeed debates from the nineteenth and twentieth centuries about who should learn literacy, how and what they should be taught and the likely outcome for individual and society, have all been pushed back into earlier periods.

In Britain the first great national political debates on literacy took place at the beginning of the nineteenth century. In the last years of the eighteenth and early years of the nineteenth centuries, observers of British society were acutely aware that illiteracy was a common and probably undesirable phenomenon. They also recognized that it was far from evenly distributed around the country. By the middle of the nineteenth century, educational surveys and the reports of the Registrars-General had made it clear that much of Lowland Scotland and the northern counties of England enjoyed levels of literacy higher than any comparably sized area elsewhere in the British Isles, and furthermore higher than their state of economic and social development might suggest. The proportion of children of school age who were being educated in the northern counties of England equalled that in Scotland and was actually greater in the case of Westmorland.[2] By contrast, Wales and Monmouthshire, along with the agriculturally precocious southern and eastern counties, were remarkably illiterate.

The same contrast was true of industrial areas. For example, in 1833 a report on Scottish mill workers showed that 96% could read and 53% could write compared with 86% and 43% respectively among a comparable group in England.[3] Materials were at hand for contemporaries to make more wide-ranging comparisons of literacy in the form of signatures of brides and grooms on the marriage register,

[2] J. Sinclair, *Analysis of the statistical account of Scotland* (1826): 79–80.
[3] T. C. Smout, *A history of the Scottish people* (1972): 42–3.

statistical summaries of which were published for each registration district from 1838 in England and 1855 in Scotland. Some 90% of Scottish men and women could sign the marriage registration document in 1870 compared to roughly 80% of English people.[4] Scotland certainly had a slight lead at this time. The distinct regional zoning of illiteracy in mid nineteenth-century Britain can be seen from the proportions of brides and grooms unable to sign their names in full as presented in the reports of the Registrars-General of Scotland, and England and Wales for 1855.

While less marked than in Continental countries such as Germany, France or Italy, this zoning was not a new discovery. Middle- and upper-class observers were however convinced that the deleterious impact of urbanization and industrialization on the 'morals' of the nation was unprecedented and warranted firm action. Industrial areas of the north of England in particular were believed to be peopled by ill-educated, godless and wretched human beings, torn from their closely supervised rural world. These commentators were not slow to draw conclusions from the example of Scotland. In a letter to J. C. Colquhon MP, The Revd Richard Burgess paraphrased the Member's recommendation for a 'free', universal system of popular education to be set up in England on what was supposed to be the Scottish model, since '"its results have been the elevation of the people from the lowest to the highest point of civilization, from disorder to comfort, from barbarous ignorance to intelligence". And all this is a matter of history which cannot be denied.'[5] Education was to be an antidote to the detrimental influence of economic change. It was one element of the fondly held bourgeois belief that mankind could be perfected through institutions. Great faith was placed in the value of education. Observers cast around for examples of proven success in other countries as a justification for change in England and for a model of how that change should be brought about. They did not have far to seek. The tradition of universal and effective education in the rural lowlands of Scotland was the focus of envy and admiration in England, especially among those convinced of the need for state intervention in schooling. Compared to Scotland and the other Protestant countries of Europe, education in England was felt to lag behind, dragging with it 'lower orders ... more ignorant and less

---

[4] *18th annual report of the Registrar-General of births, deaths, and marriages in England [1855]* (1857); *Reports from commissioners vol. 18. First detailed annual report of the Registrar-General of births, deaths, and marriages in Scotland* (1861); E. G. West, 'Resource allocation and growth' (1973): 64–5.
[5] R. Burgess, *A letter addressed to J. C. Colquhon esq., M.P.* (1838): 3.

civilized'.[6] Even Switzerland in the early nineteenth century might have had better educational provision per capita.[7]

Nor was belief in the superiority of Scottish literacy and education confined to the early nineteenth century. As early as the 1700s Daniel Defoe lamented of England 'how full of Ignorance are the dark Villages in our Land of Light?'[8] It was accepted, though not without question, that Scotland had enjoyed a substantially superior progress in education and literacy when compared to England. According to Sir John Sinclair, who wrote at the start of the nineteenth century, 'in former times, the commons of Scotland were considered to be the most enlightened people of that rank in Europe'.[9] However, by the nineteenth century even this performance had been called into question. In the face of the unprecedented social problems created by an increase in population, notably in the towns, and by the spread of industrial employments, it was conventional wisdom that Scottish education and literacy declined from their previously excellent standards. In his 1826 *Analysis of the statistical account of Scotland*, Sinclair allowed that 'Scotland is not now so superior to other countries in regard to extent of education, as is generally supposed. It probably was the case about a century ago.'[10] In the 1830s Scotland seemed to some observers 'a half-educated nation', its valuable educational heritage threatened by lack of proper resources.[11] During the eighteenth century however a state-instituted national education system had apparently produced a palpably better-educated country than England. Education and literacy were also seen as having a wider social dissemination among the Scottish population. How was this to be explained?

One advocate claimed in 1840 that it was the statutory provision of parochial education in Scotland that had produced 'the industry, enterprize, and foresight of our Scottish fellow-subjects, and above all, their household virtues and earnest patriotism . . . in their domestic piety and reverence for the public institutions and ceremonial of religion'.[12] It was assumed that the exhortations of John Knox and the Calvinists at the Reformation had combined with a variety of state legislation to ensure educational provision on a generous scale during the seventeenth century, and to produce by 1700 what one eminent authority has termed 'the most enlightened peasantry in the world'.[13]

---

[6] *Recent measures for the promotion of education in England* (1840): 32; *Substance of the Marquess of Lansdowne's speech* (1839): 11.
[7] Sinclair (1826): 79–86.
[8] D. Defoe, *A Review of the state of the British nation* (1708): 318.
[9] Sinclair (1826): 83.   [10] *Ibid*. 80.
[11] G. Lewis, *Scotland a half-educated nation* (1834).
[12] *Recent measures* (1840): 20.   [13] G. Clark, *The seventeenth century* (1972): 305.

Many aspects of this picture of Scottish education were drawn from the statements of intent set out by the Calvinists in the mid sixteenth century. Their manifesto, the *Book of discipline*, advocated that since

God hath determined that His Church here on earth shall be taught not by angels but by men; and seeing that men are born ignorant of all godliness; and seeing, also, how God ceaseth to illuminate men miraculously . . . it is necessary that your honours [the secular magistrates] be most careful for the virtuous education and godly upbringing of the youth of this realm.[14]

The Protestant aspiration that all should have access to the Word of God for themselves was to be accomplished by a system of universal education – a schoolmaster in every parish backed up by a legally enforceable assessment of the landowners to pay for him which would provide basic literacy for rich and poor alike. The wish for greater educational provision was common to all religious reformers of the sixteenth century, but only in Scotland was the church able to recruit the aid of the state in implementing legislation to realize this aim. Acts of the Scottish Parliament were passed in 1616, 1633, 1646, 1696 and 1803 to implement this aim. This was of course quite different from the English system which, until the late nineteenth century, relied on philanthropic endowment, public charities and private fee-paying schools. Apart from intermittent ecclesiastical exhortations to the parish clergy 'to teach the children . . . to reade and write' there was no English equivalent of the Calvinist church's national campaign backed up by secular authority.[15]

National education systems were only slowly implemented outside Scotland in the eighteenth and nineteenth centuries. Of other European countries, Poland did not have a National Education Commission until 1773 and in England state provision was strictly limited until the 1870s. There were attempts to institutionalize the provision of education throughout Europe at various times in the early modern period, but these enjoyed only limited success.[16] Scotland's early tradition of state legislation on educational provision was seen as the key to her success in literacy, despite the fact that the constant reiteration of acts during the seventeenth century suggests their limited effectiveness. Education was not compulsory in any case even after 1696 –

---

[14] J. Knox, *The history of the Reformation in Scotland* (1905): 382.

[15] *Injunctions and other ecclesiastical proceedings of Richard Barnes, bishop of Durham* (1850): 19; J. Scotland, *The history of Scottish education* (1969); R. O'Day, *Education and society 1500–1800* (1982).

[16] S. Litak, 'The parochial school network in Poland' (1973): 46; R. Chartier, D. Julia and M. Compère, *Education en France du XVIᵉ au XVIIIᵉ siècle* (1976): 27 (hereafter Chartier); M. Roberts, *Gustavus Adolphus* (1953): 437; B. Vogler, 'La politique scolaire entre Rhin et Moselle' (1976): 351–2.

though the kirk often exhorted parents to send their children to school – and in nearly all cases it was certainly not free. Compulsion did not come until 1872, 'free' schooling until 1891. It is well known that the parochial system was supplemented by a large number of private, fee-paying schools similar to those found in many European countries. Still, the belief remained among an important section of opinion that the Scottish 'national' system, where heritors (landowners) were forced to pay most of the cost of education, was bound to be superior to the English 'voluntary' one where local demand and charity were the main means of creating educational provision.

Some of the claims made for the Scottish educational system were far from modest. Sir John Sinclair believed: 'education is so cheap, and the people are so impressed with a sense of its importance, that in almost all the lowland parishes, the younger part of the population, *without a single exception*, are taught to read English, and instructed in the principles of religion'. 'However humble their condition, the peasantry, in the southern districts, can all read, and are generally more or less skilled in writing and arithmetic.'[17] When in the 1740s Tobias Smollett created the character of Roderick Random, he made him a Scotsman, since 'I could at a small expence bestow on him such an education as I thought the dignity of his birth and character required, which could not possibly be obtained in England.' He has Random at one point explaining to a bemused lady how 'it was not to be wondered at if I had a tolerable education, because learning was so cheap in my country, that every peasant was a scholar'.[18] As early as 1708 Daniel Defoe compared the ignorance of much of the English population with their Scottish counterparts who reaped the benefits of statutory provision of schools and teachers in every parish 'by which means the poorest People have their Children taught and instructed'.[19] The Report of the Education Commission (Scotland) of 1868 repeated the claim that the Scottish educational system was 'thoroughly appreciated' by the middle class, and 'sedulously employed . . . both for itself and for the class whose labour it uses; and here is their superiority to the English; and the reason of the success of Scotch skilled labourers and Scotsmen of business everywhere'.[20] In this fashion beliefs about the workings of the Scottish educational system were used as arguments and examples to justify action in other countries.

---

[17] Sinclair (1826): 89, 99.
[18] T. Smollett, *The adventures of Roderick Random* (1748): xxxv, 224.
[19] Defoe (1708): 318.
[20] Quoted in J. Gray, A. F. McPherson and D. Raffe (eds.), *Reconstructions of secondary education* (1983): 41; hereafter Gray.

Defoe's remark points us towards another aspect of the legendary Scottish educational system: the idea that it was unusually accessible to high- and low-born alike. Lord Brougham spoke of his wish that able members of the lower orders should compete directly with their social superiors for jobs.[21] Carried out in the light of a vague moral obligation to recognize ability 'which providence has scattered so profusely and so impartially among every rank of men', this was part of the continued struggle by elements of the Scottish intelligensia 'at least for the ideal that education, consisting at the minimum of reading, writing and arithmetic, ought to be for all'.[22] Scotland might be economically backward, but by striving for this goal it gained moral kudos and intellectual standing. Sir John Sinclair opined that wherever 'teachers are liberally educated, and capable of instructing youth in the important branches of education, persons of the lowest birth rise to rank and eminence'.[23] Of course, as the Kirk Session of Crail in Fife noted during the 1790s, 'the people in general are not able to afford a liberal education'.[24] Without searching too closely for evidence of this aspiration being put into practice, the Scots have developed a sentimental notion of 'lads o' pairts' – poor but gifted boys able to pursue upwards social mobility through education. This notion forms an important part of their national self-image.[25] Education was available to all social classes and could promote social mobility. There were of course the well-publicized examples of lower-class boys like Carlyle who made good through education. This does not mean that there was equality of educational attainments between social classes, but that there were no obstacles to education 'which unfairly discriminated against children of particular backgrounds'.[26] Poor but gifted boys would not be prevented from bettering themselves by the lack of an education.

The belief that the educational system was performing its intended function has meant that no real examination of its actual workings has been undertaken. Historians have in fact adopted two distinct general attitudes to these sorts of nationalist assertion, and 'judgements have swung violently from extremes of praise to equally uncritical condemnation'.[27] A recent and highly influential version of the 'optimistic'

---

[21] C. F. Kaestle, 'Elite attitudes towards mass schooling in early industrial England and America' (1976): 181.
[22] *Moral statistics of the Highlands and Islands of Scotland* (1826): 34; Smout (1972): 442.
[23] Sinclair (1826): 83.
[24] J. M. Beale, 'A history of the burgh and parochial schools of Fife' (1953): 333–4.
[25] Scotland (1969): 68–9.
[26] Gray (1983): 198; R. D. Anderson, *Education and opportunity in Victorian Scotland* (1983): 6–8.
[27] W. Ferguson, *Scotland 1689 to the present* (1968): 198.

approach is Lawrence Stone's classic article of 1969. Stone sees the creation of a system of free, compulsory, state-supported schools as the reason for Scotland's superior mid nineteenth-century literacy, and for what he believes was the 'dramatically different' evolution of literacy in the two countries from the late seventeenth century onwards.[28] Scotland in the mid and late eighteenth century was 'one of the best educated countries in Europe', with education on a far larger scale at all levels and far greater social mobility, the system 'catering for an unusually wide range of social classes'.[29] Many historians have followed Stone's assessment and have thus contributed to the legend of Scottish literacy. For Kenneth Lockridge, New England, Scotland and Sweden 'stood out among the western nations of the early modern era for the rapidity, breadth and peak of their rise in literacy'.[30] Only New England, parts of northern Germany and perhaps Scotland had attained nearly universal male literacy by the end of the eighteenth century. Scotland in this scenario was truly a star performer in the early modern period.

A more cautious assessment is provided by Christopher Smout, who addresses more directly the question of whether the system collapsed in the early nineteenth century as Webb believed, or whether in fact it had never actually attained the standards of comprehensiveness claimed for it.[31] Smout suggests that in the Lowlands the parochial schools and the adventure schools were able to create a rural society in which almost everyone seems to have been able to read and write by the mid eighteenth century. Over the period 1780–1830, however, educational provision deteriorated with the redistribution of population to urban and industrial areas, and along with it levels of literacy fell.[32] In other words, the 'universal literacy' of the Scottish Lowlanders lasted less than a century, though they retained high levels in many areas into the early nineteenth century. However, the superiority of Scotland's literacy in the second half of the seventeenth century and most of the eighteenth is still implicitly accepted. Even recent critical studies of the role of literacy in social and economic development have accepted this general scenario.[33] Only the very latest work is balanced enough to point out that there was a steady build up of legislation over the seventeenth century, but no uniform and regular process of advancement in either education or literacy.

---

[28] L. Stone, 'Literacy and education in England 1640–1900' (1969): 126–9.
[29] *Ibid.* 135.
[30] K. A. Lockridge, 'Literacy in early America 1650–1800' (1981): 188.
[31] Smout (1972): 421–50.   [32] *Ibid.* 427, 442–3, 450.
[33] H. J. Graff, *The literacy myth* (1979): 229.

Indeed, a formidable range of unsubstantiated claims have emerged associated with the explanatory and celebratory myth of Scottish literacy; they are neatly rehearsed by L. J. Saunders in his influential study *Scottish democracy*, published in 1950. It was 'widely admitted that there should be a range of educational opportunity and a right of passage for the 'lad o' pairts' who had no initial advantage beyond his own ability, industry and energy'. Accepting uncritically the idea that anyone however poor could benefit from educational provision, Saunders goes on to portray the 'parish school as an equalizing agency in so far as it was a common school designed for education of children of all classes'. As an end in itself, education

helped to define the worth and duty of the individual in terms that were relatively independent of class and circumstance. The average parish school gave the oncoming generation an early experience of a simplified world in which there were few artificial distinctions; it inculcated some universal standards of self-respect and an appreciation of intellectual and moral effort. The result was to create a community of values that made for an easily recognizable national character and outlook.[34]

The essence of the 'democratic' tradition in education was a stress on equality of opportunity plus the selection of gifted individuals for upwards social mobility through education. Other implications are said to follow. Because the children of all social classes *might* sit together in the schoolroom, it is assumed that class distinctions were diminished, a key feature of Scottish 'democracy'.[35] As we will see below this is no more than an assumption. It has, however, fed into a variety of historiographical traditions, one of which is to be found in the debate on the origins of the Scottish Enlightenment, an unexpected phenomenon in such a backward country. Thus Clive argues that the 'national system of education, though in practice never quite as ideal as in conception, enabled many a poor father's boy to go on to one of the universities as well prepared as his socially superior classmates'.[36] In the burghs of sixteenth- and seventeenth-century Scotland 'sic as are puir shall be furnished upone the comone expenses'.[37]

The argument is that Scotland's unique educational system was a powerful influence in making her society not only different from but better than that of England. Yet even in the southern kingdom one historian speaks with more enthusiasm than judgement of greater social mobility through education in the eighteenth century than in the

---

[34] L. J. Saunders, *Scottish democracy 1815–1840* (1950): 242–3.
[35] Scotland (1969): 80–1.
[36] J. Clive, 'The social background of the Scottish Renaissance' (1970): 225.
[37] Beale (1953): 17.

nineteenth, with 'thousands of craftsmen and farmers sending their sons to Universities . . . the sons of agricultural labourers climbing to the top of the social ladder'.[38] Stories of social mobility through education were common in English Sunday schools at the end of the eighteenth century and can also be found in seventeenth-century chapbooks.[39] These sorts of story also form part of the self-image of the Scots, for to be Scottish is

to set less store by differences of rank in one's behaviour towards, and judgements of, other individuals. To the extent that one does differentiate, it is to do so on the basis of merit; that is, on the basis of the extent to which universal human qualities are realised in a person's behaviour.[40]

Approaches to the history of Scottish education and literacy offer an excellent example of the impact of this ethos on popular as well as academic thinking.

A less tangible but very real legacy was then the special understanding surrounding the educational system. George Lewis lamented the loss of Scotland's identity in his influential 1834 treatise *Scotland a half-educated nation*.

In all but our parochial churches and parochial schools, we have lost our nationality. In these alone we survive as a nation – stand apart from and superior to England. . . . These are the only institutions around which linger Scottish feelings and attachments: in the support, extension and improvement of which may yet be rallied all the patriotism and piety of Scotland.[41]

Views about the distinctive nature and particular importance of Scottish education continue to influence national consciousness and attitudes towards educational change. The Scots persist in seeing the purposes, workings and achievement of their educational world in the light of an historical understanding of past experience which may or may not bear any resemblance to reality.

Scots have, over the centuries, attached a particular importance to the generous public provision of educational opportunity, and they have, on occasion, framed and revised policies and practice in the light of a certain historical understanding of the place of public educational provision in the life of the nation.[42]

Thus 'the present is explained as the realization of an inheritance that is made potent for the future through the public consent it commands'.[43] In the twentieth century accessibility to education is judged by reference to the tradition laid down by John Knox and the Reformers at the

---

[38] N. Hans, *New trends in education in the eighteenth century* (1951): 210.

[39] T. W. Laqueur, *Religion and respectability* (1976c): 193–4. M. Spufford, *Small books and pleasant histories* (1981).

[40] Gray (1983): 39.   [41] Lewis (1834): 75.   [42] Gray (1983): 38.

[43] A. McPherson, 'An angle on the geist' (1983): 219.

time of the Scottish Reformation, to principles associated with the ideal of individual social mobility, and to the expedient motive of general economic prosperity. Scottish literacy is legendary. It has reached the status of a myth, a story which people tell about themselves 'first, to explain the world and, second, to celebrate identity and to express values'.[44] Literacy itself was an emotive topic, but when linked with politics it became still more potent, both as a source for conflict and as a focus of identity.

It is by no means unusual for education and literacy to be at the centre of a political debate: witness the disputes between republicans and conservative churchmen in nineteenth-century France or the arguments about the role of the Lutheran church in education in nineteenth- and twentieth-century Sweden. In Scotland, however, debate has taken the form of axe-grinding rather than objective investigation of the impact of education on literacy. As Geoffrey Elton once pointed out, Scottish historians hold their history very dear but do not study it too closely in case the results of their enquiries interfere too much with their preconceptions.[45] Scottish education and literacy are too often studied as a way of asserting Scotland's special identity and celebrating her particular values rather than as a means of discovering what Scotland's educational history really was.

Because of Scotland's long nationalist tradition, it is easy to promote controversy about literature, society and culture, but difficult to induce constructive debate. There are numerous accounts of schools and educational legislation but few attempts have been made to analyse the image of Scottish literacy in its social context. Scholars have produced a large amount of painstaking research into actual events and influences, but when it comes to explaining the events and fitting them into a theoretical framework historians have too easily resorted to the simplest notions and to apparently commonsense logic or simplistic pseudo-psychology. Indeed, the perceptive reader will not be slow to notice that most of the above remarks about literacy are almost purely conjectural. They are implicitly quantitative but offer almost no information on actual levels of literacy.

Even the most basic statistics on Scottish literacy attainments for any period before the nineteenth century are lacking. Anecdotes and snippets of suggestive information are virtually all that can be found.[46] In 1521 John Major opined that 'the gentry educate their children neither

---

[44] Gray (1983): 39.
[45] B. P. Lenman, 'Reinterpreting Scotland's last two centuries of independence' (1982): 217.
[46] O'Day (1982): 229.

in letters nor in morals', and indeed Grant Simpson estimates only 60% of the Scottish nobility could sign their names in the second half of the fifteenth century. A century later a bond of association dated 1567 showed that only 16 of 216 barons were illiterate.[47] A marked improvement had taken place. In the Highlands on the other hand the position remained bad. The principal men of late sixteenth-century Kintyre could read and write, but the bulk of ordinary tacksmen and smaller chieftans were illiterate.[48] Fifteen of sixteen Inverurie burgesses could not sign a document drawn up in 1600. Of 161 witnesses before Argyll Justiciary Court in the early eighteenth century 41 men and 4 women could sign their names.[49] We do have evidence on schooling and the extent of bookownership or production. These provide useful indirect estimates of literacy, but are much more valuable if seen in the context of actual ability to read and write. The need for quantitative information on the extent of literacy among the men and women of early modern Scotland is clear.

England is better served, but proper figures on the regional distribution of literacy in the late seventeenth and early eighteenth centuries are similarly sparse. David Cressy's survey has nothing to say about this period for the north of England, which he finds emerging from widespread illiteracy in the early seventeenth century.[50] In the late sixteenth and early seventeenth centuries northern England was allegedly still in an 'economically and commercially primitive' condition.[51] The low levels of literacy found there when compared with those elsewhere in England have been explained by the supposedly 'backward and culturally impoverished' nature of the economy and society.[52] Yet by the late eighteenth century the north showed high literacy levels except in industrial areas. What had happened in the intervening century?

Historians require proper quantified information on literacy in Scotland, but there is also a pressing need for systematic comparison between Scotland and England. Too often, by concentrating on Scottish history for itself, writers have effectively considered it by itself, thus contributing to the myth that it is irrelevant to broader structures and trends in European society and economy.[53] On the title page of George Lewis's famous 1834 treatise thrown up by the great educational debate we find the warning: 'measuring ourselves by ourselves we are not

---

[47] Scotland (1969): 38; G. Simpson, *Scottish handwriting 1150–1650* (1973): 10–11, 25.
[48] A. McKerral, *Kintyre in the seventeenth century* (1948): 149.
[49] Scotland (1969): 49; J. Imrie (ed.), *The justiciary records of Argyll and the Isles* (1969): x.
[50] D. Cressy, *Literacy and the social order* (1980).
[51] B. E. Supple, *Commercial crisis and change in England* (1959): 5.
[52] D. Cressy, 'Social status and literacy in north-east England' (1978): 23.
[53] J. G. A. Pocock, 'British history' (1974).

wise'. Alas, this caveat is too often ignored by Scottish historians, especially those who deal with education.

Attitudes to the study of Scottish history have admittedly changed substantially since the publication of Christopher Smout's *History of the Scottish people* in 1969. Even within the last five years significant advances have occurred in the writing of Scottish history, both in the breadth of the comparisons made with other countries and in the methods and concepts of analysis which have been employed.[54] Yet for the period before 1800 many of the developments which have taken place in social and economic history elsewhere in Europe and North America have passed by Scottish history. Quantification, the use of techniques drawn from cognate disciplines such as sociology and anthropology, and concern with the experience of the masses rather than with social elites, have all made comparatively little progress. Topics such as the extent of literacy, local geographical mobility, social stratification, popular religion or the nature of urban development are only beginning to be studied. There are too few examples of the sort of exemplary comparative work done by Larner, Mitchison and Devine, or for that matter the excellent conferences on Scottish and Irish social and economic development.[55]

Instead, Scottish history is often distinguished by a peculiar form of navel contemplation. In the interests of preserving the identity of 'a kingdom, once proud and independent', T. F. Henderson set the example of elucidating national features shown in Sir Walter Scott's beloved ballads: 'the interest of the stories themselves, and the curious picture of manners, which they frequently present, authorize them to claim some respect from the public'.[56] This defensive antiquarianism has dominated the writing of Scottish history, and has fostered the notion that it is interesting only when embellished with romantic or stirring stories. Scottish literature of the eighteenth and nineteenth centuries was designed to preserve an existing national identity rather than positively asserting a new one, as was the case with nineteenth-century America or twentieth-century Russia.[57] Indeed historians of Scotland have themselves fostered the impression that little of

---

[54] For example L. M. Cullen and T. C. Smout (eds.), *Comparative aspects of Scottish and Irish economic and social history* (1977); T. M. Devine and D. Dickson (eds.), *Ireland and Scotland 1600–1850* (1983); R. A. Houston, 'Comparative aspects of society in Scotland and north-east England' (1981); R. A. Dodgshon, *Land and society in early Scotland* (1981); I. H. Adams, *The making of urban Scotland* (1978).

[55] C. Larner, *Enemies of God* (1981); R. Mitchison, 'The making of the old Scottish poor law' (1974); T. M. Devine, 'Social stability and agrarian change' (1978).

[56] T. F. Henderson (ed.), *Sir Walter Scott's minstrelsy* (1902): 161.

[57] D. Craig, *Scottish literature and the Scottish people* (1961): 165.

importance happened there before the late eighteenth century. Writers like Daniel Defoe were prepared to describe Scotland as an ordinary country 'for the Admonition of those People, who think *Scotland* a desert, a wast howling Wilderness, a Place of wild Folks that live in Mountains, live they know not how, and feed upon they know not what, and not at all like other parts of the World'.[58] They were, however, no less inclined to propagate their own particular preconceptions. More commonly, Scotland has been treated as an oddity on the social and geographical periphery of Europe, 'a kind of *terra incognita* ... a half-mythical country where strange things might exist which it was irrational to look for in any place nearer home'.[59] To some extent the same is true of Wales and Ireland, though these countries have distinctive historical developments and historiographical traditions.[60]

Nor is it too much to accuse English historians of similar faults in their approach – the result of excessive concentration on England alone at the expense of proper comparisons with Scotland, Ireland and Continental Europe. Recent work which explicitly addresses itself to this issue has depended for its impact on a reductionist perspective of other societies in an attempt to demonstrate that English society did not experience a transition from feudalism to capitalism in the fifteenth and sixteenth centuries and was indeed unique in its historical experience.[61] Commonly Scotland is considered only when she began to disturb the political stability of her more important southern neighbour.

Perspectives on British history are not merely Anglo-centric, but also show a heavy concentration on the south and east of England. Most if not all work on northern England has focused on the classic period of the Industrial Revolution.[62] Before 1750, the commercial importance of London and the south-east goes some way towards explaining this bias, and by the late eighteenth century the enormous industrial expansion of parts of the north of England makes that area much harder to ignore. For the earlier period, we are still burdened by the legacy of Macaulay's assumption that civilization stopped north of the Trent and that the barbaric north was only saved from its primitive poverty by its exposure to the benign effects of London.[63] Hughes has argued that

---

[58] Defoe (1708): 318.   [59] P. H. Brown, *Early travellers in Scotland* (1891): ix.
[60] L. A. Clarkson, 'The writing of Irish economic and social history since 1968' (1980).
[61] A. Macfarlane, *The origins of English individualism* (1978); A. Macfarlane, *The justice and the mare's ale* (1981).
[62] E. Hughes, *North country life in the eighteenth century* (1952); T. S. Ashton, *The industrial revolution* (1955); E. Gilboy, *Wages in the eighteenth century in England* (1934); P. Deane, *The first industrial revolution* (1965).
[63] Macaulay, *The history of England* (1903): 294 and *passim*.

until the late eighteenth century the north of England had a 'greatly retarded social and political development'.[64] Until the considerable expansion of industrial production – notably coal and textiles – in the eighteenth century, the north is assumed to have had little relevance to English national development, except perhaps as a problem area, interesting only in so far as it shows the survival of economic, social and political forms which had disappeared much earlier from the more developed parts of the country. Drawing on a long tradition of commentators from the sixteenth century onwards, literature of the nineteenth and twentieth centuries portrayed the area north of the Lancashire/Cheshire border or the Trent as a distinct part of England: a region with a long military history and an unusual social structure. The dominant images of the landscape meanwhile were of darkness, drizzle, smoke and wind: for many people these vicarious views formed their first and most enduring picture of the north. Harsh, uninteresting, unprepossessing: the prejudices which underlay this caricatured image were reinforced in the late nineteenth century by pseudo-scientific studies, such as that of Conan Doyle, which purported to show that in the north people had only half the per capita intellect of those in the south.[65] In the absence of any evidence to the contrary, the stereotype established in this literature perpetuated the conventional viewpoint that the north passed from being backward and agricultural to being industrial and culturally substandard. Of course, this literary and historiographical stereotype was not wholly condemnatory. Writers from Defoe to Disraeli stressed the vital, wealth-creating and poor but morally superior nature of the northerners over the luxury-loving and parasitic southerners. However, these comments simply reinforce the stereotype rather than providing an accurate assessment of social realities.

Recent work has begun to show that the stereotype of economic and social backwardness in the north of England is misleading in a number of important respects, especially after the sixteenth century.[66] Detailed analysis of a national sample of probate inventories has suggested that, as Daniel Defoe noticed, the north-west of England had a higher material standard of living, if we judge by the possession of pewter instead of wooden utensils, silverware, beds and bedlinen: probably higher than the southern counties in the late seventeenth and early eighteenth centuries. Alan Macfarlane's important study, *The origins of*

---

[64] Hughes (1952): xviii.
[65] D. C. D. Pocock, 'The novelist's image of the north' (1979).
[66] J. V. Beckett, *Coal and tobacco* (1981); Macfarlane (1981); J. Langton, *Geographical change and industrial revolution* (1979).

English individualism, suggests a much greater identity of experience between areas of England in key respects, such as the extent of social and economic polarization, the way in which kinship structures were relatively unimportant, the size and composition of households.[67] A recent doctoral dissertation has suggested that the Border area was much more peaceful in the sixteenth and seventeenth centuries than is conventionally assumed.[68]

The notion that Scotland and northern England were curious but not very important is matched by the view that for most purposes Scotland and England during the early modern period were discrete entities with thoroughly distinctive institutional and social developments. This is questionable. As one would expect in geographically contiguous regions, there were strong economic ties between northern England and southern Scotland'. Scotsmen were commonly to be found in Cumberland, Westmorland and Yorkshire, thanks to the presence of the cattle-droving routes which passed from the Highlands through south-west Scotland into north-west England before branching out southwards. Many of the notorious Tyneside keelmen came from the Forth basin of eastern Scotland.[69] By the eighteenth century, the grain trade stretched from London all the way to the Northern Isles and was important in the economic integration of diverse regions of Britain. In the 1760s Kendal was sending coarse woollen cloth via Glasgow to the colonies for export, and the manufactories in and around that town were using large quantities of wool from Scotland and county Durham.[70] In the early eighteenth century, developments in the woollen trade fostered a greater economic integration of the southern counties of Scotland with northern England. Eighteenth-century Glasgow had historic connections with Yorkshire and Lancashire in the fine-yarn trade.[71] Bibles printed in Scotland were cheaper than English-produced ones, and were widely sold in eighteenth-century England. As well as people and products, ideas about religion, politics and education trafficked in both directions.[72] Such contacts could of course exist between regions

---

[67] M. Chaytor, 'Household and family in Ryton' (1980). Personal communication from Dr Lorna Weatherill.

[68] C. M. F. Ferguson, 'Law and order on the Anglo-Scottish border' (1981).

[69] A. R. B. Haldane, *The drove roads of Scotland* (1952); J. Fewster, 'The keelmen of Tyneside in the eighteenth century' (1957; 1958).

[70] T. Pennant, *A tour in Scotland 1769* (1774): 259.

[71] C. Gulvin, 'The union and the Scottish woollen industry' (1971): 137; T. M. Devine, 'The English connection' (1983a): 17.

[72] C. J. Hunt and P. C. G. Isaac, 'The regulation of the booktrade in Newcastle upon Tyne' (1977): 169; D. J. Withrington, 'Education and society in the eighteenth century' (1970): 169.

with fundamentally different social, economic and cultural characteristics, but we shall argue that in the case of north England and Lowland Scotland there were considerable social similarities. Many of them are extremely difficult to pin down, but in studying literacy this book represents an attempt to analyse just one comparative aspect of society in Scotland and England.

Our main concerns will be with the extent of reading and writing, with the pathways to literacy and with the practical uses of literacy rather than with creative literature. We shall make only a few references to post-elementary learning. Throughout, literacy is used as a social indicator. The works of Harvey Graff and others have argued that literacy should no longer be treated anecdotally or as a peripheral subject in the traditional manner, which concentrates on analysing literature and arguing from strings of examples in a way 'relatively unconcerned with questions of context, development, change, typicality, or representativeness'.[73] There is less of a tendency now to deal with education largely on its own terms. Literacy can provide important insights into social structures and change, yet cannot be understood properly outside the context of socio-economic inequality, political and institutional forms and ideological assumptions. Interactions between these factors may mean that structural measures such as urban–rural or male–female differentials, may have differing importance at different times. We have also to consider what was taught and what reading, writing and learning actually meant. Education and literacy must be seen in their proper social, economic and political setting. Literacy is part of a whole social system, understanding of which depends on an awareness of context coupled with international comparisons. Only by comparing areas with different economic, institutional and social characteristics can we hold certain factors constant while assessing the significance of others. Literacy, like inheritance or household size and composition, can be seen as one of the 'grids that allow us to distinguish between different cultural zones'.[74]

This book has at the same time a number of implications for analyses of the elements of distinctiveness in Scottish and English society. The social structure of the two countries is assumed to have been quite different in the early modern period, one crucial difference being Scotland's legendary educational system. Comparison of literacy profiles in the two countries may help to question this, and may for example help to expand the horizons of *British* history, too often treated as synonymous with English history. At the same time the importance of

[73] H. J. Graff, 'Literacy in history' (1975): 468.
[74] E. Le Roy Ladurie, 'Family structures and inheritance customs' (1976): 37.

regionalism in Britain can be assessed. We can for example investigate the differences between Highland and Lowland Scotland or those between the north of England and other areas.

To create a firm comparative framework we need to know actual levels of illiteracy among men and women, among different social groups, in town and countryside and the extent of regional variations over time. We have to assess the various factors promoting literacy in Scotland and England, the interaction between oral and literate culture, and the uses of literacy in a variety of situations. A broader comparison between Britain and the rest of Europe is essential if we are to weigh up the importance of certain supposedly unique features, such as religion or schooling, in encouraging literacy. Were Scotland and England like Sweden, Switzerland, France or New England in their literacy regimes and what do the superficial resemblances or divergences mean in the wider social, economic and political context of these different countries? Only when we have made such comparisons will we be in a position properly to assess the claims of contemporaries and historians alike: to see whether Scotland's supposedly superior literacy truly was 'a matter of history'.

There are three specific notions to which we must address ourselves, two relating to Scotland, but one with rather wider implications. First, Scotland is said to have possessed palpably better educational facilities than England in the past. The latter are alleged to have produced a highly literate society at an early date and furthermore one in which access to education was remarkably open irrespective of social origins. Second, literacy is thought to have been higher than in England and this contributed to the relatively harmonious and open nature of Scottish society. Third, education and literacy are considered to have been key factors in civilizing and improving both individual and society by opening up new horizons of thought and wider opportunities for social mobility. Sir John Sinclair celebrated what he saw as the achievement:

the great body of the people in the more southern part of Scotland, having very generally obtained the blessings of education, the art of reading and writing, and a knowledge of the elements of arithmetic, in those districts, have been placed within the reach of almost every individual; while persons of all ranks, being taught to read the Bible from their earliest years, and being instructed in the catechisms . . . have received the rudiments of a religious education, such as they could not have had the same means of obtaining, in almost any other country.[75]

[75] Sinclair (1826): 79.

A neat summary of the alleged benefits perceived by the apologists for Scottish education is provided by Smout – the

opportunity for everyone who had talent to make his way in the world however humble his origin, a relative absence of social tension due to the easy mixing of children of all classes in schools, and a literate and intelligent working class better equipped both to work productively and to refute the disturbing arguments of the radicals.[76]

All well and good, but we need to compare the intended and perceived benefits of literacy with its actual function in society.

In the next two chapters we shall analyse the comparative levels of literacy in areas of northern Britain. We can then offer some explanations of the similarities and divergences, and can assess the importance and meaning of literacy in Scottish and English society. We need to ask whether Scotland's history of education and literacy gave her a special identity compared to England or other parts of Europe. We conclude by considering some of the implications of a specifically comparative approach to the history of European societies.

[76] Smout (1972): 423.

2

Structures and trends in illiteracy in the seventeenth and eighteenth centuries

Social dimensions of illiteracy

There are many ways of understanding literacy and there are a variety of ways of measuring it. Traditionally the most common mode of analysis is through a study of the provision of education or the production, ownership and borrowing of books. Unfortunately these tell us little directly about the literate skills of early modern people. They are very much indirect indicators from which we must infer abilities to read and write. The results they produce are necessarily vague about the distribution of literacy in any given population. This is not to say that such measures are without value, for they have advantages when it comes to considering aspects of literacy not directly dealt with by the best available criterion, which is the ability to sign one's name in full on a document. Those who can sign their full name on a document are deemed literate, while people who could only sign their initials or a mark are counted as illiterate. The merits of this measure compared to the indirect ones already mentioned are discussed more fully in chapter 5. It is sufficient to say for the present that the great advantage of signing ability is that it is a universal, standard and direct gauge of literacy. Found in most countries of Europe from the sixteenth and seventeenth centuries onwards, documents which bear signatures or marks allow us to compare literacy in different regions, among different types of people and over time. Generally available, these signatures or marks offer a standard medium for comparison and above all one which involves no problems of inference. Manual skill is being measured directly.

Signatures and marks are found on all sorts of documents in the early modern period. Not all are suitable for our purposes. The best

20

type of document is one in which a representative cross-section of the population is covered or where we have enough information about the individuals who are included to control for any bias in the way they were selected. For this purpose subscribed marriage registers are ideal, since most people married at some stage in their lives (usually in their twenties or thirties for the first time at least). Unfortunately, signed or marked marriage registers only survive in England from the 1750s and do not appear in Scotland until a century later. Another reliable source is the depositions recorded in civil and criminal courts. Deponents were drawn largely at random from the population as a whole, and the short statement of biographical information which commonly precedes a testimony means we can divide the population into social groups, town- and country-dwellers and even age groups in some cases. This allows us to control for any biases and to assess the importance of social and cultural factors on literacy. The deposition was usually concluded by a signature or mark. The problems in selecting a source and in interpreting the statistical results which we can derive from it are discussed more fully in an appendix. The analyses presented in this chapter are based on depositions at the English Northern Circuit assize court and the Scottish High Court of Justiciary for the period from the mid seventeenth century until the beginning of the last quarter of the eighteenth century.[1]

The extent of illiteracy in Scotland and England before the nineteenth century has been largely a matter of conjecture until now. It has been assumed, however, that from the later seventeenth century at the latest, levels of illiteracy in Scotland were low compared to England and much of the rest of Europe.[2] Equipped with a set of reliable sources from which to derive our universal, standard and direct measure of literacy, we are now in a much stronger position to offer firm statistical information on Scotland instead of simply anecdotes and impressions or extrapolation from educational legislation. Using court depositions it is possible to assess levels of literacy among males and females, among the various social classes of Scotland, in towns and in the countryside. We can go further by comparing both structures and trends in Scotland with those found elsewhere in England, Europe and North America in the period 1600–1800.

When we make these comparisons, it appears that the levels and the profile of illiteracy in Lowland Scotland are extremely close to those for northern England, and that the evolution of Scotland's literacy was not

---

[1] PRO ASSI45; SRO JC6/1–14; SRO JC7/1–30; SRO JC10/2–6, 8; SRO JC11/1–33; SRO JC12/1–22; SRO JC13/1–22; see appendix 1.
[2] Stone (1969).

dramatically different from that of a number of other European countries. Scotland's achievements in literacy were among the best in
Europe, but they were not unique, and in many ways the spread of
illiteracy among her population was unremarkable. The distribution of
signing ability among Scotland's population turns out to have been
much less distinctive than that of New England, where by the end of
the eighteenth century almost all men could sign, or contemporary
Sweden, which had achieved mass reading ability among both sexes.
At the same time there were differences between Scotland and
England, but they are nothing like as pronounced as one might believe
from some of the older literature on this subject. The achievements of
Scottish society with its state educational system were rather less exalted than we might expect. Literacy over Lowland Scotland as a whole
was not particularly high compared to northern England. Attainments
were firmly related to factors such as social class, economic need and
the sort of environment in which people lived and worked. Indeed
they tended to mirror the existing divisions in early modern Scottish
society just as they did throughout Europe in the pre-industrial period.
The image of Scottish literacy in the past which forms so strong a
component of the twentieth-century perceptions of Scotland seems to
be rather different from the reality which we can measure.

If we are to show that literacy was related to social position in seven-
teenth- and eighteenth-century Scotland, we need to have some idea
about the social and occupational composition of Scotland's population. The outlines of English social structure are already known.[3] There
was a clear if fluid hierarchy of wealth, status and power headed by the
gentry and aristocracy. These, the political and social elites, were the
unchallenged leaders of society and the only true class in pre-industrial
Britain. Below them came the yeomanry, an economically diverse
group who formed the 'stout midriff' of English society. The lower
echelons of the rural world were made up of husbandmen (small
farmers) and finally by cottagers and landless labourers. This is of
course a rural hierarchy and indeed the large majority of the population lived in the countryside and were closely involved in agriculture.
Those in the secondary and tertiary sectors, craftsmen and tradesmen
plus professionals, fit alongside this ranking. Professional men were
the wealthy and highly qualified 'pseudo-gentry', most of whom lived
in the towns. Those in the secondary sector ranged from humble village
craftsmen and shopkeepers to wealthy merchants or goldsmiths in the
larger cities. Contemporaries saw the social order in this way and their

---

[3] Laslett (1971); K. Wrightson, *English society 1580–1680* (1982).

comments fit in neatly with the distribution of wealth, status and power identified by historians.

Work on Scotland is much less developed, and the sort of detailed contemporary comments by figures such as Gregory King and Sir Thomas Wilson, which have served as guidelines for historians of the early modern period in England, are absent. Some general outlines are however available. Bishop Leslie described the three estates of Scotland as churchmen, nobility and burgesses.[4] One early seventeenth-century Kirk Session meanwhile spoke of 'the maisteris, frie holdaris, fewaris, propriators and servitors of the ground'.[5] Descriptions of Scottish society have tended to concentrate on legally defined relations or have referred to various forms of ownership or occupation of the land.[6] In England the importance of legal distinctions such as those between copyholders, leaseholders and freeholders is recognized by historians to have been less important for understanding the social order than was once thought. We are not yet certain if the same is true of Scotland. Town-dwellers are treated as anomalous because they do not fit into the 'feudal' categories in such classifications. However we can offer some rudimentary ideas about the distribution of wealth and status between different occupational groups, and also some indication of the variations within groups. Armed with this information we can see whether the distribution of literacy followed the social order, as in much of Europe, or cut across it, as in Sweden or New England. Our discussion will centre on wealth and occupations rather than on legal or tenurial status.

We start at the lowest point in the social scale – dependent persons such as servants. To a twentieth-century observer, a servant would mean a domestic. However, most English servants of the early modern period were probably servants in husbandry, 'hired not to maintain a style of life, but a style of work, the household economy'.[7] Yet the employer might use a servant for a variety of purposes. The better-off lairds and gentry would employ domestics, footmen, gardeners, agricultural workers, brewers and wetnurses; some of these employees might be craftsmen, such as smiths or wrights, or even semi-professionals such as clerks and estate agents.[8] Thus Scottish baillies who presided over the baron court in the absence of

---

[4] P. H. Brown, *Scotland before 1700* (1893): 173–83.
[5] SRO CH2/471/1: fol. 1.
[6] I. D. Whyte and K. A. Whyte, 'Some aspects of rural society in Scotland' (1983); B. P. Lenman, *An economic history of modern Scotland 1660–1976* (1977a): 30–3; Adams (1978): 58–9.
[7] A. Kussmaul, *Servants in husbandry* (1981): 4.
[8] NCRO 2DE; SRO GD18/737 fols. 55–60; SRO CC8/8/14: fols. 299–304.

landowners have been classed as professionals, but could also appear
in the sources as 'servant', especially when described by their
employer. The upper classes employed the widest range of servants,
including this type of professional person who might enjoy a status
close to that of their employer, who would be drawn from less localized
origins and who would have wider social and geographical horizons
than most ordinary servants. There are examples where servants
themselves employed servants.[9]

It is clear that the term servant could be used to cover a wide range of
people who were essentially employees – anyone in a dependent position in fact. Alexander Braidfoot was described in a Justiciary Court
deposition as the 'tenant or servant' of Patrick Howstoun of Drumas-
toun. George Barclay was 'sub-tenant, servant to John Scott, tenant in
Craiglockhart'. A servant could be a·book-keeper; Mathew Finlayson
was 'writer and one of the servants to the African Companie'. William
Megat described himself as 'servant and journeyman' to a Potterraw
shoemaker in his first deposition, 'cordiner' in his second. The 'servants' at Bells Mill, Edinburgh, who deponed before the Justiciary
Court about a riot there in 1740 were probably factory workers.[10] The
range of occupations and social status was considerable. Persons describing themselves as 'servant' rarely made wills, but the wide range
of wealth revealed in the inventories of those who did is a further
indication of the potentially misleading nature of the term. James
Simpson servant in Dalkeith had no goods or gear but £262 Scots
owing to him, mainly money which he had lent out and outstanding
debts owing to him for livestock. For others, like Agnes Thompson,
her only moveable asset was the cloth she had helped to make while
she had been in service.[11]

Service was specific to certain stages of the life cycle and in some
parts of Scotland, such as the north-east, servants were 'part of the
class of small-holders, occupying subordinate positions in the rural
order but generally with eventual access to small scraps of land'.[12] Yet
for others this subordinate status could become permanent, especially
after they were married. Andrew Corsbie, under the censure of Lasswade Kirk Session at Whitsunday 1661 for fornication, petitioned to
be allowed to marry before he had completed his penance, since 'he

---

[9] SRO E70/8/1: 51, 57.
[10] In order, SRO JC6/12: 12 November 1688; Houston (1981): 182–3; SRO CC8/4/380:
   Leach v. kin of Menzies; SRO JC6/14: 22 April 1701; SRO CC8/4/380: Salter v.
   debitors; SRO JC7/23.
[11] SRO CC8/8/48: (1614); SRO CC8/10/15a: (1651).
[12] M. Gray, 'North-east agriculture and the labour force' (1976): 90.

could not be in service without marriage'.[13] Lifelong service became a structural feature of society in areas such as Berwickshire from at least the early eighteenth century. In the western Lowlands and the north-east, however, those who worked as servants and labourers in their teens and twenties might continue to aspire to holding a plot of land of their own later in life. In north-east England and south-east Scotland there was a form of married servant called a 'hind' who lived in tied cottages, working for keep and a small cash wage plus perquisites, such as the right to keep limited amounts of livestock.[14]

South of the Border both husbandmen and labourers might style themselves 'hired servant'. In England by the mid eighteenth century a working justice of the peace stated that the term 'servant' was never used of those hired for less than one year: these were labourers.[15] In earlier periods the usage is more ambiguous, but by the nineteenth century the term 'labourer' replaces 'servant' as an indicator of wage labour. There are however also ambiguities about the use of the term to describe employees or subordinates. Robert Helme of Tynemouth in Northumberland described himself as a servant to the Earl of Northumberland, but the context of the deposition he made to Star Chamber makes it clear that (at the age of sixty-four) he was a bailiff with the responsible job of collecting tithes.[16] In 1607 Ralph Delaval of Seaton Delaval in the same county sent some 'servants' to recover distrained cattle. Other evidence shows that some of these were substantial tenants on the Delaval demesne.

Nevertheless, life-time wage labour was relatively less important in Scotland compared to England. Most families had at least some land, and few were wholly dependent on piece work or day labour.[17] Comparatively few people are described as labourer or workman in any Scottish source, and 'labourer of the land' often means a farmer in sixteenth- and seventeenth-century documents: closer in meaning to the French 'laboureur' or farmer. In an urban context the usage may however be nearer to that in England. Between 1500 and 1800 there was a marked increase in the proportion of the English working population who depended largely or completely on wage labour for subsistence. This was true of both agriculture and of industry, especially in the south and east, but also in parts of Yorkshire.[18] In areas of

[13] SRO CH2/471/3.
[14] W. S. Gilly, *The peasantry of the Border* (1842); Kussmaul (1981): 7; M. E. Goldie, 'The standard of living of the Scottish farm labourer' (1970): 9–10.
[15] PRO ASSI45: 24/3/32; PRO ASSI45: 25/4/53; Kussmaul (1981): 6.
[16] NCRO 1DE/18, 19, 113.   [17] Whyte and Whyte (1983): 37–8.
[18] Devine (1978); Wrightson (1982); P. Hudson 'Proto-industrialization' (1981): 44.

Yorkshire or the north-west where partible inheritance fragmented holdings to the extent where plots were too small for subsistence, participation in manufacturing was encouraged.[19] The 'really poor', labourers with no livestock, were nevertheless fewer in the north: 13–30% of all 'labourers' (if we follow Everitt's classification), compared to 22–39% in the eastern counties and 38–47% in the Midlands. In the pastoral north-west, reduced population pressure and better non-agricultural employment opportunities created more advantageous conditions for the poorer farmers and labourers during the second half of the seventeenth century.[20] In the Pennines and the East Riding of Yorkshire hemp and flax were grown on labourers' plots along with peas and corn. 'In the Pennine fells and the lowland areas of the far north, cottage farmers were relatively few and never well-off, but not often totally indigent, and the labouring community was relatively equalitarian in its social structure', compared to the Midland and eastern counties where there were more and more poor labourers.[21] The position of the poorer members of society would have been better in the north. In the early seventeenth century the north of England had the highest percentage of cattle per labourer in any area outside the Midland forest area, but average inventoried wealth in the period 1610–40 was easily the lowest in England.

Grouped along with labourers in the tables below are coalworkers, among whom there also existed a range of skills, workplaces and remunerations. The commonest designations in England are collier and pitman, in Scotland collier and coalhewer, but mine records outline a wide variety of actual tasks among specialist workers such as sinkers or miners. The group of literate Cumberland miners who deponed in an assize case of 1751 were probably more independent and used different productive techniques than those labouring in the pits of south Lancashire or the Northumberland and Durham coalfields.[22] In Scotland at least, coalworkers were well paid but also proverbially illiterate and troublesome.

The small farmers with by-employments designated 'labourers' by Everitt were the rough equivalent of Scottish cottars or sub-tenants. These shadowy figures rarely surface in early modern Scottish records though they were probably extremely numerous in some

---

[19] Hudson (1981): 42; A. Appleby, *Famine in Tudor and Stuart England* (1978); C. M. L. Bouch and G. P. Jones, *A short economic and social history of the Lake counties* (1961): 240, 244–5.

[20] A. Everitt, 'Farm labourers' (1967): 413–28.   [21] *Ibid.* 420.

[22] Langton (1979); T. S. Ashton and J. Sykes, *The coal industry of the eighteenth century* (1964); PRO ASSI45: 24/3/37.

areas.[23] There were only thirty men described as 'cottar' in the Justiciary Court depositions and at 80% illiterate they were worse off than labourers or servants. The social and economic status of sub-tenants varied over Scotland. In the north-east and Perthshire they could be substantial landholders, while in the south they more characteristically had small plots of land rented for cash and the specified labour services of themselves and their families. In the southern Lowlands 'as town size became larger, the number of genuine sub-tenants diminishes but the number of cottars and cottagers increases'.[24] Subtenant was not a total state and temporary employment could be had in dyking and ditching, for example, while there were also a variety of non-agricultural employments. In the Lowlands at least many cottars had craft and trade occupations and poll tax records describe such people as 'cottar-tailor' or 'cottar-weaver' for instance. To be a cottar without a trade was felt so unusual by the tax assessors as to merit special comment.[25] For those with more marginal agricultural holdings some form of by-employment was essential.

The difference between cottars and small tenant farmers could be slight in terms of wealth, especially in the north-east Lowlands of Scotland. Even in the southern Lowlands, William Scot, tenant in Heriot town, had a valued rent so small that he was worth more as a cottar paying the minimum poll tax of 6s Scots.[26] Indeed before the eighteenth century agricultural changes there were usually opportunities for a servant or cottar to aspire to the position of tenant farmer in his own right. In parts of the western Lowlands and the north-east this continued to be true into the mid nineteenth century.[27] Certainly, tenants with a sure claim to a piece of land probably enjoyed higher status than the often itinerant and lowly cottars. And on average, tenants as a group were clearly superior to cottars and sub-tenants in their wealth as well as their social standing. Tenant farmers were the backbone of rural society in early modern Scotland, but variations in their holding size and prosperity were marked.[28] Renfrewshire at the end of the seventeenth century was a county where smallholdings rented for £20–40 Scots a year predominated.[29] In the barony of Lasswade in the late seventeenth century rents varied from £5 Scots to

[23] I. D. Whyte, *Agriculture and society in seventeenth century Scotland* (1979a): 38–9; SRO GD18/1200.
[24] Dodgshon (1981): 214. [25] SRO E70/13/5; E70/13/7; E70/8/8.
[26] SRO E70/8/1: 91. [27] Dodgshon (1981): 213.
[28] F. J. Shaw, *The northern and western islands of Scotland* (1981): 48.
[29] Whyte and Whyte (1983): 35.

£480, not including payments in kind which were roughly propor-
tional in value to those in cash.[30] On such commercialized estates, this
one owned by the Clerks of Penicuik, differences in housing show the
increasingly distinct stratification of rural society which went with the
polarization of wealth.[31]

The increased size and decreased number of farms which diminished the number of cottars and sub-tenants and swelled the ranks of
the landless population during the eighteenth century would tend to
create 'a new upper class among the tenants'.[32] There was a shift in the
overall balance of landholding to single tenants during the eighteenth
century, but the fall in tenant numbers in the Lowlands during the
seventeenth century shows an earlier adjustment to market pressures
than is often assumed.[33] Unfortunately there is no way of assessing the
socio-economic position of members of this group from the designations given in the court depositions. Almost anyone could be involved
in renting land, especially in areas around towns. Of 119 men recorded
in documents in St Andrews University Library who leased land in
areas of Fife and Perthshire between 1660 and 1750, forty-one were
described as tenants, nine as landlabourers, four as gardeners. However thirty-eight or nearly one-third were craftsmen, tradesmen or
professional men among whom maltmen were the largest single
occupational group with twelve representatives. Many of the latter
group lived in the town of St Andrews and rented plots ranging in size
from one acre to sizable farms in the countryside around the royal
burgh. Even lairds might rent land on their own behalf. One prominent landowner, Hay of Leys, himself took a tack or rental of land in
Perthshire belonging to a minister called Patrick Johnstone.[34]

At any one time tenant farmers were probably the largest single class
in Scottish society. However, surprisingly few appear who are described as such in the High Court minute books. We can speculate that
in this largely agricultural society farming occupations were so
common that either the fact that someone was a tenant was simply not
stated or that any other designation was used to identify individuals.
Thus a farmer who worked part time as a weaver or blacksmith might
give that as his occupation. The notion of a 'default' designation helps
to explain the implausibly small number of tenant deponents and
possibly also some of the many deponents for whom we have no
indication of occupation or social status. In the parish of Lasswade in
Midlothian between the mid seventeenth and mid eighteenth cen-

[30] SRO GD18/721.   [31] Whyte (1979a): 168.   [32] *Ibid*. 145.
[33] Dodgshon (1981): 207–8, 216–17.   [34] SAUL Hay of Leys MS 881.

turies it was usually only substantial tenants paying more than £100
Scots a year in money rent who are described as tenant or farmer in
other sources, such as the Kirk Session register, estate papers or court
records. Occupations are not recorded for seven out of the fifty Lasswade fathers who apprenticed their sons to Edinburgh companies
between 1583 and 1755. All turn out to have been tenant farmers when
they appear in other records.[35] In the Fife and Perthshire tacks which
we have just mentioned, 23% of all men who rented land had no
occupation or status given on the lease. Before the second half of the
eighteenth century tenant farmers are heavily under-represented
among matriculands at Glasgow University, probably because farming
was regarded more as a way of life than as an occupation.[36] Proportions
of farmers' sons increased from 5% to 25% between the 1760s and
1830s. It seems likely that those whom we are picking up in depositions
as tenants in fact formed the elite among the farming population: the
equivalent of English yeomen in the hierarchy of wealth and status.

One type of tenant whose position we can assess more accurately is
the gardener. Some men who were thus described were only hired
servants, but the term was more usually applied to those who were
involved in intense cultivation of small plots of fruit and vegetables in
areas close to the larger towns.[37] Adam Smith felt that 'a gardener who
cultivates his own garden with his own hands, unites in his person the
three different characters of landlord, farmer, and labourer'.[38] Access
to an urban environment and close involvement in markets, plus their
appreciable prosperity, explains why, despite their smallholding sizes,
these men were more literate than tenant farmers as a whole: 18%
illiteracy among the 34 gardeners compared to 34% among the 198
tenants.

In England the nature of the social hierarchy in the agricultural
sector is clearer, with the broad categories of yeoman, husbandman
and labourer forming a powerful analytical classification despite the
sometimes substantial wealth variations within the groups.[39] This
tripartite classification is of less value in some parts of the north of
England, since the term yeoman seems to have been used promis-
cuously of all sorts of men. The legal definition of a yeoman was a 40s

---

[35] Houston (1981): 47, 431.
[36] W. M. Mathew, 'The origins and occupations of Glasgow students' (1966): 78.
[37] G. Robertson, *General view of the agriculture of Midlothian* (1793): 21; SRO GD18/740:
fols. 40, 124.
[38] A. Smith, *The wealth of nations* (1977): 156.
[39] M. Spufford, *Contrasting communities* (1974): 37–9, 72.

freeholder, those with 'estates of inheritance' according to some
authorities.[40] Used more to describe general social standing rather than
as an indicator of exact socio-economic status, the term carries
overtones of independence and respectability. The Northumberland
justices licensed Robert Key and Edward Watson of Shotton to buy
grain, 'yeomen ... being married men and not servantes to any
man'.[41] Throughout the seventeenth century and much of the
eighteenth, the term 'yeoman' is used in all sources relating to Northumberland and Durham as a blanket term, and the designation 'husbandman' is employed very rarely except in assize depositions. In the
records of Durham Consistory Court, for example, there is an abrupt
shift in terminology during the 1590s from 'husbandman' as the most
common appellation to 'yeoman', and this fashion continues into the
second half of the eighteenth century. Conceivably the society of
northern England was so equalitarian in terms of wealth and status
that all could enjoy the same designation. This seems unlikely. Rather
than reflecting social reality the predominance of yeomen in the assize
sample may simply be a taxonomic artifact. A similar shift in fashions
of description seems to have taken place in southern England over the
seventeenth and eighteenth centuries. The term 'yeoman' came increasingly to be applied to the humbler type of farmer, who would
have been called 'husbandman' in the early seventeenth century.

One important difference between England and Scotland in the early
modern period is that most of the land in Scotland was owned by a
handful of proprietors: the nobility and the lairds. Small proprietors
may have been more numerous in the sixteenth century than during
the period of this study, but except in the western Lowlands and parts
of Fife there was no class of numerous small owner–occupiers as we
find in contemporary England.[42] In Scotland the most basic social
division was between those who owned the land and the bulk of the
population who only occupied it. Adam Smith put it quite simply: 'the
station of farmer' was 'inferior to that of proprietor'.[43] Those who had a
heritable interest in land were described as being 'of' a place, while
those who simply rented find themselves 'in' that place.

To all intents and purposes the gentry of Scotland are completely
literate, but again this category covers a range of wealth – £4 to
£2000 in moveable goods among sixteenth-century inventories of one
sort of proprietor, the feuer. A feu was a perpetual lease of land in

[40] Bouch and Jones (1961): 95.   [41] NCRO ZAN M15C19.
[42] Adams (1978): 58; Whyte (1979a): 29.   [43] Smith (1977): 494.

exchange for a fixed annual rent.[44] Social status also varied considerably from the 'bonnet-lairds', who might be poorer than a substantial tenant farmer, to the mighty barons who owned hundreds of thousands of acres. At Lochwinnoch in Renfrewshire the average rent paid by small feuers was £33 Scots compared to £26 Scots for tenant farmers.[45] Highland 'tacksmen' are an intermediate group, as are 'portioners' or heirs to sections of a heritable property. These are rather vaguely described as 'a kind of landed middle-class' by one authority.[46] All could hide under the addition 'of'. There are variations in wealth and status within this group, but on average lairds stand clear of tenant farmers.

Similar variations in socio-economic status may explain the illiteracy of sections of the gentry in the north-east of England at the end of the sixteenth century better than the blanket attribution of a backward economy and society to the area.[47] Henry Misson noted 'the abuse of every man's calling himself gentleman in England' at the end of the seventeenth century.[48] Lastly, professional men, defined in broad terms here as those who made their living wholly or mainly through reading and writing, men who could also own land and might be described in depositions by their landholding or their occupation. In England as in Scotland, professionals could style themselves gentlemen: Michael Talbot, 'practitioner of phisick, gent', for example.[49] According to Guy Miege in his *New state of England*:

Gentlemen are properly such as are descended of a good family bearing a coat of arms ... On the other side, anyone that without a coat of arms, has either a liberal or genteel education, that looks gentleman like (whether he be so or not) and has the wherewithal to live freely, is by the courtesy of England usually called a gentleman.[50]

The new professional classes were what Everitt calls 'pseudo-gentry'. Again, their total literacy limits such problems of comparison and the identification of precise socio-economic status in this analysis.

Finally, we turn to the largest and most heterogeneous group in our criminal court samples, craftsmen and tradesmen. By far the biggest

---

[44] M. H. B. Sanderson, *Scottish rural society in the sixteenth century* (1982): 142; Dodgshon (1981): 101.
[45] Whyte and Whyte (1983): 35; Larner (1981): 44; Sanderson (1982): 135–50; Shaw (1981): 191.
[46] J. A. Di Folco, 'Aspects of seventeenth century social life' (1975): 15; Whyte (1979a): 157.
[47] Cressy (1978): 20–3.
[48] Quoted in P. Clark, 'Migration in England' (1979): 63 n22.
[49] PRO ASSI45: 15/2/29.
[50] Quoted in P. Borsay, 'The English urban renaissance' (1977): 593–4.

single occupational group in the Scottish depositions was the merchant one. The term 'merchant' had a very general usage. According to John Gibson in 1777, 'by merchants are to be understood those who buy and sell'.[51] According to Defoe, English merchants were actually 'mercers and drapers, shopkeepers', while in Scotland they were 'merchant-adventurers, who trade to foreign parts and employ a considerable number of ships'.[52] In some towns like seventeenth-century Southampton the confusion of terms is obvious, but in fact the reverse would seem to be true in practice, since in England merchants are distinguished from shopkeepers, grocers and chapmen, whereas in Scotland the term has a fairly catholic usage.[53] Accused of fathering a bastard, Thomas Stewart was described as a 'merchant, widow man travelling up and down about his merchandise': possibly a chapman or perhaps a substantial trader.[54] Scottish merchants had widely varying economic interests, ranging from the localized concerns of burgh traders and village shopkeepers in a small town like Cupar to the wealthy Edinburgh and Leith men who owned their own ships and who had sums to invest in the unsuccessful Darien scheme.[55] Some were grand men selling luxury goods and owning shares in trading ships; some were landowners in their own right. Others were humbler and less influential. These latter probably formed the bulk of the merchant community in most Scottish towns.

Poll tax records reveal substantial variations in wealth between members of the same craft or trade. At Musselburgh in Midlothian in the 1690s most merchants were worth 500 to 5,000 merks Scots in stock, though others had upwards of 10,000 merks. One shoemaker was assessed at 'less than 5,000 merks' and was probably a master craftsman, since he employed both an apprentice and a journeyman. The other sixty-nine shoemakers in the parish paid the minimum of 12s Scots tax and can be classed as small-scale independent craftsmen. Among weavers, 97% paid the same minimum sum as did all the tailors.[56] Edinburgh merchants were a socially and politically dominant group within the city, but there were enormous variations between the resources of individual members of this occupation. A 1565 tax roll for Edinburgh shows that 70% of the assessment was raised from the top 25% of the merchant community. Personal wealth at this time varied

[51] Quoted in T. M. Devine, 'The social composition of the business class' (1983b): 164.
[52] D. Defoe, *A tour through the whole island of Great Britain* (1978): 590.
[53] A. J. Willis (ed.), *A calendar of Southampton apprenticeship registers* (1968): xxi.
[54] GRO OPR691/5: 3 July 1692.
[55] Di Folco (1975): 323; J. S. Marshall, 'A social and economic history of Leith' (1969): 15; I. F. Grant, *The social and economic development of Scotland before 1603* (1930): 382.
[56] SRO E70/8/10.

Table 2.1. *Occupational illiteracy of Scottish and English male deponents,*
1640–99 and 1700–70

	England		Scotland	
	1640–99	1700–70	1640–99	1700–70
Professional	(80) 3	(103) 0	(238) 3	(377) 1
Gentry/Laird	(211) 0	(74) 0	(132) 1	(188) 3
Craft & Trade	(551) 43	(673) 26	(248) 25	(983) 18
Yeoman/Tenant	(287) 49	(300) 26	(31) 26	(201) 32
Husbandman	(110) 75	(83) 42	not applicable	
Labourer	(196) 85	(148) 64	(22) 82	(73) 68
Servant	(62) 73	(86) 50	(121) 58	(397) 55
Soldier	(51) 55	(35) 46	(40) 65	(121) 39
Unknown	(863) 62	(225) 30	(540) 51	(1,149) 47
Total	(2,411)	(1,727)	(1,372)	(3,489)

In all tables, the figures in round brackets are numbers sampled, those unbracketed are percentages illiterate.

from £20 Scots to nearly £30,000 Scots, though on average Scottish merchants were less wealthy than English. Only 7 out of 205 Edinburgh merchants were worth more than £12,000 Scots in sixteenth-century testaments and one-third left less than £500 Scots of moveable property in their testaments. Among craftsmen, meanwhile, the top 15% of payers of a 1583 tax accounted for 56% of the assessment.[57] Tailors were prominent in the craft 'aristocracy'.

We shall have more to say about specific craft and trade occupations shortly. In the meantime, the foregoing discussion has given us the broadest outline of the make-up of the society of Scotland and England in the sixteenth, seventeenth and eighteenth centuries, and has provided some background for the discussion of literacy which follows. Table 2.1[58] allows us both to consider comparative levels of illiteracy among males in delineated occupational groups in Lowland Scotland

---

[57] M. Lynch, *Edinburgh and the Reformation* (1981): 52–3; M. H. B. Sanderson, 'Edinburgh merchants in society' (1983): 183–4.

[58] Deponents at the Durham Consistory Court between 1716 and 1800 had a similar profile of illiteracy and, among all groups except craftsmen and tradesmen, levels are nearly identical. Crafts and Trades were 17% illiterate (N = 204), Yeoman 26% (N = 134), Labourers 67% (N = 15). Numbers are too small in all other groups except Gentry and Professionals, who were all literate. For comparison with marriage bond subscriptions for the diocese of Durham see Houston (1982c). In the 1620s Cressy (1978): 20 shows 50% craft and trade illiteracy, a much lower figure than the 73% we will observe below in table 2.4 for the 1640s based on assize depositions. Conclusions on levels of illiteracy may then depend on the sources used to a much greater extent than is currently assumed.

and northern England, and to gain some impression of relative change between the seventeenth and eighteenth centuries in these groups. The story of the Highlands and of women is told in two short sections at the end of the chapter.

For northern England the social distribution of literacy is very much in line with patterns discovered elsewhere in the country during the sixteenth, seventeenth and eighteenth centuries by David Cressy and Roger Schofield.[59] Literacy was closely associated with occupation and thus with socio-economic position as defined both by contemporary observers and by historical analyses of the distribution of wealth and perceived social status.[60] Not surprisingly, the gentry and those who used writing as part of their work were nearly all able to sign their own names. Separated by a wide gulf, craft and trade occupations were closest in their attainments to the landed classes and the professionals, and were very much on a par with yeomen farmers in both periods. There is another clear gap between these categories and the lower echelons of the agricultural hierarchy – the small husbandmen farmers who were usually much poorer on average than yeomen, along with labouring people and servants. Labourers and servants did experience improvements in literacy, but these were not as great as among the middling strata of society who saw their illiteracy halved between the seventeenth and eighteenth centuries. The same is true of soldiers.

What of Scotland? The assertions about easy access to education for all social groups in seventeenth- and eighteenth-century Scotland, which we set out in the introduction, would lead us to expect that any social hierarchy of literacy would be less clearly defined than in England. In fact, the profile is similar, with literacy firmly related to social status and economic utility. The lack of contemporary outlines of the social order with which to compare this hierarchy is unfortunate. It would be naive to judge the extent of social stratification by the one criterion of literacy differentials, but table 2.1 shows that attainments in this field were firmly tied to social position.

For lower class groups such as labourers and servants levels of illiteracy in Scotland and England are remarkably close but Scottish servants saw less of an improvement since they started from a better initial position. The same can be said of Scottish tenant farmers who actually saw increased illiteracy over time. We may however be able to attribute at least part of this apparent change to the small numbers in the earlier period. English yeomen in the north had more than caught up with their Scottish counterparts by the eighteenth century. As we

[59] Cressy (1980); R. S. Schofield, 'Dimensions of illiteracy' (1981).
[60] Cressy (1980); Houston (1981).

have suggested, 'tenant' or 'farmer' may have been reserved for the more prosperous members of the primary sector in Scotland. Even if we add yeomen and husbandmen together to allow for terminological confusions and the range of wealth and status in the tenant farmer category the levels come out nearly identical. The really pronounced difference between Scotland and England is in levels for craftsmen and tradesmen. In seventeenth-century Scotland this group was a mere 25% illiterate, a score which had fallen slightly to 18% by the subsequent period: only 8% ahead of northern England rather than 18% as had been the case earlier. To some extent this is a product of the composition of the grouping. As we shall see shortly, Scottish merchants were nearly all literate and comprised 19% of the craft and trade group over the whole period, compared to just 4% in England. There is a greater range of craft and trade occupations in the English sample – perhaps the result of a more advanced division of labour in the more economically developed country – but a larger proportion came from manual occupations with lower literacy than was the case in Scotland. This would tend artificially to raise levels of literacy in the craft and trade category for Scotland. The superiority of the Scottish group may be attributable in part at least to a compositional effect. The same is true of the servant grouping. Scottish servants show superior literacy only in the seventeenth century, but again this may be explained by the larger proportion of those employed by lairds and professional people: around one in four of all servants in Scotland compared to one in six in England.

There are two important points to emerge from this simple analysis. First, Scotland enjoyed superior literacy to the north of England only during the seventeenth century, a time when the full impact of the introduction of its state education system was only beginning to be felt, but also one when her economy and society were said to be comparatively backward. Secondly, the improvements which did occur between the seventeenth and eighteenth centuries were largely confined to the middling groups in society. The social elites were already literate by the mid seventeenth century, while for the lower orders literacy levels effectively stagnated. Scottish literacy is slightly superior to English for some occupational groups and at some points in time, but there is still a clear hierarchy of illiteracy. Social divisions were just as marked as in England, despite Scotland's allegedly open access to education.

At the same time, we must allow that the actual composition of occupational groups may produce the impression of higher literacy in Scotland than was actually the case. Two occupational categories

Table 2.2. *Illiteracy among male servants to masters in different occupations in northern England and Lowland Scotland, 1640–1770*

Occupation	Northern England	Lowland Scotland
Gentry/Laird	(25) 24	(101) 32
Professional	(1) 100	(32) 6
Craft & Trade	(24) 33	(41) 39
Yeoman/Tenant	(9) 44	(6) 83
Unspecified	(89) 71	(338) 68
Total	(148)	(518)

illustrate this point in more detail. Grouping occupations is bound to blur the possibly complex range of signing abilities both within one designation and even more so within broad categories. Those described as 'servant' in their depositions offer a neat example. Variability in the functions and status of servants to masters or mistresses in different occupations is strongly suggested by divergences in their literacy attainments. Servants to weavers or other craftsmen need not necessarily have been employed in the craft but could have been performing residual agricultural tasks or domestic duties.[61] Nevertheless, the occupation or social status of the employer does give a rough guide to the servant's status. Table 2.2 compares illiteracy levels among servants deponing before Scottish and English criminal courts, and uses the same occupational groupings as in table 2.1. Numbers are very small for some categories, such as farmers' servants and those working for northern English professionals, but a hierarchy of sorts does emerge which shows the same characteristics as that for 'independent' males. At the same time we notice the similarity of literacy levels among servants employed by masters in the same occupations. The less aggregated our sample is the harder it becomes to maintain assertions about Scotland's superiority in literacy. Even those men who shared the same designation may have a widely differing economic and social status. The gradations of status which existed within single occupational designations, such as 'servant', are reflected in ability to sign. As we would anticipate, lumping together diverse terms is bound to conceal even more variations between individual occupations. This aggregation is however essential if we are to have numbers large enough for reliable statistical analysis.

Another example of the injustices done to the subtle hierarchy of illiteracy within occupational groupings can be seen in table 2.3, which

[61] Kussmaul (1981): 14.

offers a selection of individual occupations from all those which we have lumped together in the craft and trade category. The range of occupations in the English column is narrower simply because numbers were too small for some groups to allow reliable figures to be given. There are two main points to notice. First, there is a wide range of literacy between the occupations. Merchants, for example, are all literate in the English sample, and nearly all can sign their names in full among Scottish deponents. Butchers and sailors are much less adept. Again, even specific occupational terms, such as 'merchant' or 'weaver' or 'shoemaker', can conceal the precise scale and nature of economic activity. The difference in status between a journeyman and a master within a traditional guild context could be marked, and that between 'master manufacturer' or capitalist entrepreneur and his employees similarly so. Subtle and unannounced shifts in usage may have occurred over time which produce apparent but unreal changes. There is no way, however, in which we can compensate for this possibility. Yet in a society where the division of labour was comparatively poorly developed, occupational designations have a clear association with wealth and status. The occupational spectrum was complex and diverse in both Scotland and England, but apparent differences between certain crafts may be illusory. There was a greater standardization of nomenclature during the seventeenth century, and outside London the distinction between, say, marikin-makers, cordwainers and shoemakers was more apparent than real.[62]

This brings us on to the second important point about table 2.3. What is extremely interesting about this table is the close similarity of literacy levels between particular occupations in Scotland and England, notably for merchants, innkeepers, smiths and shoemakers. In the case of butchers and sailors English deponents are actually more literate than their Scottish counterparts. Among the individual occupations we can compare, the main differences are between those men involved in making and working cloth. As we have already noted, this may be attributable at least in part to variations in the meanings of the occupational terms. There were probably more independent cloth-workers in Scotland than in northern England, where the putting-out or domestic system was further developed. Production was organized by merchant capitalists who put out raw materials and bought back the finished cloth to be marketed. Not all cloth was produced in this way, however, and there were still many independent clothiers and clothworkers.

[62] J. Patten, *English towns 1500–1700* (1978): 274–7.

Table 2.3. *Occupational illiteracy among male craftsmen and tradesmen in northern England and Lowland Scotland, 1640–1770*

Occupation	Northern England	Lowland Scotland
Merchant	(44) 0	(231) 2
Wright	– –	(77) 6
Maltman	– –	(35) 9
Baxter	– –	(30) 13
Brewer	– –	(24) 21
Chapman	– –	(28) 21
Innkeeper	(113) 22	(57) 23
Tailor	(65) 43	(84) 24
Stabler	– –	(23) 26
Weaver	(109) 48	(129) 26
Clothworker	(167) 53	– –
Smith	(78) 37	(81) 27
Carter	– –	(23) 30
Shoemaker	(73) 30	(76) 30
Butcher/Flesher	(94) 31	(41) 46
Miller	– –	(25) 56
Sailor	(42) 43	(25) 60
Total	(785)	(989)

The large and economically heterogeneous county of Yorkshire provides interesting examples of the varieties of relationships to the mode of production which could exist among those engaged in cloth production. In the West Riding the woollen industry was dominated by independent rural artisans who served apprenticeships and worked to traditional rules and regulations in making blankets and coats. During the early eighteenth century lighter-weight, un-fulled worsted cloth production expanded, but this was run by well-off merchant capitalists putting out to domestic wage earners who, especially around Halifax, formed a growing landless proletariat of specialist weavers. These had very small landholdings which contrasted with the larger, more self-supporting concerns of the lowland area around Leeds.[63] It is tempting to see the difference in literacy between those described as weaver and clothworker as a reflection of this, but we can only speculate about the relationship of these changes to literacy attainments.

Production of woollens was by far the largest industrial employment in the seventeenth and eighteenth centuries: 45% of fathers in a sample of early eighteenth-century Lancashire and Yorkshire baptism

[63] Hudson (1981): 38–43; where no figures are given in the tables, numbers are too small for reliable analysis.

registers were somehow involved in textiles.[64] Changes in productive organization and techniques from mainly self-employed clothiers making woollens to wage-earning weavers producing worsteds in the late seventeenth and early eighteenth centuries may have encouraged continuing weaver illiteracy, though independent smallholder-craftsmen calling themselves clothiers remained common, especially in more remote upland areas.[65] The development of the Yorkshire worsted cloth manufacturers attracted considerable numbers of unskilled workers. The impact of this trend varied geographically, but the sample is too small to allow consideration of local variations in the literacy of, say, 'weavers' versus 'clothiers' or 'clothworkers', even if one could rely on the accuracy of the distinction. It is interesting, however, to contrast the relatively high illiteracy of weavers with their reputation as literate radicals in the later eighteenth century. The key point to notice here is that the composition of the craft and trade grouping may have a more powerful bearing on observed literacy levels than did actual differences between the attainments of individual occupations in Scotland and England.

The figures we have presented so far cover long time-spans and may conceal important differences in the exact timing of changes in illiteracy between the two countries. With the exception of craftsmen and tradesmen in the two regions of Britain, and of Scottish servants, numbers are unfortunately too small in most categories to allow the sort of breakdown into ten-year time periods which we see in table 2.4. Among crafts and trades in Scotland levels of illiteracy fell steadily between the middle and the end of the seventeenth century, then stayed at roughly the same level until the 1720s, with only a slight rise into the 1760s when the very low score of 8% was recorded. This is so different from the general trend of *rising* illiteracy that we must wonder whether small numbers of the predominance of city- and town-dwellers was responsible. As we shall discover shortly those who lived in towns enjoyed higher literacy than their rural counterparts. Interestingly, however, a similar mid eighteenth-century drop is recorded for northern English craftsmen and tradesmen, but only as far as 19% illiterate. Servant illiteracy also rose and fell over time and with the exception of an initial fall in the first decades here is no detectable trend towards consistently improving or declining literacy.

---

[64] M. Drake, 'An elementary exercise in parish register demography' (1962): 430–1; J. Langton, 'Industry and towns 1500–1730' (1978): 176.
[65] Langton (1978): 183.

Table 2.4. *Occupational illiteracy among male craftsmen and tradesmen in northern England and Lowland Scotland and of Scottish servants by decade, 1640–1770*

Date	Northern England	Lowland Scotland	
	C & T	C & T	Servant
1640s	(66) 73	–	–
1650s	(71) 44	(17) 47	(18) 89
1660s	(92) 37	–	–
1670s	(69) 36	(50) 36	(19) 68
1680s	(103) 38	(82) 24	(47) 43
1690s	(150) 38	(99) 17	(37) 57
1700s	–	(79) 22	(60) 60
1710s	–	(170) 22	(73) 56
1720s	(73) 44	(180) 14	(62) 42
1730s	(113) 23	(169) 15	(58) 53
1740s	(111) 22	(110) 17	(64) 56
1750s	(187) 31	(201) 21	(66) 61
1760s	(189) 19	(74) 8	(14) 57
Total	(1,224)	(1,231)	(518)

It is worth remembering that while craftsmen and tradesmen are representative of the most economically active groups in the population, their experience is not typical of all sections of the community. If we can regard the Scottish educational system as responsible for these differentials it seems to have worked disproportionately well for members of the middling ranks in society. With lairds, professionals and crafts and trades so literate by the mid eighteenth century, improvements in aggregate literacy during the subsequent century were almost wholly attributable to the lower classes. For England, craft and trade illiteracy fell dramatically in the mid seventeenth century then stagnated until the second quarter of the eighteenth, and while some of the gains were lost in the 1750s a further drop ensued in the 1760s. Literacy rose first and fastest among the upper and middle ranks of society in the sixteenth, seventeenth and eighteenth centuries. It was only after this that significant advances could take place for the lower orders.

The occupations where Scotland had the lead over England in literacy attainments were principally craftsmen and tradesmen plus farmers. We have already questioned just how marked the divergence really was by pointing to the profile of illiteracy among individual occupations and to the composition of these groups. Further disaggregation may help to make the point clearer and to bring to light some

Table 2.5. *Occupational illiteracy among males in areas of northern England and Lowland Scotland, 1640–1770*

Occupation	4 N. counties	Yorks.	Scotland
Craft & Trade	(257) 27	(879) 35	(1,231) 19
Yeoman/Tenant	(232) 40	(315) 34	(232) 31
Husbandman	(28) 43	(154) 62	–
Labourer	(57) 67	(251) 77	(95) 72
Servant	(36) 47	(86) 61	(518) 56
Total	(610)	(1,685)	(2,076)

of the more subtle aspects of regional as opposed to national differences in literacy in early modern Britain. If, for example, we break down the northern English sample into the four northernmost counties, where literacy was so high in the mid nineteenth century and compare these with Yorkshire an interesting pattern emerges which we find in table 2.5. With the exception of yeomen, male deponents have appreciably higher occupationally specific literacy in Northumberland, Durham, Cumberland and Westmorland than was the case in Yorkshire. The Scottish lead in these large occupational groups remains over both categories, but is halved in the case of the four northern counties. Levels for labouring men are close in any case between the two countries, but for servants the northern counties of England are well ahead of Scotland. As is the case with yeomen, who were frequently conflated with husbandmen in the north-east at this time, wealth and status variations within occupational categories may well be exerting an influence on relative levels in the two countries. Lower literacy levels among farmers may have something to do with the rather backward agriculture of county Durham and parts of upland Northumberland, Cumberland and Westmorland.[66] The near-total absence of husbandmen described as such in the Consistory Court sample and the comparatively small numbers for the four northern counties, coupled with the nearly identical illiteracy levels between yeomen and husbandmen – a pattern not duplicated in Yorkshire – does indeed suggest that the terms overlap and that we should not take too much from the apparent inferiority of farmers in the northern counties.

We can further broaden our understanding of the dimensions of illiteracy. Occupation and literacy are closely related to one another. But there are other environmental influences which played a part in

[66] R. I. Hodgshon, 'The progress of enclosure in county Durham' (1979): 96–8; A. Young, *A tour through the north of England* vol. 3 (1770): 113–16.

determining literacy. One of the more powerful was the type of community in which a person lived. Both Scottish Justiciary Court and English assize depositions typically name the witnesses' exact place of residence, and this makes it possible to determine not only the county but also the type of community in which deponents lived – whether in towns or in rural villages. The impact of town-dwelling on illiteracy has already received some attention for England, and a standard classification of towns has been suggested which conforms with John Adams' seventeenth-century *Index villaris*.[67] This is a list of settlements in England broken down into cities, market towns and villages. To some extent this is a crude classification which conceals differences in size and economic function between towns. Boroughs like Leeds and Halifax with many townships, for example, were not wholly urban environments. The breakdown does however seem to work well until the late eighteenth century when non-market industrial centres began to proliferate. It is especially reliable for the north of England where there was considerable stability and continuity of market centres throughout our period. Comparing the status of market towns in 1640 with 1792 John Chartres, for example, has discovered that only Learmouth, Elsdon and Rothbury had disappeared from the list of Northumberland market towns. The seventeenth-century creations of Hawkshead and Ambleside were qualified successes, but Shap failed to establish itself.[68] Fairs were few and far between in the north of England compared to the rest of England and Wales, and these should not therefore distort the residential classification by creating unexpected population concentrations.

Nevertheless not all market towns were the same. Some, like Whitehaven or Berwick, were clearly prospering as specialist centres but others were losing some tertiary functions to bigger centres such as Newcastle. Whitehaven saw considerable commercial and industrial development but secondary and tertiary sectors did not expand as fast as, say, Newcastle's in the later seventeenth century.[69] The town failed to continue its path of industrial development into the second half of the eighteenth century and lost its trade in tobacco to Glasgow at that time. Clearly the towns and cities in our classification had a different and changing range of social and economic functions. Newcastle and York form examples of high-order service centres in an increasingly integrated urban hierarchy.[70] The prosperity of Newcastle was increasingly

[67] J. Adams, *Index villaris* (1690); R. A. Houston, 'The development of literacy' (1982b).
[68] Personal communication from John Chartres of the University of Leeds.
[69] Beckett (1981): 201–4.   [70] Langton (1978): 190.

associated with the coal trade and with a range of heavy industries in and, more particularly, around the city. With increasing social segregation of residence there was still a complex occupational zoning, and also a narrow wealth distribution with 76% of the population assessed for the hearth tax of the 1660s being identifiable as a 'quasi-proletariat'.[71] Civic rituals reinforced the town's corporate identity and also its links with regional and national society. Other towns in northern England were much smaller. Kendal had only 2,000 inhabitants in 1700 and Penrith a mere 1,350. Even the city of Carlisle could muster only about 3,000 souls.[72]

For Scotland a similar classification is a good deal harder to create. The primitive state of Scottish local history plus the lack of a standard classification of towns and villages such as Adams' *Index villaris* for England makes it difficult to present any definitive list of active towns. It is comparatively easy to discover the legal status of a settlement but much harder to determine the size of potentially 'urban' communities or the range of functions they provided in the secondary and tertiary sectors. Ian Whyte's claim that 20% of Scotland's population at the end of the seventeenth century lived in burghs should not be taken to imply an 'urbanized' country.[73] Nor is the picture static. During the seventeenth and eighteenth centuries there was a high failure rate among burghs. Some royal burghs such as Falkland and Lanark suffered relative decline, Lanark at the hands of nearby markets.[74] In 1692 the densely settled area around Lanark had a number of centres 'who have all weekly mercats and severall fairs of great value'.[75] The fortunes of individual burghs varied enormously. Alloa developed from a small collier village to flourish as a respectable trading and industrial town with a thriving mixed economy in the late seventeenth century. The same is true of Dundee, and of Perth in the eighteenth century, but Culross stagnated completely from the seventeenth century onwards.[76] Given the backward state of Scottish social and economic history before the nineteenth century it is extremely difficult to gain anything but the most general outline of the occupational structure and socio-economic function of most towns. With 30,000 and 15,000 inhabitants respectively in 1700, Edinburgh and Glasgow stand out as easily the largest and most economically diverse centres in Scotland

[71] J. Langton, 'Residential patterns in pre-industrial cities' (1975).
[72] Beckett (1981): 2.   [73] Whyte (1979a): 9.
[74] *Ibid*. 185–9; W. H. Mackenzie, *The Scottish burghs* (1949): 49.
[75] *Register containing the state and condition of every burgh in Scotland [1692]* (1881): 122–3.
[76] Adams (1978): 55, 81–2; Pennant (1774): 76.

before the second half of the eighteenth century.[77] With the combined
functions of a capital (though it lost the royal court in 1603 and Parliament in 1707) and (through Leith) a port, Edinburgh was 'the metropolis of the nation', 'the residence of our nobility, and fixed place of our
solemn judicatories'.[78] Glasgow was growing rapidly from the mid
seventeenth century onwards and increased its population six-fold
between 1700 and 1800.[79] Unable to match Edinburgh's prestigious
status it nevertheless became an important commercial, industrial and
administrative centre during the eighteenth century. Defoe remarked
with approval on the expansion of trade and manufactures in early
eighteenth-century Glasgow.[80] By the 1760s Glasgow could rival Manchester as a manufacturing town, and had a great advantage as a port,
capturing the tobacco trade from Whitehaven and Aberdeen and
building up one in sugar.[81]

With more than 2,000 paid hearths in the 1690s – some 10,000
inhabitants – Aberdeen and Dundee were the largest of the remaining
towns of Scotland, the latter with a flourishing long-distance trade by
the mid eighteenth century.[82] Greenock, Stirling, St Andrews,
Kirkcaldy, Linlithgow, Ayr, Hamilton, Montrose, Perth, Inverness,
Kelso and Dumfries had 900–1,200 hearths or some 4–5,000 people.
Finally Paisley, Kilmarnock, Musselburgh, Tranent, Prestonpans,
Dalkieth, Bo'ness and Falkirk were the only other towns which could
number more than 500 hearths.

Provisional work by Ian Whyte of the University of Lancaster on
burgh schedules of the 1690s poll tax does suggest that towns with less
than 250–300 pollable persons did not possess a full range of craftsmen,
tradesmen and professionals. Peterhead and Fraserburgh make the
grade, but places like Culross were little more than industrial villages.[83]
At the end of the sixteenth century most burghs of barony were small
and had highly localised economies. Burghs of barony were settlements
which had been granted the right to contain burgesses, to hold local
markets and to have limited jurisdiction over criminal and civil cases.
Finally, there were many fairs and markets held throughout Scotland.
Acts of Parliament created 246 non-burghal markets between 1660 and

---

[77] Whyte (1979a): 9.   [78] SRO GD18/3025.   [79] Lenman (1977a): 42.
[80] Defoe (1978): 602–3, 606.   [81] Pennant (1774): 231–2, 121.
[82] Whyte (1979a): 9; M. W. Flinn (ed.), *Scottish population history* (1977): 191; D. Loch,
A tour through most of the trading towns and villages of Scotland (1778): 27.
[83] Adams (1978): 53.

1707.[84] A complete list of all those settlements treated as urban communities is given in appendix 3. Size alone is not an adequate criterion though it was broadly associated with the range of functions performed by towns.[85]

Nor is the title of burgh a reliable indicator. Scottish burghs are usually distinguished by the legal privileges which they enjoyed over trade. Royal burghs like Aberdeen or Stranraer could engage in foreign trade, while burghs of barony or regality could strictly trade only inland. The former also had exclusive inland trade rights over a defined area.[86] The status and functions of the royal burghs diverged considerably and varied over time. In 1769 Thomas Pennant found Elgin had great cattle fairs, but little other trade.[87] In his late-eighteenth-century description of Scotland, Knox singled out Wick, Dornoch, Dingwall and Fortrose as places carrying the 'high-sounding appelations of royal boroughs, but which, in reality, are nothing more than ruinous villages, exhibiting all the symptoms of decay, poverty, and distress'.[88] Commerce was open in the burghs of barony, and craftsmen and tradesmen were encouraged in order to foster trade. To some extent these legal positions were mirrored in the size and economic functions of settlements. Markets could exist, for example: 'designed to serve the small-scale but frequent and regular needs' of the burgh and its hinterland and, in the case of Edinburgh and Glasgow, there were separate markets for a variety of particular products.[89] There were however a number of burghs with trade privileges which were not used: 'paper' burghs. Indeed there was a wide range of functions performed in different types of burgh. Some places such as Rosline in Midlothian had burgh charters which allowed them trading privileges, but were in fact little better than villages with only a few hundred inhabitants. Certain settlements described as burghs were not even this big.[90]

Table 2.6 gives a breakdown of levels of occupational illiteracy in

[84] A. R. B. Haldane, 'Old Scottish fairs and markets' (1961); Mackenzie (1949): 93.
[85] J. Patten, 'Village and town' (1972).
[86] Whyte (1979a): 180–1; Adams (1978): 40–2.   [87] Pennant (1774): 146.
[88] J. Knox, *A view of the British empire* (1784): 17.   [89] Whyte (1979a): 180, 187–9.
[90] Note that a literacy profile for towns with more than 4,000 inhabitants compared to smaller burghs within the 'town' classification revealed that differences between towns were much less important than between towns and rural parishes, or between towns and Edinburgh or Glasgow. Furet and Ozouf's study of eighteenth- and nineteenth-century France, *Reading and Writing* (1982), suggests that towns with as few as 2,000 inhabitants still showed superior literacy to rural areas. K. Lockridge, *Literacy in colonial New England* (1974): 63–4 regards a population of only 500 to 1,000 inhabitants as the critical size for urban status (and literacy) in eighteenth-century New England.

Table 2.6. *Occupational illiteracy in communities of residence, Scottish male deponents, 1650–1770*

Occupation	Edin./Glas.	Towns	Villages
Professional	(208) 0	(263) 2	(107) 5
Laird	(25) 0	(43) 0	(143) 4
Craft & Trade	(349) 10	(596) 16	(257) 39
Tenant/Farmer	(14) 29	(31) 6	(171) 37
Labourer	(15) 53	(34) 76	(36) 72
Servant	(105) 37	(89) 43	(255) 67
Soldier	(46) 39	(19) 42	(16) 44
Unknown	(58) 21	(235) 32	(1,176) 54
Total	(820)	(1,310)	(2,161)

different communities of residence over the period 1640–1770. For nearly all occupational groups in Scotland, except soldiers and servants, experience of living and working in Edinburgh or Glasgow produced appreciably higher levels of literacy than in other towns. Rural-dwellers lagged far behind town-dwellers in the craft and trade and servant categories, but again, levels for labourers and soldiers are much closer. The rather low scores for tenant farmers can in part be attributed to small numbers plus the fact that in towns tenants might well be shopkeepers. It is worth remarking, nevertheless, on the close ties with the land retained by early modern town-dwellers.

From the 1680s onwards in Scotland we can consider changes from decade to decade in craft and trade illiteracy in the three types of community, though we must bear in mind that urban crafts and trades were richer than their rural counterparts, and that there would be more high-status, low-illiteracy trades in the bigger towns – merchants, goldsmiths, booksellers and others. Table 2.7 shows that Edinburgh and Glasgow levels were fairly constant over time and approached the exceptionally low level of 1% illiterate obtaining among London craftsmen and tradesmen during the 1720s.[91] Edinburgh was in many ways Scotland's powerhouse of modernization. Economically, 'Edinburgh is not considerable for trade, but depends chiefly for its support upon the college of justice, the seminaries of education, and the inducements which, as a capital, it affords to genteel people to reside in it.'[92] Edinburgh was the main centre of elite culture in seventeenth- and

---

[91] D. Cressy, 'Literacy in pre-industrial England' (1974): 235.
[92] H. Arnot, *The history of Edinburgh* (1816): 258.

Table 2.7. *Illiteracy among Scottish male craftsmen and tradesmen in different communities of residence by decade, 1680–1770*

Date	Edin./Glas.	Towns	Villages
1680s	(21) 10	(44) 20	(14) 50
1690s	(36) 14	(41) 15	(7) 43
1700s	(19) 5	(43) 23	(16) 31
1710s	(48) 8	(87) 26	(28) 39
1720s	(68) 3	(77) 17	(32) 31
1730s	(44) 9	(86) 13	(35) 29
1740s	(31) 10	(42) 10	(36) 33
1750s	(23) 13	(110) 9	(62) 47
1760s	(36) 11	(31) 6	(7) 0
Total	(326)	(561)	(237)

eighteenth-century Scotland. It was also an important town for publishing and distributing chapbooks, one where access to all forms of oral and literate culture, such as newspapers, plays and sermons, was unusually comprehensive. The capital was also an important centre of new attitudes to business and society. 'The literate gentry who moved into Edinburgh and began to make money in government and the law were ... opening up a gulf between themselves and the local community as they ... rejected its traditional ways of doing things and sought to impose their new ideas.'[93] English copy books were on sale in Scotland's capital in the 1570s and 1580s.[94] 'Seminaries of every description could not be too much multiplied in Edinburgh, where the *great manufacture* was that *of the mind*.' Education in eighteenth-century Edinburgh was increasingly geared to the needs of a society whose main concern was with commercial activity. Along with the development of an elite culture there was an increasingly secular, utilitarian emphasis on education at the expense of religion and the classics. Much smaller than other European capitals, such as London or Paris, at the end of the seventeenth century Edinburgh nevertheless had concentrations of literate people. Paris, with 1% of Europe's population, had 4% of its literate population and 7% of its reading public.[95] Edinburgh was more like Newcastle, Amsterdam, Antwerp or Cracow in its size and in the sorts of literate media available.

---

[93] J. Wormald, *Court, kirk and community* (1981): 165.
[94] A. Somerville, *Autobiography* (1951): 48, 60; Simpson (1973): 30; Sinclair (1826): 106.
[95] G. Parker, 'An educational revolution?' (1980): 214.

There are, however, signs that Edinburgh and Glasgow were losing their slight lead over other towns. The mid-eighteenth-century rise in illiteracy among craftsmen and tradesmen may offer the first indication of the situation observable in the early nineteenth century, when towns like Dundee and Paisley were much better placed in terms of education and literacy than were Edinburgh or Glasgow.[96] In these smaller towns illiteracy fell steadily from the early eighteenth century, in contrast both to the largest urban centres and rural areas. Indeed levels for craftsmen converged to parity among all 'urban' centres by the mid eighteenth century. The economic problems which many smaller burghs had experienced during the seventeenth century were being resolved. Population growth and industrial development in the late eighteenth century are said to have spoiled the excellent results produced by the Scottish educational system in the Lowlands. Edinburgh suffered particularly badly. A number of commentators remarked upon the influx of poor Highlanders into the capital during the eighteenth century.[97] We shall see shortly that these would be highly illiterate people. Nor was the city a homogeneous social environment: the College Kirk parish was called 'the paroch of beggars', while the Canongate was the wealthiest, 'frequented with persons of the greatest quality in the nation' and the Tolbooth or North West parish was similarly affluent.[98] Outside the city limits were communities of less skilled workmen, especially weavers, anxious to escape guild restrictions. Suburban parishes with a poorer socio-economic make-up (often specializing in unskilled textile manufacture) seem to have had much lower literacy than the inner parishes inhabited largely by merchants and professionals. The contrast between London and Middlesex, which in fact contained many of the capital's suburbs, is instructive here.[99] When London craftsmen and tradesmen could boast illiteracy levels as low as 1% during the 1720s, those in Middlesex had 13%. There were wide variations, then, within the city as well as between the main urban area and the rural parts. The shifting balance of population towards the suburban and the poorer socio-economic groups could decisively influence the levels of literacy in Edinburgh and Glasgow during the eighteenth century.

A similar phenomenon is observable in some European towns. Analysing differences in literacy between central and suburban parishes of towns in seventeenth- and eighteenth-century Normandy,

[96] R. K. Webb, *The British working class reader* (1955): 23.
[97] Smout (1972): 424, 441–2; Saunders (1950): 294; Arnot (1816): 258; Robertson (1793): 26.
[98] SRO GD18/3025.   [99] Cressy (1974): 235.

Longuet concludes that spatial variations in literacy were due to the predominance of weavers, spinners and carders in the suburban parishes rather than to a poorer educational provision.[100] Small numbers and the sometimes poor quality of residential information prevents more detailed analyses for Scotland, but it is possible that while the smaller Scottish towns became, like some of those on the Continent, a homogeneous literacy environment, Edinburgh and Glasgow retained marked differentials between central and suburban areas. Interestingly, the gap between (improving) urban and (stagnating) rural literacy was actually widening over time for this group. It would appear that the Scottish educational system, said to have functioned best in the rural Lowlands, was beginning to experience problems at a much earlier date than the late eighteenth century. Finally, it is worth noting that Edinburgh's advance to pre-eminence in elite culture was associated with rising mass illiteracy.[101]

The role of towns in pre-industrial Scotland seems to have been more of a stimulus to economic development rather than parasitic upon it as was Dublin, or some Continental towns, such as Madrid. Scottish burghs were created that 'trade and travelling should be fostered'.[102] Again there were many cultural and economic opportunities created by the growth of markets for agricultural produce, which also fostered the growth of towns and the integration of local areas into regional economies. The seventeenth century therefore saw the growth of urban populations in old towns such as Edinburgh and new ones like Bo'ness.[103] Agricultural improvements created a greater marketable surplus, allowing more of the population to engage in the secondary and tertiary sectors of the economy, thereby creating more demand for agricultural produce within the towns and so on.[104] Internal and overseas trade was on the increase, especially in raw materials such as coal, salt and wool. In both society and economy, towns were an important force for change.

For the north of England a similar profile of higher urban than rural literacy can be observed in table 2.8. We can also assess change over time among key occupational groups (table 2.9). Two points are clear. First, the superiority of city-dwellers is shown in all social categories. Second, the differences between towns and village communities was rather less marked than the city/town one, except in the craft and trade category.

[100] Y. Longuet, 'L'alphabétisation à Falaise' (1978): 225.
[101] Smout (1972): 421–50; O'Day (1982): 236.
[102] Adams (1978): 26.   [103] *Ibid*. 49–51.
[104] E. A. Wrigley, 'Parasite or stimulus' (1978b): 304–5.

Table 2.8. *Occupational illiteracy of males in communities of residence in northern England, 1640–1770*

Occupation	City	Town	Village
Professional	(62) 0	(64) 2	(43) 2
Gentry	(60) 0	(67) 1	(113) 0
Craft & Trade	(243) 16	(466) 29	(462) 46
Yeoman	(39) 21	(101) 40	(420) 37
Husbandman	–	(27) 63	(159) 59
Labourer	(34) 68	(70) 80	(215) 75
Servant	(33) 42	(34) 59	(55) 64
Total	(471)	(829)	(1,467)

Table 2.9. *Occupational illiteracy of males in communities of residence in northern England, 1640–1700 and 1725–1770*

Occupation	1640–1700			1725–1770		
	City	Town	Village	City	Town	Village
Craft & Trade	(104) 23	(190) 35	(221) 57	(139) 11	(276) 25	(241) 36
Yeoman	(17) 35	(48) 48	(206) 50	(22) 9	(53) 32	(214) 26
Labourer	(13) 85	(40) 83	(129) 86	(21) 57	(30) 77	(86) 58
Servant	(16) 63	(12) 83	(15) 80	(17) 24	(22) 46	(40) 58
Total	(150)	(290)	(571)	(199)	(381)	(581)

The same profile need not have been true of sixteenth- or nine-teenth-century towns. In the sixteenth century, London grew, but towns elsewhere had mixed fortunes and overall their share of a rapidly expanding population fell.[105] In the nineteenth century, administrative and tertiary services were standard features of large towns, but other factors such as industrial employment could depress literacy, and the balance between manufactures and services would influence overall literacy and the place of towns in the 'urban hier-archy'. During the late seventeenth and early eighteenth centuries, however, towns of all sizes grew despite population stagnation, stimu-lated by rising real wages and thus a greater demand for industrial goods and the variety of services offered by towns. Newcastle's popu-lation doubled between the 1660s and 1730s to about 29,000, and along

[105] Much of this paragraph is based on P. Clark (ed.), *Country towns in pre-industrial England* (1981): 11–24; E. A. Wrigley and R. S. Schofield, *The population history of England* (1981): 467, 472.

with other county towns developed a considerable gentry presence. By the late eighteenth century market towns throughout England were showing greater literacy levels than rural areas, having developed as agricultural service centres with more occupational specialization, a position they had not enjoyed a century before when these functions were more confined to a few urban centres.

Traditional market towns and cities provided widespread opportunities for reading and writing. Most county towns had two or more booksellers in the early eighteenth century, while provincial centres had up to six.[106] Chapmen were concentrated in the towns and cities: more than half of their number licensed in returns during the years 1697–8 lived in market towns, and Newcastle had more than forty licensed pedlars.[107] When their society was not damaged by population growth, towns possessed superior educational facilities, and the many advertisements for private schools in early provincial newspapers suggest that urban schooling may not have suffered as much after the Restoration as is sometimes thought.[108] Though 'old style endowed grammar schools teaching ordinary town boys were in decline in many places after 1680, those concentrating on instructing and boarding the offspring of the well-to-do ... did a handsome business'.[109] In traditional provincial centres of the type doing so well in the late seventeenth and eighteenth centuries – Newcastle, Bristol and Norwich for example – continuity of residence was increasing over time and the less mobile elements of the urban population may have found themselves better placed to benefit from education and the economic and cultural stimulus provided by the towns.

In both Scotland and England fewer apprentices moved to large towns from rural areas than we should expect given the urban/rural distribution of the population as a whole. More apprentices were drawn from within or very close to cities such as Newcastle in the later seventeenth and eighteenth centuries than had been true of the sixteenth century.[110] Socio-economic polarization which occurred over the sixteenth and seventeenth centuries meant that local village schools became principally elementary schools while the 'new rural middle class' sent their children to the grammar schools in the towns. English boroughs from the sixteenth century onwards probably saw a flourishing school as a sound investment in status. Changes within the

---

[106] Clark (1981): 18.
[107] Spufford (1981): 120.
[108] J. Simon, 'Schools in the county [Leicestershire]' (1968a).
[109] Clark (1981): 24.   [110] Houston (1981): 347–67.

cultural environment of towns helped to produce concentrations of literate people.[111]

Yet the whole explanation may not lie with developments in the towns themselves. Towns in the early modern period drew large numbers of their inhabitants from rural areas, especially during periods of population increase, though inter-urban movement was fairly common, particularly among long-distance movers. Most migrants moved after the end of any formal schooling at ages between fifteen and thirty, and most had predominantly rural contacts prior to moving into towns, suggesting that urban schooling may not provide a full explanation of urban–rural literacy differentials.[112] Differential literacy might exist between natives and migrants, though the relationship is not constant but depends on the status of the migrant and the reason for moving. We might expect some groups, like apprentices, who moved to towns to better themselves would be more literate than the lowly subsistence migrants drawn to towns by the prospect of poor relief or casual work. The importance of this latter category was apparently decreasing over the seventeenth century. In eighteenth-century Leeds, for example, natives were much less literate than immigrants, while in some Lancashire industrial towns the reverse would be true, since migrants were mainly low status rural-dwellers coming to take up unskilled industrial jobs.[113] Late eighteenth-century northern industrial towns attracted predominantly unskilled, illiterate workers, but the late seventeenth-century commercial and service centres may have been most attractive to more skilled, wealthier and therefore more literate persons.

Scottish towns share some of the same features which would promote literacy, though it is not clear whether the same shake-down of market centres occurred between the sixteenth and eighteenth centuries as in England. Where small towns were able to cope with population increase during the eighteenth century, rapidly expanding urban centres experienced similar problems to those of English manufacturing towns.[114] In the present state of research, there is no way of telling whether rural–urban or inter-urban migration was selective of literates or non-literates, or even if the relationship holds constant over time. Certainly educational provision seems to have been better in the towns. By 1500 there was a grammar school in every town of any size in Scotland, and larger burghs of the eighteenth century were well pro-

---

[111] J. Simon (1968a): 32–3; J. Simon, *Education and society* (1967): 374.
[112] Clark (1979): 70–2.
[113] M. Yasumoto, 'Urbanization and population in an English town' (1973): 84–5.
[114] Smout (1972): 438–9; Saunders (1950): 267–79; Scotland (1969): 104.

Table 2.10. *Craft and trade illiteracy in Lowland Scotland and areas of northern England, 1640–1770*

	1640–99	1700–70
Village		
Four northern counties	(34) 56	(62) 32
Northumberland & Durham*	–	(100) 19
Yorkshire	(177) 58	(171) 37
Lowland Scotland	(41) 59	(216) 36
Town		
Four northern counties	(24) 50	(42) 17
Northumberland & Durham*	–	(65) 19
Yorkshire	(160) 33	(225) 26
Lowland Scotland	(119) 18	(477) 15
City		
Four northern counties	(50) 20	(44) 2
Northumberland & Durham*	–	(48) 6
Yorkshire	(49) 27	(93) 15
Lowland Scotland	(80) 18	(269) 8
Total	(734)	(1,812)

* From Durham Consistory Court depositions 1716–1800.

vided with schools offering increasingly diverse curricula. Commercial development 'formed a positive and compelling inducement to curricular change and development in the burghs', such as Perth.[115] All town-dwellers were supposed to send their children to the schools, but in fact this remained a middle-class pursuit.[116] Immigration to towns may help to explain differential literacy, since it is usually claimed that Scottish *rural* education was that country's strong point. Table 2.10 shows that it was only in small towns in seventeenth-century Scotland that craft and trade illiteracy was substantially superior to English.

How does this chronology compare with elsewhere in England? While no comparable studies broken down by type of community exist, we can see that London underwent a similar late seventeenth- and early eighteenth-century rise in those sections of the population participating in and influenced by commercial expansion. From 19% illiteracy in the 1670s and 23% in the 1680s, London craftsmen and tradesmen saw an improvement to 7% in the 1690s and a mere 1% by the 1720s. Members of the same occupational group living in increas-

[115] Scotland (1969): 16; Withrington (1970): 169–70, 180–1.
[116] Scotland (1969): 75; Smout (1972): 444.

ingly urbanized Middlesex experienced a fall from 24% and 28% to 18% and 13% over the same periods of time.[117] Perhaps other towns in the seventeenth century were joining London as socially and economically dynamic centres. Developing regional economies and expanding internal and overseas trade meant that despite London's continuing importance other growing towns were beginning to perform significant catalytic roles in social change. Interestingly, however, the illiteracy of London craftsmen and tradesmen continued to fall after the late seventeenth-century pause, while in the north-eastern cities the early eighteenth century was a time of stagnation. The chronology of changing illiteracy shown in the north-east was not true of Norfolk and Suffolk craftsmen and tradesmen (living in all types of community). From 38% illiteracy between the 1640s and 1670s, a slight increase occurred in the 1680s and 1690s to 39%; even in the 1720s the level had only improved to 34%.[118]

We can press still further in our search to peel back these layers of literacy by combining analyses of both the county and the community where the deponents lived. Even with a sample numbering over 4,000 for England and nearly 5,000 for Scotland there is unfortunately only a single occupational category with adequate numbers for such an analysis: the craft and trade one. Looking to table 2.10, we can see that Scottish towns and cities are actually superior to those of northern England in the seventeenth century, while rural inhabitants are nearly identical in their literacy scores. The lead of Edinburgh and Glasgow over Newcastle, Durham and Carlisle is fairly slender, though it is more prominent over York. Aggregate literacy levels in the city of York derived from signed or marked entries in the marriage registers of the second half of the eighteenth century show that illiteracy among males was more common there than in rural parishes of Yorkshire during the period 1750–80. Population increase and opportunities for industrial employment were keeping literacy down to the levels of the cloth-producing town of Leeds.[119] The economy of York, which relied on distributive and service sectors, stagnated between 1650 and 1750, and it must be counted as one of the least successful of provincial capitals.[120] Newcastle, on the other hand, was not only an important port but also a successful shopping and professional centre at this time. By the period 1725–70 craftsmen and tradesmen in all parts of the four northern counties are ahead of their Yorkshire counterparts and in the case

[117] Cressy (1974): 235.   [118] *Ibid*. 235.
[119] Yasumoto (1973): 83–4.   [120] Clark (1981): 26.

of the cities very close to the effectively complete literacy of London crafts and trades at this time. The presence of unskilled craftsmen in the Yorkshire communities may well have depressed levels compared with the four northern counties, where independent craftsmen and tradesmen were more the norm, and where industrial concentrations apart from coalmining and some clothworking around Kendal were less developed.[121] At the same time, towns and cities could boast more specialized and richer crafts- and tradesmen, such as goldsmiths, merchants and stationers, who had lower illiteracy than many ordinary craftsmen and tradesmen.

As industry expanded in the north of England the experience of towns would begin to diverge. Traditional centres where population growth was not so rapid as to damage educational provision would fare well, as would non-industrial towns where the stimulation of occupations connected with the expansion of trade, which was itself stimulated by increased agricultural and industrial output, encouraged people to seek out at least some education. Meanwhile towns which had an expansion of industry, both factory and putting-out, experienced falling literacy levels.[122] Early nineteenth-century Halifax, which had seen prosperity 'prodigiously encouraged and increased by the great demand of their kerseys' since the late seventeenth century, provides an example.[123]

Further evidence of dramatic improvements at the end of the seventeenth century in Newcastle's comparative position is given in the signatures to bonds demanded by the Cordwainers company of that city. From the Restoration to the Revolution one shoemaker in four was illiterate, but by the 1710s and 1720s only 3–4% could not sign their names in full.[124] The guilds of Newcastle and Carlisle continued to be strong until the end of the eighteenth century, though it is also worth noticing that in York the stranglehold of the guilds was blamed for the economic stagnation of the town during the eighteenth century. Given the emphasis these bodies placed on having educated apprentices, the higher literacy of crafts and trades in the northern cities is easier to understand. In Scotland too, Edinburgh and Glasgow craft and trade companies remained vital into the late eighteenth century. In fact, the proximity of literacy levels between the four northern counties and Lowland Scotland by this stage is strikingly reminiscent of the sort of

[121] Beckett (1981).
[122] W. B. Stephens, 'Illiteracy and schooling in the provincial towns' (1977): 32–3.
[123] Defoe (1978): 495, 515; Stone (1969): 103.
[124] R. A. Houston, 'Illiteracy among Newcastle shoemakers' (1982e): 145.

profile we observed in the introduction for the 1850s. Again it seems that the more we disaggregate literacy figures the greater is the resemblance between adjacent regions of northern Britain. If we are looking for explanations of literacy we may have to examine factors common to areas of both countries and thus not related to the much-stressed institutional differences between them.

In conclusion, we can attempt an estimate of overall male illiteracy in mid eighteenth-century Scotland which can be compared with England. We must allow for occupational biases in the depositions, difficult though this is in the present rudimentary state of knowledge about Scottish society. Imperfect though they are, taxation documents provide the best snapshot picture of social structure. In the 1690s poll tax schedules we find the proportion of adult male payers who were tenant farmers varying from 15% in Berwickshire and the Lothians to 20% in Lowland Aberdeenshire and some 35% in Renfrewshire.[125] These are maximum percentages, since any omissions from the poll tax schedules would be of those below the level of tenant. There were probably fewer tenant farmers by the mid eighteenth century in view of the trend towards increasing size and decreasing number of farms during our period. An estimate of some 25% for the 1750s and 1760s would seem realistic. Perhaps 20% of the adult males were craftsmen and tradesmen, and less than 5% lairds and professional men. This leaves half of the male population or more in the low-literacy labourer, cottar and servant category. Allowing for the levels of illiteracy obtaining among these groups we can suggest an estimate of some 35% adult male illiteracy in the mid eighteenth-century Scottish Lowlands: slightly higher than the English national average of 40% taken from subscriptions to marriage registers, but very much in line with the four northern counties' figure of around 36%.[126] Because marriage registers cover almost the whole population there is no need to adjust the figures from the assize records. We have a ready-made representative sample with which to compare the Scottish deposition statistics. The level for the Highlands of Scotland was much higher at around 55–60%, as we shall discover shortly. This suggests that the rise to nearly universal literacy which we can see in Scotland during the 1850s must have come at some stage during the later eighteenth or early nineteenth centuries. At the same time we have seen that the contrast between Lowland Scotland and northern England is not as marked as we might expect from some of the balder assertions about Scotland's educational superiority. However the divergence between literacy

[125] Whyte and Whyte (1983): 34; Flinn (1977): 192–3.
[126] R. A. Houston, 'Illiteracy in the diocese of Durham' (1982c): 249.

levels in Lowland Scotland and Yorkshire is more marked. Scottish literacy was higher in the post-Restoration period for the middling orders in society, but by the eighteenth century there is little distinction between the areas of northern Britain. Perhaps the differences in levels of literacy in parts of Britain were not constant over time, the mid nineteenth-century superiority of Scotland being attributable to conjuncturally specific circumstances rather than being a permanent or enduring feature. Certainly, the importance of secular factors such as the social hierarchy or experience of living in a town were as important for Scottish writing ability as they were for English. There is little reason to see literacy as unusually widespread in Scottish society. And we should be rash to claim that Scotland's experience was 'dramatically different' from that of her southern neighbour.

Some possible reasons for these patterns will be discussed in chapter 4. Wider European comparisons over a longer time-span are drawn at the end of the following section of this chapter, and there is an account of literacy in Scotland and England as a whole in the period from 1638 to 1644 in chapter 3. But so far all of our remarks have been about the writing abilities of men and boys. We must now turn to a more detailed examination of women's literacy.

The experience of women

Girls and women formed more than half of the population of early modern Britain, but except in bald outline little is known of their writing abilities. We know from a variety of local and regional studies of England and Europe that until the nineteenth century women were usually much less literate than men. Just as signing ability was related to social and economic status and to a variety of identifiable secular factors, so too was it much less common among women than among men. This divergence of experience was a general and persistent feature of European societies in the pre-industrial period. Even in the fifteenth and sixteenth centuries when the clergy formed a literate elite, most nuns could not sign their own names. Indeed, before the middle of the seventeenth century female illiteracy in Scotland and England alike was generally worse than 90% and probably closer to 95% or 100%.[127] In England between 1640 and 1760, 42% of all male assize deponents were illiterate, while in Scotland between 1650 and 1770 the comparable level was 32%. The level for women is identical in both countries at 81%. These figures are not weighted in any way to

---

[127] M. Dilworth, 'Literacy of pre-Reformation monks' (1973): 71; Houston (1981): 190.

allow for the occupational composition of the sample: they are simple aggregates. If the social make-up of the sample was important, the proportion of deponents drawn from occupational or status groups which had high or low literacy would clearly influence aggregate figures.

The mere fact of being female created a distinctive experience of literacy, but we cannot be sure that gender-specific differences were more significant than those which can be related to position in the socio-economic hierarchy. Most analysis of British literacy tends to ignore the question of differences in female literacy which can be attributed to social status. Characteristically, all women are lumped together without regard to their occupation or social status, a convenient practice which nevertheless obscures important variations in levels of illiteracy.[128]

There is one immediate problem when we try to probe deeper into the structures of illiteracy among females. This is that women are almost never given an occupational or status designation of their own in early modern documents, despite the importance of their involvement in the labour force. The only appellation which women enjoyed in any numbers was that of servant, though very occasionally terms such as midwife, shopkeeper, innkeeper, mantua-maker, apprentice or portioner are used in the court records. One middle-aged woman earned her living in the 1760s as a chapman [*sic*] in Cumberland.[129] 'Singlewoman' is a frequent but unhelpful designation in seventeenth- and eighteenth-century assize records, along with the more ambiguous 'spinster'. The former designation is found more commonly in English towns and cities where female employment opportunities were expanding in the late seventeenth century, and may indicate a woman who was economically independent. There is bound to be a bias if we exclude all female labour apart from servants. Daughters of high-status fathers would be much less likely to have had experience of service than their more lowly counterparts, for the majority of whom service in another household formed a normal part of growing up.[130]

Thus we require some surrogate measure of female social status. Fortunately women are sometimes described in early modern documents in relation to a father, husband or master, giving an oblique indication of their social position. Women did not derive all their status vicariously from father or husband. What is more we undoubtedly lose some of the more subtle nuances in the social position which women

---

[128] Cressy (1980): 119–21, 144–5.   [129] PRO ASSI45: 28/2/22.
[130] Kussmaul (1981): 14–15.

claimed for themselves or were allocated by their peers. The status of widows may have fallen after the husband's death, for example, either through poverty or through loss of a male adjunct in a society dominated by men. In sixteenth- and seventeenth-century London, subtle differences in status existed between young women who lived in their parental home or away from it and between those whose fathers were alive or dead.[131]

In view of the difficulties in our sources we must make do with an indicator of status which is possibly removed from actual experience. Nevertheless the occupation or social status of a male relative or employer does seem to offer a broad guide to female social status. For unmarried women living in the parental home it would be difficult to establish a distinctive position in society, though women who headed their own households must have been more independent. For married women or widows the tendency towards social endogamy at marriage would offer a further reason to believe that the status of husband and wife would be similar. Parity in wealth, reputation, age and status was seen as an important criterion when selecting a marriage partner.

Table 2.11 reveals that a social profile of illiteracy existed for women which was very similar to the one we observed above for men. In Scotland as in England the (small numbers of) daughters, wives and widows of professional men and of the nobility and gentry were much more likely to be able to sign their names than other women. Such high-status women would have had better access to education in schools and at home and, in the case of landowners, can be seen taking a close interest in household and estate management from an early date.[132] Women at this level of society were economically involved and not legally disadvantaged to any great degree. Highly proficient female calligraphers like Esther Inglis who worked in late sixteenth- and early seventeenth-century Scotland came from this sort of background.[133] Some women received a training in Gaelic bardic composition, while a handful could boast the accomplishments of Katherine MacLean, wife of the Earl of Argyll, who was said to be 'not unlernyd in the Latyn tong, speckyth good French' and had a range of other cultural skills.[134] Even at this level of society, however, literacy was not universal as was the case with men.

---

[131] V. Brodsky, 'London women and the marriage market' (1981): 97–100.
[132] A. Clark, *The working life of women in the seventeenth century* (1919); Sanderson (1982): 171.
[133] Simpson (1973): 30–1.
[134] J. Bannerman, 'Literacy in the Highlands' (1983): 223.

Table 2.11. *Occupational illiteracy of female deponents in northern England and Lowland Scotland, 1640–1770*

	England		Scotland	
	1640–99	1700–70	1640–99	1700–70
Prof. & Gentry	(17) 24	(10) 0	(16) 35	(63) 25
Craft & Trade	(60) 78	(94) 69	(35) 71	(251) 72
Farmer/Tenant	(24) 88	(31) 68	(1) 100	(42) 86
Labourer	(20) 95	(24) 88	(5) 100	(40) 90
Servant	(39) 85	(51) 75	(52) 92	(214) 88
Total	(160)	(210)	(109)	(610)

Lower down the social scale we find a similar story. Female servants were highly illiterate and much more so than males in the same occupation. In both Scotland and England women who were servants to gentry and professionals had appreciably better literacy attainments than those working in craft and trade households or businesses. Five out of the fifteen English women in the former category were illiterate, and 47% of the thirty-two Scottish, while for the latter scores were 85% and 89% respectively. Women servants in all other groups including those where employer's occupation is not known were 89% illiterate in Scotland and 93% in England. The wives, widows and daughters of craftsmen and tradesmen form an intermediate group with levels around 70% among criminal court deponents during both the seventeenth and eighteenth centuries. Women from the lowest ranks of society and those still in service were almost wholly illiterate. It is only at this social level that male illiteracy among labourers and servants begins to approach that of females.

Numbers are admittedly small, but there is little if any evidence of improvements among the various social groups over the two centuries. Most social groups did see improving literacy, but only in the case of English yeomen women is there any strong evidence of a substantial rise in the proportion able to sign. A quarter of women related to gentry and professionals were illiterate, though the small numbers in the English sample and that for seventeenth-century Scotland make it difficult to offer any unequivocal judgements on the comparative literacy of this group. We cannot make any definite statements about changes in the literacy of Scottish women of tenant farmer status, since only one deponent fell in that category during the seventeenth century. The leases from Fife and Perthshire which we used to discuss the status of those who leased land do however show 80% illiteracy among ten women between the 1690s and 1720s. We

Table 2.12. *Occupational illiteracy of Scottish female deponents by decade,*
1680–1750

	Date						
Occupation	1680s	1690s	1700s	1710s	1720s	1730s	1740s
Craft & Trade	(18) 61	(26) 81	(38) 84	(41) 76	(35) 63	(35) 66	(53) 72
Servant	(32) 91	(35) 89	(39) 90	(34) 85	(39) 85	(24) 96	(38) 84

can find little to choose between Scotland and England if we compare the two countries, though England may have had a slight superiority in female literacy in the eighteenth century.

For Scottish women servants and the wives, widows and daughters of craftsmen and tradesmen there are enough deponents to allow a decadal analysis of changes in illiteracy (table 2.12). For female servants levels fluctuated around 90% from the late seventeenth to the mid eighteenth century, though for crafts- and tradeswomen there does seem to have been some fall in illiteracy during the second quarter of the eighteenth century. As with men in this category levels actually increased again during the 1740s and 1750s to reach scores close to those of the 1720s. The ratio between literate men and women was becoming more favourable to women over time in England. Between 1580 and 1640 there were eight literate males for every female; in the 1690s this had fallen to three to one, and to two to one by the 1750s.[135] However, the lack of any general improvement for women comparable to that for men meant that the numerical gap between the sexes in literacy attainments was widening over time, unlike contemporary France.[136] Gender did play an important role in determining literacy attainments, but position in the social hierarchy could also exert a powerful influence. We cannot escape the fact that an economic, social and political system which was dominated by the wealthy exercised considerable restrictions on the lower socio-economic groups amongst women as well as men (see table 2.13).

There is further evidence that women were subject to the same identifiable economic forces which shaped male literacy attainments. Like their craftsmen and tradesmen husbands and fathers, women living in towns were more literate than their rural-dwelling counterparts though, as with males, the exact occupational composition of this group is important to literacy levels. Scottish women associated with merchants were 26% illiterate, the equal of laird women, whereas

[135] O'Day (1982): 190.
[136] J. Houdaille, 'Les signatures au mariage' (1977); Longuet (1978).

Table 2.13. _Occupational illiteracy of Scottish and English female deponents in different communities of residence, 1640–1770_

Occupation	England			Scotland		
	City	Town	Village	City	Town	Village
Craft & Trade	(48) 60	(57) 74	(42) 81	(82) 60	(121) 63	(79) 96
Servant	(23) 78	(22) 73	(31) 87	(71) 93	(70) 84	(101) 92

weaver, smith and tailor related females were all worse than 80% illiterate. Innkeeper and wright women enjoyed an intermediate position at 48% and 67% respectively. All the percentages we have just discussed are based on categories which contain at least twenty women. There are too few female assize deponents in individual occupational groups to repeat this analysis for England.

The type of community in which an individual lived had as much importance for the literacy of women as it had for men. For Scottish women servants there is little to choose between city-, town- and village-dwellers. In both countries the profile of male and female differentials corresponds closely, especially among craft and trade occupations which would be most subject to the literacy-enhancing effect of economic need. Among men and women as a whole the homogenization of illiteracy levels in town and country which had occurred in parts of France by the late eighteenth century seems to have eluded British society, though in the city of York at least we know from the evidence of marriage registers that aggregate male and female levels had converged by the 1800s.[137] Among identifiable social groups, however, the gap between male and female attainments was no less pronounced in British towns and cities than in the countryside, again unlike France.[138] Employment opportunities for women were increasing in English towns of the later seventeenth and early eighteenth centuries, and like men more literate women may have been drawn to the towns. Educational provision was also better in towns, and every town of any size had a girl's academy by the mid seventeenth century.[139] Still, the influence of towns could not overcome the fundamental divergence between male and female illiteracy.

Already we can see some of the economic and social dimensions of high female illiteracy. However, the wide divergences in aggregate male and female illiteracy cannot be understood properly outside the

[137] Longuet (1978): 215–20; Yasumoto (1973): 84.
[138] Houdaille (1977): 71; Chartier (1976): 94.   [139] O'Day (1982): 187.

context of male attitudes towards women. The extent to which women could gain access to education and learning was closely determined by the social role allocated to them. Low female literacy was justified and perpetuated by strongly held opinions on their existing intellectual capacities and social importance.

The assumed inferiority of women was a major and pervasive feature of early modern European society. Views about the fickle and imperfect nature of female judgement restricted their chances of being called as witnesses in court cases. But these views also informed the desire to educate them with 'womanly virtues', since the 'mother of a family is a moral power, fertilizing the mind, and opening the heart to ... every virtue'.[140] Strong belief in the imperfection of women is clearly seen in attitudes to menstruation in the seventeenth century.[141] Meanwhile, the overwhelmingly masculine emphasis of Scottish social and ecclesiastical institutions which characterized the seventeenth century had its origins in the accepted priorities of Celtic society reinforced by the assumed sanction of divine approval at the Reformation. 'The ritual and moral inferiority of women was preached along with their new personal responsibility', which was to be aided by education and religious awareness.[142] Women had a new personal responsibility, but the means to fulfil it were denied them, thanks to the pessimistic outlook of members of the political and intellectual elites concerning their possibility for improvement. For Luther and Calvin and the Counter-Reformation Catholics the education of women was not seen by itself but as part of a much greater enterprise which involved the christianization of women, though the education they were to receive was to be restricted.[143] The consequences of this attitude to female education were neatly summarized by an early sixteenth-century writer. Joannes Vives spoke in his *Instruction of a Christen woman* (1529) of

the unreasonable oversyght of men, whiche never cease to complayne of womens conditions. And yet havyng the education and order of them in theyr owne handis, nat only do litell diligence to teache them and bryng them up better, but also purposely with drawe them fro lernyng, by whiche they might have occasyons to ware better by them selfe.[144]

It was assumed that girls should not be given the same education as boys since they would not be able to understand it and would in any case lack any opportunities to use additional learning. Thus the limited

---

[140] Gilly (1842): 32; see appendix 1.
[141] P. Crawford, 'Attitudes to menstruation in seventeenth century England' (1981).
[142] Larner (1981): 101; R. Mitchison, *Life in Scotland* (1978): 34.
[143] Chartier (1976): 238.
[144] Quoted in S. W. Hull, *Chaste, silent and obedient* (1982): 57.

education they received was used both as a sign of their inferiority and as a means of perpetuating it. Defoe, Locke and Swift felt that women should receive more of an academic education, but again these views were dictated by a very traditional conception of woman's role in the home. Defoe was one of the few writers who actually believed in encouraging women to be independent by giving them educational and economic opportunities. Misogyny was not universal. Yet few voices were raised to suggest that in an 'age of enlightenment' women should receive an education equal to that of men in the pursuit of reason. In his *Compleat woman* of 1639 Duboscq argued that reading 'is even necessary for all *women*, what kinde of spirit soever they be of, while it affords a certaine lustre to such as have it in an eminent degree, and lessons much their *imperfection* who have it not so great'.[145] Indeed, women's literature stressed their moral and intellectual inferiority and their duty to be subject to their husbands. Women, according to one Scottish worthy,

are taught what their parents or guardians judge it as necessary or useful for them to learn, and they are taught nothing else. Every part of their education tends evidently to some useful purpose, either to improve the natural attractions of their person or to form their mind to reserve, to modesty, to chastity, and to economy; to render them both likely to become the mistresses of a family, and to behave properly when they have become such.[146]

This was, of course, exactly the attitude of which Mary Wollstonecraft complained in her influential late eighteenth-century work, *Vindication of the rights of woman*. She developed 'a profound conviction that the neglected education of my fellow-creatures is the grand source of the misery I deplore, and that women, in particular, are rendered weak and wretched by a variety of concurring causes, originating from one hasty conclusion': that they were women rather than people.[147] Women suffered from 'a false system of education, gathered from the books written on this subject by men who, considering females rather as women than as human creatures' sought to mould their learning to male preconceptions.[148]

Arguments adduced by the political elites and by savants such as Rousseau to justify the ignorance of women were also used to keep knowledge from the lower orders.[149] Certain forms of learning were defined as necessary for political and cultural participation, while

---

[145] *Ibid.* 131; K. Rogers, 'The feminism of Daniel Defoe' (1976).
[146] Sinclair (1826): 128. Sinclair borrowed those thoughts on the subject from Adam Smith.
[147] M. Wollstonecraft, *Vindication of the rights of woman* (1975): 79.
[148] *Ibid.* 79.   [149] *Ibid.* 154.

popular culture was defined as largely irrelevant. The same thing happened with women, their position as purveyors of oral culture being undermined by a growing emphasis on literate forms. Many of the 'necessary' forms were reserved for men of the higher social classes. The attitude of dominant groups to women's literacy was informed by the same preconceptions as those regarding the masses. English thinkers of the sixteenth century argued about whether women provided guidance and protection for men or whether by nature they were bound to seduce them to evil. For some, education would enhance female virtue and religious faith while helping them to make an advantageous marriage. Detractors argued that it would hinder these desirable developments. As in contemporary France there was no dispute among established (male) thinkers about the social role of women, only about how best to prepare them for the tasks of bearing and socializing children and of keeping house. This attitude began to ease in the early eighteenth century as more sympathetic views were aired in periodicals such as the *Gentleman's Magazine*. However, the climate of opinion stayed deeply traditional in the main.[150]

These pessimistic and misogynist attitudes were reflected in the frequent separation of boys and girls in schools and in the different subjects taught to them. In Catholic countries convents were available for educating girls separately, but in Protestant Europe other forms of segregation were used.[151] In seventeenth-century Fife boys outnumbered girls among poor scholars paid for by the Kirk Sessions. On occasions female children were sent to the parish schools only when there were not enough boys to make a decent living for the teacher.[152] In Scotland male and female children were sometimes taught together in parish schools, but even then boys usually outnumbered girls and the sexes were often not learning the same lessons.[153] The burgh school of late sixteenth-century Ayr was unusual in teaching girls to read *and* write.[154] The minister of Bathgate in West Lothian in the 1790s told how 'labourers have often paid for teaching their sons [to learn to] read, write and sometimes arithmetic, and their daughters to read, and often to sew and write'.[155] There may have been a shift in emphasis over the eighteenth century towards greater curriculum equality between boys

---

[150] N. McMullen, 'The education of English gentlewomen 1540–1640' (1977): 87; Hull (1982): 106–24; Chartier (1976): 231–2; J. E. Hunter, 'The 18th-century Englishwoman' (1976).

[151] Chartier (1976): 233–5; M. Laget, 'Petits écoles en Languedoc' (1971): 1399, 1403, 1409.

[152] Beale (1953): 44–5, 224.   [153] Scotland (1969): 68, 81.

[154] W. Boyd, *Education in Ayrshire* (1961): 16.   [155] Scotland (1969): 56.

and girls.[156] Young women from the upper classes certainly had access to a wide range of education in eighteenth-century Edinburgh, though parents were still reluctant to see these as relevant to the 'useful accomplishments' fitting for 'the important duties of wives or mothers'.[157]

In England too in the late eighteenth and early nineteenth centuries girls occupied a high percentage of places only in inferior schools, though the numbers of boys and girls in all types of school lumped together was equal.[158] Girls were conventionally taught reading, sewing and knitting but were usually not given writing instruction in either Scotland or England.[159] Boys, where possible, received reading, writing and arithmetic. It was unusual in the eighteenth century for observers to advocate teaching of writing to poor boys and even rarer to girls. More common was the attitude revealed in the bequest of Bartholomew Hickling of Loughborough, who made provision for the poor girls of that town to learn the alphabet, spelling and reading, along with 'good manners and behaviour, the grounds and principles of the Christian religion'.[160] The much-vaunted classical education of the humanists was confined to only a few women of the highest social rank in sixteenth- and seventeenth-century England. Women's education was often confined to a few 'appropriate' topics, and girls commonly attended schools for a much shorter time than boys.

Contemporary attitudes towards women go a long way to explain the different education meted out to boys and girls. In Scotland, as in New England, 'women were discriminated against as women'.[161] Restricted curricula and duration of education for girls also imply that the ratio between those able to read and to sign was much worse for women than for men. Indeed, nineteenth-century evidence suggests that signing ability understates the proportion of the population who were able to read much more for women than for men. A criterion of literacy based on signing ability probably serves to enhance sex-specific differences in illiteracy when compared with one based on reading ability.

However, the picture is not entirely gloomy. The frequency with which women can be found teaching dame school in Scotland and England is just one indication of greater female participation in literacy

---

[156] *Ibid.* 109.   [157] Sinclair (1826): 127–8.   [158] Laqueur (1976c): 153.

[159] McMullen (1977): 100 shows that upper-class women did learn to read and write; Scotland (1969): 109; Spufford (1981): 34–5; F. G. Thompson, 'Technical education in the Highlands' (1972–4): 268.

[160] Quoted in J. Simon (1968a): 35.   [161] Lockridge (1974): 52.

than we might imagine.[162] There are even examples of women running parish schools. One seventeenth-century schoolmaster of Auchtermuchty in Fife, who also worked as a notary public, defended himself against the charge of neglecting his teaching by claiming that while he was away 'his wyffe did supply his absence, being able to teach bairnes as well as himself'.[163] Women are often to be found in the market place in early modern court records, an arena in which they would become familiar with skills such as reading and counting. In the essential task of running a household these would be important capabilities. The need for literacy was less developed than a trader's would be in casting accounts and writing receipts, yet it was suited to the context of economic and social life. At the same time the market place was particularly important as a centre of oral culture – the verbal dissemination of news and ideas in which women were involved to a considerable extent.[164] Women were certainly discriminated against in a systematic way, but this does not mean that we should denigrate their achievements or regard their cultural position as substandard to that of the literate man or to men in general, any more than we should do for the poorer levels of early modern society. Excluded to some extent from the literate mode of writing, which was deemed suitable for 'important' matters, women nevertheless played a full cultural role in early modern society. There may even have been a separate women's tradition of ballad composition and recital within the broader Scottish tradition – an emphasis on 'marvellous' rather than 'martial' topics, for example.[165] Oral modes of communication would have been preserved longer by women and by the lower, less literate classes among men in the transitional periods between restricted and mass literacy – the seventeenth and eighteenth centuries.

There is however no escaping the fact that women's ability to sign was everywhere far behind men's in early modern Britain. How do the differentials in Scotland and England compare with other countries and what can these tell us about the relative status of women? The sort of profile we have seen for Scotland is shown in all sources and in all European countries until the late nineteenth century.[166] In colonial New England male testators were 30% illiterate between 1705 and

---

[162] Sinclair (1826): 95.   [163] Beale (1953): 42.
[164] E. P. Thompson, 'The moral economy of the English crowd' (1971).
[165] D. Buchan, *The ballad and the folk* (1972): 76.
[166] R. A. Houston, 'Literacy and society in the west' (1983b); specific examples are drawn from Lockridge (1974): 39; M. Rodriguez and B. Bennassar, 'Signatures et niveau culturel' (1978): 25; W. Urban, 'La connaisance de l'écriture en Petite Pologne' (1977): 257; Cressy (1980): 113, 119–21; Houdaille (1977): 68.

1715, female 60%; in the years 1787–95 levels were 10% and 45% respectively. At the Toledo Inquisition during the centuries from 1525 to 1817 Spanish men were 37% illiterate and women 87%. The weighted national average illiteracy of the adult male population of France during the 1740s was 60%, while that of the female population was 81%. By the 1790s these figures had fallen to 51% and 70% respectively. Only in periods of time or among occupational groups where male illiteracy was very high did female levels ever begin to approach them. In Little Poland in the late sixteenth century, 96% female illiteracy was matched by 82% male. In the English diocese of Norwich during the 1630s husbandmen were 86% illiterate, while women as a whole were 94%.

The relative literacy of women compared to men is comparable in all the countries of north-west Europe and North America. Scotland is no exception. A starker contrast can be found between these parts of the world as a whole and the Mediterranean and eastern Europe. We can see in France that for most women their inferior legal and economic status was reflected and indeed reinforced by their backwardness in literacy.[167] However, discrimination in access to education is especially obvious in Pyrenean dioceses where educational provision was poor in any case, but where women received a particularly raw deal. In the diocese of Tarbes in the late eighteenth century, 62% of eligible boys can be found attending school, but only 2% of girls. Female enrolments did not match their proportion in the population until the 1880s. In the northern diocese of Reims, proportions attending school were almost equal for boys and girls at around 86%.

Areas of south and west France with relatively low male literacy to start with saw the slowest rate of female improvement.[168] The social position of women in southern France and indeed much of the Mediterranean world was much more of a subordinate one than in north-western Europe and this is reflected in comparative literacy attainments. Male deponents before the Toledo Inquisition improved their aggregate illiteracy from 43% during the sixteenth century to 27% by the second half of the seventeenth and then to a mere 8% during the years 1751–1817. For women, the respective scores are 96%, 100% and 82% illiterate.[169] In the rather more economically and culturally advanced environment of northern Italy in the eighteenth century, women with enough wealth behind them to enter into dowry contracts

---

[167] Chartier (1976): 90.
[168] *Ibid.* 42–3; F. Furet and W. Sachs, 'La croissance de l'alphabétisation en France' (1974): 726.
[169] Rodriguez and Bennassar (1978): 32.

Table 2.14. *Illiteracy in an Italian community, 1806–14*

	% illiterate	
Economic sector	males	females
Primary	84	99
Secondary	46	83
Tertiary	32	86
Residual	3	30

and who lived in the city of Turin were as literate overall as men from the neighbouring rural areas.[170] This was unusual in the Mediterranean world where time, residence and social status did little to bring women up to the level of men. At the market town of Vigevano in Lombardy between 1806 and 1814 the illiteracy of women was much higher than that of men and table 2.14 shows that the role of occupation and social status in stratifying literacy was considerably attenuated for females in this farming and silk-working community.[171] The primary sector was agriculture, the secondary industrial and commercial, the tertiary involved the provision of services. Outside the towns in Italy, gender was far more important than other factors in determining literacy differentials. For males, working in the secondary and tertiary sectors brought far higher levels of literacy than for farmers, but for women the enhancing effect of connections with non-agricultural employments was much attenuated.

A similarly stark profile obtains in eastern Europe. In the early seventeenth century most literate women came from the nobility, though even here literacy fell off quickly among the poorer sections, and wives of the minor nobility were 85% illiterate whereas nearly all women from the lordly classes could write. Some upper-middle-class women could sign their names, but there is a wide gap in literacy attainments between the social elites and the rest of society. Again, female school attendance was very low in Poland: in the diocese of Cracow at the end of the eighteenth century only 26% of all schoolchildren were girls.[172] This contrasts with the higher levels of female literacy in Britain and its more even social distribution, attributable in part to the bridging effect of craft and trade women. Conceivably, the structure of illiteracy for women who lived in Highland Scotland was similar to that obtaining in southern and eastern Europe. In other words,

[170] M. R. Duglio, 'Alfabetismo e societa' a Turino' (1971): 501.
[171] G. Vigo, 'Istruzione e societa'' (1972–3): 134.   [172] Urban (1977): 257.

male literacy was low, but female literacy was abysmally so. We shall examine illiteracy in Highland Scotland in the next section, but there were so few women deponents from this region at the High Court that it is impossible to derive reliable percentages from this source.

Female illiteracy reflects women's social position. Socio-economic conditions and education preserved differences between the sexes as they did between social groups. We are told that English women had an exceptionally favourable legal and social position, and their literacy attainments do indeed seem to have been somewhat higher than for those in Scotland or indeed elsewhere in Europe.[173] Where Scottish men were slightly superior to their northern English contemporaries, women in Scotland fell slightly behind their English sisters. Nevertheless, the attainments of Scottish and English women were not far out of line with north-west Europe as a whole. The contrast is much more marked between this part of the Continent and its southern and eastern regions.

Literacy was not a cultural necessity even in north-western Europe, yet there is no escaping the fact that many women could not write and would have needed help to participate effectively in the same range of economic and cultural activities as men. Given the structures of illiteracy this would mean in all likelihood seeking the advice and skills of a man, probably from a high social class. Lower female literacy illustrates women's inferior social position, but it was also one of the ways in which their status was justified and perpetuated. Literacy and education were of course only two of the many contexts in which social roles were defined and reinforced. It may also be significant that women never appear as central characters in the stories circulated in chapbooks and told in Sunday schools which portrayed social advancement through education.[174] Writers may have assumed that it would have been implausible to do so given the assumptions of their readers.

The relative independence and social position of women in Scotland is unclear. The one thing we can say is that the rhetoric of open access to education in early modern Scotland did not extend to females any more than it did to the bulk of the poor. If there were few 'lads o' pairts', there were even fewer lasses.

The highlands and islands

So far we have only been discussing northern England and Lowland Scotland. Yet in the seventeenth century nearly half of Scotland's

---

[173] Macfarlane (1978).   [174] Laqueur (1976c): 153.

population lived north of the Tay, while in 1755 Dr Alexander Webster's private census showed that 36% of her people lived in the Highlands and Islands.[175] Even into the late eighteenth century, Highland Scotland was a wild and remote area where traditional social and familial loyalties limited the extent of assimilation to the institutional changes taking place elsewhere in Scotland. Illiteracy was high at the time of the first national survey contained in the Registrar-General's report of 1855 and remained so until the end of the nineteenth century. In the 1850s, inability to sign one's name was much more common in the Highlands than in any Lowland county except for the most heavily industrialized ones around Glasgow. Even here, many inhabitants were recent immigrants from the Highlands or from Ireland. This much we saw in the introduction.

For earlier periods, the picture of literacy which we have is necessarily sketchy on the Highlands proper. Until 1747 there were large parts of Scotland called 'heritable jurisdictions', where certain crimes could be tried locally at private courts. These jurisdictions were areas of territory ranging from plots of a few hundred acres to many thousands possessed by a landowner in which he had certain specific legal privileges. He might be allowed to try cases of minor theft and assault only, but in places like Argyllshire that jurisdiction might cover all except a few of the most serious crimes which were reserved for royal courts, such as the High Court of Justiciary. Areas like this could be all but independent from a legal standpoint. Common throughout Scotland until 1747, these jurisdictions were especially important in the Highlands and the Western Isles. Despite some erosion of their functions by the royal courts and the Edinburgh lawyers during the early eighteenth century, the heritable jurisdictions continued to reserve a large amount of legal business to themselves, meaning that there are very few deponents at the Justiciary Court who came from the Highlands proper.

Nevertheless, we do possess enough information to discover whether the nineteenth-century pattern of low literacy in the Highlands was already present in the seventeenth and eighteenth centuries, or if it was a later development associated with the growing cultural split between the culturally and economically advanced Lowlands and the backward Highlands.

Taking the whole period from 1650 to 1770, the differences between the attainments of residents in the Highlands and those who lived in the rest of Scotland are striking. We are limited to certain occupational

[175] J. G. Kyd, *Scottish population statistics* (1952); Whyte (1979a): 9; Shaw (1981).

Table 2.15. *Occupational illiteracy of males in areas of Scotland (rural dwellers only), 1650–1770*

Occupation	Highland	Lowland
Craft & Trade	(63) 59	(257) 39
Farmer	(63) 70	(171) 37
Servant	(100) 83	(255) 67
Total	(226)	(683)

groups and, since there were no towns to speak of in the Highlands proper except perhaps Fort William and Stornoway, comparison is restricted to the 'village' category only. Table 2.15 shows that Highland craftsmen and tradesmen had 20% higher illiteracy than their Lowland counterparts, while Highland tenant farmers were nearly twice as badly off as the Lowlanders. Even in the middle of the eighteenth century estate rentals in Easter Ross show that adult male illiteracy (presumably among tenant farmers who leased land from the proprietor) was 50% or worse compared to an average of 35% in Lowland counties.[176] We can assume that cottars, landless labourers and women who would not usually appear in sources such as estate papers were still more disadvantaged. Servants too had appreciably lower literacy in the upland regions of the north and west of Scotland. *The moral statistics of the Highlands and Islands of Scotland*, published in 1826, provides further evidence of this pattern by revealing low school attendance and high illiteracy. Of 22,501 people who lived in seven west-Highland parishes during the early nineteenth century, 86% could read neither Gaelic nor English.[177] The Highland/Lowland split is even clear in the later sixteenth century. Only 7% of subscribers to a Lowland Bond of Association in 1567 were illiterate, but thirteen out of twenty-seven 'principal men' of Clan Grant could not sign a defensive bond during James VI's reign.[178] Particularly high illiteracy seems to have been a firmly established feature of Highland society by the start of the seventeenth century.

A superficial explanation of this low literacy in the Highlands would stress economic backwardness and communications difficulties. Certainly, the period from 1650–1780 has been identified as one of serious socio-economic problems for the area arising from an imbalance

---

[176] I. R. M. Mowat, 'Literacy, libraries and literature' (1979): 2.
[177] V. E. Durkacz, *The decline of the Celtic languages* (1983): 123.
[178] Simpson (1973): 25; Bannerman (1983): 216.

between population and resources. Among the area's many problems, much of the Highlands was far removed from access to an authorised market centre even in the early eighteenth century.[179] Settlements were dispersed, transport and communications poor and the deeply traditional economy offered few non-agricultural employment opportunities. Low per capita wealth, the social and economic dominance of a few landowners, lack of towns and the small numbers of independent tradesmen all helped to hold down literacy levels.[180] A larger proportion of the population were tenant farmers in the Highlands – one-half of adult males compared to about one-third in the Lowlands – but their socio-economic status was closer to better-off Lowland cottars. Landholdings were much smaller on average than those in the Lowlands, with arable plots being particularly small. A Highland tenant farmer may have been little better off materially than a Lowland cottar.[181]

At the same time the provision of schooling was much poorer than in the Lowlands. This is not to say that educational facilities were not available in the Highlands. The inventory of Samuel Ferguson in Nether Comes of Fall, Argyllshire, shows an outstanding debt of £362 Scots for nine years' boarding for his son William with Alan McLeale of Shuna, plus a further £13 Scots for books given to William while boarding during the years 1687–96. Janet, his first daughter, had had nine months' boarding and schooling with Mr Robert McRuddir.[182] Dated 1748, the testament of Duncan Fisher of Duren, sometime writer in Inverary, includes provision for his children's 'education, cloathing and maintenance to conform to their rank and quality'.[183] A grammar school existed at Stornoway in the late seventeenth century, and the synod of Argyll was vigorous in trying to promote education, notably in Skye.[184] There were also bursaries for Highland boys to attend Lowland schools, and in the seventeenth century some Highland lairds could send their sons to Lowland schools for 'that piece of learning which tends so much to form and polish their minds and to compleat them as gentlemen'.[185] The 1609 Statutes of Iona went so far as to stipulate that wealthy and powerful Highlanders were to send their children to Lowland schools in order to obtain an education in English and to pick up (acceptable) Lowland values. Education was available for those who could seek it out and could afford to pay for it.

[179] Dodgshon (1981): 277; Whyte (1979a): 183, 185.
[180] Shaw (1981); Dodgshon (1981): 287.
[181] Whyte and Whyte (1983): 34; Dodgshon (1981): 289–91.
[182] SRO CC2/5/2: 7 November 1698.   [183] SRO CC2/3/11: 205.
[184] Shaw (1981): 145.   [185] *Ibid*. 146; *Ecclesiastical records* (1837): 49.

More typically, however, we hear of scanty educational provision often stretching little further than learning practical skills such as weaving, knitting and spinning. This was scarcely 'technical education' but more a means of making profitable use of idle hands.[186] With little prospect of instilling intellectual competence into the mass of the Highland (or urban) population, reformers strove for the basic elements of 'moral' education. Inculcating habits of work would help to correct the idle, lawless ways which Lowlanders believed dominated the lives of their Highland counterparts. Some education in English was given in Highland schools as in the case of the girls who attended the spinning schools set up by the Commission for Annexed Estates in the mid eighteenth century.[187] These were unusual. Schools were generally few and far between in the Highlands. This remained true even after the early eighteenth-century drive by certain philanthropic bodies, of which the Society in Scotland for Propagating Christian Knowledge is probably the best known.[188] Founded in Edinburgh in 1709 the SSPCK was a firmly Presbyterian association whose aim was to educate and civilize the people of the Highlands. This body sought to Protestantize and anglicize the popish and ignorant people of the Highlands by setting up schools and by providing schoolmasters. By 1732 there were only 109 schoolmasters paid by this body, and even the Commissioners of Supply had failed to plant schools in 175 Highland parishes by 1758.[189] Just as teachers were in short supply, it was hard to find Calvinist ministers who could speak Gaelic and who would be prepared to preach in the Highlands. Presbytery minute books are filled with the often embarrassing wrigglings of clergy trying to evade a hardship posting to the barren north. In the proverbially backward Highlands were to be found 'wide and spacious paroches ... where ignorance, popery and profanity does much abound'.[190]

Schools were few and their geographical catchment area sometimes impracticably huge. Highland parishes were extremely large, far too big for one schoolmaster to cover all eligible children, and charity or private schools must have filled many of the gaps. Observers recognized that even parishes which had an official school would be inadequately provided for without additional charity or private adventure schools. In the Northern Isles, references to schoolmasters are chiefly confined to the main settlements, but, as in the Western Isles, the

---

[186] F. G. Thompson (1972–4): 249.   [187] Durkacz (1983): 71.
[188] Scotland (1969): 62; C. Withers, 'Education and anglicisation' (1982).
[189] F. G. Thompson (1972–4): 250.   [190] SRO CH2/424/8: fol. 361.

sporadic mention of teachers suggests an inability to sustain fixed schools in particular localities for any length of time.[191] As late as 1707, there were no legally settled schools in Caithness, except for Wick and Thurso. Only one was to be found at this date in Sutherland (at Dornoch) and a mere handful were located in Argyll.[192] The first recorded school of any kind in Kintyre was the one at Loch-head (Campbeltown) in 1622 and there was no formally established parochial school anywhere on the peninsula at this time. Parochial establishments only began to take root in any numbers from the 1690s onwards. Highland boys could only make serious use of the parish schools as a pathway to university from the late eighteenth century.[193]

Yet there is no need to follow Dr Johnson's view that 'as mountains are long before they are conquered, they are likewise long before they are civilized'.[194] Poor and geographically remote regions are not necessarily culturally backward. Limited educational facilities and a backward economy were serious obstacles to the advance of literacy, but in the case of Highland Scotland they were exacerbated by political and ideological forces. A better understanding of the reasons behind the long-established and continuing illiteracy in the Highlands can be gained by examining the cultural relationship of northern upland areas of Scotland to the Lowlands. In particular, we need to look at the predominance of the Gaelic language in the Highlands. In parts of the northern and western isles a Norse dialect was still used into the late seventeenth century, although Highland culture was predominantly Gaelic and had strong Irish connections.[195] English was known in the few Highland towns by the early eighteenth century and it certainly spread as time went on, thanks to the immigration of English-speaking farmers, experience of military service during the Napoleonic Wars and better school-teaching methods. However, the lower classes remained Gaelic monoglots until well into the nineteenth century. Habitual Gaelic speakers formed 47% of the total population of Easter Ross in 1881, for example.

The fact that much of the true Highland zone was Gaelic-speaking had a considerable impact on literacy levels. Even in the mid eighteenth century there were people in the town of Inverness, the main location of social and economic interaction between Highland and Lowlands, who could not speak English when called upon to

---

[191] Shaw (1981): 144–5.   [192] Durkacz (1983): 28.   [193] McKerral (1948): 150, 154–6.
[194] Quoted in P. Burke, *Popular culture in early modern Europe* (1978): 31.
[195] Shaw (1981): 138–9.

depone at the Justiciary Court. Their depositions were translated by sworn interpreters before entering into the written records. Alexander Cameron in Kylross, a 22-year-old bachelor, was 'examined and interrogate by Alexander Baillie Town Clerk of Inverness sworn interpreter for the witnesses who speak the Irish language'.[196] The same opportunity was given to deponents to sign their names, and the fact that many did not was simply because they had not learned, rather than because of any indirect language bias. Speaking Gaelic was not necessarily incompatible with sign-literacy and, indeed, a Gaelic letter-writing tradition existed from the late sixteenth century. In March 1687 six landowners from the Western Isles involved in the Argyll Rebellion appeared before the court. Three declared on oath that they could not write, while two stated that they were unable to speak English. One Gaelic-speaker was illiterate, but the other signed well.[197]

The low illiteracy of the Highlands is not an illusion, but has to be understood in the wider context of Gaelic culture and its proscription during the seventeenth and eighteenth centuries. Until the eleventh century, 'Gaelic was the medium through which information was communicated in the governmental, cultural and symbolic systems of the Scottish State, and was institutionalized in the Church and the bardic schools'.[198] Gaelic survived in the central and north-east Lowlands until the thirteenth century, and in parts of the south-west until the sixteenth century, but English was overwhelmingly the dominant language of the Lowlands by 1500.[199] Like early Ireland, there seems to have existed a literate caste whose work was transmitted orally to the non-literate masses of society. Recent research lends no credence whatsoever to Samuel Johnson's slander that 'neither bards nor Senachies could write or read'.[200] In 1582 a traveller in the Western Isles commented how 'their songs are not inelegant, and, in general, celebrate the praises of brave men; their bards seldom choosing any other subject. They speak the ancient Gaelic language a little altered.'[201] Seventeenth-century Gaelic poetry derived from a long oral tradition. Manuscript anthologies were compiled in the early sixteenth century by enthusiasts like James McGregor, dean of Lismore.[202] Gaelic was not a dead language by any means in the sixteenth and seventeenth centuries but formed part of a vital oral and literate culture.

---

[196] SRO JC11/7: 12.   [197] SRO JC6/12.
[198] K. M. Mackinnon, 'Education and social control' (1972): 126.
[199] Durkacz (1983): 215.
[200] S. Johnson, *A journey to the western islands of Scotland* (1775): 260.
[201] Brown (1893): 235.   [202] NLS Adv. MS 72.1.37.

However, acknowledgement of the legitimacy of Gaelic as a language was gradually withdrawn after the Reformation when its association with Catholicism became an embarrassment. Under Walter Scott's influence the trappings of Highland society became a chic curiosity in the mid nineteenth century. By the twentieth century, the hegemony of the dominant English language and Lowland culture was complete and Highlanders themselves accepted the negative attitudes towards their society. For the period between the sixteenth and nineteenth centuries the story is one of attempts to extirpate Gaelic and Catholic traces from Scottish society, a trend particularly noticeable in the anglicization programme which lasted from the late seventeenth century to the late eighteenth century.[203]

James VI's writings show early signs of a hostile attitude, and the 1609 Statutes of Iona prescribed education in the Lowlands for the heirs of lairds while simultaneously proscribing the activities of the traditional purveyors of Gaelic oral culture. This was one of a variety of legal and military measures designed to break down the traditional culture of the Highlands – a body of language, religion and social customs held to be a threat to the law-abiding Protestant people of the Lowlands. When they were not over-romanticizing the Highlands, Lowlanders and English alike were scathing in their condemnation of its society and culture. Highlanders, for example, were 'indolent to a high degree'.[204] John Knox was one of the few eighteenth-century writers to point out that it was hardly surprising that people were idle in the interior of the Highlands since there were no towns, manufactures, fisheries or harbours to employ them.[205]

Various measures were taken during the seventeenth and, more noticeably, eighteenth centuries to remove what was seen as a dangerous anachronism. Attempts were made to bring about agricultural improvements, social changes which would loosen traditional loyalties and economic ones which would give Highlanders the chance to be more industrious. English was to be the language of advancement and opportunity for the individual and for Highland society as a whole. Under the aegis of the SSPCK, campaigns of preaching were instituted to win the Highlanders from their syncretic Catholicism. A key instrument in the pacification and Protestantization of the Highlands was the move to augment the quantity of education as a means of extirpating Gaelic. The 1616 Education Act insisted upon

---

[203] V. Durkacz, 'The source of the language problem in Scottish education' (1978): 28; MacKinnon (1972): 127; Withers (1982); Mowat (1979): 1–3.
[204] Pennant (1774): 193.   [205] Knox (1784): 87.

education in English so that the 'Irish language which is one of the chief, principal causes of the continuance of barbarity and incivility in the Highlands may be abolished and removed'.[206] Civilization and Christianity were seen as synonymous with the English language and Protestant religion, ignorance and popery with Gaelic and the survival of Catholicism. Education in Gaelic was therefore firmly opposed by both church and state.

This attitude towards the vernacular language among those with the intention of extending and reorienting education was a serious hindrance to learning. Sir John Sinclair pointed to the great success achieved by the small number of Gaelic schools run by the SSPCK once attitudes to education in the Gaelic had begun to soften in the late eighteenth century, since with Gaelic 'it is not a new language that is taught, which would require a great additional labour, but only a new mode of applying one, with the words of which the scholar was already well acquainted'.[207] More usually schools were used as agents of cultural transformation in the direction of English speaking and Lowland values – an evangelical emphasis almost bound to fail. The aim of the SSPCK was straightforward. It sought to provide schools 'for teaching the principles of our Holy Religion in the English language and by time wearing out the Irish'.[208] Rote learning in a language which pupils may not have understood was unlikely to encourage literacy with the result that reading ability was low among Gaelic speakers. English learned at school would be quickly forgotten when children lived in a Gaelic-speaking environment. The result can be seen for example in the Statistical Account of the Isle of Harris in the 1790s which stated that only 108 of 2,536 inhabitants could read or write and that Gaelic speakers were particularly illiterate.[209] Recent work by Charles Withers on the 1826 *Moral statistics of the Highlands and Islands* confirms the pattern over the whole region: in the mainly Gaelic speaking parts of the north-west Highlands inability to read was common, but on the east and west Highland margins with a strong tradition of speaking English literacy was well developed.

The problems inherent in such an approach to education are clearly seen in the example of one young man educated in the Highlands and 'born again at Cambuslang' during the 1740s:

When I was about twelve year old I was put to school and was taught to read the Bible in English and Psalm Book in Irish or Highland language, being

---

[206] Quoted in O'Day (1982): 227.   [207] Sinclair (1826): 94.   [208] SRO GD 95/1/1: 294.
[209] Sinclair (1826): 92.

taught from my infancy to speak Irish and afterwards by hearing some people about me speak English I came to learn that language; but I could have read most of the English bible before I knew anything of the sense or literal meaning of what I was rendering.[210]

In the eighteenth century the SSPCK recognized that many Highlanders could read English without actually understanding it. To a considerable extent they only had themselves to blame, since, until the end of the eighteenth century, the Society steadfastly refused to countenance anything but learning in English. James Kirkwood recognized that 'children cannot be taught at first to read the Irish because some letters and syllables in that language are not pronounced'.[211]

There may also have been conscious resistance to anglicization. English was portrayed as the language of social and economic mobility and may have been perceived as such by some ambitious and well-informed parents. In 1721 the SSPCK affirmed that failure to learn English excluded Highlanders 'from all Commerce, Conversation and Correspondence with the rest of the nation', and debarred them from 'employments, Stations or offices that might afford them advantage'.[212] Others may have chosen not to have their children taught for political reasons, or simply because this would distance them culturally from the rest of the family. Instruction was in an alien language and conducted by people from outside the community: factors which must have prevented any quick progress.

By the late eighteenth century, insistence on English teaching was relaxed to some extent, but by then the harm had been done. Language was alienated from literacy by the attempt to import an alien cultural and linguistic norm in order to dilute the strength of association which the people had with their Gaelic past. Other steps were taken in this direction. Highland boys apprenticed to Lowland masters by the Commissioners for Annexed Estates were required to return to the Highlands to practise their trade. This was one method of introducing English into Gaelic communities. This attitude of antipathy to Gaelic was the dominant one in the eighteenth century, though the situation was improving in the early nineteenth century when the fear of Jacobitism receded and the evangelical Christians, along with the Edinburgh Gaelic School Society, began to provide instruction in Gaelic.

A further problem in education was the lack of vernacular literature

---

[210] Quoted in T. C. Smout, 'Born again at Cambuslang' (1982): 124; Durkacz (1983) is used extensively in the following discussion.
[211] Quoted in Durkacz (1978): 38.   [212] SRO GD95/1/2: 170–1.

from which to learn. Legal documents written in Gaelic did exist, but the only printed books in that language before the 1690s were religious. The first, which came out in 1567, was a translation of Knox's liturgy. The superiority of the Welsh language in this respect is clear when we realize that the same year saw the publication of a complete Bible in that tongue. There was no Gaelic New Testament till 1767 and no complete Bible till 1801. Some Irish Bibles were distributed, but without much success since Gaelic was not an identical language, and because the Scottish church was either indifferent or actively hostile to it. Only 350 titles were ever printed in Gaelic before 1850, 80% of them after 1800.[213] The Commissioners of the Annexed Estates ordered copies of books on agricultural improvement by Young and Dickson to be given to the factors of certain estates 'for the benefit of the tenants'. Most of them would have spoken only Gaelic. Preaching and catechism was provided in Gaelic, sometimes by reluctant Lowland ministers who happened to speak it and who were sent by their presbyteries to the Highlands.

The fact that there was no Gaelic foundation for literacy when a drive for Highland education started in the eighteenth century seriously hampered its advancement. Coupled with the opposition of church and state to Gaelic, this meant that attempts by figures such as James Kirkwood to bind literacy and learning to the Gaelic language were doomed to failure. The same was not true of the other minority language in Britain, Welsh, which had popular scriptural books in the seventeenth century and which was not proscribed by official bodies. The campaign of Griffith Jones worked by 'binding Welsh to religion and education, and stabilizing bilingualism by giving Welsh a role in community life'. Wales was not free of attempts to integrate its people to the dominant culture and polity of England. Welsh grammar schools only catered for the English-speaking gentry.[214] However, the Welsh language was not attacked in the same way as Gaelic.

The Gaelic experience seems to have been more typical of European developments, at least in so far as literature was available largely in the dominant language of religion and politics. Indeed, the existence of discrete linguistic regions within and sometimes transcending national boundaries was a common feature throughout early modern Europe. The precocious Friesland peasants who owned books in the seventeenth century had to read them in Dutch rather than their own local dialect. Vernacular editions there certainly were in sixteenth- and seventeenth-century France, but rarely in regional dialects such as

[213] Durkacz (1978): 29–31; Durkacz (1983): 15, 34; Mowat (1979): 9; Smout (1972): 432–3.
[214] Durkacz (1978): 39; O'Day (1982): 39.

Breton, Provençal or Poitevin. Catechism might be available in patois, but reading and writing was taught in French.[215] In France, Belgium, Prussia and Spain linguistic zones were broadly coterminous with literacy ones. Stendhal's comment on the triangle between Bordeaux, Bayonne and Valence, where 'they believe in witches, they cannot read and do not speak French ... they are unbelievably ignorant', echoes those made of the Highlands of Scotland in the eighteenth and nineteenth centuries.[216] In areas of France like Brittany, linguistic differences are associated with identifiable social and economic characteristics which also account for low literacy: a feudal social structure, for example, which contrasted with the predominance of small independent farmers in French-speaking areas. Again, this is true of the Scottish Highlands. However, we cannot relate this simply to economic structures any more than we can to geography. Countries such as Norway and Switzerland, along with the Hautes Alpes region of France, all had literacy levels approaching or even exceeding socially and economically precocious parts of Europe. It was the gap between vernacular usage and the official language of education, politics, business and ritual which created areas of high illiteracy every bit as much as environmental factors.

In areas like Languedoc where the local dialect was well established, illiteracy was higher than in areas where the dominant official language obtained. *Langue d'oc* was spoken, not written, and schools teaching Latin or French within the patois regions were bound, like English schools in the Gaelic Highlands, to have a limited effect. Despite the late eighteenth-century campaign to replace patois with French in provincial schools, as late as the 1890s there were still educational problems existing in Provence as a result of the insistence on teaching in French among a largely Provençal-speaking population.[217] Like Highland deponents at the eighteenth-century Justiciary Court, delegates from the Midi who participated in revolutionary assemblies in the 1790s had to have interpreters. Of course, the political and social context of the countries was quite different. Language was not proscribed as a dangerous instrument of conservatism in Languedoc as it was in the Scottish Highlands.

Nor is there any automatic connection between regions of patois and

---

[215] J. de Vries, 'Peasant demand patterns and economic development in Friesland' (1975): 222; N. Z. Davis, *Society and culture in early modern France* (1975): 197; P. Butel, 'L'instruction populaire en Aquitaine' (1976): 16; J.-R. Armogathe, 'Les catéchismes et l'enseignement populaire' (1974): 111.

[216] Quoted in Furet and Ozouf (1982): 318.

[217] Chartier (1976): 107; L. Trenard, 'Histoire des sciences de l'éducation' (1977): 466; T. Judt, 'The impact of the schools' (1981): 264–5.

illiteracy. We must also take into account the emphasis on oral communication in some areas and the rejection of schools and of the dominant language and culture by some communities or some sections of society. Yet the impact on literacy of the relationship between dominant and peripheral language was much the same. In its drive for ideological orthodoxy, the early modern Scottish state, like that in France, sought to assimilate the sorts of distinct regions which had typified the medieval polity to uniform, national political and cultural norms. Administrative integration and linguistic assimilation were to be achieved by institutional changes, such as the abolition of heritable jurisdictions or the introduction of schools where learning was taught in the dominant, 'national' language. Even in England the existence of regional dialects may have created problems of communication between inhabitants of different areas. Separate languages survived longer than is sometimes thought. Cornish was the prevailing tongue west of the river Tamar during the fifteenth and sixteenth centuries and was only really eradicated during the eighteenth and nineteenth centuries.[218] Unlike Gaelic or Welsh, Cornish was not a medium of worship and was swamped by the vigour and cultural buoyancy of English.

Linguistic differences also mirrored social ones and reinforced developing cultural splits during the seventeenth and eighteenth centuries. The divide between predominantly oral communication in Gaelic or Provençal or Poitevin and the oral and literate world of English and Latin or French and Latin was marked, and bridged only by the elites who could communicate in all the available media. As in southern France, when the Scottish elite who spoke both languages and could mediate for those who were Gaelic-speakers chose to turn their back on the traditional culture, it would become isolated and peripheral to mainstream cultural developments. This happened in the Highlands of Scotland during the seventeenth, eighteenth and nineteenth centuries, as it did in southern France where the elites came eventually to reject patois in favour of integration into the national culture. The mass of the patois speakers were left illiterate and culturally isolated.[219] Finally, the example of Flemish shows how, where a regional language is restricted to religious and learned matters and leaves the bulk of the population without a literate means of communication, literacy will remain low.[220]

Through neglect, poverty, language and geography the literacy of the Highlands lagged far behind the rest of Scotland until the late

---

[218] Durkacz (1983): 214.   [219] Shaw (1981): 154–64.   [220] Chartier (1976): 107–8.

nineteenth century. Whatever the disadvantages the Highlands laboured under they were seriously aggravated by the search for religious, cultural and political hegemony waged by the Lowlanders. Until the nineteenth century, church and state were wholly opposed to bilingual education in the Highlands, this insistence being part of a drive for political integration and cultural unification. We cannot understand literacy properly without setting it in its full cultural and political context.

3

Illiteracy in mid seventeenth-century Britain

We have dealt in some detail with the period between the English Civil War and the onset of the Industrial Revolution in Britain. One aim of this book is to fill in gaps in our knowledge about this century. However, we cannot entirely ignore earlier times. As far as the decades between the accession of Elizabeth and the reign of Charles I are concerned the picture is relatively clear, at least for England. The important work of David Cressy has shown that the later sixteenth and early seventeenth centuries was an important period throughout England of substantially improving literacy for yeomen, and for craftsmen and tradesmen, but less so for women and the lower social ranks among men.[1]

Of this earlier period there is unfortunately precious little we can say for Scotland. Sources are scanty and their reliability is open to question. Of 379 males who subscribed the 1581 Confession of Faith in the small town of Kinghorn in Fife, 84% were illiterate, as were all 414 women.[2] Some patchy figures can be gleaned from the Justiciary Court 'Small Papers' – loose documents of the court – which suggest that levels of literacy among key groups were remarkably constant between the last quarter of the sixteenth century and the mid seventeenth century. Of twenty-nine craft and trade deponents at the Justiciary Court whose testimonies were subscribed between 1575 and 1660, 48% were illiterate, and nine of eighteen for 1661–80. Many more depositions survive for this period, but most are innocent of any holograph subscription. These figures are close to levels obtained for comparable social groups from Durham Diocese Consistory Court depositions between 1580 and 1630.[3] Unlike the same class in the north of England,

---

[1] Cressy (1980): ch. 7.   [2] SRO CH2/472/1.   [3] Cressy (1980): 146.

however, the Scottish gentry class were all literate from the late sixteenth century. The levels for the Restoration period also sit well with
the 47% illiteracy of craft and trade deponents who appeared before
the Justiciary Court in the 1650s: see table 2.4. For Scottish workmen
and servants the numbers are again small at twenty-two in the earlier
period (91% illiterate) and only ten (80% illiterate) for the later.[4]
Aggregate female illiteracy stayed above 90% over the century 1575 to
1680 for the 103 deponents who appeared before the Justiciary Court
and whose testimonies survive in the Small Papers.[5] The seventy or so
years to 1650 seems to have been a period of comparatively stable
literacy in Scotland compared to the changes of the following century
and a quarter. From the slight evidence we have there seems to be little
sign of an 'educational evolution' of the kind which took place between
1540 and 1640 in England.

Given the small sample size and long time-span involved we should
not place too much faith in these figures for the late sixteenth and early
seventeenth centuries. We shall probably never find documents which
would allow reliable quantitative analysis of literacy in Scotland in the
century before the Scottish Revolution. However, there are sources
which allow us to assess adult male illiteracy in the mid seventeenth
century for both Scotland and England: oaths of loyalty associated with
the political and religious upsets of the period from 1638 to 1644. These
were variously called Covenants or Protestations. The snapshot picture of literacy across mainland Britain at one point in time which we
can glean from the Covenants is useful, because we can study not only
the adult male population as a whole, but we can establish the geographical distribution of literacy: crucial tasks if we are to discover
whether Scotland did indeed have a distinctive experience of literacy in
the period before the Industrial Revolution.

Throughout its long history the National Covenant in Scotland was
essentially a 'defensive bond' designed ostensibly to protect the
person of the king, but used in the seventeenth century as a political
instrument to unite Presbyterian Scotland against the religious innovations of Archbishop Laud. The Solemn League and Covenant of 1643
was intended specifically to ensure support for the English Parliamentary cause provided the churches of England and Ireland were
made Presbyterian like that of Scotland. The 1638 Covenant was so
phrased as to possess 'popular politico-religious appeal', and when
sent out all were exhorted to sign it.[6] According to contemporaries it

---

[4] Houston (1981): 207.   [5] *Ibid.* 190.   [6] G. Donaldson, *Scotland* (1974): 190–1.

was received with universal approbation, one observer claiming that it was signed 'in a very short time by almost the whole kingdom'. The impression that 'the enthusiasm of the people everywhere was unprecedented' is probably an exaggeration, and regional or local variations in religious zeal would necessarily influence the proportion of the adult male population signing in any one parish.[7] However, Hugo Arnot noted that 'few, in their habits, were disposed to resist it. Fewer still durst avow their disinclination towards it.'[8] Meanwhile, for the inhabitants of Dundonald in Ayrshire the Covenant was sworn 'with the wonderful applause of all the congregation without exception, shewing thare reddiness of mind by the elevation of hands, cheirfulness of countenance, tears and all the expressions of joy that the gravitie of the meeting could admit'.[9]

Local factors could promote particularly full subscription. The laird of Edzell was a zealous Covenanter and would have exerted personal pressure on parishioners to ensure subscription. Presbyteries, such as St Andrews in Fife, ordered that the Solemn League and Covenant be subscribed by all, while that of Ayr prescribed that the names of 'all schifters and refusers' should be written down. Penalties for not taking the 1643 bond were severe, amounting to confiscation of goods.[10] The atmosphere of the time augurs well for the completeness of subscription. Popular concern with political and religious matters may also have encouraged widespread subscription and even have fostered literacy. In 1639, Dalkeith presbytery ordered its ministers to make more of private worship in families, especially now 'instructions for familie worship and exercising of prayer and catechising are come out in print'.[11] As in England, political and religious debate may have increased the desire of adults for literacy.

Many copies of Covenants from the 1630s and 1640s survive, but because of the way subscriptions were collected for some of them they cannot all be used with equal confidence as indicators of literacy. The criteria used to select those Covenants felt to be reliable enough for the analysis of literacy among those which have survived is outlined in detail in an appendix. To summarize these, the ideal is to have a set of subscriptions collected over a short period of time within a delimited geographical area, such as a parish, and known to cover a uniform section of the population – adult males, for instance. Some Covenants

---

[7] J. D. Mackie, *A history of Scotland* (1978): 204.   [8] Arnot (1816): 86.
[9] SRO CH2/104/1: fol. 146.
[10] *Ecclesiastical records* (1837): 15–16; Mackie (1978): 215; J. K. Hewison, *The Covenanters* (1908): 388; J. H. Pagan, *Annals of Ayr* (1897): 25.
[11] SRO CH2/424/3: 14 November 1639.

are open-ended in their date of subscription, raising the problem of re-subscription or the distorting effect of geographical movement among the population. In others, the place of residence of subscribers cannot be determined accurately. In this respect the 1643 Covenant is superior, since the 1638 document was often signed by prominent Covenanters in Edinburgh before being sent out into the localities for general subscription. Some Covenants were signed by nobles or ministers only: a particular problem with the 1638 examples. Preferred were Covenants such as that from North Leith, which was notarially attested 'at the north kirk of Leith the sevant and fyftane dayis of Aprill' 1638 by persons 'all indwellers in the north syd of the brig'.[12]

Who were the subscribers of the Covenants? Hostile commentators characterized them as illiterate cobblers and tanners, paupers, lunatics and children. Occupations are listed in some Covenants on a random basis, and among the individuals we can find local lairds, farmers, tradesmen and craftsmen. At Maybole, for example, we can identify smiths, coopers, tailors, cordwainers, merchants, wrights, fleshers, baxters and a group of sub-tenants.[13] The impression is less of those on the margins of society than of a cross-section of the local community. A more accurate generalization might be that adult male churchgoers comprised the bulk of subscribers. Rosalind Mitchison has compared the personnel in the Dundonald Covenant with those persons who appeared in the Kirk Session records for that parish, and concludes that the poor, miscreants and transient persons were under-represented, along with those fortuitously absent through illhealth, bad weather or business.[14] Rather than being over-represented, these low-status sections of the community were probably excluded to a greater or lesser extent. We have already seen from deposition evidence that the former group are likely to have comprised the less literate elements of society. If the same sort of shortcoming is true of all the parishes considered here, the figures in table 3.2 may be under-estimates of adult male illiteracy. Attempts to maximize subscription among parishioners were sometimes made – at Edzell and North Leith, for example, where the Covenants were left open for subscription at more than one church service.[15]

Considerable care seems to have been exercised in the collection of names for the Covenant – a diligence not shown in the amassing of signatures to other locally organized petitions. In situations as public

---

[12] North Leith Covenant in New College Library (NCL), Edinburgh.
[13] SRO GD103/2/150.   [14] Mitchison (1978): 43; NLS Adv. MS 23.3.16: fol. 7.
[15] NCL.

and important as the signing of the Covenant, a notary public would be on hand to take the names of the illiterates and to enter them on the document according to legal form above his own attestation that they were present, consented to being included and could not write despite being given the opportunity to do so. Illiterates publicly announced their assent to the Covenant. The only possible distortion is likely to arise when men who could write decided not to do so for some reason.

The most closely comparable English sources for the mid seventeenth century are the various oaths of loyalty subscribed by adult males between 1641 and 1644. The reliability of these documents and the patterns of illiteracy they show have already been discussed in some detail by David Cressy in his monograph *Literacy and the social order*, and we need only offer a short summary here. The oaths were drawn up to enhance national solidarity at a time of political uncertainty and subscribers vowed to preserve Protestantism, liberty and the law. All those above the age of eighteen were to take the oath which, like the Scottish Covenants, was well received by a determined people. Stronger oaths were contained in the Vow and Covenant of 1643 and in the Solemn League and Covenant of 1644 which were again administered in the localities. Only 'demonstrably authentic and complete' examples of these oaths have been used in this study and the levels of adult male illiteracy in certain English counties shown in table 3.1 are based on these.[16]

Table 3.1 shows the number of parishes in each county with surviving, usable returns, the number of subscribers to the oath in those parishes, mean illiteracy in all parishes plus the range of scores within a county. There are some variations between counties, but those within them are more striking. Cheshire, Huntingdonshire and Sussex are the most noteworthy instances, though the widest variations appear between parishes with unreliably small numbers of subscribers. The rich London parishes had easily the lowest average illiteracy of all. Among other counties, mean illiteracy ranges from 76% in Nottinghamshire to 52% in Chester city. Overall illiteracy is around 70%. Contrary to Stone's belief, there is no conclusive evidence that illiteracy increased in the north and west of England, nor that it was related to upland zones. At the same time, Cressy seems to be exaggerating when he claims that the north of England was steeped in illiteracy compared to the south.[17] There are few surviving returns for the north of England, but these reveal levels of illiteracy only slightly higher than the average elsewhere in non-metropolitan England. In contrast to the

---

[16] Cressy (1980): 73.   [17] Stone (1969): 100. Cressy (1980): 75.

Scottish sample, town parishes are under-represented in table 3.1 though there is definitely evidence of superior urban literacy in some town parishes. Few usable urban returns, smaller parishes in England and thus smaller numbers leave the issue of suburban versus inner parish literacy unresolved, though we might suspect that richer inner parishes were likely to have lower illiteracy. How do these scores compare with contemporary Scotland?

English returns are grouped by county, but the small number of Scottish parishes in table 3.2[18] are arranged alphabetically according to whether they are 'urban' or 'rural'. As in the case of England, literacy levels for adult males in individual communities vary considerably from 32% unable to sign in the Edinburgh parish to 90% at Edzell. However, six of the eight town parishes fall in the narrow range 46–54% illiterate and this sets them well apart from the 70–90% spread of the predominantly rural communities. We shall examine the social and economic nature of the parishes in more detail, but it would be well to remember this basic division.

How do we explain the different levels of illiteracy in the Scottish parishes? First, there is a geographical dimension to consider. Most of the surviving Covenants which are sufficiently inclusive for analysis come from parishes in Lowland Scotland. Nevertheless, they do provide a reasonable geographical spread and offer a useful selection of contrasting economic types, which are outlined below. By casting our eye down the counties we can see that geographical location does not appear to account satisfactorily for the considerable variations between communities even within the urban and rural categories.

The division between Highland and Lowland is seen as a particularly crucial one in pre-industrial Scotland. In his *Britannia*, William Camden claimed that 'With respect to the manners and ways of living, it is divided into the *High-land-men* and the *Low-land-men*. These are more civilized, and use the language and habit of the English; the other more rude and barbarous, and use that of the

---

[18] Sources: Ayr, National Library of Scotland (NLS) Adv. MS 20.6.17b.; (there is a transcript in *Ayr Advocation* for 8 October 1874: NLS Adv. MS 20.6.17a); Borgue, SRO SP13/160; Dalmellington, Scotland (1969): 49; Dundonald, SRO CH2/104/1: fols. 146–50; Edzell, New College Library, Mound, Edinburgh; Galston, in the kirk session register for 1638–44, in the keeping of the minister, the Manse, Galston; Gartly, SRO SP13/161; Inveresk, NLS Adv. MS 20.6.18; Kilmany, SRO 'File T258' (photographic copy); Kinneil and Bo'ness, New College Library; Legerwood, Edinburgh University Library LaIII 229/1; Menmuir, NLS MS 3279; Newbattle, Museum of the Society of Antiquaries, Queen St, Edinburgh, OA19; North Leith, New College Library; North West Edinburgh, NLS Adv. MS 23.3.16; Stranraer, Mitchison (1978): 45; Forfarshire, NLS Adv. MS 34.5.15; Ceres, Beale (1953): 99; Abercorn and St Andrews, St Andrews University Library.

Table 3.1. *Adult male illiteracy in England, 1641–4*

County	N parishes	N subscribers	% illit.	range
Berkshire	(12)	(725)	74	93–57
Buckinghamshire	(3)	(156)	71	75–69
Chester city	(5)	(736)	52	82–30
Cornwall	(116)	(15,868)	72	92–47
Derbyshire	(3)	(316)	74	77–61
Devon	(38)	(4,903)	72	87–57
Dorset	(9)	(573)	70	77–47
Durham	(2)	(247)	74	77–68
Essex	(16)	(1,081)	63	85–36
Hertfordshire	(1)	(85)	74	
Huntingdonshire	(28)	(1,933)	67	80–7
Lincolnshire	(48)	(3,152)	73	94–50
London	(4)	(609)	22	33–9
Middlesex	(3)	(392)	62	77–41
Norfolk	(4)	(146)	72	89–56
Nottinghamshire	(49)	(3,845)	76	93–27
Oxfordshire	(4)	(288)	66	71–58
Shropshire	(1)	(67)	66	
Somerset	(4)	(904)	64	85–37
Staffordshire	(3)	(312)	64	71–63
Suffolk	(6)	(294)	45	58–36
Surrey	(18)	(1,228)	68	91–49
Sussex	(28)	(1,797)	71	82–59
Westmorland	(7)	(797)	74	94–62
Yorkshire	(2)	(639)	74	74–73
Total	(414)	(41,093)	70	94–7

Irish.'[19] Illiteracy was substantially more common in the Highlands between 1650 and 1770, and in the mid eighteenth century adult males in that part of Scotland were 20–30% less literate than their Lowland counterparts. There are unfortunately no truly Highland parishes among the surviving Covenants – hardly surprising in view of the lack of commitment to Presbyterianism there. Gartly, Legerwood and Borgue are at least upland parishes, and do certainly have above average illiteracy. However, they are not unique but are matched or even exceeded by Dundonald, Kilmany and Edzell. The gap between upland and lowland is not as wide as we should expect from the Highland/Lowland differences we saw above among farmers, servants, craftsmen and tradesmen. There is no reason to see a necessary connection between upland, northern communities and illiteracy any

[19] W. Camden, *Britannia* (1695): 885.

Table 3.2. *Adult male illiteracy in Scotland, 1638–44*

Parish and county	Key	Total subscribers	% illit.
Towns			
Ayr, Ayrshire	A	(386)	46
Ceres, Fife	Ce	(68)	60
Inveresk, Midlothian	I	(707)	52
Kinneil and Bo'ness, West Lothian	KB	(303)	53
North Leith, Midlothian	D	(357)	51
St Andrews, Fife (town only)	SA	(628)	54
Stranraer, Wigtownshire	S	(183)	52
Tolbooth (Edinburgh), Midlothian	Ed	(729)	32
Rural parishes			
Abercorn, West Lothian	Ab	(265)	81
Borgue, Kirkcudbrightshire	B	(217)	87
Dalmellington, Ayrshire	Da	(222)	81
Dundonald, Ayrshire	D	(222)	83
Edzell, Forfarshire	E	(211)	90
Galston, Ayrshire	Ga	(335)	70
Gartly, Aberdeenshire	Gr	(170)	83
Kilmany, Fife	K	(210)	89
Legerwood, Berwickshire	Le	(150)	82
Menmuir, Forfarshire	M	(54)	70
Newbattle, Midlothian	N	(383)	76
Forfarshire	–	(1,058)	76
St Andrews, Fife (landward part)	SA	(223)	88
Total		(7,081)	

more than there is in seventeenth-century England. Newbattle, Galston and Menmuir have slightly below average illiteracy and are rather more 'modern' in the sense of being more agriculturally specialized and integrated into developed market systems. In the case of Menmuir, the numbers involved are so small that one or two signatures either way would alter the proportions considerably. What we can say is that simple generalizations about geographical location offer little help in explaining literacy differentials. We shall have to go into more detail.

In periods with better documentation there is more opportunity to carry out a full analysis of the possible reasons for differing literacy levels. Thus for late eighteenth- and early nineteenth-century England, Schofield shows that parishes which underwent appreciable falls in illiteracy

were more likely to have had an ordinary day school, but not a Sunday school, a wider dispersion of landownership, a higher percentage of inhabitants in

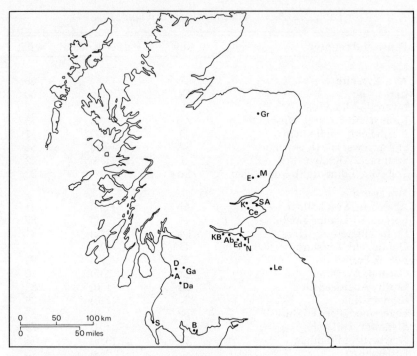

Location of parishes with surviving covenants used in table 3.2 (For key see table 3.2)

non-agricultural occupations, and to have expended less per capita on Poor Relief in the 1830s than had parishes in which illiteracy increased.[20]

There is no chance to perform such a detailed parish level investigation even at one point in time for seventeenth-century Scotland. Consider-able effort would be required to repeat the detailed analysis conducted by Margaret Spufford on education and literacy in parts of sixteenth- and seventeenth-century Cambridgeshire. For a variety of reasons, Scottish local history is poorly developed compared with English, and the range of secondary literature on subjects not related to religion and genealogy is narrow.[21] Even where documents are available, the amount of labour involved in constructing a proper outline of the socio-economic characteristics of the Covenant parishes would be too great for such a general study. A simple sketch is therefore all that is offered here. Nevertheless, this will provide us with an adequate con-textual framework within which to see the variations between literacy

[20] R. S. Schofield, 'Dimensions of illiteracy' (1981): 209.
[21] I. D. Whyte, 'Scottish historical geography' (1978).

levels shown in table 3.2. We can at least offer some tentative suggestions about the sorts of environment where people became or were induced to become literate.

The three parishes outside the central Lowlands – Borgue, Gartly and Legerwood – are, broadly speaking, examples of relatively backward mixed farming areas with a bias towards pastoral agriculture. Borgue, contiguous to the small market town of Kirkcudbright, seems to have been a prosperous farming and fishing parish in the early seventeenth century. 'This parish abounds with plenty of corne, wherewith it furnishes many other places in the Stewartrie.'[22] At some time before the 1680s there had been a weekly market in one of the parish's settlements, but this had fallen into decay. Half a century later, however, Defoe singled out this region as one with favourable resources sadly under-exploited. The agricultural and undeveloped economy of the area had implications for social structure, the civil and criminal court records for the south-west in the seventeenth century making frequent use of the term 'labourer-farmer'. This part of Scotland underwent significant economic and social changes around the end of the century, notably consolidation of farms and erection of enclosures for cattle farming. In the early seventeenth century the area was dominated by large numbers of small tenant farmers.

The largest town in the south-west after Dumfries, Stranraer was only made into a royal burgh in 1611. It was more prosperous than many parts of the region, thanks to its combined functions of port and administrative centre – it was the seat of a presbytery, for example. On the other side of Scotland, Legerwood lay on the edge of the rich Merse farming region of Berwickshire, part of an area where Dodgshon has shown commercial pastoral farming to have been much more developed than was once believed.[23] Moving north to Aberdeenshire, the parish of Gartly is situated in the Grampian mounts, where constraints of geography and climate dictated the dominance of pastoral farming. An early eighteenth-century account described the parish as set in 'a country very pleasant and fertile of Corns and Pasturage'.[24] This was not however a truly Highland parish, since it was within striking distance of the prosperous coastal plain of the north east.

[22] W. Macfarlane, *Geographical collections* vol. 2 (1907): 65; information on Borgue derived from A. Fenton, 'Scottish agriculture and the Union' (1974): 77; Defoe (1978): 596–9; J. B. Henderson, *Borgue* (1898): 19, 22; T. C. Smout, 'The foreign trade of Dumfries and Kirkcudbright' (1958–9); SRO JC26; SRO CC8/6/14; R. A. Houston, 'Parish listings and social structure' (1979); Lenman (1977a): 68–9.

[23] R. A. Dodgshon, 'The economics of sheep farming in the Southern Uplands' (1976).

[24] Macfarlane, vol. 1 (1906): 36.

For the remaining Covenant parishes listed in table 3.2 we are dependent on the Lowland counties of Forfarshire, Ayrshire and the Lothians. The two Forfarshire parishes are located on the fertile plain north of Dundee. Both were involved in the production of grain for local markets and for the expanding coastal trade with centres of demand such as Leith and Edinburgh. All sorts of grain were cultivated 'in such plenty as to suffice not only for home consumption, but for a supply to the inhabitants of other countries'. There was also a 'great abundance of cattel, sheep and horse, especially [in] the brae country'.[25] The small parish of Menmuir near Brechin was a rich grain-producing part of the Panmure estates. Nearby Edzell was equally fertile, but soil variations meant that before the eighteenth-century improvements sheep and cattle farming were relatively more important than at Menmuir. There were few alternative employments even in the late eighteenth century, when it was said that the people got their living wholly or in large part from the cultivation of the ground. A mid seventeenth-century Edzell farm account book shows oats and bear as the main crops in an infield–outfield system.[26]

The Forfarshire Covenant relates to a swathe of parishes between Arbroath and Kirriemuir, including Alyth and Kinnel. Initially this example was felt to be unsuitable for inclusion, but the illiteracy level which emerged was highly plausible given the average attainments elsewhere. The area was fertile and agriculturally precocious, containing in addition a number of flourishing towns which were particularly concerned with trading grain in return for the large surplus of pastoral products from the uplands.

Though situated south of the Tay estuary, Kilmany in Fife can nevertheless be compared legitimately with the Forfarshire parishes. Between the mid sixteenth and mid seventeenth centuries, Fife was a prosperous region. Thomas Tucker spoke of it as 'one of the best and richest countyes of Scotland'.[27] Sibbald described the area in the late seventeenth century as 'generally green and fertile', with plenty of 'very good arable land: for the abundance and goodness of wheat, bear and oats produced here, and for the numbers of sheep and black cattle bred here, this part of Fife may compare with the like quality of ground in any of the best parts of Britain'.[28] It was also the greatest Covenanting county outside the south-west. Figures like Sir Thomas Hope

---

[25] A. J. Warden, *Angus or Forfarshire* vol. 2 (1881): 237, 253, 267.
[26] See Smout (1972): 123, 130; Whyte (1979a): 231; [Old] *Statistical Account of Scotland* (hereafter *OSA*), vol. 10 (1794): 108; Lenman (1977a): 17.
[27] J. A. Di Folco, 'The Hopes of Craighall' (1979): 2.   [28] Di Folco (1975): 3.

the Lord Advocate, who was sympathetic to the early Covenanting movement, owned property in central and northern Fife. Less commercially developed than the Panmure estates, Kilmany was still an important arable parish sending grain surpluses to the nearby royal burgh of Cupar. In the eighteenth century, the minister asserted that 'agriculture is the universal employment . . . It gives subsistence to almost every individual in the parish.'[29] Ceres was made a burgh of barony in 1620 to provide both a commercial nexus and impetus to the newly acquired Craighall estates south of Cupar. The estate itself was a commercially oriented one, tenants paying rents with cash they raised by selling grain at the Ceres markets. In 1659 there were twelve tenancies on the estate, plus some forty-nine 'acremen' holding small plots.[30]

The strongly Covenanting county of Ayrshire provides three further examples. Ayr itself was an important royal burgh with wide commercial horizons including trade with Ireland and Continental Europe. In 1641, for example, burgesses were buying Spanish salt to ship to Glasgow. In conjunction with Kilmarnock and Maybole, Ayr was an important leather-working centre in the late medieval and early modern period and there was an important woollen market there in 1642. Ayr was the centre of a prosperous agricultural and trading area and the town was well populated by craftsmen, tradesmen and professionals. This important town formed a focal point for religious unrest before the Reformation and acted as a gateway for Protestant literature coming into the west of Scotland.[31] Just north of the royal burgh the parish of Dundonald was influenced by its proximity, providing foodstuffs for the burgh population. It too was tainted by Protestantism before the Reformation and the parish chapel was broken into in a display of anticlericalism.[32] In 1604 Timothy Pont the mapmaker spoke of the county as 'fertile in corn and store, being of a deep fat clay soil much enriched by the industrious inhabitants liming their grounds'.[33] Weaving and leather work were practised, and there was a small but viable port at Troon.[34] Finally in this prosperous region was Galston, adjacent to the cloth and leather working town of Kilmarnock and like it involved in the production of bonnets, shoes, gloves and woollens. Mixed farming and dairying dominated agriculture. Again it

---

[29] *OSA*, vol. 19 (1797): 429.   [30] Di Folco (1979): 4–5.
[31] Adams (1978): 43; W. Dodd, 'Ayr' (1972): 302–82; Pagan (1897): 64–6; J. D. Marwick, *The River Clyde and the Clyde burghs* (1909): 90.
[32] I. B. Cowan, *Regional aspects of the Scottish Reformation* (1978): 8.
[33] Quoted in T. C. Smout and A. Fenton, 'Scottish agriculture before the Improvers' (1965): 83.
[34] Adams (1978): 43; J. H. Gillespie, *Dundonald* (1939); *OSA*, vol. 7 (1793): 615–18.

had a long pedigree of Protestant activism. George Wishart preached there in the 1540s.[35]

The remaining parishes are located in what contemporaries saw as the most economically precocious part of Scotland, the Lothians. Bo'ness provides a good example of the small towns which grew rapidly in the seventeenth century as a result of coal-mining activity and the building of a harbour which reflected growing prosperity and which acted as the focus for further urban development. Coal and salt works formed the industrial element of the parish's economy, while expanding trade in grain was associated with increased agricultural production in the landward areas within easy transport distance of the port. Regulations covering Kinneil barony reveal the central importance of agriculture, and there were continual attempts to prevent damage to arable land caused by horses pulling carts or sleds from the coalworks. Until 1634, Bo'ness belonged to the parish of Kinneil, but in that year the inhabitants 'becoming numerous' built a church to house the expanding population.[36] The dominance of merchants among those listed in the poll tax records of the 1690s emphasizes that trade was more important than manufactures at this time. More than 10% of taxpayers were involved in trade of some kind. Though far fewer than 50 of the 500-plus payers have the designation 'merchant', others, such as skippers, were taxed on stock of some kind.[37] Sailors and skippers were prominent among those giving donations to a fund set up for building a church in the parish in 1636. The regality court book covering the years from 1669 to 1692 shows considerable numbers of craftsmen and tradesmen, including maltmen, meal-makers, fleshers, bakers, brewers, tailors, shoemakers and carriers, among litigants and defendants.[38] Indeed, Bo'ness had the largest recorded volume of sea trade of any Scottish port by the later seventeenth century. Like most burghs there was a high percentage of heritable proprietors among the population.[39]

Of the parishes near Edinburgh, Newbattle was probably more economically significant in the seventeenth century than in the eighteenth. A supplier of coal, lime and agricultural products to Edinburgh, Dalkeith and the surrounding countryside, Newbattle was populated by tenant farmers whose inventories show the sort of mixed

---

[35] *Register containing the state and condition of every burgh in Scotland* (1881): 80; J. Hendrie, *History of Galston parish church* (1909); Cowan (1978): 17.

[36] Adams (1978): 51, 55; Lenman (1977a): 21; Smout (1972): 138; SRO SC41/93/1; *OSA*, vol. 18 (1796): 423; J. Barrowman, 'Slavery in the coal mines of Scotland' (1897–8): 274.

[37] Flinn (1977): 191; SRO E70/13/3.   [38] SRO SC41/93/1; SRO CH2/540/67.

[39] Flinn (1977): 193; SRO SC41/93/1 (1669).

farming typical of much of early modern Scotland. Testaments show a sprinkling of weavers, merchants and other tradesmen and craftsmen especially in the main nucleated settlement which had 130 paid hearths at the 1690s tax. There were some 900 communicants there in 1648.[40] On the coast just east of Edinburgh, Inveresk was a large parish, again agriculturally precocious, with a well-developed use of lime and manure at an early date. In this area, the 'great trafique of mercheandis' in towns like Musselburgh, Tranent and Prestonpans stimulated agricultural development.[41] Manufactures were introduced in the late seventeenth century, but at the time of the Covenant trade in skins, wool, wood, salt and coal was the most important commercial consideration.[42] The hearth tax of the 1690s shows little apparent wealth differentiation: 76% of 701 paid hearths were single ones, while only 6% of payers had four or more hearths. Nevertheless, poll tax material for the same decade does provide evidence of occupational diversification on a considerable scale. Of 568 taxpayers with occupational designations, 14% were weavers, 12% shoemakers and 5% merchants, alongside a wide range of non-agricultural designations such as fishermen, smiths, bakers, brewers, tailors and other clothworkers, masons and a handful of professionals like clerks and surgeons.[43] The area had a tradition of Protestantism and was one of those where the preacher George Wishart is said to have found enthusiastic audiences in the 1540s.

Between Edinburgh and the coast just west of Inveresk lay North Leith. Much smaller than adjacent South Leith, the economy of the parish was closely related to trade and to Edinburgh. Writing in 1689, Thomas Morer felt Leith 'may be called the warehouse of Edinburgh, to supply the merchants and other citizens'. A 'commodious haven for ships' made it an important port for both coastal and international commerce, and contemporary observers were agreed that trade was more economically significant to the parish than manufactures in the seventeenth century.[44] In the early seventeenth century, mariners, fishermen and skippers are prominent in the Kirk Session records wherein we can detect coastal trade ties with the Forth estuary and international ones with English and Dutch traders. North Leith was

[40] Whyte (1979a); *Reports on the state of certain parishes in Scotland [1627]* (1835): 87–9; F. J. Grant, *The Commissariat records of Edinburgh: register of testaments* (1897–9); SRO E69/16/1; *OSA*, vol. 10 (1794): 212–14; SRO CH2/424/3: 2 November 1648.

[41] *Reports on the state of certain parishes* (1835): 135.

[42] Defoe (1978): 573; Adams (1978): 24; SRO Ch2/424/3: 31 May 1650; J. Paterson, *History of the regality of Mussleburgh* (1857): 37–71, 146–7, 151–3.

[43] SRO E69/16/1; E70/8/10.   [44] Brown (1891): 285; 243; 226; Whyte (1979a): 232.

also an overspill community of Edinburgh, favoured by tradesmen and craftsmen wishing to avoid the taxes and guild restrictions of the city. Groups of hammermen, tailors, wrights and coopers, bakers, timbermen, weavers, maltmen, husbandmen and gardeners had pews confirmed in the kirk during 1641–2.[45] In Edinburgh itself one Covenant survives which can be related to a single parish: the Tolbooth or North West Kirk. A survey of houses in 1678 reveals 513 households or about 2,500 people – possibly more, since urban households were generally bigger than rural. Like all Edinburgh parishes the spread of wealth and social status among the population was considerable. Notarial attestations show numbers of merchants, tailors, baxters, stablers, skinners and weavers, among others. Wills and court records suggest a parish well endowed with merchants and professional men.[46] Like the London parishes with surviving Protestation Returns, the Tolbooth was a wealthy community.

We have already seen that geographical location and agrarian patterns seem to provide little help in explaining even the broad outline of differences between the parishes. There is no necessary connection between either ecological environment or agricultural development and literacy. What other reasons can there be for the variations we saw in table 3.2?

Information on illiteracy among a delimited section of the population within a small area at a precise point in time gives us the opportunity to assess more accurately than with crude aggregates the likely relationship between schooling and illiteracy. We will deal only with the parish where the Covenant was subscribed, though the extent of geographical mobility in this society means that it is uncertain whether people would necessarily have received education in the place where they ended up residing. Finding out where a person was educated is impossible on any systematic basis. Discovering the presence or absence of educational institutions is only slightly less problematic. Pinning down the existence of a school at one moment in time is difficult enough, but establishing evidence for continuity and effect is harder still. Even where the local records, such as Kirk Session minutes and accounts, do survive for the early seventeenth century they rarely allow us to determine whether schools were around for long enough to influence subscribers to the Covenants. Indeed evidence on the availability of schooling is at best patchy.

It may also be contradictory. At Newbattle in 1626, two elders of the

---

[45] SRO CH2/621/1; Mackenzie (1949): 84, 135.
[46] *OSA*, vol. 6 (1793); 559–63; SRO CC8/4/2–499; F. J. Grant (1897–9).

Kirk Session were appointed to assess the proficiency of the poor scholars supported by church charity, suggesting the existence of a functioning school. A decade earlier a doctor or assistant was felt necessary to fill the temporary vacancy created by the absence of the precentor and schoolmaster, again implying that a supply of education existed.[47] But in 1627 it was claimed that Newbattle had 'no satled schole nor any fundation for ane'.[48] The 1627 reports from which this quotation is drawn may be biased, because of their aim to produce increased funds from reluctant heritors, meaning that paucity of provision may be exaggerated. In the presbytery minutes of 1629 it is recorded that Newbattle school was 'decayed' through lack of pupils.[49] The reason was not failure of provision or a secular downturn in attendance but the competition presented to the official school by a 'common' or adventure school in another part of the parish. Turnover of teachers and the resulting fluctuations in educational provision may explain the anomalies. The employment of the doctor (assistant) from Brechin grammar school as reader at Menmuir in March 1637 was the result of this problem of maintaining continuity. We know that Menmuir had a reader-cum-schoolmaster in 1628, since the teacher of eighteen months' standing complained about delays in payment of his stipend.[50] Teachers seem often to have been poorly paid and unhappy men who were anxious to move on quickly in search of better opportunities.

Dundonald certainly had a viable school at this time which dated from 1605 and was probably one of the first post-Reformation foundations in the area.[51] The parish could manage less than one in five literate adult males. Musselburgh had a grammar school, though it was claimed that the outlying areas were less well provided for.[52] Galston's low illiteracy seems hard to reconcile with the evidence of the pittance paid to the session clerk 'in respect of the small number of bairnes'.[53] In 1647 the school was located at an innkeeper's house, then in a barn. There was not even a minister settled at Kilmany in 1611, but a schoolmaster can be found by 1649.[54] Other sources indicate that there was no school in 1647 or 1658 and still none in the 1690s.[55] For

[47] SRO CH2/276/1: 18 January 1626, 30 November 1617.
[48] *Reports on the state of certain parishes* (1835): 87, 75–6.
[49] SRO CH2/424/1: 19 March 1629.   [50] SRO CH2/264/1: 2 April 1628.
[51] Scotland (1969): 60; Gillespie (1939): 496–508; SRO CH2/104/1: fols. 155–6.
[52] SRO CH2/424/3: 10 April 1650; Paterson (1857): 71–8.
[53] Hendrie (1909): 36–7; Boyd (1961): 22; Scotland (1969): 63.
[54] Beale (1953): 19; Di Folco (1975): 98, 126–7; D. J. Withrington, 'Lists of schoolmasters teaching Latin' (1965): 128–9.
[55] *Ecclesiastical records* (1837): 49.

Borgue, we have no local records which could give information about educational provision before the eighteenth century, and while there was a burgh school at nearby Kirkcudbright from the 1570s at the latest, parishes adjacent to Borgue seem to have been poorly served.[56] Dalmellington has no record of outgoings to pay for the schooling of poor children in the 'compt of the distributione for pious uses' in the earliest surviving Kirk Session register of the 1640s – usually the most reliable indication of educational availability.[57] There was a session clerk in 1641 who may have acted as a schoolmaster, and money was given to 'ane cripple lass called Anable ... to buy ane Byble'. The payment of 6s 8d to George Inglis 'ane poore scholler' in 1642 was more likely to have been a bursary to attend college in Glasgow. All four Ayrshire parishes had ministers and readers, according to the 1574 Book of Assignations; the existence of a reader would suggest the possibility of education.[58]

All these remarks about settled schools refer of course to officially established schools with a building and a proper salary for the teacher, and do not take account of the possibly large number of temporary schoolmasters who may have supplemented educational provision. We know, for example, that there were numerous private adventure schools in Fife from the 1590s onwards.[59] In 1614 the Kirk Session of North Leith determined that the reader should have a monopoly of teaching in the parish and expressly forbade two women from keeping schools. In 1633 the reader (who usually doubled as parish school-master) complained about Janet Bilbowie, who ran a school 'to learn bairnes to reid', and following a further complaint in 1639 the minister and elders ordered three women to cease keeping schools 'prejudicial to the reader'.[60] In the early seventeenth century John Stevinson, 'workman', was delated to the Session for verbal abuse of the reader and for complaining about the alleged injustice of having to pay the reader's stipend thrice yearly. Schools were certainly operating in pre-Covenant Leith.

Towns as a whole were well provided with educational facilities, their schools subject to the Town Council rather than Kirk Session and heritors as in the rural areas. Ayr had a schoolmaster by 1608 at the latest and indeed had probably been able to boast one before the Reformation. By 1621 Mr William Smythe was employed as reader and

[56] J. A. Russell, *Education in the stewartry of Kirkcudbright* (1971).
[57] SRO CH2/85/1.   [58] Boyd (1961): 12.   [59] Beale (1953): 10.
[60] SRO CH2/621/1: 18 August 1614, 22 December 1633, 29 November 1639.

musician, Mr John Bonar as schoolmaster and session clerk.[61] Edinburgh, meanwhile, was well endowed both in the quality and quantity
of its educational provision. However, we cannot ignore the fact that
towns drew a significant proportion of their population from surrounding rural areas in the early modern period, especially in periods
of rapid expansion, such as that being experienced at Kinneil and
Bo'ness in the early seventeenth century. These people would have
been educated elsewhere in all likelihood and could not have owed
their literacy to superior schooling unless, of course, they had originated in other towns. The difficulties of relating educational provision to
illiteracy levels are clear.

However, simply showing that schools did or did not exist in a
parish does not offer a complete analysis of the availability of
schooling. The parishes of Scotland and the north of England were
often large, and weather or the location of the school relative to geographical obstacles could exert a crucial influence on the effective
availability of education.[62] Without the aid of additional teachers the
one schoolmaster provided for by statute would have been quite
unable to cope with the large population inhabiting some extensive
parishes.[63] In 1646 the presbytery of Cupar enquired whether 'parishes
that ar large and great may take themselfes to the least alternative
contained in the act of Parliament made anent Schooles, viz. a hun-
dreth merkis, or may be stented higher, according to the largenes and
proportione of other parishes'.[64] Meanwhile in 1650 Dalkeith presbytery asked Inveresk heritors 'to see to the teaching of children able to
read in the outparte of the parioch' by setting up schools.[65] St Andrews
presbytery believed 'the woeful ignorance, rudeness, stubborness,
incapacity seen among the common people proceed from want of
schools in landward and not putting bairns to school where they
are'.[66]

However, if we accept Withrington's conclusion that lack of
evidence for a school does not indicate for certain that one did not exist,
and assume that there was a school in all the Covenant parishes or at
least in one or more neighbouring parishes, we are still left with considerable variation to explain. What evidence there is points to a lack of
any necessary connection between school provision in local areas and
levels of literacy. The same was true of part of England, where 'no

[61] SRO CH2/751/1/1; CH2/751/2.   [62] Smout (1972): 425; Beale (1953): 96.
[63] Gilly (1842): 32–3, 36.   [64] *Ecclesiastical records* (1837): 116–17.
[65] SRO CH2/424/3: 10 April 1650.   [66] Quoted in Scotland (1969): 50.

correlation whatever' has been discovered between the work of school-masters in the diocese and the literacy of twenty-one Cheshire parishes demonstrated in the Protestation Returns of 1642.[67] Except at the grossest level this is also the case for seventeenth- and eighteenth-century France.[68] We should be extremely wary of assertions which automatically link increased provision of education to enhanced literacy levels, since any one of a number of intervening variables could play a powerful role.

If we glance back to our earlier analysis of urban–rural literacy differentials a more satisfying explanation of observed differences in illiteracy amongst the Covenant parishes emerges. The gap in attainments between predominantly rural parishes and those with a significant burgh element is clear. The mean illiteracy of Inveresk, Kinneil and Bo'ness, Ayr, Stranraer, St Andrews, Ceres, North Leith and Edinburgh is 47% – more than 30% lower than average rural levels. The explanation seems to have been the concentration of literate occupations in the towns. Taxation records show, for example, that the Tolbooth parish had a high proportion of substantial households headed by lairds, merchants and professionals. Of 323 male taxpayers not described as servants or wives and children in the 1694 poll tax assessment, 7% were lairds, 26% professionals, and 54% craftsmen and tradesmen of whom 43% were merchants.[69] As we have already seen, the first two groups would be almost completely literate, while craftsmen and tradesmen were much more literate than the mass of the agricultural population.

Towns contained concentrations of rich and well-educated people. In 1630 the Scottish Parliament voted a taxation to meet Charles I's extraordinary expenses in visiting Scotland and to help pay off his debts in buying heritable offices.[70] The tax was to be paid yearly at Martinmas from 1630 to 1633 inclusive. Landowners were assessed on their holdings and in addition the king was to receive 5% of the net annual rents possessed by burgesses and others. Those liable for the taxation were to give up an inventory of their debt and credit, which was to be recorded by the clerk of the burgh court in the case of town dwellers. The inventories for 1630 to 1633 survive for the royal burgh of St Andrews.[71] These provide information on the literacy of the wealthiest inhabitants in the town, since the Act ordered 'the parteis upgivers

[67] Spufford (1981): 37.   [68] Parker (1980): 215–16.   [69] SRO E70/4/6.
[70] *Acts of the Parliaments of Scotland*, vol. 5 (1870): 209–10.   [71] SAUL B65/20/1.

of the saids inventorie everie partie subscryve his awin inventar himselffe if he can write'; if the person could not write the clerk was to subscribe for him in open court. These documents only cover the well-off who lent out money at interest. The lowest annual rent principal was 950 merks relating to a merchant's widow and the highest, 18,100 merks, was the wealth of a merchant. Six women out of eleven in the 1630 inventory were illiterate: four the wives or widows of merchants, one an absent skipper's wife and one a schoolmaster's widow. Only six of the thirty-two men, mostly merchants, skippers and lairds, were illiterate. This is not a representative sample of all the people in early seventeenth-century St Andrews, but it does show the sort of wealthy bourgeoisie who lived in towns of that sort.

Some other parishes styled as rural do in fact contain an officially established burgh: Dundonald, Edzell and Newbattle. We must distinguish however between 'real' and 'paper' burghs and the level of commercial activity in them. Even in the early eighteenth century, 'most burghs were mere villages' with privileges granted but largely unused, forming 'tiny pockets of ... activity within a vast rural setting'.[72] Margaret Sanderson points out that the distinction between town and country was much less marked in the sixteenth century than it was to be in the eighteenth or nineteenth centuries.[73] Nucleated town settlements formed only part of the remaining town parishes which retained large 'landward' sections. Mussleburgh, for instance, was the only recognized burgh in Inveresk parish, but its privileges over imports and exports made it a key place in the shift of trade from the ports of western East Lothian to those nearer Edinburgh, which has been identified as a significant feature of seventeenth-century economic change.[74] There were some 2,000 people living in the town of Dunfermline in the 1690s, but a further 3,000 in the landward part of the parish.[75] Many burgesses and indwellers were farmers, and contact with the land was also maintained by social mechanisms such as inter-marriage between laird and merchant families. In the case of St Andrews, where the place of residence of household heads is recorded, about three-quarters of the subscribers of the Solemn League and Covenant lived in the town itself, the rest in the landward part of the parish. Comparison between the literacy of the two parts of the parish is highly instructive. In the landward section of the parish, illiteracy among the adult males was 88%: very much in line with levels in rural parishes elsewhere in Scotland. In the town proper the level

---

[72] Lenman (1977a): 34; Donaldson (1974): 210, 241; Adams (1978): 57.
[73] Sanderson (1982): 183.   [74] Smout (1963).   [75] Beale (1953): 7.

was much lower at 54%, again close to what we should expect in a burgh.

The eight burghs with substantially lower illiteracy were far from homogeneous in their socio-economic composition, but they certainly possessed appreciable commercial development and occupational diversification. They all had high proportions of their inhabitants working in the secondary and tertiary sectors. Both the range of urban functions and the extent of 'urbanization' varied to a considerable degree, with none able to match the catalytic effect of Edinburgh's combined status as a port and capital on literacy or her dense urban population. The comparatively low illiteracy of Newbattle may be explained by its intermediate position, since it was almost a suburb of the important market town of Dalkeith. Fragmentary poll tax records do suggest that it possessed more non-agricultural occupations even than neighbouring Lasswade, where some 25% of adult males were craftsmen or tradesmen.[76] The towns in our sample were not industrial to any marked degree and showed higher literacy, thanks to the stimulation of occupations connected with the expansion of trade. Analysing differences in literacy between central and suburban parishes of towns in seventeenth- and eighteenth-century Normandy, Longuet concludes that spatial variations in literacy were due to the predominance of weavers, spinners and carders in the suburban parishes, rather than to a poorer educational provision.[77] The occupational composition of the 'urban' parishes provides us with the most likely explanation of superior aggregate literacy levels in mid seventeenth-century Scottish towns.

In order to provide some sort of estimate of overall literacy levels among adult males, we must assess the likely urban–rural balance in seventeenth-century Scotland, and also the positive or negative impact of geographical bias and under-subscription of the Covenants. Estimates of the proportions living in towns in seventeenth-century Scotland vary considerably from around 5% to as high as 20%.[78] Something slightly above the first figure is probably the most reasonable estimate of those dwelling in towns big enough to influence literacy levels. We can therefore suggest a figure of perhaps 75% illiteracy for the Lowlands of Scotland. It is extremely likely that the levels in the Highlands were much higher – we might guess that 90% or more of adult males were unable to sign their names, though this is highly speculative. The uncorrected figure for adult male illiteracy in England at the start of the Civil War is perhaps 5% better than for Scotland.

---

[76] SRO GD18/3028; E70/8/8.   [77] Longuet (1978): 225.
[78] Whyte (1979a): 9; Adams (1978): 57; Donaldson (1974): 238.

Stone was then broadly correct in his estimate that Scotland was behind England in the mid seventeenth century.[79] It is tempting to speculate that, unlike the later period, the north of England lagged slightly behind the rest of England, but very close to Lowland Scotland at around 75% illiterate. The position was of course reversed in the period from 1650 to 1760 with the north of England and Scotland rising to national prominence. However, the nature of the town–country balance and the biases occasioned by under-subscription (discussed in appendix 1) are not altogether clear, and we should not make too much of this. Towns are under-represented in the surviving English returns, meaning that aggregate literacy levels would be too low. However, those who did not subscribe were probably among the least literate members of local communities. The two may cancel each other out. Thus the Lowland estimate is probably a minimum one. Illiteracy in mid seventeenth-century Scotland was rather higher than that in contemporary England.

What can we say in conclusion about the achievements of Scottish society in the field of literacy? Scotland was one of the countries where Strauss believes religious reformers of the sixteenth century were able to aspire towards a programme of schooling of the best available sort, backed by the state's political and financial authority. After 1525 another example, Germany, had school ordinances originating from the church which aimed to provide schools for the masses with the emphasis on religious education through catechism. Lutherans as much as Calvinists saw popular education as essential to the survival and growth of their church.[80] It seems clear, however, that just as the Scottish Reformation was not established overnight, so Knox's idea of universal education was not achieved by the time of the Covenants. We should be surprised if it was. The Calvinist church had clearly experienced difficulties setting itself up in the late sixteenth century and was simply not strong enough to carry out its programmes. In the Highlands it did not manage in some instances to install itself until the eighteenth century. Not until 1616 did the state back the kirk's demand for a school in every parish, and only in 1633 was a provision for taxing heritors to pay for it instituted – even then with the let-out clause 'where convenient means can be had'. There was no compulsion to pay until the Act of 1646. Poverty and apathy, or even antipathy, prevented the implementation of the pious hopes encapsulated in the *Book of discipline*.

---

[79] Stone (1969): 121.   [80] G. Strauss, 'The state of pedagogical theory' (1976): 69–70.

Scotland and Europe 1550–1800

We now possess firm figures on illiteracy in Scotland from the time of the Scottish Revolution to the eve of the Industrial Revolution. Able at last to cut through the claims and counter-claims about Scottish literacy, we can say that the experience of Lowland Scotland was not greatly different from that of northern England. Scotland's tradition of literacy may have been different from that of England, but the practical results of that ethos did little to mark out Scottish society from that of her southern neighbour. It is essential to compare and contrast if we are to discover the special features of society which mark out different cultural areas. But we should not stop at comparisons within the British Isles. Only by comparing Britain with other parts of Europe are we likely to be able to assess what distinctive features Scotland and England may have possessed.

First of all, what can we say about levels of literacy in countries as a whole? In the third quarter of the sixteenth century, Poland was a country with which Scots and English had trading ties. It had an adult male illiteracy level of about 88%, not directly comparable with mid seventeenth-century Britain, but at least suggestive of levels somewhere between Highland and Lowland Scotland.[81] At the other end of the Continent, in early seventeenth-century Andalucia, perhaps one-half of the male town-dwellers were illiterate, again remarkably close both to the Scottish 'urban' figure and to the five Chester parishes analysed by Cressy, which show 52% illiteracy.[82] Moving closer to Britain, marriage registers for Amsterdam in 1630 show 43% of bridegrooms to have been illiterate – higher than the Edinburgh or London figures, but almost certainly covering a wider range of parishes than the rich central ones in the Scottish and English capitals which we have analysed, and thus containing more persons from the lower end of the social spectrum.[83]

For the mid eighteenth century, figures for the proportions of adult males able to sign in regions of Britain are again close to estimates we have for other areas of north-west Europe. The nationwide survey of subscriptions to French marriage registers carried out for the years 1686–90, 1786–90, 1816–20 and 1866 by a retired schoolmaster called Louis Maggiolo during 1879–80 has been followed up by numerous local studies, which reveal that the area north and east of an imaginary line between St Malo and Geneva had adult male illiteracy of 35–40% in

[81]   A. Wyczanski, 'L'alphabétisation et structure sociale en Pologne' (1974): 713.
[82]   Rodriguez and Bennassar (1978): 41; Cressy (1980): 75.   [83]   Parker (1980): 214.

the 1760s, and in one group of departments the figure was as low as 26%.[84] This survey concentrated on rural France and it is likely that the level was rather lower if we take account of higher urban literacy. In the south and west of France, illiteracy was far more common. Men in France as a whole were 61% illiterate in the 1750s and 56% in the 1760s. There were considerable similarities between north-eastern France and much of Britain. South and west France were more like the Highlands of Scotland. The average figures suggested in chapter 2 for both Lowland Scotland and England in the mid eighteenth century are not far removed from the level of 39% illiterate found in a sample of Belgian parishes in the later eighteenth century.[85] The differences between Scotland and nearby parts of Europe at this time have been exaggerated. These are, of course, superficial similarities which take no account of the widely differing social context of illiteracy in different political, institutional and economic circumstances. Nevertheless, they do at least hint at the existence of a sort of 'background' literacy in north-western Europe which owes little to religion, school provision or other specific factors, but more to some underlying socio-cultural similarity.

What of the more detailed profile of literacy structures and trends? In broad outline, nearly all of the patterns we have discussed in this and the previous two chapters are characteristic of the rest of early modern Europe. Linguistically distinct regions were more illiterate than places where the dominant language prevailed. Women are generally less literate than men, rural people less than urban, the lower socio-economic groups less than the wealthier and more exalted.[86] In Scotland and England the main improvements during the period 1650 to 1770 were among the middling groups in society. In this respect, Britain was similar to northern France where most of the substantial improvements in literacy over the eighteenth century occurred among the middle classes. The labouring population did not catch up until the nineteenth century.

This is not to say that the patterns were exactly the same across Europe. The sexually and socially specific differences in Britain are less pronounced than in, say, sixteenth- and seventeenth-century Poland.[87] In that part of Europe the peasants who formed three-quarters of the population were 98% illiterate during the last quarter of the sixteenth century, compared to around 30–50% for contemporary

---

[84] Houdaille (1977): 68–9.   [85] Cressy (1980): 181.   [86] Houston (1983b): 270–3.
[87] Urban (1977): 257.

English yeomen and 80–90% for husbandmen.[88] Artisan levels for Languedoc are again lower at some 70% illiterate in the small town of Narbonne in the 1560s and 1570s. At this period 97% of agricultural labourers were illiterate, as were 90% of peasant farmers.[89] The rural population of the comte Nantais was almost wholly illiterate during the sixteenth century, and any signatures on sixteenth-century documents were made by nobles, officers or merchants.[90]

There was a much wider social spread of literacy in contemporary England and Lowland Scotland than we find in the southern and eastern parts of Europe. A social hierarchy of literacy persisted into the later eighteenth century in Scotland and England, but was again less pronounced than the sharp cultural divide in, say, Basse-Provence between bourgeois and notables on the one hand, and the mass of illiterate peasants on the other.[91] *Travailleurs de terre*, very small farmers with only 1 to 3 hectares, retained their near-total illiteracy in the southern parts of France into the late eighteenth century.[92] *Ménagers*, with 7 to 15 hectares, had a much better position by the late seventeenth century and had seen really substantial improvements by the late eighteenth century. As in the case of eastern Europe, the exact comparability of agricultural designations is unclear, but the overall impression is of a much starker set of social contrasts in the attainment of literacy in the east and south of the Continent than was true of Scotland and England or, for that matter, northern France. A comparatively small percentage of the population of seventeenth- and eighteenth-century Russia and Poland was involved in independent craft or trade activities, making the gulf between gentry and aristocracy and the peasantry all the more stark.[93] In sixteenth- and seventeenth-century Spain the clergy, nobility, professionals, merchants and some shopkeepers and artisans were literate, but countryfolk, the urban proletariat and many craftsmen and tradesmen were not.[94] Durham diocese gentlemen, many of whom were still illiterate in the late sixteenth century, may show some similarity with the differing attainments we can see among nobles and gentry of divergent wealth and social status in contemporary Poland, but only at this early date. In the

---

[88] Cressy (1974): 234.   [89] Davis (1975): 195, 210.
[90] J. Meyer, 'Alphabétisation, lecture et écriture' (1974): 346.
[91] M. Vovelle, 'Y a-t-il eu une révolution culturelle?' (1975): 140.
[92] Chartier (1976): 100–1.   [93] J. M. Hittle, *The service city* (1979).
[94] M. Chevalier, *Lectura y lectores en la España* (1976): 14, 20.

main, Britain and much of north-western Europe had an identity of experience which was rather different from the south and east. Analysis of the social, economic, religious and cultural factors which might explain why people became literate follows in chapter 4.

4

The reasons for literacy

Describing structures of illiteracy is comparatively easy. Explaining change over time and differences or similarities in the historical development of literacy between Scotland and England, or even between different regions within a country, is more difficult. Historians have conventionally turned to schooling as the main explanation. Because of the political and ideological significance of the school in the nineteenth and twentieth centuries, writers have assumed that it is central to the history of literacy in the pre-industrial period. If one assumes this, and by implication that there is a direct connection between schooling and literacy, then interpretation of structures and trends is fairly straightforward. Indeed, analyses of educational provisions have tended to dominate the literature on British literacy.[1] But the study of schools alone is not likely to provide an adequate explanation of structures and trends in illiteracy. We need to know why schools were provided, but we must also understand why people wanted to be educated. We have already made some suggestions about possible explanations of the profiles of illiteracy encountered in chapters 2 and 3: the role of economic need in different sorts of community, for example. Some remarks were also made about the political context of education and literacy with regard to women and to linguistic minorities, an aspect to which we shall return. The present chapter offers a more detailed and systematic analysis of the reasons why men and women should wish to learn reading and writing. It will try to assess the complexity of motivation and of the process of learning. The following section analyses educational provision in schools and the various informal ways of learning – where and when people learned to read and write – and suggests that the importance of the former may

[1] Simon (1967); O'Day (1982); Scotland (1969); H. M. Knox, *Two hundred and fifty years of Scottish education* (1953).

110

have been overstated. The second half of the chapter deals with the comparative effects of different institutional, economic and religious structures in promoting literacy in Scotland and England, arguing that, while important, the role of all three factors in promoting literacy was not nearly as simple as is often supposed.

Historians of British education have tended to follow the pre-occupations of Defoe, Malthus, Brougham, Smith and others in con-centrating educational debate on the various forms of school provision. They have picked up from the classical economists an em-phasis on the supply side of education at the expense of mass demand. In his study of oral and literate culture in north-east Scotland, Buchan, for example, claims that 'the most significant guide to levels of literacy is the existence or non-existence of schools'.[2] A large body of tedious studies of educational provision and school curricula has resulted from this concentration. Schooling was surely of great importance in the history of literacy, but findings on other European countries suggest that there were additional and powerful influences at work. The case of France, where for the mass of the population until the seventeenth century extra-scholastic forms of learning were the norm, should warn us against too heavy a stress on this path to literacy.[3] A growing body of local studies in that country are pointing to the conclusion that there was no mechanical correlation between literacy and schooling. The example of Sweden provides an even stronger warning, since by the late eighteenth century near-universal reading literacy had been attained almost entirely without the aid of schools.[4] Unfortunately, there is little hope of analysing the relative importance of different modes of learning in any systematic way. Nevertheless, we may be able to counteract the over-simplified views of schooling and literacy which exist in some of the literature.

Let us first deal with the various approaches to the history of edu-cation in Scotland and England between the sixteenth and nineteenth centuries. We can then offer a broader discussion of different modes of learning in the early modern period.

The school

In recent years the debate on British schooling has tended to concen-trate less on the curricula available in Scottish and English schools and more on the extent of provision of different types of school in the two

---

[2] Buchan (1972): 190.   [3] Chartier (1976): 293.
[4] E. Johansson, 'The history of literacy in Sweden' (1981).

countries.[5] Part of the nationalist tradition in the study of Scottish education has been to stress the importance of state legislation in providing schools in every parish, paid for by taxation of landowners. This system contrasts sharply, we are told, with the English pattern where private, fee-paying schools and philanthropic endowments constituted the bulk of educational provision. Historians of Scotland boasted proudly of the achievements of the parochial school system. For their part, historians of England used their northern neighbour as a reference standard for what could be achieved. Recent work, especially that of Rosemary O'Day, has portrayed the educational histories of the countries in less black-and-white terms, but it is difficult to escape from the assumption that Scotland and England enjoyed 'dramatically different' educational histories.

The distinctiveness of Scotland's educational system lies in the way it became centralized and controlled at an early date. Roman Catholics had tried to advance education and literacy during the mid sixteenth century. However, the Protestant reformers of the later sixteenth century argued vigorously for the provision of schools 'for the preservation of religion', and in the interests of the general good of society through the cultivation of talented individuals. Their aim was to create a national, universal and religiously-oriented system which would be compulsory. What is more, they were much more successful than the Catholics. True, their aspirations were not realized overnight, but in 1616 an Act of the Scottish Parliament specified that a school should be established in every parish 'where convenient means may be had' for supporting one, and that a suitably qualified teacher should be found to staff it. A further Act of 1633 ratified this statute and gave to the bishops the task of overseeing its implementation. The Act of 1646 was more explicit about requiring landowners to pay for the creation of a school and to provide a salary for the teacher. Church authorities were to oversee the foundation of schools. This Act was repealed in 1662 as part of the general political reaction to the legislation of the Scottish Revolution period. However, the economic dislocations of the 1690s produced the final and most important Act of the seventeenth century, the Act of 1696, which settled the salary for existing teachers and compelled heritors or burgh councils to fund them. In other words, the Act made a legal provision for the capital cost of a school and teacher. Finally in our period, an Act of 1803 was passed to augment salaries fixed in 1696 but severely eroded by the inflation of the eighteenth century, and to tighten up control of the schools in a period of social and ideological flux.

[5]   O'Day (1982); Withrington (1965).

The state legislation outlined so baldly in the previous paragraph provided the core of the Scottish educational system. Endowed schools were rare and charitable foundations were relatively unimportant, except for the SSPCK which provided most education in the Highlands until the nineteenth century. The actions of the state were vitally important, though we should recognize some qualifications to this apparently remarkable achievement. First, the progress of education was not constant, and the values embodied in legislation and contemporary writing were neither uniform nor continuous over the three centuries from 1560 to 1872. Second, education was not free, it was not compulsory and it was not universal until the very end of the nineteenth century. Third, local circumstances, such as the attitude of landowners and the size of the eligible population in any one parish, remained important in deciding the effectiveness of the parish schools even in the eighteenth and nineteenth centuries. Fourth, church initiatives and the kirk's oversight of schools and schoolmasters were crucially important throughout our period: the achievements of the 'state' education system were the product of efforts by burghs, the kirk and the Privy Council as well as the Scottish Parliament.

Some efforts have been made to assess the distinctiveness of Scotland's statutory provision of education on the actual availability of schooling by examining the role of parish schools, endowed schools and private adventure schools in Scotland and England. English education is conventionally seen as being based on charitably endowed and private, fee-paying schools, whereas in Scotland the state-instituted parish system was the key feature. Endowed schools were rare in Scotland compared to England, and more common in towns than in rural areas. During the eighteenth century, for example, a bequest had been left to the parish of Prestonpans in Midlothian to teach twenty-four poor boys reading, writing, arithmetic and stocking-knitting.[6] Efforts to test the success of church and state in Scotland in implementing the desiderata embodied in the *Book of discipline* have suggested that the Calvinist hope for schools in every parish was closer to success by the end of the seventeenth century than was once believed. There were settled schools in nearly all the parishes of Fife by 1660, and in large parishes like Torryburn there were four schoolmasters in 1653.[7]

Earlier studies tended to concentrate on discovering the presence or absence of a schoolhouse and the provision of a formal salary under the

[6] Scotland (1969): 92.
[7] Beale (1953): 28–9; see also D. J. Withrington, 'Schools in the presbytery of Haddington' (1963).

terms of the Acts of 1616, 1633, 1646 and 1696.[8] Seventeenth-century church visitations concentrated on the 'way to gett Schools fully setled' with schoolhouse and salary, but local records such as Kirk Session payments show that it was easier and more common simply to employ a teacher.[9] Combining visitation records with local parish documents probably offers the greatest chance of discovering whether a teacher of some kind was present. Thus in the Lothians in the 1690s at least sixty-one of sixty-five parishes had a school of some kind, forty-nine of them grammar schools; forty-eight of sixty Fife parishes had grammar schools, while fully fifty-five had schools of some sort.[10] In 1711 the ministers of Dalkeith presbytery in Midlothian could report a school-master in every parish and two in some, in the latter case both with salaries.[11] Most Lowland parishes could boast a teacher by the end of the seventeenth century. It was only in the Highlands that resources were by and large insufficient to provide teachers, schools and materials even to teach the English language – a vital precondition for effective reading in English. We have already seen some of the problems in identifying the presence of schools in our discussion of literacy in some mid seventeenth-century Scottish parishes. Indeed, a teacher was probably the most important factor in the equation, since even without a formal schoolhouse or properly organized salary he could still educate children.

The situation was not however so straightforward as a simple exposition of the presence or absence of officially instituted schools would suggest. Much Scottish education was provided in private adventure schools which were neither church- or state-controlled nor privately endowed. A recurring complaint made by official parish schoolmasters in seventeenth-century Scotland was that their emoluments were reduced by the existence of competition from private teachers.[12] Kirk Sessions usually sought to suppress private schools in the interest of the official master, or at least to limit their functions to practical education in sewing or knitting or their pupils to girls, the poor or the very young.[13] Burntisland Town Council allowed an independent teacher to instruct 'young children both male and female to read, write and make counts, the male children not to exceed eight years of age'.[14] Yet the continued reiteration of schoolmasters' complaints throughout the seventeenth century suggests that in the

---

[8] Boyd (1961); A. Bain, *Education in Stirlingshire* (1965).
[9] *Reports on the state of certain parishes* (1835); *Ecclesiastical records* (1837): 138; Withrington (1965): 124–5.
[10] Withrington (1965): 128.   [11] SRO CH2/424/9: fol. 334.   [12] Sinclair (1826): 81.
[13] SRO CH2/471/1: 20 December 1646, 16 January 1647; Beale (1953): 47.
[14] Beale (1953): 276.

face of popular demand the Kirk Session could not eradicate adventure schools.

Most private schools were in fact subscribed for by local people. In Scotland, parents might combine to hire a teacher on a short-term, informal basis. Such contracts would leave little trace in official records. In the large parishes of seventeenth- and eighteenth-century Scotland, for example, outlying farmers might club together to hire a teacher for the winter months.[15] In Robert Burns' Ayrshire, a small group of local tenants engaged a schoolmaster on the removal of the existing one, guaranteeing him a small salary and lodging in their houses.[16] Formal contracts with teachers were rare, but that does not mean that families did not club together to hire a teacher for the winter. It is quite clear that not all education was provided through official channels.

Indeed, some seventeenth- and eighteenth-century Scottish parishes were prepared to tolerate adventure schools to provide for the needs created by distance of settlements from the parish school or increasing population size. Wemyss in Fife provides an example.[17] During the eighteenth century pressure of population forced the realization that the private adventure schools were an essential supplement to the overstretched parish schools. By the late eighteenth century in Fife there were probably as many children taught in venture schools as in parochial ones, possibly more.[18] A report of 1818 suggested a ratio of two pupils in private schools for every one in parochial establishments, though this excluded Sunday schools, dame schools and elite institutions.[19] The same may have been true of parts of Scotland in earlier times. Even in the 1660s the Kirk Session of Lasswade seems to have recognized John Urquhart, schoolmaster, in Rosline, as well as the official Session clerk and precentor George Skirvin, who lived and worked in Lasswade town.[20] Private adventure schools were especially important for girls and the children of the poor. Historians now acknowledge the variety of educational provision in post-Reformation Scotland. They recognize that the parochial school network was important, especially in the rural Lowlands, but they also appreciate more fully the significance of private, fee-paying schools.

A similar wind seems to have been blowing through the study of English education. What was seen as England's belated progress in education during the nineteenth century is, in fact, the growth of

---

[15] Sinclair (1826): 95–6.   [16] J. G. Lockhart, *The life of Robert Burns* (1830): 13.
[17] Beale (1953): 43, 223–4.   [18] *Ibid*. 279–81; Smout (1972): 426.
[19] E. G. West, *Education and the industrial revolution* (1975): 60.   [20] SRO CH2/471/3.

centralized political control of formal learning rather than of education itself. School provision was much better than once assumed, the lack of state provision not apparently holding back educational advances. All the main marketing centres of seventeenth-century Leicestershire had schools, for example, including town schools as effective as endowed ones.[21] As early as the 1940s, W. G. Hoskins showed that besides grammar schools 'a great number of villages had schools of their own, run by a schoolmaster in the village church, whose salary was paid by the villagers out of the church rate'.[22] With a tradition of popular education which dated back to before the Reformation, there were many schools already in existence before the late sixteenth-century boom and well before the Society for Propagating Christian Knowledge, with its claims to have brought about a major increase in elementary education.[23] From the 1730s, and probably earlier, to the early nineteenth century both charity schools and philanthropic endowment were much less important than the private school which, 'created by and wholly dependent on local demand, was at the cutting edge of . . . educational advances'.[24] Throughout England from the sixteenth century to the nineteenth we find places where 'we have no endowed School. A poor Man teaches the Children to read, who takes all the Care of them that can be expected from him.' In England as in Scotland adventure schools were numerically important. Seventy-seven parishes did not reply to Archbishop Herring's question about education provision in the province of York. However, 392 parishes reported that they had no school, 162 reported private schools, 289 had endowed or charity schools, though mostly with sums which could not have maintained a schoolmaster unless he had also been charging fees.[25] Most of the existing literature on schooling deals only with formally established schools which leave traces in documents of the early modern period. Thus we should regard the known number of schools in an area as the minimum figure for educational availability. Lancashire and Cheshire, for example, had 6 schools in 1480, 30 in 1548 and 109 in 1603, but there were surely many more which have escaped mention in the records.[26] Indeed the variety of educational provisions

---

[21] J. Simon, 'Town estates and schools' (1968b): 20.
[22] W. G. Hoskins, *Midland England* (1949): 88.
[23] B. Simon, *Education in Leicestershire 1540–1940* (1968): xiv; H. M. Jewell, 'A survey of secular educational provision in the north of England' (1982).
[24] T. W. Laqueur, 'Working-class demand and the growth of English elementary education' (1976b): 195.
[25] S. L. Ollard and P. C. Walker (eds.), *Archbishop Herring's visitation returns 1743*, vol. 3 (1929): 210; figures taken from Laqueur (1976a): 257, 272.
[26] C. A. Haigh, 'Slander and the church courts' (1975): 11.

was considerable. Dissenting academies were important from the late seventeenth century until the late eighteenth. Finally, English Sunday schools were helping to improve the overall standard of literacy for many children, especially in the period 1780–1850 when educational resources were becoming strained by population increase and urbaniz-ation.[27] As in Scotland, parents might club together to hire a school-teacher for a limited period of time. This procedure was adopted in mid seventeenth-century Lancashire in the experience of the autobiographer Adam Martindale.[28] In Britain as in France, it is possible to speak of an almost anarchic diversity in forms of schooling. Schools run by religious orders are obviously missing from post-Reformation Britain, but there was still a wide variety of types of institution.

Indeed, where previous work emphasized the differences between Scotland and England predicated on the tradition of enlightened phil-anthropic endowment versus equally enlightened state provision, we know that there were indeed 'schools in England administered by local authorities comparable to the smaller burgh and parish schools of Scot-land'.[29] Joan Simon identifies the English school system of the sixteenth century as 'a nucleus of organized schools in the main centres, then parish schools interspersed with lesser foundations in the countryside and, on a more casual basis, curates and schoolmasters engaged in teaching'.[30] In Scotland, meanwhile, official parish schools were not the end of the story. They were aided by private adventure schools which had existed from the sixteenth century or earlier, but which became in-creasingly important over the eighteenth century. If we believe in the paramount importance of schools there is no reason to believe that one system was necessarily more effective than the other in terms of pro-vision of places. Just as levels of literacy in Lowland Scotland and north-ern England are rather similar, perhaps the profile of provided and private education was closer than is sometimes assumed.

Recent work by West on early nineteenth-century British education provides powerful support for this sort of viewpoint. West shows the problems of comparing school attendance figures not compiled accord-ing to a common criterion and often put together to make a polemical point.[31] He concludes that there is probably no substantial difference in the proportion of the eligible population attending school in Scotland and England in the early nineteenth century. For earlier periods, other supposedly distinctive features of Scotland's post-Reformation edu-cational history are being questioned. It is becoming clear that many

[27] H. Silver, *English education and the radicals* (1975): 7; Laqueur (1976c): 89, 120, 123.
[28] R. Parkinson (ed.), *The life of Adam Martindale* (1845): 34–5.   [29] J. Simon (1968b): 4.
[30] J. Simon (1967): 376.   [31] West (1975): 98–106, 71.

features of the Scottish educational system hitherto perceived as specifically Calvinist were visible well before the Reformation. This is in addition to the probable similarities between types of educational system in Scotland and England, and suggests greater similarity between the countries and greater continuity over time than was traditionally assumed. Educational provision does follow certain divergent paths in seventeenth- and eighteenth-century Scotland and England, but the contrast in practice is much less than the apparent differences in the legal background would lead us to believe. In fact, the historian 'is faced with a multiplicity of types of school, each the product of differing traditions as well as the interplay between these traditions and specific circumstances'.[32]

Testing the connection between education and literacy on a regional or national level is extremely difficult until we reach the nineteenth century. One method which has been used with some success is as follows. Given information on the age of deponents we can discover when they were born and calculate from this the decade in which they were likely to have been educated. We can then check for any connection between the changing availability of education and trends in literacy at the date at which it was probably acquired.

We have eschewed any attempts at analysing literacy attainments among different school generations. Ages are not given with any regularity in English assize depositions between 1640 and 1760, and even in Scotland the numbers for each decade are rather small given the size of the Scottish population in this study. Age information is given for only 4,500 men and 1,100 women during a period of 120 years. We would expect a rough correlation between greater educational provision and enhanced literacy in the following years among younger people exposed to its influence. This is the sort of pattern recovered by Cressy for sixteenth- and seventeenth-century England.[33] Such an analysis is bound to be extremely superficial, however, and quickly loses credibility when tested in small areas. There is, for example, no correlation between the activities of schoolmasters in the diocese of Chester and levels of signing ability on the Protestation Returns of twenty-one Cheshire parishes in 1642.[34] We are reminded of the situation in eighteenth- and nineteenth-century France where a broad correlation does exist between good educational provision and high literacy in the regions of the country north and east of a line between St Malo and Geneva, and poorer provisions associated with lower literacy in the south and west. However, at a less heavily aggregated level we

---

[32] O'Day (1982): 40.   [33] Cressy (1980):157–74.   [34] Spufford (1981): 37.

run into problems with areas like the Hautes Alpes, which had only an average quantity of education on offer, but could boast very low illiteracy.[35] At the same time there is no certainty that the provision of schooling was equally effective for all social classes in Britain. Given the small numbers in each decade, there is no hope of an analysis of occupational illiteracy by decade of education in our northern British sample.

Finally, we can note in passing that political events do not appear to have had a great impact on literacy any more than they did in France. There were identifiable short-term effects, as in Scotland during the 1690s or in England in the Civil War years, with what Adam Martindale called the consequent 'discouragements that many lay under to send their children [to school] in those dayes of constant alarmes'.[36] Yet the long-term impact on education and literacy was slight.

The period 1500 to 1800 saw the beginnings of a transition from restricted to mass literacy. Many more people than ever before became literate in this period and schools certainly had their part to play in bringing this about. But we should also ask why more people did *not* become able to read and write. For women and linguistic minorities we have already examined some of the limiting forces. Before turning to the many non-scholastic ways people could take to learn reading and writing, we might consider some social and economic factors which would hold down levels of literacy attributable to formal education among certain poorer sections of society.

By limiting access to and duration of schooling one powerful influence was the financial burden of educating children. A key feature of Scotland's distinctive educational history is said to have been the opportunities offered to any gifted child, however poor, to gain access to a school. He would be paid for out of charitable funds. In reality, however, 'free' education was only available for a tiny minority of attenders at Scottish schools. For the majority, some form of payment for their education would be required. Until the work of Christopher Smout on the standard of living in Scotland is complete we have no household budgets which we could analyse to discover how much disposable income would have been available to the average family to spend on education.

An example from France sheds some light on this aspect. Vauban's *Dixme royale* of the late seventeenth century illustrates the cost of education in France. This was a survey by a royal minister to assess the taxability of the French population. A labourer earned ninety *livres* per

[35] M. Fleury and A. Valmary, 'Les progrès de l'instruction élémentaire' (1957): 75.
[36] Parkinson (1845): 34.

year for an average 190 days work. Two-thirds were spent on bread. Including fixed charges, it cost the labourer three *livres* five *sous* to keep a child at school for the five months it was usually open: 4% of his total income but 10% of his disposable income after buying food.[37] To call the income disposable is not entirely correct, since a further fifteen *livres* would be required to pay taxes and still more would be needed for rent and consumer goods.[38] The labourer's income might be supplemented by a small plot of land or by the work of wife and children or by some form of by-employment, such as weaving. It is clear, though, that education would have to compete with other pressing claims on the family budget. Most of the poorer people of France could only afford to educate their children when things were going well for them economically. In France, school attendance dropped appreciably in years such as 1693–5 and 1711–13 when grain prices were high, since the proportion of income left over from the family budget after subsistence needs had been met was reduced. This illustrates the economic marginality of many rural producers in France, and the same is true of certain parts of Germany in the years 1589–94.[39]

This detailed example from France is not irrelevant to Scotland. These same forces may have been at work in Scotland, especially at times such as the 1690s which saw severe grain shortages, high food prices and heavy mortality. Scotland is said to have possessed a 'high pressure' demographic regime like that of France or Sweden, where subsistence crises (high grain prices associated with increased mortality) remained an important feature of the demographic regime until well into the eighteenth century. Extra resources for education may have been harder to come by there than in England. England, however, appears to have possessed a less stringent balance between population and resources and may have avoided this sort of connection.[40] She was a richer country than Scotland and thus had (*ceteris paribus*) more resources to spend on education.

Even so there were serious constraints on the availability of education for the inhabitants of England. In seventeenth-century England it might cost £4 to lodge a yeoman's son in a grammar school for a year. The wages of a day labourer would add up to only £15 over the same period, less than half what it would cost to keep a youth at the Inns of Court.[41] Many children would never hope to benefit from the 'Educational Revolution' about which Lawrence Stone has written with

[37] Chartier (1976): 42.   [38] P. Goubert, *The Ancien Régime* (1973): 117–18.
[39] Chartier (1976): 52; Vogler (1976): 341.
[40] M. W. Flinn, *The European demographic system* (1981); Wrigley and Schofield (1981).
[41] Wrightson (1982): 186–7.

such enthusiasm.[42] It would cost £30–40 to support an Oxford commoner for a year in 1600, rising to £80–100 by 1750: well out of the range of most fathers' pockets.[43] Curtis is happy to claim that since restrictions of cost 'fell oppressively only on the boys from the very lowest ranks of society, they allowed a broad representation from the other groups to enjoy the advantages of education'.[44] What happens to girls we are unsure, but it is clear that British society was filling up from the bottom and we must recognize that, as the lower and poorer ranks became relatively more numerous, a larger proportion of the population would have been denied access to education. In terms of available resources for education Scotland probably lay somewhere between France and England. But the general point is obvious enough. Economic constraints exerted an enduring influence on the ability of the poorer classes to attend school.

In addition to direct financial outlay there were also indirect losses occasioned by parents being deprived of child labour – what economists call an 'opportunity cost'. In the twentieth century, childhood is a clearly delineated phase in an individual's life. In earlier centuries children were expected to make an economic contribution to the family budget from an early age: perhaps as young as seven or eight years old.[45] They were expected to work as well as play and work was often the main priority. Life could be precarious in the early modern world and the more productive hands a family had the better were its chances of material well-being.

The phenomenon of child labour was of course a particular worry to those eighteenth- and nineteenth-century observers concerned with the moral welfare of the working class. The minister who wrote the Statistical Account for Coilton believed that the 'great obstacle to the education of the poor is that the people can employ their children profitably at an early age'.[46] In the industrial town of Kilmarnock in Ayrshire during the 1840s it was seen that 'the greatest enemy to education in this and other commercial towns, is a disposition on the part of poor parents to avail themselves of the fruits of their children's industry'.[47] At Bathgate in West Lothian in the 1790s, 'many parents are too poor to keep their children long enough at school; and some are tempted by the prospect of gain, to send them too early to the loom'. 'Since the introduction of cotton manufactures' at Strathblane, 'a great

---

[42] L. Stone, 'The educational revolution in England' (1964).   [43] O'Day (1982): 198.
[44] M. H. Curtis, 'Education and apprenticeship' (1964): 62.   [45] Spufford (1981): 26–7.
[46] Sinclair (1826): 139.
[47] *New Statistical Account of Scotland*, vol. 5 (1845): 560 (hereafter *NSA*).

many parents take away their children from school, before they have learned to read to any good purpose, in order to receive the pittance given for their labour'.[48] In 1855 men and women living in the urbanized and industrialized county of Dumbarton were as illiterate as those in Sutherland, thanks to the influence of industry and the immigration of unskilled, illiterate Highlanders and Irish to the western Lowlands. Again, Scotland is not alone in this. Michael Sanderson has shown the detrimental effects of education and literacy arising from opportunities for child employment and the pressure of expanding population on limited educational resources in Lancashire between 1780 and 1840. Of Lancashire, one Dr Percival said that 'the children employed in the factories are generally debarred from all opportunities for education and from moral and religious instruction'.[49]

In the great manufacturing districts, especially in Lancashire, and in most of the large trading towns, the schools frequented by the poorer children are in such a state that it is hard to say whether there is worse provision made for their bodily health or for their mental improvement.[50]

It has been argued that younger children were more likely to receive an education since the parents needed income from older offspring to be able to educate them. Analysis of birth order and education in an English context reveals no such necessary connection, but the logic of the connection provides a valuable illustration of the kind of constraints created by the cost of schooling and by the opportunities for child employment.[51] In short, 'the facility with which work can be procured for children, and the tender age at which, from necessity, they are often withdrawn from school, are operating in a moral and religious point of view, seriously to the disadvantage of the rising generation'.[52] For many children formal learning may have been sporadic or curtailed. Hartley glasshouse apprentices in late eighteenth-century Northumberland were educated part time, 'when their business will admit in order to learn writing'.[53] Of course, comparatively few people were involved in industrial work in either Scotland or England before the second half of the eighteenth century. By far the largest proportion of the population worked in agriculture where there was more free time in which children could be educated. Yet, while the effects of continuous employment in industry on

[48] Sinclair (1826): 139.
[49] Quoted in M. Sanderson, 'Education and the factory in industrial Lancashire' (1967): 267.
[50] *Speeches and observations of Lord Brougham* (1837): 10.
[51] L. A. Tilly, 'Individual lives and family strategies' (1979): 143–4; D. C. Levine, 'Education and family life in early industrial England' (1979).
[52] *NSA*, vol. 5 (1845): 543–4.   [53] NCRO 2DE/4/6/12.

access to schooling are plain, even in agriculture there were difficulties in ensuring continuity of attendance. In fact, some commentators believed that work in industry was crucial to create the extra income needed to educate children. The report of the Poor Law Commissioners in Scotland in 1843 suggests that in areas without appreciable industrial employment real wages were too low for decent food, let alone for education for one's children.[54] But in agriculture, too, cost and opportunity cost could be a serious constraint on education for the poorer classes. Of the peasantry in the Border counties of Scotland and England, Gilly wrote that irregular, discontinuous school attendance was related to the need for children to work in the fields, inability of parents to pay for education and badly located schools.[55] The seventeenth-century Puritan divine Richard Baxter regretted that in his native county of Shropshire tenant farmers 'cannot spare their children from work while they learn to read, though I offer to pay the schoolmaster myself . . . so that poverty causeth a generation of barbarians'.[56] A seventeenth-century Lancashireman called William Stout recalled how:

As we attained to the age of ten or twelve years, we were very much taken off the schoole, espetialy in the spring and summer season, plow time, turfe time, hay time and harvest, in looking after the sheep, helping at plough, goeing to the moss with carts, making hay and shearing in harvest, two of us at 13 or 14 years of age being equall to one man shearer; so that we made smal progress in Latin, for what we got in winter we forgot in summer, and the writing master coming to Boulton mostly in winter, wee got what writing we had in winter.[57]

In the Highlands and Islands of Scotland during the eighteenth century 'the inhabitants were not only poor . . . but were often obliged to employ their children in farming work and herding, which either entirely prevented their attendance at school or rendered it too irregular to be beneficial'.[58] The issue of opportunity cost may have been the stimulus behind Lasswade Kirk Session's offer to pay 'for a Bible to William Falconer's son to encourage him to keep him at school' in July 1683.[59] Opportunities for education were not automatically better in agricultural as opposed to industrial communities.

However in agriculture, unlike industry, there were slack periods when children might receive schooling. The early nineteenth-century working-class autobiographer Alexander Somerville and his sister left school in the south-east of Scotland in the summer of 1819 to herd

[54] I. Levitt and C. Smout, *The state of the Scottish working class in 1843* (1979): 108–13.
[55] Gilly (1842): 36; Sinclair (1826): 91.   [56] Quoted in J. Simon (1968a): 53.
[57] J. H. Marshall (ed.), *The autobiography of William Stout* (1967): 70.
[58] Sinclair (1826): 92.   [59] SRO CH2/471/9.

cows, but returned during the winter.[60] Contemporaries recognized the seasonal variations in attendance. A visitation of the parish school of Carrington in Midlothian during July 1683 revealed that it was 'ordinarily well frequented as to the season of the year'.[61] Kingsbarns Kirk Session recorded in September 1666 how some parents in that part of Fife 'withheld their children from the school in harvest and summertime'.[62]

In addition to seasonal fluctuations in school attendance there were also the dislocating effects of geographical mobility, a common feature of this society. The frequent movement of farm labour in south-east Scotland and north-east England at Martinmas when children would be receiving an education was felt to be damaging to their moral development.[63] Duration of education was not great, and regular attendance was not enforced. The report of the Dick Trustees on education in north-east Scotland in 1832 revealed that the mean age of entry to school was five and a half years, at leaving fifteen years, but that attendance was highly discontinuous.[64] The same was clearly true of earlier centuries. This whole issue of opportunity cost explains why, even where truly free education was available, as in some towns, comparatively few people would be able to avail themselves of these opportunities. Poverty and the need for child labour were important factors in holding down the literacy of working people.

Effective access by the lower orders to education was also restricted by middle-class dominance of provision. SSPCK schools set up to bring learning to the masses were quickly infiltrated by sons of better-off farmers, and it was several decades before they were debarred from so doing in 1749. Charity schools established in the mid eighteenth century in Edinburgh became the preserve of children of reputable burgesses and others of high status, both in town and country, rather than the poor whom they were ostensibly designed to help and who were forced out by increased fees. Smout concludes further that the grammar schools and the universities were largely the preserves of the middle class in Scotland.[65] To take one example, the grammar school on the Isle of Lewis in the seventeenth century catered for the sons of local landowners, ministers, merchants and professional men.[66] Smout's findings also suggest that those from poor backgrounds who did make good seldom did so through the universities. As in seventeenth-century France or, say, Nördlingen in Germany in the early

---

[60] Somerville (1951): 15.   [61] SRO CH2/424/5.   [62] Beale (1953): 93.
[63] J. F. Duncan, 'Scottish farm labour' (1919): 503.
[64] Saunders (1950): 289.   [65] Smout (1972): 450; Scotland (1969): 99.
[66] Shaw (1981): 146.

eighteenth century, there were some places in charity schools for the poor, though in others wealthy bourgeois dominated them because of the cheap and effective education they offered.[67] Increased educational provision did not necessarily provide equal benefits for all social classes, and augmented educational opportunity did not automatically mean greater equality of opportunity. Even where there was free education it was not always the poor who benefited. In the light of factors such as cost, opportunity cost and middle-class domination of education, the higher initial levels of literacy among the middling ranks of society and the faster rate of progress they enjoyed are easier to understand.

We have then to consider the acquisition of literacy in its wider social and economic context, assessing the connections between the stratified learning process and opportunities and constraints in access to education. Margaret Spufford's analysis of access to education provides some valuable insights into the interactions of poverty and the sort of curriculum we have described, and their influence on reading and sign-literacy levels. For most families among the ranks of society below the yeomanry, the productive labour of children was important. As we have seen, sparing them from work entailed an opportunity cost over and above the considerable money costs of schooling. Now, reading was taught at an age when children could earn little, 'whereas writing was commonly taught at an age after the meaningful earning lives of such boys had begun'.[68] Seventeenth-century English educationalists said children should be sent to school at seven or eight years of age.[69] The seventeenth-century autobiographer William Stout was roughly this age when his parents first sent him to the free school at Bolton, though he had already attended elementary dame school.[70] This early age was also true for eighteenth-century Scotland, though Sir John Sinclair did record that children were being educated from five years onwards, and sometimes those as young as three years might benefit.[71] In seventeenth-century Fife, children might get elementary education in the parish or adventure school from this age, but had to wait until they were seven or eight years old before going to grammar school. There were attempts in areas such as Fife to ensure attendance at school between the ages of five and ten. In 1647 Wemyss Kirk Session ordered both boys and girls 'having breeches and short cloathes' to come to the school by the age of seven at the latest.[72] The

[67] Chartier (1976): 81; C. R. Friedrichs, *Urban society in an age of war* (1979): 227.
[68] Spufford (1981): 27.   [69] *Ibid*. 23.   [70] Marshall (1967): 68.
[71] Sinclair (1826): 67–8.   [72] Beale (1953): 26, 38, 229.

main point to note is that reading was taught slightly before writing and that most children learned to read at about seven and to write at eight.

This is of course an unduly rigid framework. Some children were fast learners, some slow. Ralph Josselin's son started learning the elements of grammar at six and was well on in the classics before he became a teenager. William Stout's brother Leonard, on the other hand, 'very active at plow or carting, was taken from schoole' at age fourteen 'having got little learning except to read English and some little writing'.[73] Nevertheless, the general principle appears to be broadly correct. As Spufford points out, 'since the age at which paying work for a child began was the same at which the teaching of writing began, but a year later than that at which the teaching of reading began, reading was a much commoner skill than writing'.[74] Spufford assumes that sign-literacy levels 'roughly represent the proportion of these social groups which had the opportunity for schooling between seven and eight'.[75]

There are, of course, many intervening influences which add complexity to this over-simplified schema, though the broad idea seems to work. The children of Ralph Josselin, the Puritan vicar of Earls Colne in Essex, were taught to read while aged between four and ten, but did not learn to write until they had been away to school.[76] Alexander Somerville's education in late eighteenth-century Lowland Scotland gave him an early acquaintance with reading but not until much later with writing and arithmetic. His sister was less fortunate and 'went no more to school than that quarter [year], having to go to the fields to help to work for the family bread'.[77] William Stout's sister 'was early confined to waite on her brother', with the result that her education was restricted to reading, knitting, spinning and needlework.[78] In one early nineteenth-century model school, reading was taught in one year, reading and writing within three or four years. Average attendance was only thirteen months.[79] In seventeenth-century Fife, poor children maintained by the Kirk Session at the parish school were sent out when able to read the Bible. Children were to stay at school until they knew 'the grounds of religion', and it is exceptional for poor scholars to be found attending for more than five years: in fact, one or two years was the most common duration of education.[80] This fits with the estimate in the *Book of discipline* that two years was long enough 'to learn to read perfectly, to answer to the Catechism, and to have some entrance to the first rudiments of

---

[73] E. Hockliffe (ed.), *The diary of Ralph Josselin* (1908): 71; Marshall (1967): 75–6.
[74] Spufford (1981): 45.   [75] *Ibid.* 26.
[76] A. Macfarlane, *The family life of Ralph Josselin* (1970): 91.
[77] Somerville (1951): 15, 21.   [78] Marshall (1967): 68.   [79] Webb (1955): 17.
[80] Beale (1953): 98, 228–9.

Grammar'.[81] The problem of limited educational duration would be more pressing in the poor and populous parishes of the Highlands, where many children would be too poor to attend school, and as many would be too poor to stay long enough to learn to read English. Even when they did, their lack of understanding made literacy purely nominal.[82] Given the limited duration of attendance, still less reading and writing would be learnt if children had to be taught to speak English before they could start.

Finally, getting an education in writing was generally more expensive than learning to read, and many people may have been able to afford only the most basic education for their children. From the 100 children attending the English school in late eighteenth-century Kilmarnock in Ayrshire (about 10% of the eligible population) the master received 2s 6d sterling per quarter for those learning reading, 3s for writing as well and 4s for reading, writing and arithmetic. In the schools of north-east Scotland at the end of the eighteenth century, an additional fee was charged to learn writing, therefore many children were not taught this skill.[83]

In short, it does seem likely that there were widespread opportunities to learn to read, but how diffuse is quite impossible to determine accurately. The chances to learn writing were fewer. And if children only attended school for long enough to learn reading we must wonder how useful the skills they learned actually were to them. Could they read any literature or could they only stumble through passages in the Bible? Of course the argument above pertains to formal education by schooling. It is not certain whether the same priorities obtained in instruction within families – though this was certainly the case in Sweden – or in other non-scholastic modes of learning.

Before the nineteenth century it is impossible to assess the proportion of children who might have received an education, or indeed how long schooling lasted, because of the problems of irregular attendance, home learning and the existence of different types of school, some of which leave little or no trace in local records. Therefore, it is not possible to compare seventeenth- and eighteenth-century Britain with, say, eighteenth-century Poland, where less than 1% of the eligible population were in schools, or with the Low Countries where the educational system encompassed most eligible children.[84] What evidence there is suggests more open access to education in early

---

[81] Knox (1905): 384. In rural areas of seventeenth- and eighteenth-century France few children stayed at school after learning the catechism.
[82] Durkacz (1978): 34, 38.   [83] Buchan (1972): 191; *OSA*, vol. 2 (1791): 94.
[84] Litak (1973): 54, 57.

modern Britain than in southern or eastern Europe or even France where, until the eighteenth century, schooling was nearly an elite monopoly.[85] However, we cannot confirm Stone's view that Scottish education catered for an unusually wide range of social classes by comparison with its near neighbours.[86] Indeed, if judged by the ratio of official burgh and parochial schools to population it is likely that Scotland would tend to come off rather poorly, if only because of the large size of parishes. At the same time, figures on the relative spatial density of schools or the proportion of eligibles attending school are not particularly helpful indicators of an egalitarian society unless we also know what average attendances were and the social distribution of those attending.

Nor was Scotland the only country where the Protestant reformers searched out and promoted able, promising boys either by encouraging parents to continue to educate their children or (less often) by giving direct financial aid.[87] In some principalities in Germany it was argued that everyone should get an education, 'because children of working people should, for the sake of their own and our common welfare, receive in their early youth instruction in prayers, catechism, and writing and reading'. However, the gifted were to be specially encouraged. Town Councils in seventeenth-century Sweden often provided help for deserving boys to attend the gymnasia. The princely Council of the duchy of Deux Ponts in the Rhineland was committed to helping poor but able children in the hope of ensuring a good local supply of administrative talent.[88] In Scotland the emphasis was on creating religious officials. The theory that aid should be provided for poor but bright boys was not unique to Scotland. Nor was it confined to Protestantism. In parts of Languedoc, provision was made for the poor but gifted child in the belief that no child should be held back by lack of money.

We should also make it clear that Scotland was not the only state which played a role in providing education. French royal edicts of 1698 and 1724 provided for the taxation of inhabitants to supplement the ecclesiastical funding of education. The crown attempted to compel parents to send their children to school in early seventeenth-century Sweden. The level of success in these two instances was apparently low, as it was with some German princely initiatives of the sixteenth century, since governments did not institute formal controls on their administration.[89] Nevertheless, the idea was there.

[85] C. Tilly, 'Population and pedagogy in France' (1973): 122.   [86] Stone (1969): 135.
[87] G. Strauss, *Luther's house of learning* (1978): 178, 194.
[88] Laget (1971): 1407; Roberts (1953): 437; Vogler (1976): 350–1.
[89] Chartier (1976): 27; Roberts (1953): 437, 452; Vogler (1976): 351–2.

Finally, we must recognize that England too had free schools. In England, as is often pointed out, there were many philanthropic endowments of education, but relatively few funds to aid the poor boy to attend and remain in school. However, poor children probably had fewer openings than in Scotland and 'free' places were subject to the same practical restrictions of incidental and opportunity cost that we have outlined for Scotland. Schools might be called 'free' but there were incidental charges which created barriers for the poor. Grammar schools, which might be endowed at the ultimate expense of the poor, were far out of their reach.[90] English grammar schools rarely catered for the sons of lower-class fathers, such as labourers or husbandmen, dealing instead mainly with the gentry and urban middle classes. The idea of easy access to education and the possibility of social advancement is again seen to be little better than a pious hope. Almost all north-west European countries tried to make education available to the gifted poor, but we have no clear evidence that Scotland was particularly successful in this respect.

In both Scotland and England there were a variety of barriers to education which already prompt us to question any notion of 'universal education'. Most studies of literacy nevertheless do follow a line of argument which stresses the provision of places in schools as the main factor promoting reading and writing ability. Less formal means of learning have been mentioned only sketchily and even discussion of the availability of schooling has tended to emphasize the supply side of the equation – philanthropy, charitable endowment, state provision. The emphasis has been on outside agencies which created opportunities rather than on demand among the population at large for educational facilities. Historians have perhaps been too easily blinded by the claims of some nineteenth-century reformers that an unendowed school system was bound to promote ignorance. One early nineteenth-century middle-class observer claimed that education for 'our own children' would occur mainly through the 'associations of home', but 'in respect to the child of labouring man it must be done, if done at all, at school'.[91]

These sorts of bald claims about mass ignorance and apathy towards education disregard the context of child labour and employment opportunities in rural as well as industrial areas in favour of the comfortable assumption that not wishing to educate children was a sign of inner moral inadequacy. 'By blaming the poor for their poverty (and much else besides) the educationalist was *enabled* to *believe* that his was

[90] Simon (1967): 370–3; O'Day (1982): 36–8.
[91] Quoted in R. Johnson, 'Educational policy and social control' (1970): 112.

a humane, an adequate, and an essentially Christian response to potentially removable evils.'[92] Attitudes to education varied both between and within social groups, but there is no reason to accept these blanket condemnations. Much of the previous analysis has centred on schools because of the need to deal with some of the more obvious assumptions in the existing literature. Now we can start to question the emphasis on schooling and begin to expand the notion of learning to encompass a variety of contexts. It is becoming clear from other studies of literacy in Continental Europe that the study of schooling is not in itself adequate to explain the development of literacy. What of Scotland and England?

Informal learning

Formal education was not vital to the artisans who were prominent among fifteenth-century English Lollards and who 'in varying degrees and ways had become book-conscious or literate'.[93] Yet even in the post-Renaissance age when print was widely available and schooling increasingly so, autodidactic methods continued to play an important role in accounting for the literacy of the lower classes, though a grounding in basic reading and writing obtained at school may have been an important foundation for later learning. We have evidence of this process at work among all social classes. Those people, like Adam Martindale, who became literate enough to write a diary seem to have consolidated informal learning and formal schooling by a keen interest in reading. Ralph Josselin, not perhaps a very typical figure, had begun his educational career through his father's 'own instruction [and] example'.[94] He then passed on to schooling supplemented by what was to become a lifelong devotion to books. For these sorts of men the educational process involved learning from parents and peers, being taught in schools and possessing a level of personal commitment high enough to continue practising these skills.

Given the restraints on access to education during childhood which we have outlined above, it is not surprising that some adults should have returned to school later in life or to have resorted to self-help. Sir John Sinclair believed that at all social levels in Scotland, people whose education had been 'neglected in early life . . . go to school at their own expense, when they come to the years of discretion, in order to supply

---

[92] *Ibid.* 105.   [93] M. Aston, 'Lollardy and literacy' (1977): 356.
[94] Hockliffe (1908): 1–2, 31; Parkinson (1845): 5–12.

this deficiency. Nor is it unusual for schools to be resorted to by grown-up persons, after their ordinary hours of labour.'[95] Adults might develop an understanding of literacy through listening to children who were learning to read outside schools. Contrary to what Sinclair asserted, adult interest in literate pursuits was not universal. Of the men with whom Alexander Somerville lived in an early nineteenth-century labourers' bothy, three were interested in reading but the other three were indifferent and preferred drinking. A workmate of Somerville's father had been taught to read after his marriage and would walk a full twenty miles to borrow a book with which to spend Sunday in the fields reading.[96]

For those who had the urge to learn, self-teaching was important. William Stout taught himself mathematics 'without any instruction other than books'. Other diaries suggest that this approach was profitable for the already literate, but that at a more basic level one had to be shown how to read and write.[97] Women were particularly disadvantaged in access to education and may have relied more heavily on autodidactic methods. Yet curiously they may have been particularly important both as transmitters of oral culture and as teachers in their own right.

The importance of women in socialization was recognized. 'The mother of a family is a moral power, fertilizing the mind, and opening the heart to . . . every virtue.'[98] These assumptions were used as arguments to justify greater efforts being put into the education of women, since where they are 'left in a state of ignorance and degradation, the endearing and important duties of wife and mother cannot be duly discharged'.[99] However, women can be found not simply as childminders but as teachers of reading and practical skills such as sewing. Some are referred to in seventeenth-century spiritual autobiographies.[100] Female teachers were far from being unknown. Returns to Archbishop Herring's visitation of the diocese of York in 1743 include the reply from Bainton parish that 'we have no publik or Charity School endow'd. Two poor Women teach a few Children to read.'[101] During a purge of private schools which were supposedly in competition with the official parochial establishment in Lasswade in 1647, two of the three unofficial ones were run by women who were expressly forbidden to teach anything except sewing.[102] In the Western Isles

[95] Sinclair (1826): 89.   [96] Somerville (1951): 12, 90–1.
[97] Marshall (1967): 74; Parkinson (1845): 49–53.
[98] Gilly (1842): 32.   [99] Sinclair (1826): 126.
[100] Spufford (1981): 35–6; Neuberg (1971): 55.
[101] Ollard and Walker, vol. 1 (1928): 97.   [102] SRO CH2/471/2: 16 January 1647.

there was an especially strong tradition of informal teaching, as when on Tiree old women would gather children together to teach them to read. Prior to the eighteenth century much education in the Highlands was conducted on this informal, familial basis.[103]

The precise role of women in education is unclear, but there are many examples of learning in a family context. Adam Martindale's godmother gave him an ABC and, 'by the help of my bretheren and sisters that could read, and a young man that came to court my sister, had quickly learned it'.[104] When slightly older he was educated for a time by the daughter of a well-known schoolmaster who knew some Latin among her other accomplishments. Alexander Somerville was taught at home until he was eight years of age. Gilbert Burns, brother of the famous Robert, illustrates what might happen. 'There being no school near us, and our little services being already useful on the farm, my father undertook to teach us arithmetic in the winter evenings by candle light – and in this way my two elder sisters received all the education they ever received.'[105] Home education seems to have been especially important for girls, perhaps because it was cheaper and the investment was felt less justifiable than for boys. In 1824 Patrick Butler confirmed that 'the female is regarded as neither fit for any of the public offices of life, nor capable of acquiring a fortune in the event of migration, and so their attendance at school is deemed an unnecessary waste of time'.[106] In his 1764 report on the Hebrides, John Walker noted that boys were sent to school where possible, 'but the Parents consider Learning of any kind as of little Moment to the Girls, on which Account, great Numbers of them never go to any School'. At the SSPCK schools of Braemar in 1718 and Glenmuick in 1725 boys outnumbered girls by more than four to one.[107] In Scotland, schools which taught the most rudimentary reading skills were the only ones to have anything like an equal number of boys and girls attending them. Indeed, while boys from the gentry class were usually educated at grammar school in seventeenth- and eighteenth-century England, it was more usual for girls to be taught at home or in the houses of other gentle or noble families. In the mid sixteenth century one merchant's daughter wrote of how

my mother in the dayes of King Henry the 8th came to some light of the gospell by meanes of some English books sent privately to her by my fathers factours from beyond sea: whereuppon she used to call me with my 2 sisters into her

---

[103] Sinclair (1826): appx. 19; Thompson (1972–4): 248.   [104] Parkinson (1845): 5–12.
[105] Lockhart (1830): 17; Somerville (1951): 13.   [106] Quoted in Durkacz (1983): 125.
[107] Quoted in Withers (1982): 40; I. J. Simpson, *Education in Aberdeenshire* (1947): 152.

chamber to read to us out of the same good books very privately for feare of troble bicause those good books were then accompted hereticall.[108]

A statute of 1543 explicitly forbade the lower classes from reading the Bible in English, and provided that among women only those of noble and gentry stock might read it privately.

Home learning certainly took place, but how common it was is unclear. In both Scotland and England the church was keen to have families practising reading and catechism together – adults, children and servants. Parents were to encourage children in reading, while masters and mistresses were to call on servants 'often to read and hear Sermons'. Archbishop Herring was concerned in his 1743 visitation to ensure regular catechism of children and servants by the clergy of the province of York.[109] Catechism of family members was supposed to be carried out by the head of the household and there are certainly cases where this happened. One seventeenth-century Englishwoman called Margaret Corbet took notes at sermons which she then used to catechize her servants.[110] William Stout's Episcopalian parents instructed their children in the catechism. At Lasswade in December 1639 thirty shillings Scots was disbursed for 'buiks of familie exercise to distribute to the congregation'. In October 1647 the minister of Lasswade bought 120 'books of directorie worship' for elders to hand out.[111] Three years later he gave the elders twenty confessions of faith with catechisms and ordered 'caus ilk ane that can read within their bounds to get one and practice the same'.

Admittedly these examples are drawn from decades of political change and religious enthusiasm when the contest to win hearts and minds would be closely fought, but the same comments can be found throughout the sixteenth, seventeenth and eighteenth centuries. Home learning was part of the Protestant aim to secure orthodoxy by combining reading with direction. But the extent of home catechism and learning in response to the church's exhortations is not certain. In mid seventeenth-century Fife the ecclesiastical authorities ordered 'that masters of families be exhorted to use meanes for learning thair servants to read'.[112] Sir John Sinclair was surely expressing a pious hope when claiming that 'the practice of the lower classes was, to make their children read to them on Sunday afternoons, and repeat their catechisms and hymns, after which the duties of the day were closed

---

[108] Quoted in J. Shakespeare and M. Dowling, 'Religion and politics in mid-Tudor England' (1982): 97; see also McMullen (1977): 87–8, 91.
[109] Spufford (1981): 211–12; Ollard and Walker, vol. 1 (1928): 3.
[110] P. Collinson, *The religion of the protestants* (1982): 265.
[111] Marshall (1967): 69; SRO CH2/471/2.   [112] Beale (1953): 26.

for family worship'.[113] James Hogg remarked that it was common in the Borders until the late eighteenth century, though we cannot be sure how reliable his observation was.[114] In any case, David Levine points out that the transmission of literacy from generation to generation by means of the socialization process within the family was haphazard. Levine casts doubt on the efficacy of the family as a primary unit of education and socialization in England.[115] And it is all but impossible to assess whether the sort of home teaching successfully insisted upon by religious reformers in Sweden was carried out in Britain.

Of other non-scholastic means of education, the practical training of apprenticeship is perhaps the best known. Most crafts and trades companies were like the Edinburgh College of Surgeons in specifying that apprentices and servants to surgeons should be able to read and write.[116] Given the property qualifications for fathers wishing to apprentice their sons, many boys would in any case have been drawn from a more literate, middling or upper-class background. In fact nearly all of a small sample of young men specifically described as apprentices in the Scottish and English criminal court depositions could sign their own names. When he contracted with an apprentice in 1692, the Southampton hellier and plumber Michael Gissage undertook 'to perfect the said apprentice in reading and writeing', but most boys in the poor-child apprentice register for that town were already able to sign their indentures in any case.[117] Dunlop and Denman note provision for education in indentures in their classic study of English apprenticeship and child labour.[118]

At the same time, apprenticing was timed for the end of any schooling and would put boys out at what for some at least would be their most literate time of life. Poor Highland lads were indentured while aged ten to fourteen in the mid eighteenth century.[119] Of twenty-two boys apprenticed to Edinburgh companies between 1599 and 1747 and born at Lasswade in Midlothian, the youngest was thirteen, the oldest twenty-one and the mean age at indenture was fifteen and a half. Between 1640 and 1738 there were twenty-one Earsdon-born boys sent to Newcastle companies, all from a narrower age range of thirteen to sixteen, and with a lower mean age of fourteen and a half.[120]

Of course, there were opportunities for book learning during apprenticeship, which was not simply a manual education but also a

[113] Sinclair (1826): 97.
[114] J. Hogg, 'On the changes in the habits of the Scottish peasantry' (1831–2): 258–9.
[115] Levine (1979): 378–9.   [116] *Extracts from the burgh records of Edinburgh* (1869): 103.
[117] A. J. Willis (1968): lxiii, 103–4.
[118] O. J. Dunlop and R. D. Denman, *English apprenticeship and child labour* (1912): 181.
[119] Thompson (1972–4): 259–60.   [120] Houston (1981): 433.

technical one. During his indenture as an apprentice in a shop William Stout spent much time reading 'or improving my selfe in arethmatick, survighing or other mathamatikall sciences'.[121] In trades such as weaving, apprentices and master alike could work and learn from books propped up in front of them. The eighteenth-century bookseller James Lackington forgot his formal teaching from dame school, but took up reading again as an apprentice under the guidance of his master's wife and son.[122]

Less exhalted in status than apprenticeship was the institution of service. In the form of domestics and servants in husbandry, service was a fundamental aspect of English demographic, economic and social life between the fifteenth and the nineteenth centuries. Servants were young, unmarried men and women mainly between the ages of fifteen and twenty-five hired for periods of half or one year in return for their keep and a small cash fee. Significantly, they normally lived in the same house as their employer and family, a situation which could lead to sexual exploitation of young women, but also one where informal learning could take place. Joseph Mayett, a Buckinghamshire servant at the start of the nineteenth century, was already literate by the time he was encouraged to read religious books while working for a godly family. A subsequent master extended his command of reading.[123] Again some of those 'born again' at Cambuslang in Ayrshire in the 1740s illustrate the processes at work. One married man in his thirties told how he

was born in the High-lands; and my parents living far from any place where there was a school, I was not put to it, nor could I read till I was about fourteen years of age: and then, in time of my Apprenticeship, I got lessons from some about: and so at length to read the Bible.[124]

A girl who had received only twenty days of formal schooling was 'taught to read some in private houses where I served, and was brought the length of reading the Question Book [the Catechism] exactly enough but I could not read my Bible till of late I have been at great pains to learn'. Meanwhile, a tenant farmer who had only had a very imperfect school education explained how at the age of twelve he decided to learn to read so as not to be the odd man out when he got older: 'and these with whom I liv'd seeing me inclined to learn to read, both gave me liberty to learn and put me to it; and so I proceeded till I could read the Bible tolerably'. Learning was almost certainly a continuous process in which schooling might be only one component.

---

[121] Marshall (1967): 80–1.   [122] Webb (1955): 20.   [123] Kussmaul (1981): 89.
[124] All quotations from T. C. Smout, 'Born again at Cambuslang' (1982): 126.

Further details of the learning process of the atypical exemplary members of the Cambuslang revival congregation provide fascinating insights. One woman 'was put early to schools and taught to read and write and all other pieces for Education that are ordinary in Big Towns for gentlemens' daughters or people of fashion and station'. A servant girl, on the other hand, reported that she 'got some learning to read my catechism but was only twenty days at school'. Other statements indicate that rudimentary education had been provided, but that greater fluency and understanding had only been attained through endeavours later in life. Basic schooling could provide a foundation for later attainments. One girl had had a little schooling, but 'could not find leisure to learn to read' and had to teach herself 'by following the minister with my eye on the Bible as he read that portion of the Scripture he was going to lecture on', so that she came 'gradually to learn to read more than by any other way'. The Border shepherd James Hogg had a revival of interest in reading while employed as a herd at the age of eighteen, and recorded that 'the little reading that I had learned I had nearly lost'.[125] Faced with this sort of evidence we might become sceptical about Cressy's view that schooling was the only truly effective way of acquiring literate skills.[126]

It is important therefore to see education in schools as just one of many different modes of learning, and to recognize that the relative importance of informal means of education may vary between social groups, or may change with shifts in the dominant form of industrial production – rural domestic industry or the factory, for example, or even in different types of farming region. Informal education was always important in the Highlands, while in the new factory towns of the nineteenth century teaching by parents, grandparents or childminders would have grown in importance as formal educational facilities were strained by population pressure and child employment. Schools doubtless provided an important foundation for literacy, but they have to be seen in the context of other opportunities for learning which could supplement or even substitute for them. In addition, adults and children had to have some incentives to learn: the nature of these inducements forms the substance of what follows.

Demand for literacy

Broadly speaking, people could take one of two paths to literacy. They could be subject to the 'pull' of economic need or social prestige, or to the 'push' of religion and education. Much of the above discussion has

[125] Quoted in Craig (1961): 120.   [126] Cressy (1980): 39–41.

focused on the provision of schooling. However, we have begun to consider the sorts of factor which made people seek out the skills of reading, writing and counting. By looking at alternative pathways to literacy we can broaden our understanding of its importance considerably. Indeed, we should now move away from the supply side of education and literacy to examine the factors which might influence demand for and access to these resources among different social groups.

The period between the Renaissance and the Industrial Revolution was one of profound social, economic and political change. Population increase, industrial development, urbanization and the commercialization of agriculture along capitalist lines went with the expansion and integration of trade and marketing as the most significant developments in the society and economy of early modern Europe. The other principal change was the rise of the modern state and the growing intrusion of its bureaucratic mechanisms into a widening range of everyday activities in local communities.[127] Involvement with these institutions could promote literacy among some sections of the population. During the medieval period the increasing use of the vernacular in bureaucratic and religious affairs was both the cause and consequence of advances in lay literacy. Literacy only ceased to be a 'pragmatic convenience' when writing recorded a large portion of the cultural heritage in the vernacular.[128] The chances of interacting with the officials of church and state in situations requiring basic literacy would be on the increase all the time. As Margaret Spufford remarks:

The importance of reading may have been still marginal at a social level below that of the yeoman in a world in which the regular functions were predominantly oral. Yet increasingly the attender at church, at manor and hundredal court, and even at market, would find the written and printed word was physically present, if not actually necessary.[129]

There was a whole range of local, regional and central courts in Scotland and England with a variety of partially overlapping jurisdictions in both civil and criminal matters. Most individuals would have at least one encounter with such institutions during their lifetime, and especially local ones, such as the manor court in late medieval and early modern England or the Kirk Session in seventeenth-century Scotland. Written forms were becoming more important for legal and

[127] Wormald (1981); R. Mitchison, *Lordship to patronage* (1983); B. P. Lenman, *Integration, enlightenment and industrialization* (1981).
[128] M. Clanchy, *From memory to written record* (1979): 201; Aston (1977): 350.
[129] Spufford (1981): 2.

political activity. The same was true of economic life. Scottish testaments and inventories of the seventeenth and eighteenth centuries sometimes include long lists of bonds (contracts) or deeds registered with local courts of record again suggesting reasons for literacy. In other words, the growth of central and local administrations made new demands on the literacy of early modern people. This much is clear. But how do we assess the relative importance of pull factors exerted by the differing institutional structures of the two countries?

In both Scotland and England vast bodies of manuscript documents survive from the sixteenth century onwards, testifying to the importance of writing. It is extremely difficult, however, to assess whether one society's institutions placed more or less stress on writing than the other, and what impact this might have had on levels of literacy among the population at large. Scotland is sometimes described a a country where bonds and Covenants were common, ranging in importance from individual agreements to weighty oaths involving the nation as a whole – the Covenants for example. At the local level, miscreants and bad neighbours might have to sign bonds to keep the peace, as would coalworkers who their master felt had misbehaved. Bonds of Caution were recorded centrally by Commissary Courts.[130] These were formal agreements which obliged a person in dispute to find someone who would stand surety for his good behaviour. Greater use of written legal records was an important unifying force in sixteenth- and seventeenth-century Scotland. In the early seventeenth century, for example, Shetland was integrated into the Scottish legal system under the influence of Edinburgh lawyers who required much greater conformity to national concepts and procedures. Northern Britain was coming to be dominated by men whose inclination was to spend ink, not spill blood. The greater intrusion of central government into areas outside Lowland Scotland during the sixteenth and seventeenth centuries would necessitate more involvement by lairds in administration and bureaucracy.[131]

Legal and institutional integration had taken place much earlier in England and was effectively complete by the middle of the eighteenth century. English recognizances, along with other bonds and affidavits preserved in the quarter sessions and assizes records, testify to the importance of contracts in that society. In fact, legal and administrative institutions seem to have played a greater part in the lives of English people than they did Scottish, though it seems unlikely that this was more true of the northern counties than it was of other areas of

---

[130] SRO RH11/5/1: 22 May 1686; GD18/1007/2–7; CC8/15/1–20.
[131] Shaw (1981): 45, 198.

England. The superior literacy of the north of England in the eighteenth century is unlikely to have been the product of a higher level of interaction between people there and the institutions of central and local government.

Differences in court procedures nevertheless may have had a role to play in fostering literacy. There was certainly some incentive for those in trouble with the law to have enough knowledge of literate skills at least to gather an outline of what was happening. In England learning a simple neck verse could save a person from hanging.[132] Nevertheless, it is surprising how many felons appearing before the English assizes failed to save themselves by this simple expedient. Both before and after sentencing, the accused at a criminal court in Scotland could petition for mercy or improved conditions of imprisonment. They could go as high as the Scottish Privy Council before it was disbanded after the Union of Parliaments in 1707. Other court procedures were conducted in writing. The notification of a charge or citation to appear before the Justiciary Court was delivered in writing by the court messenger. The jury returned its verdict in writing and it was pronounced by the dempster.[133] However, in many instances the sentence or 'doom' preserved among the loose papers is still folded with its seal intact, suggesting that verbal notification of the contents rendered it superfluous.

Literacy might enhance understanding and confidence in the face of the awe-inspiring theatre of the court. For those using the courts to prosecute others it might also be an asset. This would be a more pressing reason in Scotland, since the Roman law obtaining there laid greater stress on written procedures. Memory was less important in Scots law and along with it oral testimony. Evidence was usually in the form of written depositions which were however read out to the jury.[134] Written interrogatories were formally presented for cross-examination, and opportunities for *viva voce* examinations were limited. Procedure was more dependent on written forms than was the case in England. However, we must recognize that there was in fact no absolute need for the accused or the prosecutor (if he or she was a private individual) to be literate. With professional writers, notaries public, on hand or with the help of friends or patrons, interaction with the literate medium of courts need not necessarily have influenced non-literates nearly as much as we might expect. Those who had already attained some reading and writing ability might be more prepared to use or appear in court or, once there, to be influenced by the

[132] Cressy (1980): 16–17.
[133] J. Cameron (ed.), *Justiciary records of Argyll and the Isles* (1949): xvii–xix.
[134] J. I. Smith (ed.), *Justiciary cases* (1972): xiv, xxv–xxvi.

environment of writing. This seems to be true of debt processes before the Commissary Courts where occupationally specific literacy rates are much higher than at the criminal courts. These courts were selective of literate people, whose involvement with them may in turn be associated with an augmented faith in the literate legal institutions of society at the expense of notions of communal arbitration. More literate people might prefer to use formal courts rather than local, informal, means of settlement. Developing legal institutions may have promoted literacy, but there was also a feedback from more literate, possibly more 'modern' elements of society who came to use and indeed to run the courts.

Legal and institutional development could promote literacy. Both the overall level of involvement with central and local government could be important as could the rate of change of administrative integration. However, we cannot be certain which was more important in Scotland and England or for that matter how the legal and political framework or the process of institutional change actually influenced ordinary men and women. Courts might stimulate literacy, but the ability to read and write might make people turn more readily to the courts. We can take one final example. We have already talked about bonds and petitions. Framed by individuals or elements of local communities, these were a common feature of early modern Britain. Designed to promote certain courses of action, petitions could unite and articulate opinion, and framing them could be a spur to literacy.

In Scotland, one reason for presenting petitions was in connection with the appointment of a minister of religion to a parish. If a ministry fell vacant in Scotland, the landowner with the heritable right of presentation was entitled to nominate a replacement. The candidate or 'expectant' would then be put through his paces, usually by being asked to present a sermon. The successful applicant would receive a 'call' or endorsement which was subscribed by the parishioners before being sent to the presbytery for approval. In cases of disputed election, a variety of petitions and counter-petitions might fly about until a decision was reached. These might split a parish on occupational lines, as in 1700 when twenty-two fishermen from Largo in Fife wrote against the removal of the minister to another parish.[135] When matters were settled the petition would be signed by heritors, interested heads of families and the elders of the Kirk Session. These latter were economically independent laymen involved in the day-to-day running of the church, uncovering and correcting moral offenders, collecting

---

[135] SRO CH1/2/3/1: fol. 19.

and distributing poor relief, supervising finance, buildings and education. Yet at Lasswade in 1659 seven of the nineteen elders who endorsed an official call could not sign their names. Elders were more literate than the remaining parishioners (sixty-four of the seventy-nine other subscribers were illiterate), but not as much as one might expect from their close involvement with administration. The elders of Lasswade at this date were mainly well-off tenant farmers and tradesmen, but it is impossible to determine whether they were any more literate than their socio-economic peers who had not experienced what we should regard as the literacy-enhancing effects of involvement in local church government.

We would imagine that Kirk Session elders or members of an English guild or four and twenty ('select vestry') would be more involved in literate activities. We could say the same of parish officials who subscribed the various oaths in England during the 1640s. Yet many civic leaders in Newcastle and Gateshead were still illiterate between 1660 and 1780.[136] Further reservations are bound to emerge when we see that 11% of the ninety-seven court messengers or officers who gave depositions before the High Court of Justiciary could not sign their names in full. Even among community leaders in the Fife burghs during the seventeenth century we do not find total literacy. Andrew Adie, the deacon of the St Andrews Hammermen's guild in 1694, could only make his initials in the minute book of the association.[137] Full command of literacy was not essential to wielding power and authority. In the mid eighteenth century, Cambuslang Kirk Session excused an alleged mishandling of funds by pleading that the elders were 'all persons in low life illiterate countrymen who had not been train'd up to writing or accounts with any Tollerable Exactness'.[138] We can see why contact with administration and familiarity with literate procedures should have enhanced literacy, but cannot at all prove that it always did so in reality. The point seems to be that despite institutional development and individual participation in or with government or administration, literacy was not a necessary result.

Alongside administrative developments changes were also taking place in the organization of economic life. Written forms could open up new ways of conducting business and could offer greater opportunities for profit or simply more security in economic relationships. In the field of agriculture, the seventeenth century in Scotland has recently been identified as less a time of stagnation before the famous agricultural

136 Stephens (1977): 29.
137 Beale (1953): 99–100; SAUL MS DA890.S1H2: fols. 114, 114v.
138 Quoted in Mitchison (1974): 86.

revolution of the late eighteenth century, than as a period of significant if gradual improvement. The spread of written leases of agricultural holdings was an important element in these changes, especially in the second half of the seventeenth century and particularly in arable rather than pastoral areas.[139] As well as being written contracts rather than verbal agreements, these leases came increasingly to be made for periods longer than the traditional three to five years. Both these developments worked to augment the security of tenant farmers who formed the backbone of Scottish rural society. Greater security of tenure meant more opportunities to try out improved agricultural techniques. Conceivably, such leases promoted literacy in the same way as the political and legal changes we have just been discussing.

For medieval England, Clanchy has argued that documents had to precede widening literacy.[140] The mechanism may however be slightly different. Written leases were related to the degree of commercially oriented agriculture. In other words long, written leases may be a product of economic advance and literacy rather than a cause. Reading and writing may have developed among tenants who, benefiting from agricultural advances, wished more security and had been taught to write in response to the commercialization of agriculture. The problems of distinguishing cause from effect are considerable. As Clanchy neatly observes of the medieval period in England:

> The gentry were not going to learn to read until documents were available and necessary. Necessity and availability also made for easy familiarity with writing, and from familiarity stemmed confidence in literate ways of doing business.[141]

More generally, English yeomen such as Henry Best and Robert Loder, as well as Scottish tenant farmers of the sixteenth, seventeenth and eighteenth centuries, were evidently subject to a number of influences which we might expect would coax or goad them into learning reading, writing and counting: building up a farm, keeping accounts, becoming committed to active participation in religion and parish government. Robert Loder's Berkshire farm account book of the early seventeenth century reveals a close awareness of accounting principles and a good head for figures. The economic integration of England in the seventeenth and eighteenth centuries, fostered partly by the growth of towns, would involve more people like Loder or Best on his Yorkshire farm in commerce and commercial agriculture.[142] Between 1640 and

---

[139] I. D. Whyte, 'Written leases and their impact on Scottish agriculture' (1979b): 9.
[140] Clanchy (1979): 57.   [141] *Ibid.* 57.
[142] C. B. Robinson (ed.), *Henry Best. Rural economy in Yorkshire* (1857); G. E. Fussell (ed.), *Robert Loder's farm accounts* (1936).

1750, for example, butter supplies for the metropolis were increasingly drawn from the Yorkshire coast, and the trade in food, fuel and raw materials on the east coast was of considerable economic importance. Trade in coal and salt between the northern counties and the south-east was well developed even in the sixteenth century.[143] In order to counter the price-setting activities of London cheese-factors, north-western producers began to participate in London markets on their own behalf. Even in the remote parts of the north and west of Scotland, farmers were assimilated to commercial markets and a money economy by their participation in the cattle trade with Lowland Scotland and England. Cash and credit notes were in surprisingly common use.[144] There were reasons present in both Scottish and English society which might induce literacy among more of the population over the period 1600–1800.

Indeed, even in the sixteenth century money was much more impor-tant in the Scottish economy than is often assumed, meaning that counting was presumably common. When specie was in short supply, credit notes were widely used, notably in the expanding cattle-droving trade.[145] Paradoxically, it was tenant farmers in areas of Scotland where transport was most difficult who would have more involvement with marketing during our period, since landlords preferred money rents to the problems of moving bulk products over difficult terrain.[146] Thus even 'backward', relatively remote, parts of Scotland would be in-volved in the cash nexus. Estates in Scotland were generating substan-tial amounts of paperwork at this time, but towards the end of the seventeenth century the amount of surviving material becomes volu-minous. In response to the ethos and reality of commercialization, more rational accounting procedures were adopted.[147] The results can be seen in the bundles of estate vouchers and receipts which fill count-less boxes in the Scottish Record Office. The whole issue of the role of numeracy in economic and social change would repay more investigation.

In the towns, craftsmen and tradesmen were involved in the giving and taking of written receipts and promissory notes.[148] Indeed, the sorts of influence which would promote literacy were to be found in a more concentrated form in towns. Certain civic rights and rites were,

---

[143] G. E. Fussell, *The English dairy farmer* (1966): 270–83; NCRO 1DE/5/18, 19; 1DE/11/2; 1DE/12/37/25, 30, 31.
[144] Haldane (1952): 46–8.   [145] *Ibid.* 46–7; Sanderson (1982): 176.
[146] Dodgshon (1981): 300.   [147] G. Marshall, *Presbyteries and profits* (1980): 155–60, 237.
[148] Thousands of these survive in the records of various Commissary Courts among the 'Processes': SRO CC8/4/1–500 for example.

for example, predicated on literacy. Urban apprentices were bound to their master by a written contract, whereas for rural servants the agreement was usually verbal.[149] Advertising and discarded print used in wrappings gave opportunities for town-dwellers to read.[150] Adam Smith pointed out that even 'a little grocer ... must be able to read, write, and account, and must be a tolerable judge of ... goods, their prices, qualities, and the markets where they are to be had cheapest'.[151] The extent of urbanization was much less in Scotland than England before the later eighteenth century, though how we assess the level of commercial development and its impact on literacy is unclear. Desire for social mobility was one reason for moving into towns, since perceived opportunities may have been greater. Some authorities argue that literacy became increasingly an end in itself, though the secular benefits expected probably continued to be a powerful incentive.[152]

The association between literacy and social advancement was less directly recognizable in Scotland and England than in nineteenth-century France where François de Dainville attributes the high secondary school enrolment of towns like Troyes and Challon to 'the ambition of the inferior strata of the Third Estate to procure their children the Latin certificate which gave them access to minor public positions'.[153] During the eighteenth and nineteenth centuries the French state's augmented need for bureaucrats, coupled with relatively easy access to upward social mobility, made it worthwhile to become literate. Early nineteenth-century English studies do tend to suggest either that parents were unable to send their children to school long enough to reap the benefits of education, or that they recognized the other objective constraints on self-improvement in an unequal society. In Poland, peasants showed little interest in education, since in the seventeenth century 'the almost complete attachment of the peasant to the land, the increased villein exploitation and the general decline of cultural standards deprived even the educated peasants of any prospects of social advancement'.[154] A similar social ethos may explain the lesser enthusiasm of the Irish living in Scotland for education, a fact remarked upon in the Statistical Accounts of the 1790s. Their aspirations and the possibilities which they perceived for advancement through education were already structured by objective social conditions.

The presence of agricultural prosperity may itself have provided an incentive to education and literacy. In the upland pasture areas of the

---

[149] Kussmaul (1981): 4.   [150] Webb (1955): 23–5.   [151] Smith (1977): 215.
[152] Wormald (1981): 177.   [153] Quoted in Tilly (1973): 122.
[154] Schofield (1981): 210–12; Litak (1973): 60.

West Riding of Yorkshire, for example, there were many small proprietors benefiting from changes in the terms of trade in agriculture towards pastoral products. According to Bigland, 'there are few parts of
the Kingdom where this respectable class is more numerous', and
around Halifax the proportion of freeholders was especially high.[155]
This may go part of the way towards explaining the higher literacy of
Yorkshire yeomen compared to those from the four northern counties
which we noticed above in table 2.5. Men like these would be well placed
to provide an education for their sons. During the Civil War the autobiographer Adam Martindale moved to a parish near Wigan in Lancashire
to teach a school since there were there 'a great number of free-holders
and considerable yeomen'.[156] Over the last decades of the seventeenth
century the number of teachers in this area was on the increase.[157]

In the period *c.*1650–1740 these sorts of men would also be well placed
demographically to provide not only a better material standard of living
for their families but also an education for their children. With population growth rates at less than one-quarter of 1% a year and a high proportion of the population in the productive age groups, the balance
between population and resources was better than at any time since the
fifteenth century and the standard of living was improving. Daniel
Defoe remarked upon the rebuilding of peasant houses in the north-
west as a reflection of the prosperity of the region at this time.[158] More of
the middling sort would be able to dispense with female and child labour
in the north through increased prosperity amongst independent producers. William Stout's father had only a modest farm of twenty-four
acres in later seventeenth-century Lancashire, but was still able to
educate his children well. Higher wages for labourers might encourage
investment not only in consumer durables but also in education. The
spread of industrial employments in the north of England also helped to
raise real wages. At the same time, the greater involvement of women at
this time in craft and trade activities, which became largely male preserves in the later eighteenth and nineteenth centuries, may have promoted developments in their literacy.[159] Furthermore, with increased
mortality and the reductions in fertility associated with a later age at first
marriage for women there would be fewer surviving children, and thus
a more advantageous ratio of productive to non-productive members of
society.[160] More money would therefore be available for education. The

---

[155] Quoted in Hudson (1981): 41; J. Thirsk, 'Seventeenth-century agriculture' (1970).
[156] Parkinson (1845):34.   [157] Spufford (1981): 21–2.   [158] Quoted in Thirsk (1970): 175.
[159] K. D. M. Snell, 'Agricultural seasonal unemployment, the standard of living and
women's work' (1981).
[160] Wrigley and Schofield (1981): 403, 443–50, 638–44.

higher proportion of fathers dying childless would also, *ceteris paribus*, mean that more charitable bequests for education might be made in wills.

However, literacy was clearly improving before the charity school movement of the early eighteenth century could have had any effect, and thus it cannot have been the reason. Certainly, the main period of endowment of education in the north was during the late seventeenth and early eighteenth centuries, whereas elsewhere in England the most prominent improvement happened a century earlier.[161] The growing prosperity shown in the probate inventories of yeomen in the north-west at this time helps to explain the forty-four new schools opened in Cumberland between 1660 and 1800, along with a further twenty-eight in Westmorland.[162] In the south and east of England, improvements both in educational provision and literacy among the middling and upper economic groups in the period *c*.1570–*c*.1630 was associated with a polarization of wealth, and may also have been linked to a reduction in the number of niches in agriculture and a consequent increase in demand for education as a means of opening up new employment opportunities. In such an environment, reasons for the continued illiteracy of labourers and servants are not far to seek. In Scotland too, studies of the effectiveness of the parochial school network of the late eighteenth and early nineteenth centuries suggest that it functioned best in areas like north-east Scotland, where there were large numbers of fairly well-off farmers who could afford a decent education for their children.[163]

But there may be other reasons for the north of England's precocious literacy at all social levels. In periods of stable or falling population such as the late seventeenth century a higher proportion of the 15–24 age group would be in service.[164] Indeed, service may be crucial here, since in the north living-in servants were still common at the end of the eighteenth century, while the day labourer was coming to replace this form of agricultural worker in the south and east. The existence in the north and west of regular alternative rural and then urban manufacturing work would encourage farmers to try to perpetuate service, as did high real wages in the period *c*.1650–1740. At the same time, pastoral farmers of the kind so common in these parts of England, and indeed in much of Scotland, had greater need for continuous labour, and the mix of rural crafts, pasture, small farms and dispersed settlements also characteristic of these regions would make servants doubly necessary. As a result, a greater proportion of the population would be

---

[161] Spufford (1981): 21–2.   [162] Beckett (1981): 4.   [163] Anderson (1983): 9.
[164] This paragraph draws on Kussmaul (1981): 23, 100–1, 121, 126.

open to the sort of informal education available from master, mistress or colleagues. More young people from relatively humble backgrounds in their late teens and early twenties would have contact with those wealthy enough to employ them as servants and who were thus likely to be able to read and write. This would also help to counteract the deleterious influence on education of earlier entry by poorer children into the labour force, because of the reduced aggregate labour supply associated with lower fertility and higher mortality.

The spatial and temporal variations in the incidence of service may then provide a partial explanation of why the north of England tended to surge ahead of the south and east and to continue this lead until the onset of compulsory, free mass education in the late nineteenth century. Moreover, it seems plausible to suggest that the impact of rural domestic industry in Lancashire and Yorkshire followed by full-scale factory development, which not only kept children away from school and strained educational resources by creating unprecedented population concentrations, but also reduced the duration of service in families other than the one of origin, may have accounted for the comparatively low literacy of these counties. The combination of these developments would reduce both formal and informal means of education for the poorer classes, especially in the towns. Similarly, the decline of apprenticeship from the mid eighteenth century onwards would tend to produce stagnating craft and trade literacy. Service may nevertheless have reinforced the other causes of high literacy in the north of England. We cannot reproduce this analysis for Scotland because of our imperfect understanding of demographic and social structures and trends there before the nineteenth century. However, it is likely that service was a common and enduring, if not a uniform, feature of agriculture in Lowland Scotland.[165]

Before turning to the social, religious and ideological reasons for becoming literate we must point out that the overall level of economic development in Scotland and northern England was not very high and cannot therefore be used as an explanation of why literacy was higher in these regions than elsewhere in Britain. Agricultural improvement came late to the area. Towards the end of the seventeenth century Camden's *Britannia* described the eastern, upland parts of Cumbria as 'a lean, hungry, desolate sort of country'. A little later Defoe deemed Westmorland 'eminent only for being the wildest, most barren and frightful' of English or Welsh counties.[166]

---

[165] R. A. Houston, 'Geographical mobility in Scotland 1652–1811' (1985).
[166] Quoted in Beckett (1981): 1.

So far we have dealt largely with secular forces which would promote literacy. However, there were also less pragmatic, more ideological reasons for learning to read and write. Religion and specifically Protestantism has been used as a general explanation of literacy advances in a number of countries. This explanation can work at two levels. First, the wish of Protestant reformers to educate the population could produce campaigns to provide instruction. Second, personal desire for religious knowledge might encourage individuals to acquire literacy in the pursuit of salvation or comfort. Some historians have attributed a leading role to religion in accounting for advances in early modern literacy. For Kenneth Lockridge, Protestant religion and the schools it brought were much more important than cultural, environmental or economic influences in accounting for the remarkable increase in male literacy in eighteenth-century New England. The role of religion is reified as a 'Protestant spirit'.[167] For authorities such as Lockridge the influence of religion was the prime motive force in enhancing literacy throughout the early modern world.

In general terms, the mechanism which connects religion and literacy is a simple one. Mervyn James talks of literacy spreading down through society because of the Protestant concern that everyone should have access to the written Word of Scripture.[168] With its stress on the individual's direct relationship with God mediated through a reading of the Scriptures, Protestantism could have a powerful impact on education and literacy. As G. R. Elton remarks, the 'explosive and renovating and often disintegrating effect of the Bible, put into the hands of the commonalty' could be marked.[169] It is true that Protestant groups such as the Lollards were promoting access to scriptural reading which 'containeth all profitable truth' in England well before the Reformation and were roundly condemned along with others who 'do wickedly instruct and inform people'.[170] The joint influence of printing and the Reformation made this development even more important. Protestantism was a force which could mediate or even perhaps counteract the material circumstances already discussed. Its effects were clear to many observers. John Patterson, a Scottish Evangelist in early nineteenth-century Sweden, believed 'this may be affirmed of the inhabitants of all the northern Protestant Kingdoms; you seldom meet one above ten or twelve who cannot read, and the most of them write their own language'.[171]

Around Europe, studies do indeed suggest a connection between

---

[167] Lockridge (1981): 186–8.   [168] M. James, *Family, lineage, and civil society* (1974): 104.
[169] Quoted in Wormald (1981): 105.   [170] Quoted in Aston (1977): 351, 352.
[171] Quoted in Johansson (1981): 152.

Protestantism and literacy in the broadest sense. In Languedoc, for example, the Protestant areas were the educated ones.[172] The struggle for religious allegiance which followed the Reformation and Counter-Reformation in Europe is said to have exercised a powerful impact on literacy trends. After the Reformation, the competition between faiths seems to have been important in fostering educational provision throughout Europe. Protestant schools in the Netherlands tended to be better than the Catholic ones and, despite official opposition, some seventeenth-century Dutch Catholics were prepared to send their children to them.[173] Contact with Protestants is said to have enhanced the literacy of Catholic communities in Provence.[174] In the Protestant provinces of Utrecht a campaign to promote religious reading was conducted during the later sixteenth and seventeenth centuries, with parents 'obliged' to send their children to the schools which the provincial government strove (not always successfully) to provide.[175] There was, however, nothing exclusively Protestant about this intense desire for widespread literacy. Huguenot towns of sixteenth- and seventeenth-century France campaigned to increase the literacy of all females rather than just a gifted few, but so too did Catholic towns as part of a wider project to win over the masses to the Christianity of the Counter-Reformation. The superior literacy of some Protestant communities in pre-Revolution France cannot be seen exclusively in relation to religion: migration patterns and occupational structures have to be taken into account.[176]

Protestantism might appeal to those already literate. We know that in parts of France and Belgium, Protestant congregations were predominantly urban in nature and drew their members disproportionately from the higher social and economic strata of society.[177] Protestant and Catholic strove to educate people in order to turn them from collective Christians into committed, individual believers. We must be wary of simplistic connections between religion and literacy. In Scotland and England, Protestantism became the official religion after the Reformation and was jealously guarded. There was no question of face-to-face competition between Catholic and Protestant schools as was found in France, the Netherlands, Germany or Poland.

---

[172] Laget (1971): 1416.   [173] For example Litak (1973): 50, 57.
[174] Chartier (1976): 105–6.   [175] E. P. de Booy, *De weldaat der scholen* (1977).
[176] Davis (1975): 77–82; Chartier (1976): 106; P. Benedict, *Rouen during the wars of religion* (1980): 90–1.
[177] Benedict (1980): 90–1; R. Van Uytven, 'Invloeden van het sociale en professionele milieu' (1968); J. Van Roey, 'De correlatie tussen het sociale-beroepsmilieu en de godsdienstkeuze' (1968).

As well as their stress on reading, the Protestants were able to promote a number of measures to encourage people to learn. They assumed that education would lead to godliness via reading. The Calvinist church in Scotland was prepared to back up its general desideratum for literacy as a path to individual spiritual renewal by requiring specific attainments as a precondition of access to the privileges of the church. Catechism was to be the main foundation of religious knowledge for the young, the poor and the ill-educated who had neither the time, ability nor inclination to grapple with proper religious literature. This form of religious learning was simple and well suited to minds which stored up aphorisms and proverbs.[178] Catechisms were published in large numbers and provided a crucial grounding in religious education and a possible starting-point for further understanding. In 1607, North Leith Kirk Session regretted that 'thair is a grit number of the pure folk within their bounds that ar ignorant of the law of god & will not heir the samen notwithstanding the paines and traveill that ar bestowit upone and taine be the pastor'. Thus all those who could not recite the Ten Commandments were to be debarred from receiving further alms from the kirk: twelve women and five men are named.[179] The level of understanding required was very low: the ability to recite the Ten Commandments, the Creed and the Lord's Prayer. The stress was on rote learning of basic religious principles. Lasswade Kirk Session specified that no children of 'ignorant' parents should be baptized. The father was to be given one month to learn the Lord's Prayer and the Ten Commandments as well as attaining 'some competent understanding of the sacraments and catechisme'.[180] Those intending to marry must be 'indifferentlie weill instruct in the chief poynts of religioun'. The Kirk Session of Ferry Port on Craig in Fife insisted that unless couples could read, their wedding was not to be conducted by the minister.[181] Synods asked as a matter of course about the catechizing of their flocks which ministers were supposed to carry out.

All this must presumably have encouraged literacy. Examinations were conducted prior to the Lord's Supper or communion to ensure 'some competent understanding to discerne the same aright at least they sall have the belief, lords prayer, and ten commandments and some good competent understanding of the two sacrements'.[182] Via the testimonial system, certificates of good character issued by the minister and elders of a parish to those wishing to move or use the facilities of another parish church, the kirk could also prevent the

[178] Collinson (1982): 232–3.   [179] SRO CH2/621/1: 471.   [180] SRO CH2/471/1.
[181] Beale (1953): 229.   [182] SRO CH2/471/1: fol. 10.

ignorant from trying to move rather than learn.[183] These restrictions were general throughout Lowland Scotland, but the level of understanding required by the kirk was extremely simple. We should acknowledge that it must have been difficult for the clergy adequately to catechize the whole population of some of the larger parishes.

However, we must notice a similar exhortation to the parish clergy in England to catechize and to ensure that their flocks attained a modest level of religious knowledge. The 59th canon ordered that 'every parson, vicar or curate upon every Sunday and Holy Day, before evening prayer, shall for half an hour or more examine and instruct the youth and ignorant persons of his parish'.[184] Bishop Barnes of Durham ordered that his clergy

duly, paynefully, and frely teache the children of their severall parishes and cures to reade and write; and suche as they shall by good and due tryall finde to be apte to learne, and of pregnant capacitie, then they shall exhorte their parentes to set them to scholes and learnyngs of the good and liberall sciences.

The clergy were to conduct a yearly examination of parishioners' 'skill and knowlede of their dewtie to God and their neighbour, of the Articles of their faithe and the Comaundments of God, and their understanding of the Catechisme and affection in religion'. Bishop Barnes further ordered that a list of those who refused to send their children, apprentices or servants to be catechized and examined should be sent to the church authorities for possible disciplinary action. The injunctions of 1538 specified that English children should be able to recite the contents of the primer (prayers) and catechism before being admitted to communion. Nobody could marry, act as a godparent or present a child to be baptized unless they were up to standard.

The Scottish Calvinists were not unique in insisting on this form of learning, but we cannot be sure about the extent to which it was practised in different countries. In early nineteenth-century Sweden, according to one observer, 'in order to be confirmed, everyone should be able to prove that, besides reading from a book, he also possessed passable skills in writing and arithmetic'.[185] Like Scotland, one could not be married unless confirmed, but, distinctively, one could not give evidence in a Swedish court without this qualification. The Swedish system was certainly effective, but it would be unsafe to assume this was also the case in seventeenth- and eighteenth-century Scotland. We

---

[183] Houston (1985); SRO CH2/621/1:484.
[184] All drawn from Barnes (1850): 15–20.   [185] Quoted in Johansson (1981): 151.

should note, however, that the framework and the will for an educational campaign to match the Swedish drive existed in both Scotland
and England alike. Unlike seventeenth- and eighteenth-century
Sweden, there are no catechism registers to provide us with comparatively exact measures of quantity if not quality of understanding.

Protestantism promoted action to educate people on the part of
secular and ecclesiastical authorities in the sixteenth and seventeenth
centuries. For the individual, too, literacy could be crucial to full and
active involvement in religion. The famous Puritan divine Richard
Baxter tells us that his father became religiously committed 'by the bare
reading of the Scripture in private, without either Preaching or godly
Company, or any other Books but the Bible'.[186] Unfortunately, we
cannot be certain of the relative extent of personal commitment to
active participation in religion in Scotland and England. Observers
such as Defoe, Pennant and Sinclair believed the Scots were better
Christians than the English, but whether they meant more personally
devout or that a larger percentage of the population attended church as
a social convention we cannot say.[187] Certainly, some historians speak
of a deep personal and societal commitment to Protestantism in
eighteenth-century Scotland.[188] Active participation may have been
fostered by, or been the cause of, higher literacy. We can see the impact
of dissent on literacy in the case of Christopher Bramley, a Yorkshire
Quaker who in 1655 had interrupted a service being given by Josiah
Hunter, minister of Ouseburn, by demanding 'where was the word,
the word was not then written or put in writing'.[189] The written statement he produced after being ejected from the church survives and can
be seen as part of the competing religious propaganda circulating in
sixteenth- and seventeenth-century England. Quakers produced tracts
and Baptists circulated their members by letter for example.[190] There
are then two possibly separate influences – the force of a strongly
evangelistic church which seeks to educate everyone irrespective of
the depth of their conviction, and the arguably stronger influence of
individuals who internalized religious ideals and sought to further
their own education. How exactly these factors interrelate is not clear.

Armed with firm figures on literacy, however, we now have the
chance to compare Scotland with other regions or countries where the
influence of Protestantism was felt. It is only by making such
systematic comparisons of different areas that we can assess properly
the impact of religion. There are two parts of the early modern world

---

[186] Quoted in Collinson (1982): 250.   [187] Pennant (1774): 88, 219.
[188] R. H. Campbell, 'The influence of religion on economic growth in Scotland' (1983).
[189] PRO ASSI45: 5/2/20, 21.   [190] Spufford (1981): xvii.

where we know that the catalyst of Protestantism brought on literacy in a remarkable way. These are colonial New England and Sweden. Scotland is said to be the third. Thus Kenneth Lockridge has argued that in New England, Scotland and Sweden 'a strong, widespread, and homogeneous Protestantism carried the society into public action to ensure basic education, and thereby carried men into universal literacy'.[191] By 1760 Protestantism was able to 'eliminate most regional, occupational, and class differences in literacy, no small event in a world otherwise marked by a series of reinforcing hierarchical distinctions'.[192] The 'forces which were sending men to school and so making them literate were independent not only of positive shifts in the distribution of wealth and occupation, but of all forces represented by wealth or occupation'.[193] The same was not true of women. The key to Lockridge's argument is that in a backward and rural region, the dynamic impact of Protestantism was able to produce a society in which literacy was the norm by the later eighteenth century and in which the social hierarchy of literacy so common in the Old World had all but disappeared. Can we say that the same was true of Scotland in the second half of the eighteenth century?

We should be rash to do so. In New England, differences between the literacy of social classes had been almost eradicated by the end of the eighteenth century. The New England school system, fostered by Protestantism which Lockridge credits with this success, cannot have been equalled in Scotland, since we have seen that significant differences in literacy persisted between urban- and rural-dwellers and between social groups. Differentials which can be related to secular forces remained. In the first place, it is clear that there was no narrowing of the gap between urban and rural literacy in Scotland over the eighteenth century, as happened in New England. Here we must compare distinct occupational groups, rather than simply aggregate figures of the type used by Lockridge, so that we can control for the changing occupational composition of urban and rural populations. Second, in the 1750s and 1760s the gap in illiteracy between Scottish craftsmen and tradesmen and servants is some 40–50% (table 2.4), whereas in colonial New England it is nearer 10–15%.[194] The figures are not directly comparable, since Lockridge's sample compares a group comprising merchants, professionals, gentry and artisans, with one made up of labourers, whereas with our data we can only contrast craftsmen and tradesmen with servants in ten-year time periods because of the small number of labourers and other occupations in the

[191] Lockridge (1974): 100. [192] Lockridge (1981): 187. [193] Lockridge (1974): 60.
[194] *Ibid*. 24–5.

Scottish sample. However, the likely contrast between Lockridge's higher status grouping which included the wholly literate gentry and that of labourers – the least literate of all male occupational groups – in the case of Scotland is likely to be even greater than 50%: the difference which we saw between the literacy of middling and lower classes in mid eighteenth-century Scotland. The comparison made here then under-estimates the gap in occupationally specific signing ability in Scotland and New England, and thus highlights the clear contrasts between the societies.

In any case, the late eighteenth-century literacy profile for Scotland is quite different from that obtaining in contemporary New England and is in fact closer to the other North American colonies, where Lockridge sees Protestantism as much less strong, or to New England in the late seventeenth century before the vigorous Protestantism could work its magic.[195] Literacy in areas of colonial America outside New England during the eighteenth century 'failed to rise towards universality because these lacked intense Protestantism and consequent school laws'.[196] Lockridge claims that the rise to universal literacy in New England was mainly accounted for by increasing rural literacy.[197] Here we should begin to question Lockridge's classifications and the biases in his sources. It is, for example, uncertain what he means by 'rural literacy', since he points to the role of population concentration in towns of more than 1,000 people in accounting for the eighteenth century fall in male illiteracy.[198] Presumably he is treating Boston as the only signifi-cantly 'urban' environment, and literacy there stagnated while smaller towns caught up. Cressy too treats the rest of England outside London as 'rural'.[199] At the same time, it is likely that Lockridge's sample of testators is more biased than he allows. Dan Scott Smith has shown that 67% of the wealthiest 40% of colonial American society left wills, but only 8% of the poorest 20% did so.[200] Given the increase in poverty in colonial New England during the eighteenth century, a larger number of poor would not be making wills, and therefore any continuing associ-ation between wealth and literacy would be concealed. Further, those who made wills may themselves have been drawn from the more literate members of particular occupational groups. Lockridge's assumption that these biases are balanced out by the deleterious impact of age and illness on signing ability is not proven. Finally, we must consider the fact that male migrants to New England were already twice as literate as their mid seventeenth-century counterparts in England. This could produce

[195] Lockridge (1981): 184, 195–8.   [196] Lockridge (1974): 83.   [197] *Ibid*. 21.
[198] *Ibid*. 62–3.   [199] *Ibid*. 65.   [200] Graff (1975): 472.

special conditions for further literacy improvements.[201] The picture of literacy in colonial North America is a complex one. Nevertheless, we can be certain that the profile of illiteracy in this Protestant part of the world was quite different from that obtaining in Scotland during the third quarter of the eighteenth century. If Protestantism was working its magic in Scotland it was working it in different ways.

We can also contrast Scotland's literacy profile with that of Sweden. In that country, widespread reading skills were attained almost wholly through home education. Egil Johansson has shown that where economic needs are the prime driving force class differences, along with the sex-specific ones observable even in New England, would persist. This is not true of reading ability in Sweden by the late eighteenth century. The Skanor catechism register of 1702 shows 67% male reading ability, but only 49% female; by 1740 this had evened out at 91% male and 93% female.[202] In terms of the ability to read and to recite the catechism, the structural divergences between the sexes and between social classes had disappeared by the later eighteenth century. On the other hand, significant improvements in sign-literacy did not occur until the establishment of a school system in the nineteenth century. However, it is certainly true of Scotland as far as ability to sign one's name is concerned. The distribution of signing ability was much more extremely polarized in eighteenth-century Sweden than it was in Scotland, again suggesting that the social context of literacy was quite different in the two countries. Scotland had many more schools per head of population than Sweden and the cultural emphasis was on reading and writing. This is why the profiles of literacy were so different in the two countries in the later eighteenth century.

These are all aggregates taken at a national or regional level from a religiously homogeneous population. There are no Scottish or English figures which might allow us to compare literacy among different occupations for Protestants and Catholics. There are no figures similar to those for Amsterdam in 1780, which show that Calvinist men were 13% illiterate, Lutherans 14%, Catholics 21%, thus suggesting that Protestantism did encourage literacy. For females, levels were 31%, 35% and 47% respectively.[203] However these are aggregate figures which do not allow for the possibility that certain high or low literacy occupations may have been over-represented among adherents of a particular faith. We must assess the importance of other factors. Indeed, Dutch material for the early nineteenth century provides a warning against assuming that Protestantism is an important force for

---

[201] Lockridge (1974): 45–6.   [202] Johansson (1981): 175–6.
[203] A. M. van der Woude, 'De alfabetisering' (1980): 262.

enhancing literacy among all social groups. In rural Utrecht between 1811 and 1820, male Catholics were as literate as Protestants among farmers and craftsmen and tradesmen, but Protestant labourers were rather more literate than Catholic. In any case, differences in literacy which can be attributed to social class were much more marked than were those associated with religion. Male craftsmen and tradesmen who were adherents of Protestantism were around 15% illiterate in this decade, while labourers of the same religious persuasion were 50% illiterate.[204] The role of religion was much less significant than identifiable secular factors – a possibility we strongly suspect also applies in Scotland. Except by assuming that Highland was synonymous with Catholic we cannot replicate these analyses for Scotland. However, it looks as though northern Britain resembles the Netherlands much more in its literacy structures than it does Sweden or New England.

Protestantism may still be important in Scotland, since religious and political unrest from the late seventeenth century onwards tended to break down the homogeneous Calvinist system and may thus have had a damaging effect on earlier achievements.[205] Religious life in eighteenth-century Scotland became as diverse as in England, France, the Netherlands or Germany, whereas in Sweden, Denmark, Norway, Finland and New England civil and religious authorities continued to be in relative harmony. Sweden in particular was a disciplined rural society with a rather small population, relatively untroubled by divergent religious opinion. In New England the control of the Puritans was firm. Despite this, the levels of literacy in seventeenth-century Scotland do not suggest conspicuous success at an early date when the Calvinist church was becoming strong throughout the Lowlands. Perhaps the time during which it could make its influence felt was shorter than has been assumed. There were even areas such as the north-east Lowlands where episcopacy remained strong into the mid eighteenth century, and where Presbyterian exhortations were little heeded.[206] These too shared in the Lowland literacy attainments.

There may be other qualifying factors. Demand for Protestant literature and preachers was evident in Angus and Fife during the 1540s. A handful of Protestants were active in Edinburgh from at least the 1530s. The Reformation built on existing Protestant sympathies to some extent at least, though there are doubts about the volume of popular support before the Reformation.[207] The strength of commitment of the

---

[204] *Ibid*. 263.   [205] Beale (1953): 171.   [206] Buchan (1972): 191.
[207] M. L. Bush, *Protector Somerset* (1975): 21; Lynch (1979): 82–3; Cowan (1978): 5–8.

Scottish population to Calvinism may have been exaggerated. Certainly, the ubiquity of church attendance in late seventeenth- and eighteenth-century Scotland has been questioned.[208] What we do about the north of England with its comparatively lukewarm Protestantism and supposed economic backwardness compared to the south and east is hard to say. Puritan concern for education remained strong into the late seventeenth century, but northern England was certainly not a notable Puritan area in the mould of counties like Essex. In fact during the early seventeenth century it was one of the parts of the realm where the Catholic faith was strongest.[209]

At a societal level we can see why Protestantism should have enhanced literacy, and can point to Sweden and New England as examples of how it did so in practice. Perhaps it did something for Scottish literacy, but precisely what is not clear and the extent of any success was palpably less than in some other countries. In Highland parts of Scotland, as in the less ecologically favoured parts of Languedoc, even Protestantism could not overcome the cultural, linguistic, geographical and economic hindrances to the spread of literacy.[210] Perhaps Lockridge is right to argue that Protestantism is what raised the levels of literacy in parts of the early modern world not favoured by other influences such as economic pull factors. Protestantism may have helped the less advantaged classes in some way. As an explanation of regional differences in literacy it is less satisfactory. Contrary to his assertions, Lockridge's catch-all explanation of Protestantism is not adequate to account for high literacy in the north of England.[211] In northern and eastern France too, literacy levels were up with the best in Europe by 1800. Here, Catholic religious orders ran schools which were important in elementary education – especially the convent schools in the towns – a strategy obviously not available to the Protestants.[212] Protestantism is simply not good enough as a general explanation. It is possible, if arguable, that Protestantism was the key to high levels of literacy for the men of eighteenth-century New England, but in the Old World the impact of religion was much attenuated by social and economic factors.

Exactly how we distinguish between the impact of differing push-and-pull factors is a continuing problem. We can see why economic and institutional developments should have promoted literacy, but we must also acknowledge that the interactions are complex and defy any

---

[208] R. D. Brackenridge, 'The enforcement of Sunday observance' (1969).
[209] C. Haigh, 'The continuity of Catholicism' (1981).   [210] Chartier (1976): 26.
[211] Lockridge (1981): 193.   [212] Houdaille (1977): 71; Chartier (1976): 245–6.

simple association. The slightly lower literacy attainments of northern England compared to the Lowlands of Scotland do indeed go along with a less strong Protestantism and with verbal as opposed to written legal procedures, but against this we must place greater market development at an earlier date and higher per capita wealth, along with a greater proportion of the population in literacy requiring occupations. We can juggle these factors around any way we like but no definite answer is likely to emerge. There is however a final and intriguing possibility.

One key element of the cultural distinctiveness of northern Britain seems to have been the strong mass desire for education evident in the eighteenth and nineteenth centuries. Basic education seems to have been a matter of pride. A day labourer's daughter who attended the religious revival meetings at Cambuslang in Ayrshire admitted that she 'kept sometimes at home because I could not read and I was much ashamed that I could not make use of a Bible in the kirk as others about me did'.[213] George Robertson similarly thought that ordinary people in the Lothians 'have always . . . been laudably ambitious of giving their children a decent education, and would be ashamed if they could not at least read the English language'.[214] Sir John Sinclair meanwhile concluded after studying many late eighteenth-century reports from ministers of religion that 'to the credit of the great body of people . . . not only tradesmen, but even day labourers are anxious, that their children should receive the advantages of education'.[215] He had before him comments such as the one from Old Luce parish in south-west Scotland that 'the poor classes consider it a disgrace, not to have their children taught to read and write', or from Galston in Ayrshire where they were said to take the 'greatest pride' in literacy.[216] At Yetholm it was said that 'parents will submit to considerable privations, rather than not send their children to school'. Concern seems to have been with mastery of basic literacy rather than the sorts of advanced curricula increasingly on offer. At Calder in Nairn 'the parents in general wish their children to read, write and get some knowledge of arithmetic, but show little desire for the learned languages'.[217]

The masses were less interested in the educational developments so stressed by historians of the eighteenth century and more concerned with the practical learning of reading, writing and arithmetic. There was also apparently a cultural dimension to these aspirations. Ministers of west coast parishes like Dailly, Girvan, St Quivox, Maybole and Kirkintilloch believed that native Scots were much keener to educate their

[213] Smout (1982): 127.   [214] Robertson (1793): 27.   [215] Sinclair (1826): 89.
[216] *Ibid.* appx. 20–1.   [217] Quoted in Scotland (1969): 57.

children than were the Irish or for that matter the English working class.[218] A similar argument can be made for Prussian Catholics who in the late nineteenth century owed their illiteracy less to religion than to the fact that many were Poles who neither linguistically nor culturally belonged to the German group.[219] Irish, like Polish, peasants placed less stress on education, possibly because of their greater attachment to the land and the apparently more limited prospects of social advancement.[220] 'The common people of England and Ireland, left to demand education for themselves, never demanded it; nor would they if left the impulse of their own device, ever have emerged from the deep, stationary and unalleviated ignorance of the middle ages.'[221] David Cressy indeed sees no social stigma attached to illiteracy in early modern England.

We must however be careful of the apparent contrast with England, since the high demand for education among the lower classes of the north was often remarked upon in the eighteenth and nineteenth centuries.[222] Cressy's comments may apply to the whole of England, and indeed Lowland Scotland, in the seventeenth century, for, as in France, a sense of shame at illiteracy may not have developed until the eighteenth century or later.[223] Perhaps the emergence of a cultural premium on literacy at the end of the seventeenth century is what caused the north of England and Lowland Scotland to surge ahead of southern parts of Britain. Writing of both sides of the Border in the early nineteenth century, Gilly believed that 'the northern peasantry set a great value on education'.[224] There was considerable working-class demand for education alongside the self-education of politically conscious workers helped by the well-known Mechanics' Institutes.[225] Particularly in the north of England there was, by the early nineteenth century, a strong and well-established tradition of weekday education, though Sunday school enrolment was low.[226]

Alternatively, a pre-existing emphasis on the social need for literacy may have been advanced by institutional and economic changes. The desire may date from as early as the fifteenth century, since the 'educational revolution' of the seventeenth century in the north of England built on a long tradition of secular education.[227] Despite the alleged backwardness of the north, school provision was better than is often

---

[218] Sinclair (1826): appx. 20, 22.
[219] C. M. Cipolla, *Literacy and development in the west* (1969): 73.
[220] Litak (1973): 60.   [221] Sinclair (1826): 73–4.   [222] Laqueur (1976c): 159.
[223] Furet and Ozouf (1982): 126–7.   [224] Gilly (1842): 32.
[225] Laqueur (1976c); Silver (1975): 12.   [226] Laqueur (1976c): 50–1, 61.
[227] Jewell (1982): 20–2.

assumed, and in most respects was up to the national average. In Scotland, the seventeenth-century superiority of some social groups cannot have been wholly based on educational provision, and may be attributable to an existing desire for literacy which has only a marginal connection with institutions. It is after all easy enough to provide schools and their provision may augment interest in education. But the demand for schooling needs to exist before they can have any effect in a society without compulsory education.

To look at this another way, the famous Scottish Act of 1496 which required Scottish landowners to send their sons to grammar schools may well have emerged from a general cultural trend towards literacy rather than being an independent force promoting it. Conceivably, we could say the same of the seventeenth-century school laws in Scotland and the Educational Revolution in sixteenth- and seventeenth-century England. One is left wondering whether for some social groups literacy was at least partly a non-functional attribute associated with social prestige rather than a direct reflection of broader needs for reading and writing. Perhaps 'literacy owed less to institutions than to the cultural basis of everyday life'.[228]

Of course, it is extremely difficult to pin this attitude down. Did it exist equally in all parts of northern England and Lowland Scotland, and was it similarly strong over time? Was the desire for learning any greater than in parts of sixteenth-century Germany, where the drive by the Lutheran church for literacy was greatly helped by a strong interest at the grass roots in reading and writing? – an interest only partly related to popular religious needs.[229] It is impossible to tell and certainly to quantify. Bernhard Vogler points out that some Rhineland communities showed a keen interest in education while others were either indifferent or actively hostile to it. The same difference in attitude can be found in parts of eighteenth-century Aquitaine.[230] The sort of attitude adopted by different communities may have been conditioned by local economic opportunities, the need for child labour, relations between secular and ecclesiastical officials or between different elements of the community and those officials. This schema may help us to understand the very considerable local as well as regional variations in literacy and attitudes towards education in early modern Britain.

We will have some further remarks on this subject in the concluding chapter. However, it is already clear that international comparisons

[228] Laqueur (1976a): 257.
[229] Strauss (1978): 194–201, 281; Laget (1971): 1399; Chartier (1976): 34–5.
[230] Vogler (1976): 343–6; Butel (1976): 10, 19–22, 26.

can provide a way of testing explanations which seem watertight when seen in one historical or geographical context. They can also make us more sceptical about the adequacy of general explanations of local phenomena. Meanwhile, let us turn to the significance of traditional oral culture and of the spread of reading and writing for the people of early modern Britain. There were, as we have seen, certain tangible reasons why early modern people might become literate. Nevertheless, these reasons were not overwhelming by any means. The main theme of the following chapters is that, although in a very general sense education and literacy fulfilled the needs of society, we must recognize the existence of possibly divergent requirements among different elements of society. What exactly were the broader uses of literacy, and what was its importance to individual and society?

5

Measures of literacy

So far, we have measured literacy by the number of people who could sign their name to a document. Most historians accept this criterion, but there is still a vigorous debate about what exactly it tells us about reading and writing as a whole. Authorities are also divided about the way in which we should understand the concept of literacy. Yves Castan argues for eighteenth-century Languedoc that sign-literacy does not mean anything apart from a desire for social prestige or a simple business requirement, and should not be used as an indicator of the presence or absence of cultural possibilities.[1] The Swedish historian Egil Johansson, meanwhile, believes that the notion of 'universal literacy' should mean that most of the population can read and compose, but not write, their own language. For eighteenth-century England, Victor Neuburg suggests 'the ability to read a book or single sheet printed in English'.[2] Indeed definitions which attempt to find meaningful indicators of literacy are almost as numerous as there are studies of the subject.

However, in order to compare Scotland with other parts of Europe we need a reliable criterion of literacy, a standard and direct measure which is available in all countries over the seventeenth and eighteenth centuries. To a limited extent we shall consider the difficult problem 'What is literacy?' However, the significance of reading and writing is dealt with more fully in chapter 6 and chapter 7, which cover the uses of literacy and education for the individual and society. For the present, our prime concern is to discuss both the reliability of signing as an indicator of literacy and some of the other ways of measuring the broad spectrum of skills we term 'literacy'. Most of the alternative measures give an indirect guide to reading and writing. Just how

[1] Y. Castan, *Honnêteté et relations sociales en Languedoc* (1974): 116–18.
[2] Neuburg (1971): 93.

useful they are and whether they tell us anything significantly different about the outline of literacy in northern Britain from the one which we have already given are the key issues to which we must now turn.

There are several criteria which fulfil one or two of our requirements, but only the ability to sign a document seems to fill all three. The early modern period was essentially a 'non-statistical age', and historians must indulge in much time-consuming labour in order to reconstruct the characteristic patterns of contemporary life. It is rare to find information of exactly the kind we should like. From the late eighteenth century, surveys of reading, writing and counting ability began to be conducted throughout England, Wales and Scotland for a variety of worthy causes. Before this time, information is a good deal harder to come by. Instead historians have resorted to inferring literacy from more oblique indicators. The production and ownership of books is often used as an indirect measure of reading ability, but as we shall see later the connection between readership, production and ownership is by no means as obvious as some historians have assumed. Even information on who borrowed books from libraries is fraught with interpretative difficulties. Other inferential measures are equally problematic, particularly the existence or non-existence of schooling. For example, Spufford argues for the seventeenth century that the appearance of large amounts of popular literature was related to a rise in the availability of popular education and literacy and was associated with an increase in schooling.[3] But which is cause and which effect? How exactly do education, literature and literacy fit together?

We have explored the relationship between education and literacy in an earlier chapter which assessed the validity of certain explanations of literacy. Let us for the moment turn to the production, ownership and borrowing of books, which are the most commonly used indirect indicators of literacy. These are known to be imperfect surrogate measures.[4] We can assume that increased book production – new titles, more editions, longer print runs – is associated somehow with a growing readership, but what exactly that relationship is remains uncertain. Even those who use the production of books as an indirect indicator of literacy acknowledge the problems involved.[5] Their argument assumes that widespread chapbook publishing must have been directed towards the lower classes and, indeed, hundreds of thousands of these pamphlets were published in the later seventeenth century. There is no direct evidence of a humble readership, but the volume of publication, the profits being made by ballad and chapbook

---

[3] Spufford (1981): 9.   [4] P. Clark, 'The ownership of books in England' (1976).
[5] Neuburg (1971): 94–8.

publishers, the well-developed distribution network of chapmen all suggest a market for cheap print.[6] Analysis of publishing and the book trade does not yield a statistical analysis of readers and non-readers, but it may point to the existence of a large and growing reading public in Scottish and English society.

At the simplest level the connections are quite plausible. Yet we are not at all sure of the actual patterns of book distribution. The relationship between literacy and demand may be mediated through wealth and marketing mechanisms, meaning that estimates, such as Spufford's that one family in three could be buying a new almanac every year in the late seventeenth century, are almost meaningless.[7] Rather than indicating growing demand on the part of an enlarged readership, increasing numbers of texts and greater profits can also be explained by technological innovations in printing, by enhanced efficiency of distribution and in relation to other intervening variables.[8]

We can point to periods when the volume of publication increased – the later seventeenth and later eighteenth centuries for example – but we cannot prove that readership amongst all social groups expanded proportionately, or if, as in nineteenth-century France, the expansion of popular literature was mainly confined to an urban public.[9] More books sold may simply mean that more were being bought by the same people as had already purchased them previously. It is not certain whether readership amongst all social groups expanded proportionately with increasing production. Finally, an example from early eighteenth-century Spain illustrates the problems of inferring literacy from book production figures. The native publishing trade in Spain stagnated at this time but not because of any declining readership. Rather, the large-scale importation of type, paper and books from elsewhere in Europe undercut domestic producers.[10]

The point is that we cannot assume a simple and direct connection between book production and book reading or ownership. Evidence of book production is highly suggestive of a widespread reading public in seventeenth- and eighteenth-century England, but it tells us nothing certain about the size or social distribution of that readership. The same is true of Scotland. By the end of the eighteenth century, Scotland was an active area in chapbook publication, Newcastle printers pirating Scottish works. In 1668 there were printers, booksellers and binders in only six centres, but by 1775 there were seventy-five places which had representatives of the book trade. The Scottish press was

[6] Spufford (1981): 45, 83–91, 120–1, 126.   [7] *Ibid*. 2.   [8] Graff (1975): 469.
[9] T. Judt, 'The impact of the schools' (1981): 266–7.
[10] D. M. Thomas, 'Printing privileges in Spain' (1979): 106.

comparatively isolated and unambitious, but the number of printers, booksellers and stationers was increasing over time, notably in Edinburgh, Glasgow and Aberdeen.[11]

Indeed, when we turn to Scotland we are faced with a wide gulf between an allegedly large reading public and a very limited range of titles, which we assume must have been filled by the Bible or cheap ephemera. Mass readership is said to have been considerable, but the 'Scottish reading public was not sufficiently large for the support of professional authors'.[12] What sort of material were the Scots reading in the seventeenth and eighteenth centuries? The number of titles published in Scotland itself was comparatively small though increasing steadily, and featured much less diversionary popular literature than in England before 1700. Proportionally more of the 4,000 titles listed by Aldis in his catalogue of books printed in Scotland were religious tracts, books on government and religious administration, treatises on politics, practical guides and almanacs.[13] These were the sort of books being published. The nature of the volumes which were owned or borrowed is discussed below.[14]

So much for the production of books. What can we say about their ownership? Apart from incidental references in heresy trials, for example, to the books people owned or read, the best way to examine bookownership systematically is to analyse probate records. Wills and inventories give us an indication of the moveable goods which were transferred after death. Books are sometimes mentioned in these documents, though there is much debate about how comprehensive their coverage actually is. Did they cover all of a deceased person's possessions? Further, inventories often lack detail on a man or woman's exact possessions, which may be referred to only in some catch-all phrase such as 'household contents'. These problems are particularly acute with Scottish inventories. In most cases, inventories concentrate on agricultural items such as grain and livestock, providing little detail on other possessions which tend to end up lumped together as 'household plenishing'. When Thomas Baikie, minister of Rousay and Egilsay in Orkney, died in 1665 his inventory mentioned simply 'a kist of books' worth £30.[15] We know that individuals possessed books but we cannot always identify what they were.

Even when the overall quality of inventories in specifying household

---

[11] Webb (1955): 30; R. H. Carnie, 'Scottish printers and booksellers' (1965): 213; H. G. Aldis, *A list of books printed in Scotland before 1700* (1904): 105–6.

[12] Clive (1970): 227.   [13] Aldis (1904): 1–103; Larner (1981): 31; Mitchison (1978): 34.

[14] See below for comparisons between readership and ownership in different parts of Europe.

[15] See appendix 2.

contents in detail improves in the eighteenth century there are still considerable variations in inclusiveness over time and space. This is especially true of Scotland, since enjoyment of the deceased person's moveable estate was possible on the presentation of any inventory, however defective. Being able to show a right to one item of the deceased person's property gave access to it all. Friends and neighbours who compiled the inventory may not have bothered to list small items. Legacies in wills sometimes mention books not found in the inventory, suggesting under-recording through negligence or the prior disposal of close possessions as tokens of affection to family or friends. This was true of England as well as Scotland. To take one example: Robert Swift was an attorney at Lincoln's Inn whose will was proved at Durham Consistory Court in 1600. He possessed a large library of religious and legal works, some of which he gave away 'as tokens of remembrance' to various people, including a bequest 'to my most deare and entirely beloved father, my ringe ... my note-book of divinitie in folio and a little Englishe Bible'.[16] It was not worth the effort of the Scottish Commissary Court officials to check in any detail for such items, especially in the case of poor people from whom little revenue could be expected in the form of the 'quot': a 5% tax on proving wills.

The limited number of books we find in inventories contrasts with contemporary comments on readership. Moral reformers like Gilly wished to believe of the agricultural workers of Northumberland that 'few of our hinds are without a family Bible with notes, and with it we remark one or two smaller Bibles'. They also hoped that 'loose productions – the vulgar ballad and the ribbald jest' were not to the taste of farm labourers.[17] George Robertson in his *Rural recollections* of the Lothians in the second half of the eighteenth century preferred to think that tenant farmers had religious and historical works such as Knox, Wodrow, Bunyan and Abercrombie, hand in hand with a thorough knowledge of the Bible. The more lowly cottars meanwhile were also well acquainted with the Bible and had books with similar themes to those of their masters, though there were fewer of them and they were mainly cheap pamphlets purchased from chapmen rather than full-sized books. He also believed that chapbooks were found in cottage 'furniture'.[18]

Chapbooks would almost certainly escape mention, but there are still very few books in the wills and inventories analysed here. This is at variance with literary evidence and, as we have noted, with information on the production and distribution of books. There were pedlars

[16] *Wills and inventories*, pt III (1906): 175.   [17] Gilly (1842): 25, 27.
[18] G. Robertson, *Rural recollections* (1829): 98–9.

purveying popular literature in the northern counties in the 1690s, and Newcastle was emerging around this time as the most important publishing and distribution centre outside London.[19] Good trade was reported for 'blasphemous and immoral publications' in the north-east of England in the early nineteenth century, but they are absent from inventories.[20] In Lowland Scotland it was said that 'even ploughboys and maidservants would gladly part with the wages they earned . . . if they might but procure the work of Burns'.[21] One minister at the General Assembly of the Church of Scotland in 1644 complained that the 'schools and country were stained, yea pestered, with idle books, and their children fed on fables, love-songs, baudry ballads, heathen husks, youth's poison'.[22] Given the volume of book production and contemporary comments on the possession of reading material, it is very hard not to conclude that probate records do not by any means give a comprehensive indication of bookownership.

Nevertheless, wills and inventories can provide us with useful and interesting information. We can examine the social and geographical distribution of bookownership, we can discover something of reading tastes and we can assess the extent of any connection between signing ability and the presence of books among the possessions of the dead. As part of a preliminary assessment of the documentation available for a comparative study of local communities in Scotland and northern England, a sample of wills and inventories was selected for two mining parishes – Earsdon near Newcastle and Lasswade near Edinburgh.[23] For the parish of Earsdon in Northumberland between 1568 and 1760, forty-nine inventories were discovered. Of these only three mention books. Oliver Ogle, gentleman of Burradon township, had a chest with 'many books of divers sorts' worth thirty shillings, while Michael Mitford, Esquire, of Sighill and a Justice of the Peace, had two Bibles, a service book and one 'statute book'. Cuthbert Bates, a Halliwell gentleman, had twenty books in his 'closet'. Books tended to be passed around a lot and they are thus unlikely to be included in one person's inventory. Only works of a reference nature were retained by an individual.

The impression we are left with from this far-from-perfect material is that bookownership was mainly an elite phenomenon in north-east England at this time. This was not apparently true of late

---

[19] Neuburg (1971): 79.   [20] R. Colls, 'Coal, class and education' (1976): 92.
[21] Craig (1961): 113.   [22] *Ibid*. 201.
[23] SRO CC8/8/1–131; DPDD Durham probate records, wills and inventories.

sixteenth- and early seventeenth-century Kentish townsfolk, among
whom attributed ownership stretched as far down the social ladder as
labourers.[24] Margaret Spufford posits the existence of a readership
from merchants down to apprentices in towns, from prosperous
yeomen to servants in the rural areas.[25] Bookownership in the north of
England also seems to have been more restricted than in the Midlands.
Between 1625 and 1649 roughly one inventory in twelve relating to a
sample of parishes in the forest of Arden near Birmingham contains
reading material.[26] However, this impression may be partly attributable to the small sample size for Earsdon, since a larger sample taken
from the region as a whole shows a much higher percentage of
bookowners. Of 260 inventories taken at random from a single year in
each decade among Durham diocese probate records for the years 1675
to 1725, 11% or twenty-nine had books mentioned in them. The
comparable percentage in an identical sample taken from the diocese
of Carlisle was eighteen.[27]

Despite the problems of inclusiveness and interpretation it does
appear that literacy and bookownership went together rather closely.
One study of Worcestershire probate inventories between 1699 and
1716 shows the patterns (table 5.1).[28] Bookownership and literacy fit
together neatly for all social classes except women. The gentry have
easily the largest proportion of inventories with books. Craftsmen and
tradesmen are superior to yeomen farmers, but are still a long way
behind the gentry. Husbandmen's and labourers' inventories only
contain books on rare occasions. In the case of women, books handed
down as heirlooms or bequeathed by a dead spouse may explain the
unexpectedly high proportions whose inventories mention books
when compared with their illiteracy. However, it is also possible that
more women then men could read and that the association between
reading and writing was different for women.

For Lasswade in Midlothian there are nearly double the numbers of
wills and inventories (ninety-five), but only six mention books, all from
the period 1660–1760 – a time as we have noticed of greatly expanded
publication in both Scotland and northern England. They list the goods
or legacies of two ministers, two widows of prominent landowners, an
indweller in Lasswade town and a merchant there. Of these, Jean
Douglas, widow of Mr Simon Ramsay of Whythill, had a particularly

[24] Clark (1976).   [25] Spufford (1981): 72.

[26] V. Skipp, *Crisis and development* (1978): 83.

[27] Based on information supplied by Dr L. Weatherill of the University of St Andrews
from her ESRC project on English probate records.

[28] J. A. Johnston, 'Worcestershire probate inventories, 1699–1716' (1978): 207.

Table 5.1. *Illiteracy and the ownership of books in Worcestershire, 1699–1716*

	% illiterate	% bookowners
Gentry	10	38
Craftsmen and Tradesmen	39	19
Yeomen	49	10
Husbandmen	76	6
Labourers	75	4
Widows	78	15
Spinsters	60	12

detailed inventory including two Bibles and a Psalm book. More usually, the number and type of books is not stated. Mr Archibald Newton, minister at Liberton, left in his legacy any four books to his fellow minister Robert Douglas and the rest equally among two other clerics. Most works mentioned specifically were devotional. John Stevenson, indweller in Lasswade, had 'a very old Bible, torn'.[29] When the Kirk Session of this parish bought books for poor scholars they were nearly always Bibles, but there is a single instance when Ruddiman's *Rudiments* of Latin grammar was purchased in August 1662.[30] Recorded bookownership was very much a preserve of the upper middle class.

A much larger sample of Scottish inventories from the Highlands and Islands has been analysed by Dr Frances Shaw of the Scottish Record Office in Edinburgh. Between them, the Commissary Courts of Orkney and Shetland up to 1700, along with those of Argyll and the Isles up to 1750, produced fifty-six individuals whose inventories *post mortem* contain mentions of books. These are listed in appendix 2, along with their exact references. Forty-six were men and ten women, and of the total, thirty-eight came from Orkney. The earliest recorded defunct died in 1612, but most of the inventories relate to the period 1660–1700 in the case of Orkney and Shetland, and to the years 1700–1750 for Argyll and the Isles. The detailed occupational breakdown of the bookowners is given in table 5.2. Of the men, 76% were professional types whose jobs required reading and writing, while the remaining 24% were craftsmen and tradesmen, nearly all Kirkwall merchants. Town-dwellers are then over-represented among recorded bookowners. Of the ten women, two were the widows of ministers, one a glover's wife, one a baillie's, one the spouse of George Mowat, deacon of the timbermen of Kirkwall, one a laird's widow; the

[29] SRO CC8/8/111/2.   [30] SRO CH2/471/3.

Table 5.2. *Occupations of males who owned books in the Northern and Western Isles before 1750*

Occupation	Number	Occupation	Number
Minister	20	Cordiner	1
Merchant	8	Notary public	1
Laird/tacksman	3	Postmaster	1
Physician/surgeon	3	Precentor	1
Baillie	2	Skipper	1
Bishop/son of bishop	2	Student of divinity	1
Advocate	1	Tailor	1

status of two of the women is unknown, but, of the remaining two, one was the dowager Duchess of Argyll and the other a lady's servant.

Again, we see that bookownership is restricted in its social and geographical distribution. Ministers accounted for twenty of the forty-six males and the remaining twenty-six nearly all lived in towns – principally Kirkwall, but also Inverary. In those cases where book titles are specified we again find a predominance of Bibles, Psalm books, histories and practical works of professional interest. William Duncanson, the postmaster at Inverary in the early eighteenth century, had 'ane old little pocket Bible and Psalm book'. Patrick Kindsay, a Kirkwall physician who died in 1682, had 'physic books in Latin and Dutch' worth £9. Mr Alex Campbell, the Commissary of the Isles, could boast four law books and a Hebrew Bible. But there were other works too. As early as the 1640s one Kirkwall merchant had 'bairns books' worth £2 as part of the goods in his booth. The diet was not wholly monotonous. But again only the ministers and lairds had anything approaching real libraries – Dugald Campbell, minister of Lismore, had some eighty titles.

One final source which we can use to augment the inventories so far examined is the receipt, either retained by the buyer for the purchase of goods and kept among personal papers, or the debts owing to merchants for the volumes bought. John Mackenzie of Delvine had accounts for books which he bought for Sir Donald MacDonald in 1707, including titles from Thomas Cutler, Thomas Ruddiman, Mrs Margaret Mossman, Mr Henry Knox and Mr Robert Freebairn. These sources are unfortunately time-consuming to analyse, since they are often dispersed among other documents. Furthermore, those who kept such receipts were mainly the landed classes whose papers survive for the historian to examine and who would probably have bought from specialist dealers with a stock of quality publications. Thus we have a double source of bias with receipts.

The sort of pattern which we have observed for areas of Scotland – ownership of mainly religious and practical works by an elite of middle- and upper-class town-dwellers – seems to resemble that found in other areas of Europe. In sixteenth- and seventeenth-century Spain or Germany only gentry, officials and clergy had real libraries, mostly containing books relevant to their work.[31] Indeed, three-quarters of all bookowners in Valladolid were gentry, officials or churchmen, people for whom the privileges of wealth, rank and occupation had brought both the opportunities to learn and an interest in literacy. At Valladolid only 45 or 12% of 385 inventories had books, while only a handful have anything approaching a broad range of topics. Artisans can also be found owning books in fifteenth-century Barcelona and sixteenth-century Valladolid or Strasbourg, as they can in sixteenth-century Edinburgh or Newcastle, but in much smaller numbers. The merchants, clergy and nobility of eighteenth-century Grenoble had books in 28% of the inventories *post mortem* relating to their social class, but for artisans and members of the lower classes the figure was only 8%. In the Protestant city of Strasbourg between 1500 and 1580 only sixteen of forty-four bookowners in a sample of 100 inventories had Bibles. These highly literate town-dwellers read a surprising variety of books. The proportion of religious books in lower-class inventories from eighteenth-century Grenoble was higher – sixteen of thirty-four had only religious books, a further eight had more than two-thirds religious works and in another five the proportion was 50%. In Scotland as in Spain merchants can be found with business guides, religious works and some travel stories. This sort of ownership does not seem to have stretched down as far as the peasantry in either country in the way we find in the agriculturally advanced area of Friesland in the Low Countries during the seventeenth century.[32]

Acknowledging the problems inherent in using inventories to discover the extent of bookownership and thus the actual social distribution of the British reading public, some recent studies of Britain in the seventeenth and eighteenth centuries have sought to infer this from the borrowing of books. Indeed, if we turn from production and ownership to borrowing and subscription, the social dissemination of

---

[31] Chevalier (1976): 28–30; B. Bennassar, *Valladolid au siècle d'or* (1967): 511–12; M. U. Chrisman, *Lay culture, learned culture* (1982): 60–9, 155; J. Solé, 'Lecture et classes populaires à Grenoble' (1974): 97.
[32] De Vries (1975): 222.

Table 5.3. *Occupational composition of book subscribers in the Glasgow area,*
1757–9

	1757		1759	
	N	%	N	%
Professional	(65)	19	(26)	5
Craftsmen & Tradesmen	(222)	68	(459)	86
Farmers	(32)	10	(44)	8
Servants & Labourers	(7)	2	(8)	1
Total	(326)		(537)	

ownership seems to have been much less exclusive. Instead of three-quarters of owners being from the upper classes, the same proportion of subscribers to the demanding range of books offered by John Howie of Lochgoin near Fenwick in Ayrshire between the 1770s and 1790s were artisans: 20% weavers, 8% each for wrights and shoemakers, 12% farmers, for example.[33] Subscribers to the books edited by John Howie were mainly from the south-west of Scotland and the Borders along with the city of Glasgow and its environs. There was said to be a 'remarkable' traffic in books around Glasgow by itinerant retailers in the early nineteenth century.[34]

Peter Laslett presents a similarly optimistic picture of the weavers, miners and cobblers who bought books in the Glasgow area during the 1750s.[35] Laslett has used the subscription lists printed inside two religious works which were reprinted in the mid eighteenth century: Isaac Ambrose's *Prima media* (7th edition, Glasgow 1757) and Thomas Watson's *A body of practical Divinity* (5th edition, Glasgow 1759). These books were subscribed to by 398 and 606 persons respectively. Only 12 women bought the 1757 volume (3%) and 11 the 1759 one (2%) leaving respectively 326 and 537 males for whom occupational information is recorded. The occupational breakdown of the men who subscribed to these volumes is given in table 5.3.

The proportion of subscribers who came from the lowest levels of society, the servants, coalworkers, workmen and labourers was tiny: 1–2%. The proportion of craftsmen and tradesmen, on the other hand, was very high: two-thirds in 1757 and nearly seven-eighths for the 1759 volume. Farmers and tenants formed a much lower percentage. Of craftsmen and tradesmen, by far the largest single group was made up

[33] R. E. Jones, 'Bookowners in eighteenth-century Scotland' (1979): 35.
[34] Craig (1961): 143.
[35] P. Laslett, 'Scottish weavers, cobblers and miners who bought books' (1969).

by weavers: 37% and 45% of all males of known occupation at the two dates. The numbers of professional men involved was surprisingly small and we must assume that they obtained their books through other channels. It looks as though a wide social spectrum was involved in reading these weighty and expensive books. The Watson volume cost six shillings sterling. However, the numbers involved are tiny given the total population of the catchment area from which they were drawn. Even the largest occupational group, weavers, could have fitted into the parish of Kilmarnock which in 1778 had 446 looms at work in it.[36] Sedentary pursuits such as weaving and shoemaking allowed reading to go on alongside work, possibly promoting well-developed reading ability despite comparatively lowly accomplishments in signing. The seventeenth-century Puritan divine Richard Baxter recorded that he had known 'many that weave in the long loom that can set their sermon notes or a good book before them and discourse together for mutual edification while they work'.[37] If they so desired, comparatively well-paid agricultural labourers such as Alexander Somerville who worked in south-east Scotland in the early nineteenth century could afford to buy books.[38]

It was also increasingly easy to borrow books. Circulating libraries were increasing in number, especially in the early nineteenth century. This picture of widespread access to and desire for reading material was not true, however, of parts of the Highlands in the eighteenth century. In Easter Ross libraries were small, scattered and under-used. There were only 16 subscribers to the library at Kincardine out of a population of 1,100 people. Even in the Lowlands, the reading material provided by middle-class philanthropists was too dull to be very popular.[39]

Now that we have looked at who owned books we can turn to another indirect measure of literacy: who borrowed books. A source which gives us information on both reading and writing would be invaluable in enabling us to tackle the problems of indirect measures of literacy and in allowing us to test some of our assumptions about the connection between reading and the ability to sign. Such a source is the subscribed borrowing book of a 'public' library. Borrowing is perhaps a better indication of readership than owning, since we are not certain whether people ever actually referred to the books in their chests. At worst they may have been little better than 'coffee-table' literature.

---

[36] Loch (1778): 36–7.
[37] Quoted in J. Thirsk and J. P. Cooper (eds.), *Seventeenth-century economic documents* (1972): 183.
[38] Somerville (1951): 82.   [39] Mowat (1979): 4, 6, 8; Buchan (1972): 193.

However, information on borrowing is much harder to come by. One of the earliest and fullest borrowing registers is the one which was kept by the clerk to the library at Innerpefray near Crieff in Perthshire.[40] From 1747 onwards the librarian kept a tally of those who borrowed books from the library. He normally recorded their name, occupation or social status, residence and the title of the volume or volumes borrowed. The reader was obliged to return the book in good condition within three months and a fine was chargeable on books lost or returned late. To make sure that an authentic record was maintained, the clerk normally required a personal subscription for each loan. Between 1747 and 1757, 241 loans are recorded. Most people borrowed one or two volumes at a time; the maximum number taken out on any one occasion was four by John McLiesh, minister of the gospel at Gask. He signed for a quarto Bible, Poole's *Annotations*, volume one, Person on the Creed and Cradock's *Knowledge and practice*. Most of the borrowers lived in the parish of Crieff itself, but some came from neighbouring communities like Muthill.

We can use this source to answer a number of important questions about who may have been reading books in the middle of the eighteenth century. First of all, while there were 241 occasions when books were borrowed there were only 130 individuals involved. Of these only 9 were women – a mere 7% of all borrowers. Book-borrowing in this part of Perthshire was overwhelmingly a male activity. Of the 121 male borrowers we know the occupation or status of 88. Fully 41 were members of the professional classes, people who would have required literacy for their jobs: mainly ministers, students, schoolmasters and lairds. This group forms 47% of all those males whose occupation we know. A further 40 men can be classed as craftsmen and tradesmen, among whom merchants, weavers, wrights and masons figure prominently. Of the remaining 7 individuals, 6 were described as servants and 1 as a farmer. These last make up only 8% of a borrowing public overwhelmingly dominated by the middling and upper levels of village society. We should not regard the servants mentioned as necessarily representatives of a truly lower-class reading tradition. One worked for a writer in Muthill and may have been a clerk, another was a minister's employee (perhaps chosen for his literacy and godliness), a third worked for a dyer.

At the same time we must stress that the number of individuals involved was very small. Take the case of weavers. There were nineteen entries in the register which record books being borrowed by

[40] NLS Mf. 9 (18); titles and spellings are as found in the original manuscript.

weavers. However, nine of these entries are attributable to John Bryce who lived in Innerpefray; a further four were borrowings by John Roben, a weaver from the Loanhead of Innerpefray. In total there were only seven weavers involved. This was a small proportion of the total weaving community in the parish of Crieff which numbered ninety-two heads of families four decades later.[41] Wrights are rather better represented: seven borrowers from the library and twenty of that trade in 1792. For tailors, the ratio of borrowers to total population is one to ten. These figures almost certainly overstate the representativeness of the borrowers, since not all actually came from Crieff. One borrowing farmer out of some forty in the parish is a dismal figure.

What is more, eighty-one of all those who borrowed during the eleven years did so on only one occasion: 62% of all borrowers, male and female. A further twenty-five borrowed on two separate dates (19%) and twelve at three different times (9%). The remaining twelve borrowed between four and eleven times during the period 1747–57. Conceivably, the books were being read by more people than just those recorded, but on the evidence before us we should have to say that regular borrowing was very far from being a characteristic experience even among the minority who penetrated the portals of Innerpefray library.

Before we go on to assess the other information which the Innerpefray borrowing register affords we must address one fundamental problem in interpreting the source. People certainly borrowed books from the library, but we do not know if they actually read them. Take the example of James Sharp in Innerpefray. Sharp was one of the most frequent borrowers from the library, signing out one or two volumes a year over the period 1747–57. Whether he read them or not is uncertain, for in June 1756 we find him borrowing volume one of Abercrombie's *Scots martial achievements* 'for the use of James Drummond of Kelty'; volume two was issued to him on 3 January 1757. Did Sharp actually bother to read what he borrowed? Perhaps, because earlier, in 1751, one of his own servants borrowed a religious treatise on his behalf. The point is that we cannot be sure that the borrower was the end user, a problem which seems to be particularly obvious with servants. William Murray, servant to the dyer John Caw in Millnab, borrowed the sixth and seventh volumes of the *History of Europe* 'for the use of my master' in April 1752. A frequent borrower was Duncan Morrison, another servant from Innerpefray, whose name and signature appears eight times over the eleven years studied. In July

41 *OSA*, vol. 9 (1793): 589.

1754 his loan was on behalf of William Brewster. Perhaps Duncan read himself: he could sign his name in full. He may have been part of a borrowing and lending circle outside the library system; possibly he read the material before passing it on; he may even have read it aloud to others or asked them to do so for him. Alternatively he could have been little more than a delivery boy for his master or acquaintances.

The position is further complicated when we find Thomas Miller the schoolmaster in Innerpefray borrowing Drummond of Haw-thornden's *History of the five King James* 'for the behoof of Mr John Muckarse minister at Kinkell'. Undoubtedly both were equally able to read the volume. The permutations are endless. There is some sug-gestive evidence of groups of people who may have formed literate book-reading communities, associations created either by kinship or by geographical propinquity or occupational ties. Alex, James and John Roben (weaver, wright, weaver respectively) all lived in Loan-head of Innerpefray. Groups of readers also came from Kirkhill and the Coblehaugh. There were four Faichneys, also from the Loanhead, who borrowed on thirteen occasions in all. Two of the men were masons. Unfortunately, we can only make some impressionistic suggestions here, since the number of surnames was limited in this area and we cannot prove that the people were actually related. We can say nothing certain about reading ability from this source and should treat the results with some caution.

The bulk of borrowers could sign their own names in the register. Only two men and three women could not write when they were asked to do so. In addition, there were a number of occasions when the clerk recorded 'lent myself without receipt', and when we have no record of ability to sign. The quality of subscription varies from the bold hand of ministers like James Reid to some of the rough holographs of tailors like James McRobbie and weavers like Alex Roben. However, the vast bulk of men could sign in full. We cannot say anything worthwhile about women from a sample of only nine individuals.

Virtually all the literature which was being borrowed can be reduced to the categories of religious, historical, philosophical or practical works. Of these, religious works were by far the commonest, mostly sermons, commentaries on the Scriptures and treatises on aspects of faith. Fully 60% of recorded loans fall into this category. The works of famous divines such as Perkins, Burroughs, Sibbes and Preston are prominent alongside titles such as the *Saints highway to happiness* and the *Life and death of the twelve apostles*. The second most popular category was historical. For example, there was a multi-volume *History of Europe* and a *History of Queen Elizabeth's reign*. Many of these historical works had a religious focus: Knox's *History of the Reformation* sat with a *History of the Bohemian persecution* and Abercrombie's *Scots martial achievements* in celebrating religious and national identity. Historical works comprised about 30% of all volumes borrowed. A typical borrower was Andrew Moir who in 1751 took out said *History of the Bohemian persecution* and a volume entitled *Wonderful prodigies of judgement and mercy*. There were few alternatives to this staple fare, or if there were they do not seem to have been particularly popular. John Morison, a wright, borrowed one example of a lighter genre, the *Garden of delights of English poetry*, in addition to the *Present state of the United Provinces*. Certain practical works were available, such as Topsel's *History of the four-footed beasts* (borrowed only by students) and Reid's *Scots gard'ner*. These practical works and some philosophical treatises such as Locke and some of the classics formed the remaining 10%.

One person who did have a wide range of reading tastes was Ebenezer Clement. Ebenezer was the son of William Clement in Powmill and in 1755 or 1756 he was apprenticed to Alexander Porteous, a Crieff dyer. He borrowed throughout our period. His first recorded loan was *Ruth's recompense*, and he worked his way through *Highways to happiness*, Hooker's *Laws of ecclesiastical polity*, *A history of the world* and the *Sight of Palestine* to MacKenzie's *Scots writers* volume one.

Ebenezer's tastes were remarkably catholic, especially by comparison with the two men and three women who could not write. In 1747 Janet Cooper was lent 'a small book on the unchangeableness of God', while Mrs Thompson in Crieff took out 'a big Bible'. Large or small, the books lent to women were, with one exception (a *History of Queen Elizabeth's reign*), religious. The reading tastes of women and the illiterates do seem to have been very limited. The illiterate Innerpefray weaver John Roben borrowed Burroughs' *Gospel revelations* for the first time in April 1754 and then again in January 1755. He did not borrow again until the last month of that year and his Christmas reading fare was the *Fulfilling of the Scriptures*. At the end of the following July he returned to his faithful *Revelations*. One assumes either that John was particularly attached to the message of this book or that he was struggling to get through it. From the small number of instances we have it seems that repetitive borrowing of the same volume was more common among illiterates and women than among the bulk of men who could sign their names in the register. Margaret Morison twice took out an abridgement of Dr Preston's works before passing on to Gouge on *God's three arrows*. Such people may have been using the volumes to teach themselves to read or as material for prayer and study meetings with friends. Certainly, for literates and illiterates alike the material borrowed was weighty, demanding and, superficially at least, far from cheerful. *Drellencourt on death* was rather popular. The emphasis on religious literature is very much in line with the other information we have on book production, borrowing and ownership.

Reading material was mainly but not exclusively religious. We can see the same pattern in other sources. The parochial and presbyterial libraries of Easter Ross, for example, were predominantly religious in their contents, though subscription libraries had a wider range of informative material.[42] Scottish witchcraft was used as a subject for English pamphlets, but as far as we can tell Scots literary diet was largely restricted to biblical studies, theological tracts and other learned works.[43] Contrary to the pious hopes of the moral reformers, however, 'religious literature circulated chiefly among "professing Christians of the middle classes"; while the [much greater quantity of] unsavoury sheets found their way, "in a very large proportion, to the homes and haunts of the poor"'.[44] Alas, this sort of ephemera leaves little trace in our records and formed no part of the Innerpefray library.

Despite the problems with this fascinating source there are some things about which we can be fairly certain. First, the broad spectrum of local society who borrowed from the Innerpefray library seem to have been able to cope with some weighty literature, suggesting a high level of accomplishment. Secondly, having said this, the number of people involved is very small. Perhaps a dozen different individuals a year borrowed books from a population of some 2,000 people in the area.[45] Nearly all the borrowers were drawn from the middling and upper ranks of society. Thirdly, the vast bulk of readers could sign their names. Not being able to sign in full did not preclude reading ability, but in virtually every case the high level of reading skill required was associated with sign-literacy. Again our universal, standard and direct criterion of literacy is vindicated.

Because they are indirect, book production, borrowing and ownership have not been used as measures of literacy in the main part of this study. They present too many problems of interpretation. The only source which allows us to be absolutely sure that people could both read and write were diaries, such as that of Adam Eyre who recorded his progress through Foxe's *Book of martyrs*, Raleigh's *History of the world* and Erasmus' *Praise of folly* in the years 1643 to 1645.[46]

---

[42] Mowat (1979): 4.   [43] Larner (1981): 168.   [44] Quoted in Webb (1955): 27–8.
[45] Lenman (1977b): xxxviii. This only covers the parish of Crieff itself. Since people from nearby parishes also used the library the proportion of the local population involved in borrowing was probably even smaller than suggested.
[46] A. Eyre, *Dyurnall* (1877): 67, 70, 100.

Clearly Eyre was not typical of the rest of society: the very fact that he kept a diary makes that plain. Diaries provide interesting insights, but even in large numbers can only provide a partial picture. Most of the statistical information on literacy presented here has therefore been based on one simple criterion. Those able to sign their names in full on a document such as a court deposition are deemed literate, while those making a mark or initials or claiming to be unable to write for themselves are held to be illiterate.

While this definition is generally accepted, it is not wholly unproblematic and can be criticized on two fronts. The first problem lies in the significance of a signature or mark in itself. Does the form of autograph give any real indication of the level of manual competence? The second is how much signing ability tells us about facility in reading and other culturally useful literate skills which could influence individual and societal development. The Innerpefray library borrowing register has given us good grounds for believing that signing ability is a reliable indicator of the cultural possibilities of literacy. However, we cannot ignore the other problems entirely.

All sorts of criticism have been levelled against the sign/mark dichotomy. In his study of the origins of lay literacy in the eleventh and twelfth centuries, Clanchy points out that the symbolism of signing with a cross was important to medieval English subscribers and need not have indicated illiteracy. Whether the same is true of post-Reformation Protestant countries is unclear, tied up as it is in the complex symbolism of popular religion. However, we can point to the fact that only a small proportion of marks were crosses, others being initials or mere scrawls. Nor were the crosses necessarily of the shape which one would expect as Christian symbols. In the medieval period, crosses were drawn as a long vertical line intersected near its top by a shorter horizontal one. This form is very rare in early modern documents. Marks in the seventeenth and eighteenth centuries could be many shapes, but the closest to a cross is formed by two diagonal lines intersecting at ninety degrees.[47] We should not assume that this is a St Andrews cross with special significance for Scotland, since we find it as commonly south of the Border.

A second difficulty surrounds the interpretation of the use of seals. For Poland, Wyczanski argues that personal signatures were a late medieval development, and that seals were the norm for authentication.[48] Clanchy refers to a similar phenomenon in medieval England,

---

[47] Clanchy (1979): 246; see Cressy (1980): 60 and Parker (1980): 213 for the range of signatures and marks found.
[48] Wyczanski (1974): 706.

and goes on to suggest that possession of a seal meant that the owner could read his own name, and further that seals were owned by people familiar with writing.[49] It is not certain, however, whether this extends beyond simple recognition of an authenticating symbol to encompass understanding of the literate message. Thus, seals 'looked back to charms and memorized objects and forward to the automation of writing'.[50] Seals were commonly used on documents such as wills and bonds in the north of England, but alongside holograph signatures or marks. They are not used on depositions before the English assizes or Consistory Court, or for that matter before the Scottish criminal courts. The relationship between the skills is a complex one, and we cannot accept Clanchy's view that there was no need to write if one had a seal.[51]

In practice sealing and signing were not mutually exclusive. Signatures begin to accompany seals on Scottish bonds of manrent from c.1500, and take over completely by c.1550.[52] Bonds of manrent were defensive agreements between powerful lords and lesser figures. An Act of the Scottish Parliament in 1540 ordered that writs must be signed as well as sealed, though in general signatures were not essential to authenticate a document.

Emulation of signatures is said to be another problem, sometimes extending to the copying of the name of the previous signatory on a document by the subsequent one. In eighteenth-century English assize depositions for the northern counties, two sisters used the same style of mark – a pair of vertical parallel lines – and this device was copied by their servant woman who followed them.[53] Geoffrey Parker illustrates the use of a *modèle*, or guide, in early modern France: a copy of a signature which was used as a guide when signing. This was not apparently a common feature of all European cultures and indeed one French scholar has concluded that people did not learn to sign without being able to write more than just their names.[54] The present writer has been unable to uncover any evidence of the use of devices like the *modèle* in Scotland or England.

There is also the issue of consistency. Was signing ability simply a one-off trick to be learned? Or could someone who signed once even be expected to do so a second time? We can test how robust signatures were in a variety of ways, both on occasions when more than one signature was required on a document and when we can trace a

---

[49] Clanchy (1979): 35, 184.   [50] *Ibid.* 248.   [51] *Ibid.* 245.   [52] Wormald (1981): 68.
[53] PRO ASSI45: 26/6/50.
[54] Parker (1980): 216; Longuet (1978): 222; Chartier (1976): 88–9; Meyer (1970): 336.

person's form of authentication over a period of time. At Durham diocese Consistory Court, for example, two depositions were usually entered in the documents, one relating to the prosecutor's interrogatories, one to the defendant's, allowing the robustness of people's ability to make marks or signatures to be assessed. Full signatures are extremely robust in the eighteenth-century depositions, while marks tend to vary slightly around a common theme. Rough marks tend to deteriorate between subscriptions, suggesting that writing was an unaccustomed effort. At the eighteenth-century Northern Circuit assizes a similar pattern is found. Where long depositions are signed at the foot of each page in the Scottish Justiciary Court minute books, consistency in forms of signature or mark, as well as in making one or other, is good.[55] These are only impressions, but nevertheless we can have confidence that our indicators of literacy or illiteracy were used consistently. Those who borrowed on more than one occasion from the Innerpefray library near Crieff were wholly consistent in making a signature or asking the clerk to subscribe for them.

It is still possible that the emotional stress of a court appearance may have encouraged a quick and easy mark rather than a signature. Men and women who could normally sign perfectly well might have eschewed the opportunity because of nervousness. This is a hoary old argument first used by the defenders of the inadequate church education system to discredit statistics of non-signers allegedly too overcome to sign the marriage register in full. In Scotland the accused person's fear of torture – or perhaps even its results – might inhibit signing.[56] However, the robustness of signatures would suggest otherwise.

One final piece of evidence buttresses our faith in the consistency of the signature/mark division even in the most stressful situations. Just after Easter 1768, six men who lived in the cot-toun of Leys in Perthshire were involved in bidding at a roup or auction to renew the lease of their landholdings.[57] The lease was for seven years, and when the hammer came down the future of the tenants would be decided. Five of the men were already in possession of the plots for which they entered bids: Thomas Em, Andrew Nicol, John Jackson, Alexander Kininmond and John Wighton. The sixth, Robert Wighton, lived in the same cot-toun but was not already a sitting tenant. The atmosphere of the roup became highly charged when outsiders began to bid against Robert Wighton. The strangers were James Sim, a baker from Errol,

---

[55] See DPDD Durham Consistory Court depositions, SRO Justiciary records in general and PRO ASSI45: 25/1/85, 86, 137, 138 for some specific instances.
[56] Smith (1972): xvii.   [57] SAUL Hay of Leys MS 906.

Table 5.4. *Male and female illiteracy by age in Scotland and north-east England*

Age	England (1716–1800)		Scotland (1640–1770)	
	Males	Females	Males	Females
<20	(8) 38	(20) 75	(259) 37	(123) 80
20s	(93) 15	(64) 72	(1,216) 35	(322) 75
30s	(117) 15	(50) 56	(1,318) 26	(207) 82
40s	(103) 14	(43) 58	(970) 32	(209) 84
50s	(101) 23	(25) 52	(539) 33	(137) 88
60+	(102) 28	(28) 86	(261) 44	(92) 84
unknown	(14) 14	(6) 33	(298) 36	(137) 85
Total	(538)	(236)	(4,861)	(1,227)

and a John Sim who may have been one of his relations. The effect which this had on the men involved is made clear when we compare the quality of their signatures and marks on the final agreement to lease the holdings with the shaky, trembling autographs with which they confirmed their bids at the auction. All were influenced by the tension but Robert Wighton's hand was particularly badly affected. We can feel their relief when the tack was finally signed. The historian of literacy can also take comfort from the consistency with which four of the men made signatures throughout the process while the other two made marks. The fluency of the holographs varies but not the type of authentication used.

Many of the subscriptions we have used to analyse signing ability in the early modern world were made in stressful situations. But the profile of literacy which we have uncovered could also be distorted by the effect of age and of injury or illness on a person's competence in wielding a pen. One piece of valuable biographical information not used in the main analysis of structures and trends in illiteracy is the age of a deponent. For England, assize depositions only rarely record the age of a witness or accused person, and for comparison with Scottish sources we must resort to Durham Consistory Court deponents during the eighteenth century. Even where ages are given these are some-times rather vague – 'above forty years', for example – and there is a pronounced tendency towards rounding up or down to ages such as thirty or forty; there was also a marked preference for certain digits such as six. By grouping ages into ten-year brackets many of the vag-aries should be ironed out, leaving the broad profile we see in table 5.4 as representative of the age distribution of literacy.

Literacy attainments vary considerably with age. Among all men and among English women there is a marked rise in aggregate illiteracy in the older age groups. The reason for this is not far to seek. In 1699 Isabel Rowan, wife of William Rowan of Dumbieck concluded her deposition by remarking that she 'hes altogither forgot her wreitting'.[58] Thomas Kennedy, a widower of the highly advanced age of eighty-eight, pleaded in 1753 that 'he cannot now write by reason of his great age and ashaking of his hand'.[59] Alexander Fraser explained to the Justiciary Court that 'he cannot write because he is lame of a finger'.[60] Old age and crippling afflictions such as arthritis could hamper people's ability to write their names. Evidence which shows that illness and age-related disabilities reduced signing ability is particularly common in wills. Thomas Young, an Edinburgh merchant, stated that he could not write himself 'in respect of the want of my perfite sight and of my sickness'.[61] The comparatively high illiteracy of the under twenties and twenties for English women and Scottish males – we might expect the younger age groups who could still remember their schooling to be the most literate – may be a result of the large numbers of low-literacy servants who were characteristically drawn from the fifteen to twenty-five age range. Many of the deponents in the prime of life were substantial yeomen and tradesmen. The trough in illiteracy which is particularly noticeable among Durham Consistory Court male deponents aged from twenty to forty-nine and women aged from thirty to fifty-nine is also suggestive of signing ability picked up through economic need in later life. For the oldest age group among Scottish women, the need of widows to run their late husband's affairs may have counterbalanced the deleterious impact of age on signing ability.

Indeed, in some cases where we have a record of an individual's signature over a number of years, we can see the other side of the process in action: an improvement in writing skills with practise. A Fife tenant farmer called Andrew Bell provides an example. In 1681 Andrew rented the land of Falside in Kingsbarns parish near St Andrews. The lease was entered into jointly with his mother, suggesting that Andrew was still quite young. He signed the agreement, though not very well, and spelt his name 'Andro'. When he renewed the lease on his own account in 1703 his signature was much more fluent and he wrote 'Andrew' rather than Andro. Age and acquaintance with literate forms had helped this man to improve his writing and to anglicize his spelling.[62]

Signatures deteriorate with age but at the same time there is no

[58] SRO JC10/6.   [59] SRO JC12/7.   [60] SRO JC7/7.
[61] SRO CC8/10/15a: 28 April 1673.   [62] SAUL UY123/1.

denying the internal variability within the signature and mark division whether the deponent was young or old. The quality of subscription varies as much as the range of literate skills artificially dichotomized by the sign/mark distinction. Some European studies use classifications based on elaborate versus simple signatures and initials or other sophisticated marks as distinct from mere scrawls.[63] We can only offer some impressionistic suggestions here. Quality of signatures is better for the upper social levels and superior in towns. For some people, such as professional scribes, signatures may be fluent and even embellished. For merchants a plain but neat signature is usual, whereas a labouring man who could sign would typically do so in a crude, wandering hand. The minutes of the St Andrews association of hammermen for September 1692 contain an agreement subscribed by ten of the members. Two made initials, but there is a striking variety in the quality of the eight signatures, from the smooth flourish of James Reid the clerk to the shaky autograph of William Cuthbert, an ordinary member.[64] The sort of differences between levels of literacy is seen when we contrast the crude handwriting, bad spelling and poor grammar in the memoranda prepared by the man who checked the loads of coal being brought to the surface at the Loanhead pits in eighteenth-century Midlothian with the comparative elegance and consistency of the coalgrieve or supervisor's correspondence.[65]

The average quality of subscription seems to vary in different areas of Britain. For instance, signatures are more bold and fluent among Cumberland deponents than among those from Yorkshire. There were also regional differences within Scotland, the confident and often flowing hand of many eighteenth-century Lowland Scottish deponents contrasting with the shaky orthography of their Highland counterparts. Unlike some Continental towns, such as Falaise in the eighteenth century, improved quantity of literacy was definitely associated with improving quality for those able to sign in contemporary Britain.[66] Before the Reformation the signatures we have on Scottish documents are very rough, suggesting that writing was still unfamiliar. More complex categories have not been used here, since they only become meaningful with very large numbers which would allow us to control for the range of variables which are examined in chapter 2. Furthermore, the documents we are using may simply state that a person could not write, so that we cannot distinguish between initials and crude marks, since the clerk of the court would note down that the

[63] Parker (1980): 211–12; Rodriguez and Bennassar (1978); Longuet (1978).
[64] SAUL MS DA890.S1H2: fol. 113.   [65] SRO GD18/995.   [66] Longuet (1978): 220.

person could not sign in full. The need for comparability with existing studies of England by Cressy and Schofield provides the other reason.

We can be fairly certain that when people signed or marked an early modern document they were giving an unequivocal indication of their level of manual competence with a pen. What of the other criticism of the sign/mark division?

The connection between signing ability and other literate skills is by no means clear. John Brodie, a horse hirer living in Aberdeen, was obliging enough to point out in 1714 that 'he himself cannot read nor write'.[67] However, Britain possesses no sources for the systematic study of reading ability before the nineteenth century to match the incomparable Swedish catechetical records.[68] From 1686 the Lutheran church in Sweden insisted that in order to marry or give evidence in court, men and women had to have partaken of communion, and access to this privilege was dependent on passing a test of basic reading and religious knowledge. Individual abilities were recorded by the vicar on a graded scale in the examination register. These annual examinations were continued from the age of six through life. Comparison between reading ability as shown in the catechism records and sign-literacy levels shows the possibility of considerable diversity between reading and writing skills, as well as illustrating that the relationship between the two need not be constant over time. In the late seventeenth century few could read and few could write. By the second half of the eighteenth century reading was the norm for men and women but most Swedes could not write. Mass reading and writing together came only in the late nineteenth century.

In nineteenth-century Britain we are on safer ground. Statistical surveys of various sections of the population reveal a close connection between signing ability and a reasonable proficiency in reading, though the criteria used by investigators to assess proficiency in reading, writing and counting are not always clear.[69] At the same time the spectrum of literate abilities would be highly complex. The documents of the Toledo Inquisition between the sixteenth and nineteenth centuries give information on eleven different degrees of instruction which can be inferred from interrogations about literacy and the ownership of heretical books.[70] In Scottish witchcraft depositions we also find incidental references to reading, writing and learning because of the judicial belief in the highly contagious nature of diabolical knowledge. In neither instance is this information given systematically,

---

[67] SRO JC11/3.   [68] Johansson (1981): 165–74.
[69] N. Tranter, 'The reverend Andrew Urquhart' (1974): 52–7.
[70] Rodriguez and Bennassar (1978): 23–4.

since witnesses and accused were not always questioned in the same way. Authorities believed that literate people would be most influential and thus concentrated on literate means of communication, creating a possibly biased impression of the extent of literacy and its importance as a form of communicating ideas. Sometimes we can infer reading and writing skills from incidental information in the records. However, this sort of information is not available in a form which can be used systematically to provide quantitative measurements of the spectrum of literacy.

Lack of information on reading ability is a serious drawback, since of the range of literate skills, reading was probably more important than writing in shaping patterns of thought. Indeed, the wider dissemination of reading skills may have been what marked Scotland out from England. We have already shown that in the case of those who borrowed books from the Innerpefray library in the mid eighteenth century there was an almost complete overlap between reading and the ability to sign in full. Yet we should pursue this issue further.

Religious emphasis in Scotland was on reading, and Sir John Sinclair stressed the widespread reading ability of the Lowland Scots. Reports by ministers on their parishes in the 1790s sometimes contain glowing accounts of how no person of either sex aged above ten or twelve was unable to read.[71] Daniel Defoe spotted that at large religious gatherings of people north of the Border there were hardly any to be seen without Bibles except the blind.[72] In England he believed that only one in twenty would have had a Bible at a comparable meeting. Leaving aside the problem of the typicality of the section of the population who attended such gatherings, we cannot be certain that the prominence of Bibles was attributable to their relative cheapness, better distribution patterns for sellers, or even the use of Bibles for purely symbolic reasons. Nor should we ignore the frankly romantic view which Defoe took of the Scots, a people whom he claimed were morally superior and who possessed what he saw as greater religious conviction than the English. The Scots lacked only the luxury and excess of their southern neighbours, according to Defoe.

At the same time he was probably unaware of the comments of a Jesuit gaoled at Wisbech in Cambridgeshire in the late sixteenth century who reported large groups of Puritans, women and children included, following Bible texts. Or the Puritan meetings of the 1580s when it was said that 'each of them had his own Bible'.[73] Or the Lancashire and Cheshire people of the early seventeenth century,

---

[71] Sinclair (1826): appx. 20–1.   [72] Defoe (1708): 318.   [73] Spufford (1981): xvii, 33.

'many converted, and many confirmed and many convinced' who took Bibles to church in order to follow the texts.[74] When Henry Newcome began his career as a preacher in the north-west of England he quickly discovered that he had to adjust the content of his sermons, since 'people came with Bibles, and expected quotations of Scripture'.[75] Or for that matter the Continental observer John Comenius, an educated man concerned with learning and its dissemination, who was surprised in 1641 to see half the congregation of a London church taking notes on the sermon. He also remarked on the large number of printers and booksellers in the city.[76] Foreigners remarked upon the frequent reading of newspapers among the labouring poor of London in the middle of the eighteenth century.[77] In the mid seventeenth century political pamphlets had a wide circulation. Again urban populations, like religiously committed ones, cannot provide the basis for confident generalizations about the whole population. Those with strong religious faith may have been helped to it by existing reading and writing abilities. Alternatively, their faith may have induced them to acquire literate skills.

Nor was the thrust of eighteenth-century Scottish comment entirely adulatory, especially in the Highlands. A petition of 1755, admittedly painting a pessimistic picture in order to secure funding from the Scottish Society for Propagating Christian Knowledge, claimed that at Glenmoriston a mere 40 out of 1,000 people were able to read, and that only the laird and his family could write. A more reliable report of 1822 suggested 70% inability to read in the Hebrides and western parts of Inverness and Ross.[78] The essential point to notice here is that literary evidence points to a strong religious literacy tradition in both Scotland and England. Despite Defoe, the Scots were not unique in their literacy even if we rely on the impressionistic comments of contemporaries.

Victor Neuburg rightly points out that inability to sign 'is not decisive proof of an inability to read', and there are indeed a variety of reasons why we might expect more people were able to read than write.[79] In particular, reading and writing were taught as quite separate skills, the former preceding the latter. Dundonald Kirk Session exhorted its schoolmasters to 'let a special care be had of the children's writing who are meet for it'.[80] In France as in Scotland and England

[74] Quoted in Collinson (1982): 243.
[75] R. Parkinson (ed.), *The autobiography of Henry Newcome* (1852): 10.
[76] V. Pearl, 'Change and stability in seventeenth century London' (1979): 6.
[77] R. M. Hartwell, 'Education and economic growth in England' (1971): 90.
[78] Thompson (1972–4): 256; West (1975): 63.   [79] Neuburg (1971): 93.
[80] Quoted in Boyd (1961): 29.

reading and writing were not taught simultaneously until the late nine-teenth century, and in some cases were actually learnt in different schools. Luther perceived writing as an advanced skill, a view followed by the Calvinists.[81]

In elementary schools, where religious demands were predominant, reading was the most important single subject and frequently the only one. The schoolmaster of St Ninians in Stirlingshire was ordered in 1750 to stop teaching poor scholars as soon as they were able to read the Bible.[82] Religious stress on reading is illustrated in seventeenth-century Scotland by the many Kirk Sessions whose only disburse-ments for poor scholars were payments for Bibles. In January 1648 the minister and elders of Lasswade scolded the boys who looked after cattle in Loanhead 'for comeing togither and playing on the sabbath day and not exercising themselves in reading or other godlie exer-cises'.[83] When setting up schools in the early eighteenth century the SSPCK provided that £24 should be given to each teacher 'for fur-nishing the necessary books and a new Bible to every schollar when taught to read the Bible distinctly. And this is all the length the Society's funds can goe.'[84]

In England, guidelines issued to teachers paid by the SPCK stated that learning to write should not come until the third year of children's education, and then only to aid catechetical instruction.[85] William Langley of Ashby specified that only three years' education should be given to the poor children for whose benefit he left money in the late seventeenth century.[86] In the early nineteenth century, 'most Sunday schools [the only schooling for many children] taught little more than reading. Indeed, in some schools, anything beyond reading was held in abhorrence.'[87] Dissenting Sunday schools were however keener to teach writing. Some early nineteenth-century moral reformers argued that writing and arithmetic were more of a threat to the established order and that lower-class education should be confined to reading. For these, the notion of a full 'liberal education' in the classical tradition would have seemed not only superfluous but dangerous.[88]

Presenting example and counter-example is unlikely to help us resolve the issue of reading ability any better than arguments based on the availability and sales of printed material. Spufford rightly regards the social diffusion of reading ability as a 'murky unquantifiable

[81] Parker (1980): 217; Scotland (1969): 66; Furet and Sachs (1974): 715.
[82] Bain (1965): 126.   [83] SRO CH2/471/2.   [84] SRO CH2/424/9: fol. 360.
[85] J. Simon, 'Was there a charity school movement?' (1968c): 64.
[86] J. Simon (1968a): 36.   [87] Webb (1955): 16.
[88] C. F. Kaestle, 'Elite attitudes towards mass schooling' (1976): 180.

subject'.[89] Isolated documents afford reluctant insights into reading ability in the seventeenth and eighteenth centuries, though we are again confronted by the difficulty of discerning the criteria used to judge this skill and the motivation of those reporting it.

These problems confront us in dealing with two promising sources for the study of reading. The 'Islington annual register of the parish poor children until they are apprenticed out' gives information on reading ability among the over-fives there between 1767 and 1810. Of 267 boys, 75% could read, while 173 or 76% of 228 girls had this ability.[90] This source reveals a much greater similarity in attainment between males and females than is shown by findings based on ability to sign. This picture again reminds us of Sweden, where the ability to sign one's name was highly stratified by wealth, status and gender, but where reading was much more evenly distributed among the population.

Much the same is true of another fascinating source recently exploited by Christopher Smout.[91] This is the 'Examination of Persons under Scriptural Concern at Cambuslang' during the religious revival movement of 1741–2, contained in two manuscript volumes which cover 75 men and 35 women. These were drawn mainly from the nubile age groups from thirteen to twenty-nine years and from the lower middling sections of society resident in and around that Lanarkshire town – tenants and craftsmen. The poorest classes are largely unrepresented and further biases are clear if we consider that the converts were already in the habit of regular religious attendance. Active participation in Protestantism has been shown by European studies to draw disproportionately from literate sections of society, even allowing for occupational distribution.[92] In early seventeenth-century England it was not uncommon for an influential preacher to be given a signed affidavit by those who acknowledged him as their spiritual leader and guide.[93] At the same time the 110 persons were specially selected as edifying examples from thousands who attended the communions in 1741–2.

In short, the 110 who were 'born again' were by no means necessarily a representative cross-section of those who attended the meeting, let alone those who made up Scottish society in the mid eighteenth century. Nor are we altogether certain whether those who said they had been taught to read and/or write actually had these accomplishments or only claimed they could do so as a boast. Yet of 109 usable

[89] Spufford (1981): xviii.   [90] Neuburg (1971): 173.   [91] Smout (1982).
[92] Benedict (1980): 90–1; Cressy (1980): 85.   [93] Collinson (1982): 242.

cases all men and all women claimed to have been taught to read. The real difference was in sign-literacy: 89% female illiteracy but only 40% male, a characteristic profile which sits well with our figures presented in chapter 2 and one which we encounter throughout Europe between the sixteenth and nineteenth centuries. If we were able to discount the unrepresentative nature of the sample the read/write distinction would offer some suggestive comparisons with eighteenth-century Sweden, where most people could read but sign-literacy was relatively uncommon, especially for women and the lower social levels. The same may have been true of another Scandinavian country. In Denmark as in Sweden nearly universal reading ability was attained by the end of the eighteenth century, but widespread sign-literacy was not achieved in either country until well after the school Acts of 1814 and 1842 respectively.[94]

However, we should not carry the comparison with Sweden too far. Reading and rote learning was all that was required there and the church instituted a rigorous campaign to teach the people. What is more, since there were very few schools before the nineteenth century, these skills were acquired in the home from parents, siblings and friends. Opportunities to learn writing were strictly limited, a situation unusual in contemporary Europe. In most European countries, except Sweden, progress in writing closely followed that in reading. Reading was learnt first, then writing within a year or so.[95] Scotland relied to a greater extent on schooling than on home instruction in reading, which was almost the only means of education in seventeenth- and eighteenth-century Sweden. In these Scottish schools, reading and writing were taught almost simultaneously. It is crucial to recognize the different context of learning in Scotland compared to Sweden. We cannot distinguish a separate home-reading campaign in Scotland distinct from school education. We must also recognize the importance of a general demand for full reading and writing literacy learnt in a variety of ways. We should expect a close correlation between reading and writing abilities in Scotland and England but not in Sweden. In fact the only other part of Europe where reading without writing is documented on any scale is in certain parts of nineteenth-century France, which had a strong tradition of Catholic religious observance.[96]

Only in the Highlands is there any hint of a pattern of home learning of reading alone, and then only in the seventeenth century before

---

[94] I. Markussen and V. Skovgaard Petersen, 'Læseindlærning of læsebehov i Danmark' (1981).
[95] Johansson (1981): 152; Vogler (1975): 266.   [96] Furet and Ozouf (1982): 174–5, 183.

schools were properly established in the area. In 1650 the synod of
Argyll stated that

because the knowledge of the English language is so necessary for the weall of
the Gospell, the scriptures not being translated in Irish, and seeing the country
cannot have schools in every church for learning English, that therefore use be
made of poor boys that can read and write English to teach the young and
others that may be made willing in the parish to read and understand the
English in the interim till schools may be erected.[97]

This suggests that home education in reading alone was a stop-gap
measure, a temporary expedient to be tried until schools were established. We do not know if this campaign achieved any results, let alone
those which the Swedes managed in the eighteenth century. However, elsewhere in Lowland Scotland at least schools were common by
the end of the seventeenth century and a close connection between
reading and writing should be expected. We should not allow loose
comparisons with other countries to persuade us that Scotland was
quite different from England in the extent of her literacy any more than
we should contemporary comments. Regrettably, the historian is left
in a similar position to the Kirk Session of Lasswade who in 1642
ordered all parishioners who could read to sing psalms in the church.
He can only wonder how many voices were raised to heaven.[98]

The use of the simple division between the ability to sign a name in
full and the inability so to do is by no means a straightforward measure
of the complex phenomenon of literacy. Nevertheless, most European
studies do suggest that despite the lack of a necessary connection
between reading and writing, because of the disparity in the facilities
for learning and using the two skills, that they do indeed parallel each
other closely. Furet and Sachs find for nineteenth-century France a
spectacularly close association between the variables of ability to sign
the marriage register and ability to read and to write for both men and
women.[99] There is no connection between sign-literacy and ability
simply to read without knowing how to write. The result of an exhaus-
tive study of European literacy concludes that being able only to read
and not write is associated with certain very specific forms of Catholic
education. The same close connection between signing and the ability
to read was true of England in the early nineteenth century.[100] As we
have seen, the way in which reading and writing were taught and the

[97] Quoted in McKerral (1948): 155.   [98] SRO CH2/471/2.
[99] Webb (1955): 21–2; R. S. Schofield, 'The measurement of literacy' (1968); Johansson
    (1981): 152; Furet and Sachs (1974): 721.
[100] E. le Roy Ladurie and M. Demonet, 'Alphabétisation et stature' (1980): 1330;
    Schofield (1968); M. J. Campbell, 'The development of literacy in Bristol and Glouces-
    tershire' (1980).

priorities of both educators and educated in Scotland and England would lead us to expect that these shared the experience of France and, indeed, much of north-western Europe. The cultural context of the countries is similar and for this reason we should expect that signatures do form a comparable indicator of literacy in all of them.

Signatures offer a 'universal, standard and direct' measure the exact position of which in the literacy spectrum is unimportant when it comes to assessing regional, social and temporal aspects of illiteracy.[101] The criterion we have adopted is direct because there is no problem of inferring abilities of the sort we find when using book production, borrowing or ownership, is universal because it is found in all parts of Europe and North America between the late medieval period and the present day. And it is standard because the same skill is tested on each occasion.

[101] Schofield (1968): 319.

6

Oral culture and literate culture

The ability to sign one's name in full on a document provides us with the best criterion which we can use for statistical analysis of literacy. Some sort of quantitative study is essential if we are to cut through the claims and counter-claims about Scottish education and learning. In the *Times Literary Supplement* of 7 April 1966 Keith Thomas stated that 'all historical propositions relating to the behaviour of large groups, for example, about illiteracy and religious activity, are susceptible of treatment in this [statistical] way, and indeed permit of no other'. This is very true, since quantitative analysis allows us both to test existing hypotheses and to generate new ones. But just as there are other ways of measuring literacy so too are there other modes of understanding it. Quantification tells us about the structures of literacy in Scottish and English society, but reveals little about the importance of literacy in cultural, social, economic and political life. We have already looked at some of the reasons why men and women might wish to become literate. It was becoming simpler, cheaper and safer to understand reading, writing and counting. Now let us examine how compelling these reasons for literacy actually were.

Much of the discussion so far has been predicated upon the common assumption that literacy is an important, desirable capability which all individuals would wish to acquire. It is also usual to accept that all societies will eventually achieve mass literacy and that until this is attained full economic, social and intellectual development cannot occur. Thus the focus of interest on the period between the Renaissance and the Industrial Revolution which saw the beginnings of the transition from restricted to mass literacy in Europe and North America.

The pervasive experience of literate culture among scholars means that oral forms tend to be seen as second best. The late twentieth century assumes that there is a great divide between literate and non-literate societies, and between persons who can and cannot read and write. Printed literature and mass literacy are historically unusual, but it is assumed that societies without them lack 'access to that part of culture which we would normally regard as among the most valuable parts of our intellectual heritage and perhaps the main medium through which we can express and deepen mankind's intellectual and artistic insight'.[1] Editing Sir Walter Scott's Border ballads at the end of the nineteenth century, T. F. Henderson begged consideration of the backward state of society, in view of which 'the reader must not expect to find, in the Border ballads, refined sentiment, and, far less, elegant expression'.[2] This sort of romantic but patronizing outlook characterizes many studies of non-literate cultures which are said to have lacked any proper means to communicate ideas and information: in short, cultures 'without deliberate intellectual probing or aesthetic insight, submerged . . . in an unmoving and communal quagmire'.[3] The other side of this tradition is to claim great things for literacy's potential for civilizing people and broadening their intellectual horizons. These are powerful assumptions, but they suffer from both anachronism and cultural arrogance.

We must question the simplistic notion of a non-literate society as somehow a culturally substandard version of a literate one, comprised of people 'less creative, thoughtful, self-aware or individually sensitive'.[4] As Buchan has argued for eighteenth-century Scotland, the oral tradition is a complex and demanding artistic form in itself: not just a poorly developed sort of literate tradition but something imaginatively quite different.[5] Until the nineteenth or even the twentieth century, literacy was not an essential skill for many Scottish or English people. We shall see that while literacy and education were important in seventeenth- and eighteenth-century Britain, the significance of oral forms remained strong and the usefulness of academic learning was not as obvious as we might assume.

First of all it is unlikely that illiteracy was a total state, since it was everywhere face to face with literacy. E. P. Thompson describes the distinction between oral and literate as

fuzzy at every point in the eighteenth century: the illiterate hear the products of literacy read aloud in taverns and they may accept from the literate culture some categories, while many of the literate employ their very limited literate

---

[1] R. Finnegan, 'Literacy versus non-literacy' (1973): 113–14.
[2] Henderson (1902): 160.   [3] Finnegan (1973): 135.   [4] *Ibid*. 144.
[5] Buchan (1972): 51–61.

skills only instrumentally (writing invoices, keeping accounts) while their 'wisdom' and customs are still transmitted within a pre-literate oral culture.[6]

Oral and literate culture were not separate and illiterates were not necessarily denied access to written forms. Those living in close physical proximity to anyone who could read had access to literacy – servants in their masters' households, labourers from their employers or neighbours in local communities, women from their husbands or fathers. People did not have to be able to read and write themselves to gain access to the products of literate culture. Reading and writing were by no means social and economic necessities for every individual. The seventeenth-century Lancashire apprentice Roger Lowe was often approached by friends and acquaintances who wished him to write out personal letters or legal documents.[7] The journal of Adam Eyre, a Yorkshire gentleman, is peppered with instances when he read or wrote for friends and acquaintances. In 1647 William Barber dropped in on Eyre after dinner 'to get mee [to] reade him some writings', and in the following year Eyre drew up a deed of sale for some land along with an apprentice indenture on behalf of a friend.[8] A seventeenth-century English chapbook called the *Country's counsellor, or everyman his own lawyer* gives the form of a will, bond, receipt and apprentice indenture for ordinary laymen to copy.[9] English communities of the seventeenth and eighteenth centuries had 'edge-lawyers', local people who would write out such documents as well as offering advice on the law. Eyre is an example.[10]

The point is that a person with the requisite reading and writing skills could be found in almost any circumstance when literacy was needed. Part of an arrangement to establish a 'stock-purse' or insurance scheme for Loanhead coalworkers in early eighteenth-century Midlothian was a provision which allowed colliers to ask for a copy of the yearly accounts.[11] Most were illiterate, but provided only one of their number could read and cast accounts they could maintain the required checks on managerial addition. As late as the 1930s George Orwell related how, at the end of a hop-picking expedition when wages were paid, illiterate people would bring their tally books to himself and other 'scholars' to check the sometimes dubious addition of the farm cashiers.[12] One assumes that a similar strategy would have been available to other low-status people, such as the seasonal harvest

[6] E. P. Thompson, 'Eighteenth-century English society' (1978): 155.
[7] W. L. Sachse (ed.), *The diary of Roger Lowe, 1663–74* (1938).
[8] Eyre (1877): 2, 49, 56, 92, 114.   [9] Spufford (1981): 60–1.   [10] Neuburg (1971): 31.
[11] SRO GD18/695: fol. 81; GD18/1017.   [12] G. Orwell, *Collected essays*, vol. 1 (1970): 92.

workers who migrated from the uplands of northern England or Highland Scotland to the Northumberland littoral or to the Lothians and the Berwickshire Merse during the eighteenth and nineteenth centuries. There were always literate intermediaries available, and Roger Schofield is probably wrong to state that there were social groups and areas of England 'which were entirely cut off from any contact with the literate culture'.[13]

In addition to these amateur scribes and intermediaries, local communities might also boast professional or semi-professional writers. In Scotland, notaries public were available even in comparatively small communities and were used particularly for writing and authenticating important documents. Notaries were professional scribes who wrote out legal documents. They existed to keep the pool of known writers closed and thus to limit the possibility of forgery. Notaries provided safeguards against forgery by the use of an individualized signum, their presence ensuring uniform standards in documents and restricting writers to a manageable number whose credentials could be checked.

From the fifteenth century, the sphere of activity of Scottish notaries public was generally wider than their English counterparts.[14] These men tended to be concentrated in towns, but there was a notary public living and working in the small village of Lasswade near Edinburgh throughout the second half of the seventeenth century. England did not develop a notarial system because of the limited influence of Roman law on bureaucratic and legal procedures. In the medieval period, reading and writing were specialist skills exercised by experts on behalf of the community. In Scotland, the development of a body of lay literate servants in the sixteenth century broke the clerical monopoly of writing and occasioned a downwards spread of literacy.[15] In the fifteenth century writing had been confined to specialists in the church, administration and law. Only the Session clerk or precentor was supposed to write in the Kirk Session register to prevent falsification. In 1702 the elders of Penicuik in Midlothian were reprimanded for allowing other hands in the Session minutes, and were warned that 'nothing be written in the registers but by the session clerk his own hand'.[16] Personal subscriptions are comparatively rare in many Scottish records. There were attempts by the secular literate to retain a monopoly of reading and writing, but these clearly did not inhibit the

[13] Schofield (1968): 313.   [14] Clanchy (1979): 235–6, 241–2; Simpson (1973): 7–8.
[15] Wormald (1981): 23; Simpson (1973): 8; Spufford (1981): 15.
[16] SRO CH2/424/8: fol. 192.

spread of literacy. The presence of professional scribes did not necessarily prevent ordinary people from writing for themselves.

Reading and writing were not social necessities and illiterates were not wholly cut off from literate ways. In the same way, those who spoke a distinct language or dialect were not wholly divorced from communication with other groups. In Highland Scotland during the sixteenth, seventeenth and eighteenth centuries three languages were in use: Gaelic (both in its literary and dialect forms), Latin and Scots, the latter two being the medium of government.[17] During this period, Latin and Scots gained ground among the upper levels of Highland society under the stimulus of increasing participation in church, university education and government, all of which were dominated by Lowland institutions. There were further influences which favoured Scots and Latin over Gaelic. Among landowners, for example, a command of English was essential for the 'service of heirs' or formal transfer of inherited property, especially in the Western Isles where male primogeniture obtained. In the Highlands proper, knowledge of Scots or Latin was rare even among the upper classes until the later sixteenth century. However, Gaelic-speakers were not necessarily isolated from the dominant external culture of the Lowlanders and upper-class Highlanders who used the English language or Latin for communication. Colin Campbell, formerly changekeeper in Tobermory but living at Auchadashennag in Argyll stated in his deposition before Argyll Justiciary Court that he had seen papers relating to the customs duty on herring but 'not having the English language not able to read and wryte did not know the contents thereof but was told'.[18]

Clearly men like Campbell were dependent on literate people, and especially on certain types of bilingual figures – 'brokers' who mediated between the 'Little' tradition of Highland society and the 'Great' one of the Lowlands, between speakers of subordinate and dominant languages.[19] In essence, the Great Tradition is a sort of cultural form which is national and uniform and dominant. The Little Tradition is local, varied and subordinate. The Great Tradition originates outside a community and is imported into it, becoming more or less firmly established by a process of constant interaction. English schools and the English language are good examples of this tradition, as we have already seen.

People adapted to the penetration of the English language. Originally an alien importation into a mainly Gaelic culture, English language and Lowland culture gradually became integrated into the existing

[17] Bannerman (1983): 214–15; Shaw (1981): 5, 31.   [18] Imrie (1969): 285–6.
[19] R. Redfield, *The little community* (1960): 42–4.

social structure, while also altering it. One way this adjustment was brought about was through people who could speak both languages. Gentry and itinerant pedlars were two examples of the bilingual elements in Highland society. In the statements of evidence in a 1716 case before the Argyll Justiciary Court involving wounding and threatened arson we are told that John Campbell of Barwilline, the accused, was heard talking to a chapman. Their conversation was overheard by John McCallum in Kirktoun of Strathphillan who told how 'sometimes they spoke in Irish and sometimes in English but that the deponent did not understand what they said when they spoke English'.[20] Lairds, clergy and pedlars had equal access to elements of both Highland and Lowland culture and could mediate for the many who knew only one of the two cultures. These sorts of people would be concentrated in towns on the edge of the Highlands such as Dunkeld, Inverness or the Falkirk cattle tryst where English and Gaelic vied for the ear of those in the streets and other public places, despite the fact that English was the 'official' language.[21] Towards the end of the eighteenth century at Crieff in Perthshire it was said that Gaelic was spoken in the town itself and up to three or four miles away to the north and west. However, in the low-lying part of the parish people could neither speak nor understand it.[22]

The third sort of intermediary or broker between different cultures was the notary public who would be versed in Latin, Scots and Gaelic. Finally there were the Gaelic bards. The core of lay literacy in the sixteenth century, some of these were skilled in both literary and dialect Gaelic as well as in Scots.[23] Gaelic monoglots were not wholly divorced from the dominant culture, but they would often have depended on intermediaries who were drawn from the social and political elite. Indeed, linguistic divisions could reinforce social ones. At Callander in Perthshire in the late eighteenth century the language spoken by 'persons of rank and of liberal education' was English, but the lower classes made do with Gaelic.[24]

The importance of oral and literate forms could vary markedly for different individuals not only in the Highlands but throughout early modern Britain. There were clearly some people, especially in the eighteenth century, who seem to have been thoroughly at home in a literate milieu, though this does not imply that they were necessarily distanced from oral forms. The diary of the reverend James Clegg of Chapel-en-le-Frith, Derbyshire contains frequent references to the

[20] Imrie (1969): 325.   [21] Haldane (1952): 141.   [22] *OSA*, vol. 9 (1793): 591.
[23] Bannerman (1983): 218–19, 229.   [24] *OSA*, vol. 11 (1794): 611–12.

occasions he spent 'at home all day reading and writing'. In 1729 he can be found buying books on a visit to Manchester. When his son was apprenticed, Clegg gave him a family Bible and received letters from him during his indenture in Manchester.[25] Adam Eyre's diary is full of occasions when he wrote and received letters, read and annotated books, or bought, borrowed and loaned them. Ralph Josselin, the Essex vicar, could read in Latin and was striving to learn Hebrew.[26] In the early nineteenth century the Scottish farm labourer Alexander Somerville preferred to associate with literate, thoughtful people, 'men above the average rate of intelligence, and many pleasant hours I had with them, conversing about books, sometimes buying books together, and frequently borrowing and lending them to read'.[27]

Both these sorts of men would have felt dissociated from the mass of their fellows, Clegg and Josselin from the illiterate and ungodly among their parishioners, Somerville from the drink-oriented culture of many of his fellow labourers. There were indeed sections of society which were tending to dissociate themselves from the traditional communal sociabilities and predominantly oral culture in both Scotland and England. The withdrawal of the upper classes, along with elements of the middling sort and even some of the lower orders, from traditional cultural forms is clear in the radical divergences in literary tastes which developed over the period 1500–1800.[28] Ballads and stories became confined to the lowest social levels in both Scotland and England. Literacy may not have been essential for social and economic life but it was spreading through British society and this was producing important cultural changes.

The importance of reading and writing for some sections of eighteenth-century society was clearly growing. However, cultural forms which were geared to oral communication remained strong even in the seventeenth and eighteenth centuries. Illiteracy was not a total state. Nor did orality and literacy form separate cultural compartments. There were certainly practices which would help to bridge the gap between any distinctly 'oral' and 'literate' mental world which might have existed. One was the convention of reading aloud and thus sharing what was read. Alexander Somerville used to read to his fellow workers in the fields of the Berwickshire Merse when he was only fourteen, and later averred that this was more entertaining and sociable than reading alone. In fact his own interest in reading had itself

[25] V. S. Doe (ed.), *The diary of James Clegg* (1978): 29, 32, 79, 81.
[26] Eyre (1877): 42, 62, 78, 92–3; Hockliffe (1908): 62.   [27] Somerville (1951): 71, 90–1.
[28] Burke (1978): 270–86; Wrightson (1982): 183–221; Buchan (1972); Spufford (1981): 14.

been inspired by tale-telling.[29] The person who introduced him to Burns could read, but preferred to recite aloud from memory when in company. James Hogg, a Border shepherd during the nineteenth century, was similarly stimulated to revive and improve his reading skills by hearing and then memorizing Burns' 'Tam o' Shanter'.[30] As late as the early twentieth century, George Orwell recalled that it was the custom for the newspaper to be read aloud in the home.[31]

Some printed literature of the period was designed for just this purpose. The layout of narrative in popular chapbooks suggests they were meant to be read slowly and probably aloud. Simple text was backed up by woodcuts which stimulated imagination so that there was 'a direct continuation of habits formed when transmission of pictures and ideas was through oral communication'.[32] We pause to wonder whether the advent of literacy really did reduce 'the importance of the oral community's entertainment, proverbs, riddling sessions and tale telling' at least before the nineteenth century.[33] Reading aloud and a preference for listening rather than reading helped the illiterate to cope with advances in literate media. In Scottish civil and criminal courts charges and statements were usually read aloud, partly because of widespread illiteracy but also to promote 'more terrification' as well as through ossified convention.[34] When Sir John Clerk of Penicuik was trying to correct his troublesome coalworkers in the Loanhead pits near Edinburgh, he ordered his officials to read out his condemnations of their behaviour and his recommendations for improvement 'over and over again' for maximum effect.[35] In less formal situations we can be sure that there was a hearing as well as a reading public for script and print. Reading aloud meant that people could learn about what was in books without necessarily being able to read the printed page for themselves.

In judicial, religious and recreational contexts the continued emphasis on the spoken word slowed down the trend towards the literate forms which have come to dominate twentieth-century culture and society. James Hogg, the nineteenth-century 'Ettrick Shepherd', believed that the publication of Walter Scott's *Minstrelsy of the Scottish Border* had a damaging impact on the singing of songs and telling of tales which 'had floated down on the stream of oral tradition, from generation to generation'. 'A deadening blow was inflicted on our rural literature and principal enjoyment by the very means adopted for

---

[29] Somerville (1951): 42–3, 47, 91.   [30] Craig (1961): 114.   [31] Orwell (1970): 588.
[32] H.-J. Martin, 'The *bibliothèque bleue*' (1978): 88.   [33] Spufford (1981): 13.
[34] SRO CH2/424/3: 13 February 1640.   [35] Marshall (1980): 240.

their preservation.' Hogg further believed that as a result people 'have ten times more opportunities of learning songs, yet song-singing is at an end, or only kept up by a few migratory tailors'.[36] In practice however the oral and literate traditions would run in parallel: as in the case of Gaelic stories and literature which complemented each other.[37] Oral and literate forms were not mutually exclusive, but existed in a sort of symbiotic relationship. At the same time the example of the north-east of Scotland in the eighteenth century reminds us that high adult male literacy does not at all preclude a strong oral tradition.[38]

The presence of writing in a society could effect oral tradition, but it is also possible that oral and literate traditions could exist simultaneously in different social groups or even within the same sections of society. Women were particularly important in preserving oral forms, especially in the transitional period from c.1700–1900 when mass literacy was attained for males, but much more slowly for females. Speaking and hearing would be more important than reading and writing for them. At the same time the older generation would preserve oral forms longer than the young during periods of improving literacy levels, and with the demise of more egalitarian and communally oriented local communities in favour of socially polarized ones, oral forms would become concentrated in the lower social groups.[39] The status of the perpetuators of the oral tradition would decline as literacy became the province of the upper sections of society and of men, and as it greatly reduced the possibilities for ordinary people creatively to participate in certain cultural forms. We may wonder about the impact on community and family relationships in the Highlands which the programme of anglicization through education might have had, since it would create divergent values and languages between old and young. Conceivably the fact that men as a group saw faster rises in literacy than women might have widened any cultural gap between the sexes. Unlike oral forms, literacy could ultimately distance some elements of society from others.

Of course, the change would have been slow, mediated through the existing means of socialization. Finally there were areas of Scotland where ballads and tales remained important. In the 1760s Thomas Pennant recorded of parts of the Western Highlands that 'the amusements by their fire-sides were, the telling of tales, the wildest and most extravagant imaginable: musick was another'.[40] What was learned from books did not immediately replace experience but only provided

---

[36] Hogg (1831–2): 257.   [37] Bannerman (1983): 224.   [38] Buchan (1972).
[39] *Ibid*. 171–89, 273–5; Craig (1961): 118–19.   [40] Pennant (1774): 195.

another way of understanding and modifying it. The printed or written page was meaningful only to those who knew already what to
expect from it, and consequently how to interpret it.

We can see the co-existence of oral and literate traditions as part of a
long and gradual change from memory to written record, one stage of
which has been documented by Michael Clanchy for medieval
England. The examples of symbiosis between oral and literate forms
which he mentions can be replicated centuries after the end of his
period. Record-keeping was helping to render information more
certain, but the extent to which memory continued to be important was
considerable even in the seventeenth century. In 1659 William Stoddart approached Lasswade Kirk Session on his return from some years
in Poland for a testimonial of his past life and honest character so that
he could marry. He was the son of John Stoddart and Marion Wilson in
Gourton who had left the parish for Edinburgh when William was a
child. The minister and elders found the parents' marriage in the
parish register for July 1619, but, since there was no baptism record at
this time, 'four aged and famous men' were found who 'declared that
they were not only witnesses to the ... marriage but were also
witnesses to the said William his baptism'.[41] Collective oral testimony
was used in the absence of proper documentation, though which form
was preferred is not clear. If anything, memory was probably less
important in Scottish legal procedures than in English, because of the
emphasis in Roman law on written records.

Pew disputes before the church courts in England offer another illustration of the process of transition from memory to written record.
John Wardell of Haughton, County Durham, a septuagenarian
gentleman stated in his deposition before Durham Consistory Court
that his father had died twenty-seven years previously at the age of
eighty; he had left Haughton forty-nine years before yet continued to
talk of the pew in question. Memory would be confirmed in the form of
a written judgement from the Consistory Court, which would form a
reference point, but which was nevertheless subject to change in the
future. Wardell admitted that his testimony was to 'the best of his
remembrance and belief'.[42] Oral tradition was selective and custom
was far from immutable. Memory could be an integrating force in the
community, as when the bounds of a parish were beaten in medieval
and early modern English parishes. But the selective element might
follow social divisions, as in the case of access to common rights or the
nature of an interest in a piece of land. In the medieval period we know

[41] SRO CH2/471/3: 6 February 1659.
[42] DPDD Durham Consistory Court depositions: Bendlowes 1758–60.

that custom established in memory and written record could be altered to suit different economic circumstances or the particular interests of certain social groups.[43] 'General belief and opinion' might be specific to certain occasions. The memories which survived as part of official records were not a cross-section of current ideas, but were those appropriate to specific conjunctures which were selected through the filter of existing political, social and institutional forms. In the same way, the forms which written language took were not derived from majority parlance but from those with social and political influence. The Gaelic scribal tradition is a good example, as is written Scots, which was an anglicized version of what most people spoke. Oral tradition may have been a way of preserving cultural identity when control of written forms was largely in the hands of the ruling elite. Oral culture was in many cases strong enough to resist mere correction and standardization from above.

There were other reasons why the dominance of literate culture was only slowly won. Print, for example, was not always preferred as a communications medium. For many purposes manuscript was still superior to print for speed and discretion. Margaret Aston tends to play down the role of print in the development of English Lollardy, which instead flourished through varying modes of attaining literacy such as rote learning and handwritten tracts.[44] Handbills inciting to riot in late eighteenth- and early nineteenth-century Scotland were generally handwritten. While the handwriting could be traced this was less easy than locating a printer if the authorities came to seek retribution. In any case, there is no direct evidence of participation in riot because of reading handbills.[45] Their role was probably peripheral to the usual oral modes of transmitting discontent, which were faster and more effective in any case. This mode of dissemination may account for the strong but comparatively ill-informed religious and political opinions of some members of British society at this time. Unnecessarily condescending though he is, Webb is partly correct to say that such ideas as the working class had 'in political and social matters came, not from the exercise of reason, but from experience, economic necessity, a vague but important sense of justice and dignity, a preference for collective action, and infection by better-informed and more active fellow workers'.[46]

Literacy itself was not an adequate precondition of radical politicization; nor did illiteracy preclude it. The 'impudent women' who made

---

[43] R. M. Smith, 'Some thoughts on hereditary and proprietary rights in land' (1983).
[44] Aston (1977): 359.   [45] K. J. Logue, *Popular disturbances in Scotland* (1979): 204–6.
[46] Webb (1955): 160.

a 'noise and clamour' over the call of a new minister to Lasswade in 1710 may provide an example. The aspirant whom they supported was 'an other than any of these betwixt whom the competition was' and in the end they 'acknowledged their folly therein'.[47] Women appear in most early modern records as implicitly ill-informed and of weak judgement, a fact which has much to do with their low literacy and their subjection to male-dominated educational ideas. Nevertheless, we do find examples of women leading and articulating opinion on occasions such as riots.[48] The likelihood is that they would have depended on oral forms of communication. This did not automatically render women unimportant. They certainly participated in what we should call political activity. The spokesperson for the coalworkers at the Loanhead mines near Edinburgh on the occasion of a lockout by the owner in 1703 was one Margaret Girdwood.[49] We can even suggest that because women were more commonly found in the market places of early modern Britain buying and selling produce they would be crucial transmitters of information and ideas gleaned from those they met.

Oral modes of communicating political ideas through the interactions of market place and tavern were of considerable importance. There were certainly attempts to influence popular political awareness through printed or written propaganda. Upper-class propaganda was sometimes formated to resemble popular pamphlets, chapbooks or news sheets and might be distributed free when a quick, widespread impact was desired.[50] Propaganda was distributed at times of political uncertainty, such as the 1640s in England or in 1710 when, at the time of the Parliamentary elections:

Rehearsalls and other news Papers were writ and scattered to perplex the conciences of the people about the succession to the crown, the state ministers Blackened, our successes abroad lessened and misinterpreted, our losses aggravated, Passive obedience and Hereditary right and the crown preachd upon.[51]

The clergyman who records this may not have been as closely in touch with the rumours circulating at this time. Indeed, oral communication was probably the most important form until much later than this. In the later seventeenth century it is likely that only the leaders of society were reached by printed propaganda. Almanacs were used for propaganda purposes at the time of the Anti-Corn Law agitation, but it is not certain whether the audience was genuinely a mass one.[52]

---

[47] SRO CH2/424/9: fols. 303–4.
[48] Logue (1979); Thompson (1971); J. Walter and K. Wrightson, 'Dearth and the social order' (1976).
[49] SRO GD18/695: fol. 114.   [50] Webb (1955): 159.   [51] Doe (1978): 3.
[52] O'Day (1982): 17; Webb (1955): 29.

The slow reception of what we might see as a distinctively literate mode of thought along with the differences between the mental worlds of those who would be classed as 'literate' is shown in methods of dating events. At the English church courts the first few lines of any deposition usually explain the circumstances which surrounded the deponent's knowledge of the events at issue. Testifying before Durham Consistory Court about events concerning the Northern Rising were two men. Robert Helme was aged thirty-six, a gentleman living in Tynemouth. The other was Robert Handforth of Ovingham, a 40-year-old yeoman. Both signed their depositions.[53] Helme referred to the event in question happening 'anno domine 1570', adding the regnal year of 12 Elizabeth during the month of November. Handforth, meanwhile, described the same occasion as 'the yere next after the commotion last past about iii weeks or a moneth before harvest that yere'. Recent significant events were used by Handforth for dating rather than the reference which Helme made to a documented time continuum. Both men provided good signatures yet seem to have been living in distinct mental worlds which depended on their existing cultural milieu and the depth and duration of their immersion in literate forms. The speed of penetration of a literate mentality seems to have varied considerably between different social groups and in different experiential contexts. The way of locating events in time which the yeoman Handforth used was characteristic of an oral culture where, before written forms had been deeply internalized, people did not feel themselves situated every moment of their lives in abstract computed time of any sort.[54] For Helme, the gentleman, the world was seen in a quite different way.

Dating procedures provide an example of the selective way literacy penetrated the mind of early modern individuals and ultimately demanded changes in the way people articulated their thoughts, both individually and collectively in society. We must allow that the literate habits and assumptions which made up a literate mentality could take many generations to spread. Even in the eighteenth century deponents can be found dating events by pre-Reformation feast days. The practical skill of literacy did not immediately and automatically bring with it all the fully literate habits of mind.[55] Assimilation of literacy was mediated through existing mental patterns in a way far more complex and selective than some recent writers like Spufford have perhaps allowed. As Thomas à Kempis said of one of these contexts, 'The voice of books informs not all alike.'[56]

---

[53] DPDD DR5/4: fols. 6v, 7.   [54] W. J. Ong, *Orality and literacy* (1982): 97.
[55] Clanchy (1979): 150; Buchan (1972): 193.   [56] Quoted in Aston (1977): 347.

This was true not only of manuscript but also of print, for which a great deal has been claimed. For Elizabeth Eisenstein, 'changes in mental habits and attitudes entailed by access to printed materials affected a wide social spectrum from the outset'.[57] Once printing was established, 'learning by doing became more sharply distinguished from learning by reading, while the role played by hearsay and memory arts diminished'.[58] Printing provided a cheap, standardized and effective way of disseminating ideas. For those who could read and understand books the effect of attitudes could be profound. The diarist Adam Eyre read voraciously and 'had varyous thoughts by reason of the varyety of men's opinions I find in reading'.[59] The immediate impact and long-term ramifications of printing could be substantial.

Yet we must be careful not to see this happening too quickly. The masses 'were not passive recipients (neither passive beneficiaries nor passive victims) of a new type of communication. Rather they were active users and interpreters of the printed books they heard and read, and even helped give these books form.'[60] Perhaps the best-known example of the interplay between oral and literate traditions is that which took place among ballad forms. Well-known stories from the oral tradition were enhanced by reading, and in turn their popularity helped to lend prestige to the printed word. Eisenstein speculates that 'most rural villagers ... probably belong to an exclusively hearing public down to the nineteenth century. Yet what they heard had, in many instances, been transformed by printing.' In England by 1700 printed ballads, chapbooks and plays had already made an indelible mark on oral tradition. Even here print may not have helped to kill the oral tradition but may have helped in its preservation and diffusion.[61] Ballads and stories might originate in oral culture, be written and possibly altered by educated, literate men before being returned to the communities from whence they had come for still further modification and incorporation into local cultures. Oral and literate cultures, Great and Little Traditions, were constantly interacting.

Oral and literate forms meshed in with one another in a way reminiscent of the syncretic religion of the medieval and early modern period. Their forms were worked out gradually in a way which lends further weight to the idea that oral culture was not a passive recipient of the supposedly powerful literate influences. A case of charming

---

[57] E. Eisenstein, 'Some conjectures about the impact of printing' (1968): 5.
[58] *Ibid.* 6.   [59] Eyre (1977): 67.   [60] Davis (1975): 225.
[61] Eisenstein (1968): 30; Burke (1978): 253–6; Spufford (1981): 9–12; Neuburg (1971): 122, 141; Martin (1978): 74.

brought before Dalkeith presbytery in May 1637 provides a neat illustration.[62] John Archer consulted a local landowner about the theft of certain goods. The laird told Archer to give him a piece of paper on which the names of the suspects were to be written, after which he would return one piece of paper with the name of the prime suspect on it. This was a traditional aspect of 'white' witchcraft detection procedures in the medieval and early modern period.[63] In seventeenth-century England the procedure adopted sometimes involved placing a key inside a book, usually a Bible. The names of the suspects would be written down on slips of paper which were placed in the hollow end of the key. When the name of the guilty person was inserted the book would vibrate in the holder's hand and the key would fall out. Writing may have been invested with a special symbolism in these situations. Ong argues that in some societies writing had a magical association – it was regarded as an instrument of secret and magic power.[64] Over the subsequent century this form of conjuring did not become a wholly literate affair, but began to die out as part of a more 'rational' approach to crime, its detection and social relations which is epitomized by the growing use during the eighteenth century of newspaper advertisements to help in the apprehension and prosecution of felons.

At the same time, written documents contained many repetitious clauses and symbols, suggesting that the importance of writing was less than it would appear. In medieval England and in early modern Scotland symbolic objects alone could serve as instruments transferring property.[65] An official register of land transactions, the Register of Sasines, was set up in Scotland in 1617. The written instruments which comprise the title and the written record contain a number of stock phrases plus symbolic steps such as the handing over of a clod of earth. The witnesses who subscribed the actual instruments of sasine were observers of the transfer of the handful of earth. This was a survival from a time when bearing witness was the most important aspect of contracts. With the written instrument of sasine buyer and seller had the best of both worlds, the certainty of symbol and written contract which conveyed conviction to literate and non-literate alike.

The same mixture of forms can be found in the transfer of moveable property. Once subscribed and sealed, wills were held up and declared out loud to be the last will and testament in a way which suggests that the oral, symbolic side may have been as important as the written one.[66]

---

[62] SRO CH2/424/2.   [63] K. Thomas, *Religion and the decline of magic* (1973): 254.
[64] Ong (1982): 93.   [65] Clanchy (1979): 232; Ong (1982): 97.
[66] DPDD Probate records 1757: Dodd v. Charlton.

Witnesses to Scottish wills were there only to attest that the document had been approved by the testator as an accurate record of his wishes. The will-maker had no need to subscribe the testament himself and the witnesses did not necessarily concern themselves with its contents. These examples may of course be pure anachronism – outdated forms which though widespread had lost their significance. The relative importance of written and symbolic forms may have shifted in favour of the former. Clanchy believes that in England wills had by 1300 come to depend primarily on correct written form rather than verbal assurances of witnesses, though nuncupative wills are still common in England even in the seventeenth century.[67] Richard Clyffe who lived at the salt pans near South Shields 'declared his testament and last wyll nuncupative, before certeine honest witnesses'. The copy in Durham Consistory Court papers states the terms of his will, recording 'whyche woordes or the lyke in effecte he sayd, spoke, declared and wylled to be done'.[68]

The importance of symbolic elements alongside written ones on documents probably declined over time, so that ultimately in literate societies writing played the part performed by collective rituals in oral civilizations. Yet there were other purely symbolic and visual aspects to some writing. For example, it is plain that at least a few of the illiterate deponents in testamentary cases could recognize the style of handwriting and the form of a common document even if they could not actually read the words contained therein. This form of recognition by comprehending an overall impression rather than specific words fits in well with the importance of certain types of visual propaganda.[69] Forgeries of medieval charters were aimed at making a document which looked the same as a preconceived notion of a charter, however erroneous that might be.[70] Forgeries of Scottish testimonials, the certificates people needed to move from one parish to another, looked like authentic documents of the kind written by parish clerks at the time, but the quality of handwriting, the precise form of words and errors in the names were a giveaway to the parish officials charged with running the system. Ability to distinguish good from bad coin suggests a familiarity with the visual as well as the tactile qualities of money. Signs in public places became increasingly common in the eighteenth century, and court depositions show that places were more and more identified by reference to these. Again, the influence of the written word could be mediated through existing forms and understandings. The use of

---

[67] Clanchy (1979): 203.   [68] *Wills*, pt III (1906): 97.
[69] R. W. Scribner, *For the sake of simple folk* (1981): 1–13.   [70] Clanchy (1979): 249.

visual symbols was particularly effective among a largely illiterate population, but even in the early nineteenth century the woodcut was still widely used in popular literature.[71] We cannot be certain what role these visual elements performed at this time, since studies of literature elsewhere in Europe have argued that illustrations which were designed to elucidate the text in early sixteenth-century publications eventually became simple embellishments in later periods.[72]

The interaction between oral and literate cultures is epitomized in one final example which deals with a transitory contact between professional purveyors of the two forms. Thomas Harrison, a yeoman of fifty-six years of age when he gave testimony before the English Northern Circuit assize court in 1764, had been born at Knaresborough in Yorkshire.[73] He was trained to be a maltmaker 'but has for several years past got his livelihood by hawking and selling books and pamphlets about the country'. Harrison bought books in the important chapbook publishing centre of Newcastle to sell in the towns and villages of Northumberland and Durham. On his travels he met a woman and her child, travelled with them for a time before splitting up after an argument. Some days later he met and drank in Newcastle with a ballad singer who told him the whereabouts of the woman and of her regrets about the row. This reminds us of the continued importance of the oral tradition both in terms of ballad singing and as a quick, effective means of passing information, rumour and propaganda in an age when other modes of communication were slow and unreliable.

What can we say by way of conclusion? It may seem perverse in a study of reading and writing to stress the continuing importance of oral culture. Yet we must recognize that while literacy could be a valuable skill, it was not by any means essential for every purpose. Once acquired, its impact on the mental world of early modern people was neither immediate nor total. Its value to individual and society was not automatic nor necessarily very great.

This is one way of looking at the uses of literacy. We can further question the benefits of literacy and education by examining what was taught in schools and the sorts of attitude which underlay the provision of and demand for education. Literacy had some practical benefits and it could be 'a good thing'. But there are many other dimensions to the way we can understand 'the uses of literacy'. Seen in their correct political context literacy and education are very far from value free. Literacy might be a simple tool which helped ordinary men and women to lead a fuller religious life and to participate in more complex

[71] Webb (1955): 25–6. [72] Chrisman (1982): 106. [73] PRO ASSI45: 27/2/47.

social and economic relationships. Education and literacy can fulfil a general social need, but they can also serve the needs of some social groups more than others. Literacy could be a force for change, but it could also be a means of ensuring social stability and continuity. If we are to weigh up the distinctiveness of Scotland's educational tradition we must consider whether the advantages and opportunities created by education and literacy were superior to those of England or of other European countries. While we have already questioned the notion of equality of access to education in seventeenth- and eighteenth-century Scotland, we can assess the importance of this myth to Scottish society, past and present.

7

The politics of literacy

Despite the continued importance of oral forms, the claims made for literacy and education both by early modern reformers and by later historians have been far from modest. We noticed in chapter 4 how difficult it is to explain why and how men and women came to learn reading and writing. In chapter 6 we also introduced the idea that historians have been influenced by a powerful intellectual tradition, which assumes that literacy is automatically a benefit to individual and society, and a value-free one at that. In Tolstoy's *Anna Karenina*, Levin's brother Koznyshev asks rhetorically: 'Can there be two opinions on the advantage of education? If it's a good thing for you, it's a good thing for everyone.'[1] This assumption, implicit and explicit, pervades writing on literacy and education.

At the same time the broad outlines of literacy attainments which we demonstrated in chapter 2 are really only a starting-point for understanding the various implications of the ability to read and write. Statistics are important if we are to test our assumptions about literacy and to generate new hypotheses which we can investigate. However, we must also explain the patterns which we uncover and unravel their importance by placing them in the context of the society as a whole. Harvey Graff sums up the importance of context very neatly when he observes that 'The measurement of the distribution of literacy in a given population may reveal relatively little about the uses to which those skills could be put and the demands they could meet.'[2] We have seen some of the political and social context of literacy and illiteracy in the sections of chapter 2 on women and the Highlands of Scotland. Now we must be much more explicit about the precise significance of literacy and education to individuals, particular social groups and the

[1] L. Tolstoy, *Anna Karenina* (1978): 264.   [2] H. J. Graff, 'Introduction' (1981): 9.

society as a whole. Literacy could clearly be an asset in economic, social and legal interactions as well as in religious life. But we need to look more closely at the attitudes of individuals and groups towards literacy and learning as well as at their practical impact on society.

The most important questions which we need to answer are first, how did people perceive the value of education and literacy, second what influence did they have in shaping Scottish and English society in the seventeenth and eighteenth centuries? Did Scotland have a special national identity which was strongly reinforced by a distinctive educational system that allowed poor but gifted boys, 'lads o' pairts', to rise in society through their own merits? If so, what were the implications for Scottish society compared to English? Why did some sections of society desire education and why did certain groups provide it? Was literacy altogether 'a good thing'? Did it help to reinforce rather than break down social divisions? Was it a force for change or a reason for stability? This chapter addresses itself to these issues.

Practical uses of literacy

The most common view of literacy is that it is an unqualified good. Reading, writing and counting are seen as central to the happiness and prosperity of the individual and to the economic and political development of a society. No less a person than the director-general of UNESCO has claimed that only mass literacy makes possible 'the liberation and advancement of man' and the ending of 'darkness in the minds of men'.[3] Less exalted personages have echoed these sentiments in asserting that literacy 'changed traditional modes of thought and slackened people's adherence to traditional beliefs and customs'.[4] Printing is seen as an important force which stimulated mental activities and intellectual exchange. Literacy is assumed to be very important for social mobility, effective political and cultural participation, economic and social development.

This questionable view has a long historical lineage. In the 1540s Protector Somerset stated firmly that if 'learning decay, which of wild men maketh civil, of blockish and rash persons wise and godly counsellors, of obstinate rebels subjects, and of evil men good and godly christians, what shall we look for else but barbarism and tumult?'[5] In the early seventeenth century, John Brinsley asked rhetorically 'what maketh a nation to be a glorious nation, but that the

---

[3] Finnegan (1973): 113.   [4] Spufford (1981): 13; Wrightson (1982): 191–9.
[5] Quoted in P. Williams, *The Tudor regime* (1978): 297.

people are a wise and an understanding people?'[6] For the eighteenth-century physiocrats, education was the surest path to political harmony. Reticence was not a common failing in early nineteenth-century commentators and their claims regarding education were no exception. Sir John Sinclair believed that 'the character of a nation' was principally determined 'by the degree in which the mass of the population is enlightened, and by the proportion of the youth, who are early taught to cultivate habits of industry, and to check their vicious propensities'.[7]

Faith in the shaping power of education was firm and enduring. The New Statistical Account of Kilmarnock spoke of education exerting 'a most salutory influence on the conduct and morals of the inhabitants'.[8] For Sir John Sinclair, the aspiration 'to raise any people in the scale of intelligence, is the best means of softening their barbarism, checking their tendency to misrule, – increasing their powers of useful exertion, – enlarging their means of happiness, – and promoting private good, social order and national prosperity'.[9] 'The universal intelligence of the people is the best safeguard of the social order, of freedom and of peace.'[10] 'When children are properly trained, sound principles and virtuous habits are spread over the whole community; and the safety, peace and happiness of society, are more effectually promoted, than by the most perfect system of civil and criminal law.'[11] Crime and illegitimacy would be reduced. In his famous pamphlet of 1834 George Lewis argued that without education society would have to pay 'for the repression of social disorder and for coercing an unhappy, dissolute and reckless population'.[12] Peace, happiness, sobriety and circumspection: much was expected from literacy. Adam Smith believed that the Scots were more law-abiding than the English, thanks to their widespread education – an idea adopted by Thomas Malthus and John Stuart Mill.[13] Brougham and others believed education would limit crime and it was often noted that illiterates were socially pathological types.[14] Moral reformers, spurred on by their pessimistic views of the ignorance of the working class and their belief in the correlation between illegitimacy and illiteracy, continued to stress education's value as a force for moral correctness. Quite what they made of the Highlands of Scotland with their high illiteracy and low illegitimacy we are not sure. Quoting Pinkerton, Sinclair talked of the way in which

---

[6] Quoted in Curtis (1964): 53. [7] Sinclair (1826): 65. [8] *NSA*, vol. 5 (1845): 560.
[9] Sinclair (1826): 71. [10] Quoted in Saunders (1950): 264. [11] Sinclair (1826): 5.
[12] Lewis (1834): 43–4; Sinclair (1826): 5, 90; Knox (1784): xlvi. [13] West (1975): 130–1.
[14] *Speeches and observations of Lord Brougham* (1837): 10; Sinclair (1826): appx. 20.

education 'enables every individual to regulate his feelings, to form right [middle class] habits of thought, and not only to promote his own success in life but the public benefit'.[15]

As an example of this, observers pointed towards the superior intelligence of all social classes in Scotland as the key to her economic advance from 1750 onwards, and by 1853 Gladstone could announce that Scotland's successful position in Europe and her advance from economic and social backwardness was due to the widespread availability of education. This was accomplished through the influence of education on Scotland's people. Its importance lay in 'opening their intellectual horizons and thus breaking the mental cake of irrational custom'.[16] These then are just some of the claims made for literacy and education. To what sort of uses could literacy be put in early modern Britain?

Dissemination of new ideas is seen as a key aspect of literacy's contribution. We can find examples in a variety of contexts. The dissemination of information (or misinformation) on obstetrics and gynaecology in Tudor and Stuart England illustrates the possibilities and limitations of both oral and literate modes of communication. A variety of specialist and non-specialist tracts were available in sixteenth-century England on this subject, but it is difficult to tell how far or how fast the innovations made by key figures in the field filtered down to the bulk of poorly educated women who comprised most midwives. Traditional practices probably persisted in large measure through the oral transmission of women's lore. 'Many midwives indeed could not read at all and were obliged to gain all their knowledge by hearsay and example.'[17] Percival Willughby passed on his newly developed techniques by example and demonstration, yet it appears that whether by this method or by reading the sort of books which contained innovations, changes in obstetric practices were slow to spread. Indeed, popular texts often perpetuated outmoded theories in an attempt to pander to the preconceptions of their public. What was put into print might fix old ideas rather then introduce new ones. Any widespread diffusion of practical informative literature on skills such as medicine might, however, have reduced popular dependence on the mysteries previously monopolized by doctors.

One example illustrates the complex process of disseminating information. In 1545 Thomas Raynald, who revised and reissued the

---

[15] Sinclair (1826): 5.
[16] Smout (1972): 432, 421; R. K. Webb, 'Literacy among the working classes in Scotland' (1954): 100.
[17] A. Eccles, *Obstetrics and gynaecology in Tudor and Stuart England* (1982): 116, 119–20.

earliest English textbook for midwives, *The birth of mankind*, claimed that gentlewomen at confinements 'carienge with them this booke in theyr handes, and causynge such part of it as doth cheifly concerne the same pourpose, to be red before the mydwife, and the rest of the wemen then beyng present'.[18] It is unclear how often literate gentlewomen attended births, but the role of example, the importance of implied endorsement by the upper classes and of reading aloud are all shown, and should serve to indicate that availability of printed didactic material was by no means exclusively important in communicating information.

Literacy is also held to be an important way of disseminating ideas on agricultural improvements. Christopher Smout has argued for Scotland that 'the peasants' literacy greatly assisted the agricultural revolution' of the late eighteenth century because 'the new farming was disseminated in Scotland in books and journals read and sometimes written by the new tenant farmers'.[19] Authorities who have compared the economic performance of Scotland with that of Ireland between 1600 and 1900 feel that Scotland had an advantage in agriculture, since 'an educated peasantry more readily turns its back on immemorial tradition because it finds on the printed page an alternative form of authority'.[20] This begs a number of questions about the readership of informative literature and the means of disseminating innovations in agriculture. In the agriculturally precocious county of Northumberland, Stuart MacDonald has concluded that improving techniques were not disseminated by reading and writing except among the wealthiest farmers.[21] Thirsk has identified correspondence between such men as a means of disseminating new agricultural techniques in the seventeenth century.[22] For most working yeomen, however, example was the principal mode of learning. The spread of innovations could be seriously hindered by social divisions which had developed in the north-east of England and the more agriculturally advanced areas of Lowland Scotland by the late eighteenth century.

The fact that there were new ideas circulating among some farmers does not necessarily mean that they will be available to or widely accepted by all. If precedent and face-to-face interaction were the most important mechanisms for dissemination, mere literacy need not have made much impact against the countervailing influence of social

[18] *Ibid.* 12.
[19] T. C. Smout, 'The role of non-economic factors in Scottish growth' (1970): 7.
[20] L. M. Cullen and T. C. Smout, 'Introduction' (1977): 10.
[21] S. MacDonald, 'The diffusion of knowledge among Northumberland farmers' (1979): 35, 37.
[22] J. Thirsk, 'New crops and their diffusion' (1974).

barriers. Nicholas Breton's countryman was of the opinion that 'we can learn to plow and harrow, sow and reape, and prune, thrash and fanne, winnow and grinde, brue and bake, and all without booke'.[23] We might wonder whether books and pamphlets brought much in the way of new information or whether they changed significantly their reliance on oral transmission and the importance of their social relationships with innovators. In the case of the most literate and most agriculturally precocious areas of late eighteenth-century Britain – south-east Scotland and north-east England – social divisions restricted improvements to large landowners and substantial tenant farmers.[24]

Mark Overton's first-rate study of agricultural change in East Anglia between 1580 and 1740 illustrates the problems in identifying mechanisms of innovation through analysis of the role of printed literature as a source of instruction and information for working farmers.[25] Eric Kerridge has described the spread of new crops and rotations as an 'Agricultural Revolution' in sixteenth- and seventeenth-century England, but exactly how these changes occurred is still unclear. There were a number of practical treatises about farming available to potential agricultural innovators in seventeenth- and eighteenth-century England, though the advice they offered was sometimes not reliable. However, using wills and inventories one can analyse the comparative levels of literacy among those who did and did not adopt new techniques advocated in the literature. In the early seventeenth century those who did innovate were only slightly more literate than their more 'backward' contemporaries and 'the written word was not an essential requirement for the early innovators'.[26] By the late seventeenth century, however, innovators with both grass substitutes and root crops are much more literate than non-adoptors: 30% illiterate as against 53%. Differences are clear between those of differing social status, a time-lag of thirty or forty years being observable in the adoption of grass substitutes and root crops among husbandmen compared to gentry and yeomen. Social status and literacy are the most significant characteristics of opinion leaders, though we now know that the former exerted a powerful influence on the latter. Overton identifies 'two movements of information through the various social groups, "horizontally" amongst the literate opinion leaders where the innovation could move quite long distances, and "vertically" by face to face contacts where information must have moved in short steps over

[23] Quoted in Wrightson (1982): 188.   [24] Macdonald (1979).
[25] M. Overton, 'Agricultural change in Norfolk and Suffolk' (1980): 218–29.   [26] *Ibid*. 219.

space'.[27] Without the initial benefit of literacy among certain intermediary 'broker' groups, innovations would have been very slow, but
large-scale adoption was firmly related to social distance and thus to the
possibility of personal example. Innovations were disseminated at
different speeds and in different ways to diverse social groups – literate
contracts were more important for turnips, face-to-face for clover.
Literacy was important but not at all in the simple and direct way which
some historians assume. Pre-existing circumstances would shape and
direct the impact of literacy on the mental world and thus on farming
practices.

In the nineteenth century, local Farmers' Associations developed for
the acquisition, generation and diffusion of information on agricultural
subjects.[28] Literature was disseminated and discussed at their gatherings, which were backed up by agricultural shows at which new technology and techniques were demonstrated, and where farmers could
meet to exchange ideas. There were many (self-congratulatory) comments about the effectiveness of these associations, but it is difficult to
assess accurately their influence on different classes of farmer. By the
1800s in Scotland we find a 'new breed of professional farmer' avidly
reading books on husbandry alongside *Farmers' Magazine*. However,
the importance of social mixing is illustrated by the examples of farmers
clubbing together to buy a newspaper and then reading it aloud at their
gatherings.[29] Indeed, one authority has concluded that most works on
agricultural improvement were little better than coffee-table books. In
any case, the most active period of publishing came after the main phase
of agricultural improvement in the late eighteenth century.[30]

A more effective way of transmitting improvements may have been
through mobile skilled labour – the principal reason suggested by
Cipolla for the spread of technological change in early modern Europe.[31]
In late seventeenth- and early eighteenth-century Scotland, skilled
labour had to be imported from England and elsewhere to staff industrial operations such as the Newmills cloth manufactory in East Lothian,
because of the problems of finding trained workers in Scotland.[32] Books
were available, but practical instruction by experienced operatives was
lacking. Demonstration rather than reading was probably the most
important mode of communicating new industrial techniques. As far as
agriculture is concerned, regular annual mobility of labour was useful to

[27] *Ibid*. 227.   [28] H. S. A. Fox, 'Local farmers' associations' (1979): 54.
[29] Buchan (1972): 182, 194.
[30] I. H. Adams, 'The agents of agricultural change' (1980): 172.
[31] C. M. Cipolla, 'The diffusion of innovations' (1972): 48.   [32] Marshall (1980): 140–97.

masters and servants in husbandry in balancing demand and supply for employment. However, this may also be an inhibitory factor because of traditional prejudices against new and unfamiliar agricultural practices.[33]

Associated with the idea of literacy as a means of disseminating ideas is the notion that once people become more literate they also become more economically productive, not to say thrifty, law-abiding, religious and discriminating. For one eighteenth-century political economist 'the only improveable riches of any nation are its inhabitants'.[34] One way of improving the productivity of the labour force was to make them better-educated. A labour force of higher quality would be more economically productive. Economic historians have become concerned with such residual factors in economic growth after land, labour and capital have been taken into account: what is termed 'human capital'. Indeed, twentieth-century policy-makers see a need to spread literacy so that more of the rural population may understand literature on agricultural improvement or contraception, and in order to broaden their intellectual and geographical horizons, since 'elementary education enlarges the pool from which society can draw the individuals who play at least a corporal's part in change'.[35]

This itself is part of a sociological and political tradition which sees in literacy the most certain path towards producing a 'modern' and economically developed society. Once a certain 'threshold' level has been reached, say 40% of the population achieve basic literacy, benefits felt likely to accrue will become apparent on a national level. Policy-makers have tended to look to past societies for examples of this tradition, and Rostow claims that literacy was a necessary but not sufficient precondition of the Industrial Revolution in Britain.[36] West has argued that there was an educational as well as an Industrial Revolution in eighteenth- and nineteenth-century Britain, the former aiding the latter.[37] The onset of industrialization is said to have been helped by the early attainment of a threshold of 40% male literacy, and early industrial development to have required higher standards of education and ability than ever before. The rate of improving mass literacy quickened noticeably after the Industrial Revolution was under way.[38]

Recent work has provided a rather more subtle interpretation of the uses of literacy in economic development. First, there is evidence to

[33] Kussmaul (1981): 68–9.   [34] SRO GD18/6106.
[35] C. A. Anderson and M. J. Bowman, 'Human capital and economic modernization in historical perspective' (1973): 252; Hartwell (1971): 76.
[36] W. W. Rostow, *The stages of economic growth* (1971): 6, 28, 30, 182.
[37] West (1975); Hartwell (1971).
[38] N. Tranter, 'The labour supply 1780–1860' (1981): 222–5.

suggest that the spread of specialized technical and scientific education was much more important for economic growth than the simple expansion of basic reading and writing abilities. Many skills, such as operating looms in a factory, had very little need for more advanced intellectual capacity than had the handlooms they replaced. The modest nature of the scale and technology of the first Industrial Revolution hardly required any great improvement in educational attainments.[39] There were certainly some benefits to be gained by skilled workers, whose success was dependent on the speed with which they could master new techniques. Literacy could be an advantage for upwards social mobility, and was vital if one was to gain promotion in the army, for example. In addition, some new specialist occupations, such as civil engineering, did require literacy. However, literacy did not necessarily bring about social mobility.[40]

Because it was of more use to the skilled worker, literacy tended to reinforce rather than alter social divisions. Specialized education in navigation and accounting of the sort increasingly available in eighteenth-century Scottish burghs and in the provincial centres of England was probably of greater economic importance than basic literacy, which did not necessarily teach people to cope with new techniques and ideas. The lack of generalized practical education was noticed in the early nineteenth century and the Highland Society advocated the teaching of farm book-keeping as a subject in parochial schools.[41] This was not widespread. Of course, a little specialized education in Latin or accounting could go a long way, but there were still some semi-professionals such as coalgrieves and oversmen in eighteenth-century mines who might be expected to have participated in improving education, yet whose accounting competence was clearly suspect.[42]

At the same time the notion of any mass access to this expanding range of education in either Scotland or England is probably illusory. Smout quotes from an 1832 survey of 7,700 children in 123 schools in north-east Scotland which shows that 96% received reading instruction, 51% writing, 30% arithmetic, 5% Latin, 2% geography and mathematics.[43] This fits in with Sinclair's remark that 'parents in general wish their children to read, write, and acquire some knowledge of arithmetic, but shew little desire to have them taught the

[39] *Ibid.* 224; D. S. Landes, *The unbound Prometheus* (1969): 343–8.
[40] M. Sanderson, 'Literacy and social mobility in the Industrial Revolution' (1972).
[41] Sinclair (1826): 88.
[42] B. F. Duckham, *A history of the Scottish coal industry* (1970): 121–2.
[43] Smout (1972): 428.

learned languages'.[44] Emphasis on practical as opposed to classical education had been growing since the seventeenth century among the bulk of those who demanded education. The benefits accruing to potentially entrepreneurial and managerial sections of the population were likely to have been more significant than the cultivation of a high literacy population before the later stages of industrialization. In Scotland as in England universities played little part in the commercial successes of the seventeenth and eighteenth centuries.[45] Towns like Ayr established a system for training youths in literature and preparing them for business.[46] The educational system in Scotland as in England did provide an excellent vocational training for the middle classes who dominated its provision. It did help to train the commercial and entrepreneurial elements in British society but was not particularly useful when it came to creating a high-quality industrial labour force.

For most of the labour force of the Industrial Revolution, literacy was not essential. In fact, what we see in the second half of the eighteenth century in England is 'an emerging economy creating a whole range of *new* occupations which required even *less* literacy and education than the old ones'.[47] As we noticed earlier, in the period from 1650 to 1770, literacy improvements were principally enjoyed by the middling orders. This is inconsistent with the idea of economic change necessarily 'demanding more literacy, creating more jobs and drawing an increasingly educated labour force up the social scale into them'.[48] Much more important than scholastic education to the continued growth of a suitable labour force was the training in new

practical skills disseminated in the home, the workshop and the factory, a training which developed along with the rise of the industrial economy rather than preceded it, and which was able to make do with a labouring population scarcely more literate than that of the immediate pre-industrial period.[49]

Industrialization did not destroy traditional skills but neither did it create a greatly accentuated demand for new capacities. It was not for nothing that Samuel Richardson asserted in 1811: 'the low and illiterate are the most useful people in the commonwealth'.[50]

Social uses of literacy

In fact, the advantage to economic development came in a rather more roundabout way since, properly applied, education could help to

[44] Sinclair (1826): 82   [45] Tranter (1981): 224–5; O'Day (1982): 271.
[46] Boyd (1961): 76–7.   [47] Sanderson (1972): 89.   [48] *Ibid.* 102.
[49] Tranter (1981): 224.   [50] Quoted in Laqueur (1976c): 125.

discipline a workforce, traditionally used to irregular rounds of mainly agricultural tasks, to the continuous and strictly regulated work demanded by industrial capitalism. Eighteenth-century schemes for 'technical instruction' in Highland Scotland were successful to the extent that

the system of technical and craft instruction to which the boys were exposed . . . brought to the region a new outlook on life and on the value of individual and corporate endeavour, on motive in industry and on the value of continuous application to work – at a time when the people of that region were regarded as being conservative in the extreme, opposed to change, and suspicious of anything which could be interpreted as potentially damaging to a way of life which had deep historical and traditional roots.[51]

A central aim of eighteenth-century education was to ensure ideological conformity among the population and to alter undesirable attitudes manifested by the lower classes. The criticisms made by respectable middle- and upper-class observers of the masses were felt to be remediable through education. Significantly, these remarks had a moral tone and seemed to concentrate on particular character or behavioural traits. They were in fact a comprehensive condemnation of the working-class way of life, of a whole spectrum of broadly cultural facets, such as a strong desire for independence and a variety of communal sociabilities often associated with drink which depended on the availability of self-determined leisure time. The criticisms were particularly directed against industrial labour. Agricultural workers had less need to be subject to the strict time-discipline of factory work. Labour discipline was already strong in northern England and Scotland, and social and economic subordination was such that employers could dispense with additional means of coercion if changes in work practices were required.[52] In the case of industry, the 'rational' requirements of capitalism dictated the need for steady labour through long hours. This sort of work regime was likely to be alien to the usual (agricultural) rhythms to which most people were accustomed: rhythms where work need not be continuous through the day and when the year was punctuated by holidays and slack periods.

Thus a less direct but potentially effective strategy for increasing labour productivity was to use schooling as a means to accustom people in youth to boring toil. This aim accounts in part for the emphasis in teaching on the habits, attitudes, the general 'moral' orientation of the child rather than either the development of skills or the

[51] Thompson (1972–4): 272.
[52] Devine (1978); E. P. Thompson, 'Time, work-discipline, and industrial capitalism' (1967); E. Hobsbawm and G. Rudé, *Captain Swing* (1973).

transmission of knowledge.[53] This is not to say that children were not given breaks during the day or that there was no concern for learning *per se*, but that these were not the only aims of education. This emphasis in education is not new to the late eighteenth century, but can be found in Scotland during the seventeenth. The clear links between class structure and education which were evident in the nineteenth century did not originate in industrial society, but had a much longer pedigree. The provision of mass education in Scotland from an early date proved valuable in making Scotland a more docile society than contemporary England, and created a system which could be used by capital once it developed the need to control labour systematically.

In England, meanwhile, the wish to use education for social and class-cultural control pre-dated educational expansion, which may itself have been encouraged by the collapse of traditional means of discipline. It has been argued that with the demise of 'gentry paternalism' in the later eighteenth century and the disappearance of a face-to-face society where the ruling groups could maintain direct control over the masses, the dominant classes were presented with the problem of winning the consent of their social subordinates by different means. Increasing participation by factory owners in education during the early years of the nineteenth century can be seen as evidence of this.[54] In late eighteenth- and early nineteenth-century Scotland intentions were similar, but there was also the spur of shoring up the damage caused to a useful system of education by urbanization and industrialization.

The provision of education was supplemented by explicit state action to discipline the workforce. In some seventeenth- and eighteenth-century European manufactories the discipline was almost military or monastic.[55] Working hours were specified and there were regulations against theft, stoppages and combinations of workers. An extreme example of the way the state backed up manufactories were the Scottish laws enforcing serfdom on coal- and saltworkers in the early seventeenth century in order to ensure labour supplies.[56] Schools were not simply important for instilling a new time-discipline but also for changing a whole way of life. According to Adam Smith:

---

[53] Johnson (1976): 48.
[54] Sanderson (1967): 267; Johnson (1976); E. P. Thompson, 'Patrician society, plebeian culture' (1974).
[55] D. Parker, *The making of French absolutism* (1983): 129; T. C. Smout, 'Lead mining in Scotland 1650–1830' (1967); Marshall (1980).
[56] B. F. Duckham, 'Serfdom in eighteenth-century Scotland' (1969).

The state derives no inconsiderable advantage from [the instruction of the common people]. The more they are instructed, the less liable they are to the delusions of enthusiasm and superstition, which, among ignorant nations, frequently occasion the most dreadful disorders.[57]

The Italian political theorist Antonio Gramsci neatly summarized this when he talked of the aim 'of adapting the "civilization" and the morality of the broadest popular masses to the necessities of the continuous development of the economic apparatus of production'.[58] The cultivation of a docile and obedient population may have been a more important consequence of education in turning the Scottish population into one that was suitable for the developing industrial world than was the promotion of superior 'intelligence'. In both Scotland and England the school was to be 'a little artificial world of virtuous exertion'.[59]

This sort of discipline could be instilled in all types of school, but it was particularly vigorously pursued in mine and factory institutions. A report of 1826 stresses the problems which could be expected if children were not subjected to 'the useful restraints of school and workshop' from the earliest possible age.[60] Michael Sanderson confirms that factory schools were 'an ideal way of exerting the social control of the firm over its workers and of raising up young labourers in obedience if not in scientific skill'.[61] Children attending these schools could be kept constantly under the eye of the owner's delegates, 'the tension of discipline' being maintained. Provision of such schools is sometimes seen as an attempt by the owner to sweeten industrial relations by showing that he cared about workers' welfare, since demonstrations of goodwill could help 'to develop company loyalty and to kill strikes by kindness'. We are sometimes at a loss to find examples of such goodwill, but the aim of the owners was still to render workers more pliant to their will.[62] Schools for collier children set up in the late eighteenth century were mainly created by paternalist landowners keen to enhance the 'morality' (tractability) of their workers.[63] 'Literacy itself was an agency through which the working class were driven or were taught to drive themselves to create wealth for their masters and to accept their values.'[64]

Desire to use education as a means of ensuring an obedient, hardworking labour force was not a development specific to the early years of

---

[57] Quoted in M. W. Flinn, 'Social theory and the industrial revolution' (1967): 15.

[58] Q. Hoare and G. Nowell-Smith, *Selections from the prison notebooks of Antonio Gramsci* (1971): 242.

[59] Quoted in R. Johnson, 'Educational policy and social control' (1970): 113.

[60] Quoted in Saunders (1950): 294.   [61] Sanderson (1967): 266.

[62] B. Duffy, 'Debate: coal, class and education' (1981): 150–1; H. I. Dutton and J. E. King, 'The limits of paternalism' (1982).

[63] Duckham (1970): 283–4.   [64] Laqueur (1976c): 242.

industrialization. At the Loanhead coalmines in the parish of Lasswade near Edinburgh during the 1690s, the landowner, Sir John Clerk of Penicuik, tried to use education to win the younger generation to his system of Calvinist, capitalist values.[65] In 1696 he provided that 'all coaliers and coale bearers who are not able to educat there children at schools give up there names to the said Sir John who is content to caus educat them at schools to read and write upon his own expenses'.[66] This was a full century before the beginnings of a general provision of schools for collier children noted by Duckham in his study of the Scottish coal industry.[67] At the same time, anyone under sixty years of age 'who is willing and desirous to learn to read the Scriptures' would be paid for by the coalowner Clerk, a reward of twenty merks Scots going to 'each old person who shall learn to read distinctlie'.[68] The connection between learning and 'acceptable' thought and behaviour which existed in the mind of Sir John Clerk is made clear in his admonition to one official of the coalworks in 1701 'not to follow the directions & example of that ungodly pack amongst who you live, remembering your sinning will be greater that the rest of the coalliers, for it is against more knowledge'.[69] Clerk was certain that education and godliness would make his workers more docile and industrious.

Education was not simply used to make the labour force more tractable and productive. There was also a firm religiously motivated desire to shape moral conformity. One prime aim of education provided or supervised by the middle and upper classes was the control of disruptive class conflict by the inculcation of shared social values. One finds this in Scotland and England in parish schools, factory schools, Sunday schools (introduced into Scotland in the 1790s) and endowed schools. Even at the most elementary level of schooling, such as Sunday schools, the Bible provided an underpinning for the social hierarchy, albeit not always a secure one, while the catechism was designed to enhance the patriarchal structures of society.[70] A conservative, evangelical tone permeates these institutions which were designed to transform the cultural patterns of the masses to forms of thought and behaviour more harmonious with the moral presuppositions and economic interests of their social and economic superiors. A proposal for setting up charity schools in the eighteenth-century Highlands spoke of 'poor young Ones, who, growing up in ignorance, are afterwards easily drawn to Thieving, Robbery and other Disorders and Vices'.[71] Edinburgh Sunday schools

---

[65] R. A. Houston, 'Coal, class and culture' (1983a).   [66] SRO GD18/695: fols. 67–8.
[67] Duckham (1970): 283.   [68] SRO GD18/695: fols. 67–8.   [69] SRO GD18/1016/4.
[70] M. Dick, 'The myth of the working-class Sunday school' (1980): 29; Sinclair (1826): 127.
[71] Quoted in Durkacz (1983): 47.

were founded in 1812 partly in response to a riot of youths there. English Sunday schools, to take another example,

attempted to remove children from the influence of inadequate or irreligious parents, the moral dangers of the town, and the influence of radical propaganda. To remedy this environmental failure, they attempted to develop the spirituality and obtain the deference of the poor.[72]

There is no need to postulate a cynical conspiracy behind this. Genuine concern for souls and morals does not by any means preclude the concept of educating the masses to be more diligent, tractable and 'honest'.

Practical education was justified in moral terms as a way of keeping the poor from idleness, but it was also useful to individual entrepreneurs to have children working for them. However, as we have already suggested, the direct financial gain from child labour in schools was probably subordinate to the wider benefits of the capitalist system as a whole which derived from the cultivation of a more tractable, disciplined workforce, docile and industrious, receptive to the new labour demands of capitalism. George Chapman, grammar school master at Dumfries during part of the eighteenth century, neatly summarized the broad interests of employers in education. In order

to reconcile the lowest classes of mankind to the fatigues of constant labour, and otherwise mortifying thoughts of servile employment, pains should be taken to convince them, when young, that subordination is necessary in society ... that happiness does not consist in indolence, nor in the possession of riches ... but in habits of industry and contentment, in temperance and frugality; in the consciousness of doing our duty in the station in which we are placed.[73]

A participant in the 1838 education controversy advocated vocational training, but at a very specific level which would make children useful in a manufacturing society, since they would be made to 'see the value of good behaviour, honesty, sobriety, and be made useful beings to their employers, and all around them'.[74] This attitude was not true solely of Scotland. In the early nineteenth century the first report of the Royal Lancastrian Association affirmed that simple literacy was of much less value than 'the frame of mind created by the discipline of education'.[75] The partial success, at best, of the reformers in altering the attitudes of the lower orders was the fault of their patronizing and culturally arrogant approach rather than any lack of effort. We can

[72] Dick (1980): 36.   [73] Quoted in Neuburg (1971): 10.
[74] G. Lewis, *An address on the subject of education* (1838): 25.
[75] Quoted in Johnson (1976): 47.

understand this sort of attitude better in the context of contemporary attitudes to the uses of education and literacy.

Whatever remarks historians may have made about the democratizing or intellectually liberating effects of literacy, one does not have to look far before discovering that these were the last things which the providers of education wanted. If we look only at the provision of schools and the espousal of education through twentieth-century eyes we can easily see them as evidence of philanthropic altruism. However, to gain a proper understanding it is vital to set these actions in the context of other attitudes: principally a wish for order and a deeply patronizing, pessimistic outlook on the awful moral condition and vicious propensities of the young, women and indeed the poor in general.

The minds of children are empty and rude: if therefore their empty minds be not furnished with usefule knowledge, and their rude minds formed with suitable manners, their native ignorance will be confirmed into a stupidity and their originale roughness into a savage brutishness.[76]

So the presbytery of Dumbarton near Glasgow revealed their prejudices in 1700. Children were sinful but malleable. Among the more forthright outlines of the depravity of the adult poor was one from the 1838 education debate which it is worth quoting at length:

Shut out from every thing that can sustain or ennoble an intelligent nature, the peasantry of England have long since displayed, in unparalleled degradation, the full effects of knowledge denied, and have now sunk into a state of mental inanition and semi-barbarism, from which, it is to be feared, the present generation can never be recovered. Rude, selfish, superstitious and profane; – their sense of right and wrong limited and often perverted; insensible to enjoyments of a higher order than those which arise from the grosser forms of sensual gratification; and scarcely ever looking beyond the apparent interests of the present hour; the great mass live and die without an effort to raise themselves above the lowest conditions of animal existence.

In the towns a different state of things prevails, yet one scarcely less to be lamented, and probably more perilous to the peace of the community. The bulk of labourers still remain in utter and hopeless ignorance; while the better class of artizans, only partially enlightened, are seldom found capable of enjoying a scientific lecture, a useful book, or a calm political disquisition . . . For evils of this description, there is but one remedy; – the cultivation and enlargement of the popular mind.[77]

We have already seen how women were recognized as important in socializing the coming generation and how it was a misogynist tradition with its belief in their inherently imperfect and ungovernable

---

[76] Quoted in Withrington (1970): 192 n.l.
[77] H. Dunn, *National education, the question of questions* (1838): 6.

natures which justified the limited steps taken to educate them. Meanwhile, working men were said to be brutalized by drink; living in dirt and depravity there was little hope for them except firm discipline in the workplace. However, there was still the aspiration that the coming generation could be taught to be more like the middle classes. 'It is in the habits and amusements of life', wrote Bosanquet, 'that the poor especially want the countenance, the encouragement, the inter-course, and influence of the rich.'[78] By example and education the lower classes were to be won over, though one suspects largely by people 'who know nothing of the lower orders but that they are not so well dressed as ourselves, and drink porter in lieu of wine'.[79]

The world which the middle-class reformers sought was one in their own image, where social and economic divisions remained clear, but where everyone knew their place. Rather than giving the workers better housing and working conditions or a bigger share in the product of their labour and allowing them the recognition of the legitimacy of their cultural patterns, the social problems created by industrializ-ation, urbanization and population growth were to be solved by a system of education which should be '*mainly* moral and religious'.[80] Education of the poor was 'the best security for the morals, the subor-dination, and the peace of countries'.[81] By training the lower classes to internalize middle-class values, schooling could act as a force pro-moting social stability.

The main thrust of education before the late eighteenth century was religious. In sixteenth- and seventeenth-century Scotland the parish clergy saw the placing of schools as an integral part of a functioning Kirk, 'a constituent part of that establishment, and absolutely essential to its prosperity and glory'.[82] A recurrent theme in the Kirk's directions to schoolteachers was to ensure that religious precepts were firmly instilled into the youth of Scotland. Indeed, all presbytery and synod exhortations to the parishes of Scotland placed a strong emphasis on Bible-reading, rote learning of the catechism and devotion to a pious life as the foundation of education. At a presbytery visitation of Dalkeith grammar school in 1731 the ministers concluded of the pupils that they 'were well satisfied with their sufficiency in profiting in their studies and had a satisfying account of the master's diligence and of his particular care to instruct the schollars in the principles of religion'.[83]

English diocesan visitations also stressed religious education from

---

[78] Quoted in Gilly (1842): 47.   [79] *Westminster Review*, vol. 7 (1827): 309.
[80] Sinclair (1826): 71.   [81] Quoted in Webb (1955): 15.   [82] Sinclair (1826): 76.
[83] SRO CH2/424/12: fol. 181.

the sixteenth century onwards. The third question posed by Archbishop Herring to his Yorkshire clergy in 1743 concerned the number of children at school and 'what Care is taken to instruct them in the Principles of the Christian Religion, according to the Doctrine of the Church of England; and to bring them duly to Church as the Canon requires'.[84] This attitude was informed by the belief that ignorance equalled superstition and immorality and that learning was bound to produce godliness. Education was to create those dispositions which were the preconditions of salvation, with individual reformation paving the way for societal regeneration. One observer from later centuries spoke for many generations when he affirmed that 'no plan of education ought to be encouraged in which intellectual instruction is not subordinate to the regulation of the thoughts and habits of the children by the doctrines and precepts of revealed religion'.[85] The wish to use education and literacy for conservative purposes was common to Catholic and Protestant churches alike.[86]

We should state categorically that the secular and ecclesiastical authorities never encouraged education except as a means of preparing people for the messages about order and godliness which they wished to transmit. There was complete agreement over the need to promote education in the interests of social stability. If literacy did liberate the mind this was by a process quite incidental to the aims of formal educators.

Educational methods reflected the desire for order and conformity. The stress on teaching via catechism in the early modern period was useful to the authorities, since it fulfilled both a religious and an educational need, but rote learning was often criticized for bypassing any real attempts to inculcate understanding.[87] Educational theorists tended towards rigidity of methods, especially in elementary teaching, and possessed a simplistic perception of learning procedures not likely to be conducive to understanding. In France, girls and boys from the lower classes were taught by imitating certain actions and repeating certain words. Even the humanist education of sixteenth-century Strasbourg was not designed to promote critical understanding, but simply to pass on an agreed body of knowledge.[88]

A similar process was at work in pre-industrial Britain. Of teaching methods at the *best* London academies for boys at the end of the

---

[84] Ollard and Walker, vol. 1 (1928): 2.   [85] Quoted in Colls (1976): 87.

[86] Furet and Ozouf (1982): 302; Lockridge (1974): 4.

[87] SRO CH2/424/4: 28 July 1653; Smout (1972): 430; Neuburg (1971): 60–1, 79; Chrisman (1982): 281; Strauss (1978): 151–7.

[88] Chartier (1976): 232; Chrisman (1982): 259.

eighteenth century, Mary Wollstonecraft wrote, 'the memory is loaded with unintelligible words, to make a show of, without the understanding's acquiring any distinct ideas: but [in her opinion] only that education deserves emphatically to be termed cultivation of the mind which teaches young people how to begin to think'. When describing the virtues of the Edinburgh Royal High School in the second half of the eighteenth century, Hugo Arnot was careful to record that learning was not just by rote but that an attempt was made to instill critical understanding of the subjects. One presumes that learning parrot-fashion was more usual in Arnot's experience.[89] At less exalted institutions the same stress on rote learning was clear. The Kirkcaldy school regulations of 1705 show a strong emphasis on rote learning and repetition, with little time left for writing.[90] The same is true of the Dundonald rules of 1640. This didactic style left little room for independent thought, though we should allow that learning by rote could help to develop memory which could, in turn, make the acquisition of reading and writing easier when it was attempted, perhaps later in life.

Emphasis on rote learning does not necessarily preclude understanding, and may provide a foundation for subsequent attainments. Dedication to learning and a concentration on memorization could make up for the lack of books or of formal schooling for some people. In this way, the presence of an oral tradition and of rote learning made the assimilation of the literate easier.

Yet it is crucial to understand that religious emphasis in education 'consisted of a stress on the acquisition of knowledge and approved doctrine and not a cultivation of critical and creative techniques'. The ideological policing performed by the Calvinist church in Scotland is well known. In England the church courts and godly parish governments strove to assert moral and religious conformity. English religious chapbooks of the seventeenth century seem more likely to bind the mind to traditional modes of thought than to open up new vistas of the imagination, to accentuate, rather than alleviate, the sort of chronic religious anxiety felt by many of their readers.[91] Nor is there any necessary reason why reading the psalms should help with other forms of literature or with Scots dialect as opposed to standard English. On the contrary, the short duration of education and the stultifying methods of teaching probably meant that many people would be ill-equipped to understand any but the most simple literature. There is no need to assume automatically that literacy by itself liberated the mind, and we have already shown that it did not necessarily replace oral modes of

[89] Wollstonecraft (1975): 280; Arnot (1816): 324.   [90] Beale (1953): 308–11.
[91] O'Day (1982): 45; Spufford (1981): 207.

transmitting ideas. We shall have more to say about literacy and education as conservative forces.

Education was to be mainly moral and religious, but 'the force of Christian morals' also had implications for the material world. The aim of charity schools such as the Trades Maiden Hospital in eighteenth-century Edinburgh was 'to prepare orphans for the business of life and the purposes of eternity'.[92] By no means absent from seventeenth-century records, this attitude became more common during the later eighteenth century, with education seen as 'the means of instructing youth, to act a part in society, advantageously to themselves and usefully to others'.[93] Eighteenth-century authorities felt that children, especially poor children, should learn a range of practical skills which would make them more useful to a society 'where more hands are still wanting'.[94] Children at the charity workhouse of Dalkeith attended school to be 'instructed in manufactories of different kinds'.[95] Girls could be taught to make stockings, for example. In June 1707 the parents and siblings of Janet McQueen were 'in distress' (poor), with the result that Lasswade Kirk Session paid for her to attend school in the parish for three months 'workin stockins'.[96] For Sir John Sinclair, it was particularly 'desireable that women should be taught some art, by which they may be enabled to contribute to their own subsistence' and 'trained to habits of virtuous industry'.[97]

Indeed, practical schools for the poor often taught only the very basics of catechism and reading, preferring to concentrate on manual productivity. An eighteenth-century example from Eastwood in Renfrewshire suggests that for poor children the Kirk Session was 'prepared to do what they could to provide them with at least the barest intellectual and manual tools of honest employment'.[98] A central feature of the programme to civilize the Highlands was a system of practical instruction alongside religious evangelization, designed to win the Highlanders from ignorance and popery. The new SSPCK charter of 1738 allowed teaching of 'some of the most necessary and useful arts of life' including husbandry, housewifery, trades and manufactures.[99] One wonders what some of the places described as schools actually did in the way of academic studies. Especially in the large towns of the late eighteenth century, infant schools meant children 'may be kept out of mischief and free from the risk of accidents

---

[92] Quoted in Scotland (1969): 95.   [93] Sinclair (1826): 69; Smout (1972): 429.
[94] A. Law, *Education in Edinburgh in the eighteenth century* (1965): 35, 42.
[95] SRO CH2/424/13: fols. 445, 464.   [96] SRO CH2/471/10.
[97] Sinclair (1826): 126.   [98] Scotland (1969): 91.
[99] Thompson (1972–4): 250, 259–60, 269–70.

– may be trained to subordination, – and may at the same time acquire ideas, which may be of singular use to them in their future progress in life'.[100] Provision of education for the poor in Scotland as in England was designed to prepare them for a preordained position in life, and not at all to provide an opportunity for social mobility. The aim of the reformers was not to liberate the mind but to regulate it along preconceived lines.

Keeping it on the desired path was less assured, however. In the late eighteenth and early nineteenth centuries Malthus, Smith, Brougham and others sought education for the masses as a means of inhibiting the unpleasant antagonisms which originated in their brutalizing environment. Reading, as one French commentator on the origins of the French Revolution claimed, could be a powerful antidote to all sorts of social ills.[101] This followed very much in the footsteps of the sixteenth- and seventeenth-century religious reformers, who believed that education would promote godliness and all its attendant virtues. The ministers of the presbytery of Middlebie were convinced that the lack of schools in south-west Scotland at the end of the seventeenth century was the cause of the political upsets there.[102] However, opinion among those who wished to keep the lower classes in their place was not always unanimous about the certainty of the connection between literacy and an obedient population. For, if schooling could inculcate habits of order and obedience it could also open minds to dangerous radical ideas which were the consequence of religious or political propaganda. The problem, succinctly put by Sir John Sinclair, was that while moral and religious instruction was desirable there was no control over the ends to which it was put, with the result that 'the great mass of people may thus be infected with principles destructive to the church and state'.[103] Even in the medieval period literacy could unleash heresy and sedition, as well as opening up new spiritual insights.[104] In Elizabethan England social policy was designed to

restrict men to the callings of their fathers, to consolidate the social order by maintaining due differences between estates; accordingly there were moves to reserve certain forms of education to gentlemen at one end of the scale while at the other the children of the poor were trained to habits of useful work.[105]

However, there were no guarantees that this would necessarily be the outcome.

By the eighteenth century in England one school of thought believed in denying education to the poor in the interests of stability, but

[100] Sinclair (1826): 67–8.   [101] Chartier (1976): 43.   [102] Smout (1972): 424–5.
[103] Sinclair (1826): 71.   [104] Aston (1977): 369; Spufford (1981): xvii.
[105] Simon (1967): 294.

another still sought 'to modify the ignorance of the poor so that they might read the Scriptures and earn a useful though humble living, grateful to their superiors and always conscious of their duty to them'.[106] In the mid nineteenth century a county Durham vicar averred that 'educational advancement is a curse to the working man without the controlling and sustaining power of religion'.[107] Yet the earlier example of the 1640s in England, the popular Covenanting movement in south-west Scotland in the late seventeenth century or the Levellers in the same region in the early eighteenth century give some hint of the radical implications of religion which could be worked out among ordinary people. In the same way, educating the lower classes so that they could read edifying and improving literature in no way guaranteed that they would not be seduced by popular recreational literature, 'the vulgar and lewd chapbooks that circulated from "that copious source of mischief, the Hawker's basket"'.[108] In the age of John Stuart Mill 'the principles of the Reformation have reached as low down in society as reading and writing, and the poor will no longer accept morals and religion of other people's prescribing'.[109] Like American elites, the Scottish ruling groups and middle-class reformers maintained a consensus on the desirability of education into the early nineteenth century which contrasted with the diffidence of the admittedly divided English commentators.[110]

At some periods it was argued by some observers that education should be denied to the poor for fear that it would give them ideas above their station. But others believed that education would provide a training in the virtues of industry, sobriety and docility. Indeed, there were variations over time, as when in the 1840s north-eastern coal-owners became convinced of the need to educate workers' children in closely controlled schools, but for Lancashire factory owners there was increased resistance to education after 1833. Attitudes to education as an instrument of control varied according to the economic climate and prevailing social conditions. Commentators, then, did recognize the absurdity of arguing that 'the most unlimited dispersion of knowledge could in itself ensure the advancement of wisdom and virtue ... but it cannot be disputed that utter ignorance is the most effectual fortification to a vicious state of mind'.[111] There was some ambivalence about whether education would ensure stability, though there was no doubt whatsoever that this was the aim. Most commonly, observers concurred in the belief that education was a good thing. Debate in journals

---

[106] Neuburg (1971): 2.   [107] Colls (1976): 96.   [108] Quoted in Saunders (1950): 252.
[109] Quoted in Webb (1955): 12.   [110] Kaestle (1976): 182, 187; Smout (1972): 442.
[111] Dunn (1838): 6.

like the *Edinburgh Review* was less about the need to educate than about how and by whom it was to be done.

The aim of providing education may have been to conserve the existing social order, but there was no way of being sure of the ends to which the newly educated might put their skills. This brings us on to the other side of the equation of learning: demand for reading and writing. Debate about the history of education has usually concentrated on the supply side of matters: the provision of schooling and the reasons why the middle and upper classes favoured education and literacy. This has been our concern so far in this chapter. However we cannot ignore the extent of demand for education or the motivations behind the search for literacy. Did the population of Scotland and England as a whole share the assumptions and aims of the articulate commentators who published in the *Edinburgh Review* or who wrote political pamphlets for the great debates on education? Or did they have a different outlook on schooling and on reading and writing?

Political uses of literacy

Faced with the overt or covert attempts of reformers to alter their way of life, the lower classes could adopt one of two approaches, assuming they recognized that education was being used to preserve the hegemony of the ruling group. They could either accept the system in the same way as they did economic exploitation, internalizing to a greater or lesser extent the official ideology of the dominant groups and using the system for what it was worth. This would mean recognizing the illegitimacy of their own cultural forms and using the schools established for their use. Alternatively, they could withdraw from the schools provided or run by their social betters. There are examples of both responses.

In the socially divided south-east Lowlands of Scotland at the turn of the nineteenth century, the autobiographer Alexander Somerville experienced the favouritism of the teacher towards the children of the better-off in the school, but his father thought very highly of the master's skill in educating children in the way those who wielded social and political power in the society thought best.[112] Somerville's father seems to have felt a vague aspiration towards social mobility and an easier life for his children, though given the objective realities of socio-economic polarization in this region, chances for agricultural labourers to rise above the level of farm baillie were very limited. 'If the

[112] Somerville (1951): 22–4.

laddie lives to be a man . . . he will need his education, and more than we can give him. If I had got schooling myself, as I am trying to give to all my sons it would have helped me through the world more easily.'[113] The tone of this statement does not suggest that this member of the working class perceived education as a means of upwards social mobility. Instead, he seems to have hoped for a reduction in the numerous troubles which the poor as a class had to meet, simply because they were poor.

Other parents failed to educate their children not because they were too poor but because of a vaguely formulated but strong doubt of the value of education in a thoroughly unequal society. Others may have been more sanguine about the possibilities. Certainly one can find instances throughout the seventeenth and eighteenth centuries where parents would refuse to send their children to a parish school if they felt a master was incompetent.[114] Of the Auchermuchty parish schoolmaster, one Kirk Session elder said in 1658 that 'there came never a good scholler out of his schoole'.[115] Parental concern seems to have been with practical learning, but it is rarely possible to discover the criterion by which a teacher's ability was judged, or even if it was the same for all social groups. Certainly, bad teachers in private schools were driven out by lack of demand. Thomas Laqueur points to the way English

Sunday schools developed from within the working class, especially after the end of the eighteenth century . . . the working class saw its real needs in pursuit of the virtues promoted by the Sunday school . . . the institution expressed qualities such as self-help, self-improvement and respectability . . . that Sunday school morality sustained a working-class culture that was not politically repressive.[116]

This was probably true of a section of the 'respectable' working class, though certainly not for all. There are many studies which show the distrust or dislike of education provided by outsiders such as employers and improving societies. Mass schooling was in a sense an artificial implantation. Faced with attempts at social or 'class-cultural' control the lower classes might, so to speak, vote with their feet. For if one set of options was to accept passively the education provided by the middle classes or to exploit it to its full potential, another was to set up schools where the values put across were those of the lower classes themselves. Desire for education need not be synonymous with a wish to use 'provided' schooling. Instead, there was a range of alternative private schools which taught basic literacy but which did not apparently try to

---

[113] *Ibid.* 18.   [114] SRO CH2/424/4: 2 November 1654.   [115] Beale (1953): 33.
[116] Quoted in Dick (1980): 29.

inculcate habits of obedience and subservience.[117] Lower-class parents who sent their children to schools which they themselves paid for seem to have had a different perception of their worth from those who used the official schools. They might even show considerable reluctance to send children to mine or factory schools.[118] The problems the Scottish Kirk Sessions experienced throughout the sixteenth and seventeenth centuries in inducing parents to send children to the official parish schools may have had something to do with opposition to them on religious and ideological grounds as much as had parental poverty. Private adventure schools genuinely did grow out of mass demand.

There is considerable evidence of indigenous demand for education among the working classes of Scotland and England, as we can see from the numerous private schools: 'genuinely popular, very ephemeral ... and very varied in their ambitions and functions'.[119] The popularity of dame or adventure schools did not simply derive from their cheapness or easy accessibility. Middle-class observers felt that these schools were mean affairs, inefficient and poorly run, when compared with the subsidized or endowed equivalent. Physically convenient and without strict rules about attendance, dress and behaviour they would, however, be well suited to working mothers and to the conventional norms of lower-class communities.[120] Public schools with teachers drawn from outside these communities might be seen as oppressively alien in their regulations and curricula. It is therefore possible to see Scottish adventure schools and English dame schools 'evolving out of the community's own needs [since] it was not and could not be their nature to seek to convert that community'.[121] Teaching at unofficial schools of the seventeenth and eighteenth centuries was a by-employment like brewing and alehousekeeping which could provide a living for economically vulnerable elements, such as single women who were likely to be representatives of the much criticized popular culture. This may be another reason why the Scottish Kirk Sessions tried to suppress private schools which taught anything beyond practical skills and the catechism, lest children be infected by unacceptable ideas. Education was after all part of the Scottish church's drive for ideological conformity. In the teeth of religious and moral evangelism parents may have been happier to send their children to private schools precisely because they would not turn

---

[117] Johnson (1970): 113–14.   [118] Webb (1955): 18.   [119] Johnson (1970): 113.
[120] Laqueur (1976b): 195, 199–201; Johnson (1976): 44–5; D. P. Leinster-Mackay, 'Dame schools' (1976): 46.
[121] Colls (1976): 90.

their children into people with different views and behaviour to their own.

Alongside the debate on the quantity of educational provision there is also one about the quality of teachers, teaching and schoolhouses. One example of the issues raised is the lack of a necessary connection between increased schooling and a higher level of literate skills. In English private venture or dame schools, for instance, books were probably less available than in charity ones. Contemporaries felt that too often schoolmasters 'fixed on that line of life only as a temporary convenience, having other objects ultimately in view'.[122] Turnover of masters in the sixteenth- and seventeenth-century south-west of Scotland was frequent. Emoluments were rarely substantial, and teachers might be driven to a range of by-employments to boost their income, as indeed were most of the less well-off members of early modern societies.[123] Robert Trotter was removed from his post as parish schoolmaster of Lasswade in 1691 for brewing ale in the school, a pursuit felt by the Kirk Session to be taking up too much time and provoking 'the complaint of all having children at the school of their bad proficiency'.[124] The economic marginality of the doctor or assistant at Dunfermline school is suggested when in 1650 his salary was increased because of the 'burden of his familie, having 4 or 5 young childrene, and of this deare yeare'.[125]

Both church and state were concerned less with whether someone could teach than with their piety. SPCK schoolmasters were expected to be able to write a good hand and teach arithmetic; this was not required of schoolmistresses. Parish schoolmasters were assessed on their reading, writing, English and arithmetic in the mid eighteenth century.[126] The teacher at the charity workhouse of Dalkeith in 1757 was only tested 'as to his reading of the English language and his knowledge of the principles of religion'.[127] Buildings were frequently said to be in a state of dilapidation, but we must be wary of taking these generalized criticisms as wholly correct because of the problems of establishing the correct ideological and material context. The lower-class idea of what constituted an acceptable building and a proper education seems to have differed from the middle-class reformers'. The latter criticized adventure schools less for their failure to teach practical

---

[122] Sinclair (1826): 81; Neuburg (1971): 89.
[123] Russell (1971): 11; Scotland (1969): 114–30.   [124] GRO OPR691/5.
[125] Beale (1953): 76.   [126] SRO CH2/424/14: fol. 334.   [127] *Ibid*. fol. 13.

skills of the sort demanded by the lower classes than for not teaching Latin and failing to inculcate moral and religious ideals.[128]

However, there may have been a further motive among the workers of the sort we have just suggested. If employers sought to use education as a means of social control, the lower orders might develop their own self-help style of learning and their own schools as a counterbalance to attempts to alter their way of life in the interests of capital. This helps to explain the growth of interest in education among both employers and employees in the new industrial areas of late eighteenth- and early nineteenth-century Britain. The well-known Mechanics' Institutes tried to promote social mobility through education. James Stirling, who ran the mine at Leadhills in Lanarkshire during the mid eighteenth century, provided a schoolmaster and an 'improving' library. During much of the eighteenth century, however, the general ethos of colliery communities was against prolonged schooling. Of course, there were exceptions, and the Leadhills miners are said to have been avid readers.[129] And in 1817 Clydesdale coalworkers realized that 'from the want of education, all those evils in a great measure, less or more, that we have suffered hath arisen; ignorance being the dupe of avarice, tyranny and ambition'.[130] These men were working out the implications of the radical programme of the 1790s which aimed to link education to political awareness as a way of ending 'the "right of ignorance and despotism" and the elevation of a generation of common people "in their own opinions"'.[131] Of course, nineteenth-century bourgeois society chose to stress the individual aspect of education and social mobility. A poor boy could rise from his class through education. Little was said except in a disparaging way about the possibility that education might create an articulate community of workers.

These, then, were some of the more positive attitudes towards reading and writing among the masses which encouraged the acquisition of literacy. If literacy was not essential, there were nevertheless occasions on which the inability to read and write could be a serious disadvantage, and such instances illustrate the way writing could be used to buttress the unequal distribution of power in early modern society. In his *Pens excellencie* of 1618 Martin Billingsley advised that no woman who survived her husband, and who had an estate left to her, ought to be without the ability to write,

---

[128] West (1975): 65.
[129] Duckham (1970): 283; Smout (1967): 126; Scotland (1969): 104; Flinn (1967): 16.
[130] Quoted in Duckham (1970): 284.   [131] Quoted in Silver (1975): 14.

for thereby she comes to a certainty of her estate, without trusting to the reports of such as are usually imployed to looke into the same: whereas otherwise for want of it, she is subject to the manifold deceits now used in the world, and by that meanes plungeth herselfe into a multitude of inconveniencies.[132]

Indeed, writing was not necessarily trusted or understood and might be viewed as a symbol of power. This attitude lies behind proverbs such as 'mony ane's deen ill wi vreet' (many a person has done harm through writing) found in north-east Scotland during the eighteenth century.[133] An illiterate Durham husbandman of the early seventeenth century was highly suspicious of his step-brother, who tried to get him to subscribe 'certain writeings . . . which I could not certainly tell what they were, but they did concerne the passing away of my said land'.[134]

In addition to vague unease about writing there were also explicit instances where its oppressive power was recognized. The burning of official documents in the Newcastle riot of 1740 provides one example of the perceived power of writing to preserve privilege. The rights of all might be dependent on the written word but they favoured those who already had property or position to protect.[135] There were cases at the English assize court when accused persons refused to sign their examination transcripts, presumably in the belief that this invalidated the confession or (among illiterates) the fear that the document could be falsified and that they would be unable to check what the justice had read out to them.[136] This refusal could also be a way of denying the jurisdiction of the court. William Holmes of Clifford in Yorkshire 'pretended that he could neither write, nor set his mark to this confession'.[137] The Covenanting rebels from south-west Scotland hauled before the Justiciary Court in the 1680s not infrequently refused to subscribe their depositions for just this reason.

The symbolic importance of writing as an instrument of oppression is seen in an example of popular protest from the late eighteenth century. During the Tranent militia riot of 1797 the mob demanded the manuscript volume containing the hated militia list, then in the keeping of the schoolmaster's wife. They believed that its destruction would put an end to the prospect of sons and husbands being conscripted for military service. In its place the schoolmaster's wife gave them an old book. Either unable to check the contents of this volume or simply not bothering to do so, the crowd retired in triumph, its symbolic needs satisfied.[138] The most important part of this action was its

---

[132] Quoted in Hull (1982): 132.   [133] Buchan (1972): 192.   [134] *Wills*, pt IV (1929): 188.
[135] E. P. Thompson, *Whigs and hunters* (1977): 258–69.   [136] PRO ASSI45: 25/1/21.
[137] PRO ASSI45: 18/5/46.   [138] Logue (1979): 85.

ritual content, a symbolic (if pyrrhic) victory over writing as a means of maintaining the interests of an outside authority against those of the local community. Written testimonials of good character operated by employers in both Scotland and England were another means of exerting control over subordinate social groups, though oral references between employers could be more important still in deciding who got work. Servants could of course make their own verbal enquiries about a prospective master and were not wholly at the mercy of employers, especially in periods of comparative labour shortage. Written documents could be a way of fixing the privileges of one individual or group over another.

Writing might also be used as a means of preserving social and sexual dominance over women. For Mary Wollstonecraft, men 'try to secure the good conduct of women by attempting to keep them always in a state of childhood'.[139] In cases of illegitimacy the church authorities in Scotland were keen to establish paternity for moral and financial reasons. Mothers might persuade the father to admit responsibility either by public admission before the Kirk Session or in a written acknowledgement. Some men adopted a range of more or less dishonest strategies to avoid the consequences. Flight abroad or into the army was one path. Another was to threaten or bribe the girl to persuade her to pass the blame onto someone else. A further ploy was to trick the woman into signing a disclaimer. Appearing before the presbytery of Dalkeith after giving birth to a bastard, Margaret Bell in Newbattle was asked about the 'line' she had subscribed absolving William Cunningham from blame for fathering her illegitimate child. She replied that 'she did subscribe a line in William Cunningham's house at his desire, he leading her hand but she knew not what was in it, only he said that it would do her no harm'.[140]

The way in which writing buttressed the basic social and gender inequalities is shown in the case of Isabel Hall, who appeared before the same presbytery in 1701. One time servant to a Lasswade miller, she had accused the powerful laird of Cockpen of being the father of her bastard. Yet a paper produced at the presbytery hearing seemed to be a retraction of this charge. Questioned, Isabel claimed that 'she knew nothing of the contents of that paper and that when she subscribed it she was made to believe it was a quit other thing, and that she was persuaded to put her hand to it by Mr Mill his fair speaches'. Mill, an agent of the laird, had used a variety of promises and veiled threats to get her to sign the disclaimer 'and when he read the paper he

---

[139] Wollstonecraft (1975): 101.   [140] SRO CH2/424/12: fol. 495.

mumbled it through his teeth and was as if he had been speaking latine and I was so frighted . . . that I knew not well what I was doing; and he said he would give me a testimonial thait would carry me through all the world'.[141] Testimonials, written affidavits of good character which were issued by employers of Kirk Sessions, could be another means of retaining control over mobile elements of the population. In this example we can see the possible advantages of literacy, the significance of writing in reinforcing existing power structures, and also, incidentally, the way in which some people saw the much-stressed Latin language as so much mumbo-jumbo.

It is clear that all forms of education were not automatically seen as 'a good thing' by all the people of early modern Britain. The uses to which education and literacy could be put were rather more value-loaded than is commonly allowed. These broader ramifications of literacy are apparent both in Scotland and in England: the northern kingdom has no particular claim to special status in these respects. The wish to use education as a way of influencing mass attitudes was common to secular and ecclesiastical elites in both countries. We have already shown that the level of literacy and its social distribution were unremarkable in Scotland when compared to other parts of Europe. A peculiarly Scottish outlook on the uses of literacy is also hard to detect. Perhaps the distinctiveness of Scottish society lies more in attitudes which saw education as open to all classes and thus a force which would promote social unity?

We noted in the introduction the stress placed by some historians on the social egalitarianism of Scottish schools. In Scottish schools, especially elementary ones, even the children of the poor could attend and as a result boys of all social classes sat together. This allegedly blurred social divisions in a way which (we are assured) could not have occurred in England. We search in vain for evidence of this distinctive ethos in practice. Instead we find a firmly elitist emphasis, especially in the grammar school which would be the most likely springboard for a 'lad o' pairts'. The landed, commercial classes formed the backbone of such schools. One of the reasons why the Kirk Session of Dalkeith were forced to sack the pederast schoolmaster Alexander Dyks from his grammar school post in the early eighteenth century was because his indecent activities 'hath occasioned several noblemen and Gentlemen's children their removing from the school . . . so that the school is almost ruined'. Dyks himself averred that 'he kept none but Gentlemen at his school'.[142]

[141] SRO CH2/424/7: fols. 70–1.   [142] SRO CH2/424/10: fols. 12, 19.

This attitude might extend as far as gross favouritism towards the children of the better-off in schools where all social classes mixed. The seventeenth-century English autobiographer Adam Martindale complained of being placed lower in his school class than boys less clever than he, but who came from richer and more socially elevated families. He believed that the teacher flew in the face of meritocratic principles because of economic need and social prejudice: the children of the better-off paid him higher fees and therefore received more favours from the teacher.[143] In Scotland as in England the quality of schools was judged by their ability to attract persons of high social status, a viewpoint adopted uncritically by some historians.[144] One reason why the minister of Heriot in Midlothian asked to be moved to another parish was because educational facilities were not good enough for his children. And in 1772 an Edinburgh teacher called Dunsmuir resigned his post following 'the objection of all ranks above the very lowest class of inhabitants' that fees were too low and that this introduced 'mean ill-dressed company' into the school.[145] So much for the democratic intellect and the happy and classless interaction of all social groups at parish and other schools. The lower classes were in any case all but excluded from secondary education in burgh schools and at university. If there was any mixing here it was between the middling sort, mainly the sons of bourgeois, and the gentry rather than among all social strata.[146]

Even if sons and daughters of lairds and labourers did rub shoulders in the rural elementary schools this does not at all prove that social harmony and the blurring of class distinctions were the result. George Lewis believed that 'the children of rich and poor, brought up at the same school, may ever after cherish kind feelings towards each other'.[147] Some early nineteenth-century commentators believed that voluntary schools were doing damage by 'separating those who are apt to be altogether separated in manhood' and thus breaking society 'into discordant parts'.[148] Omnibus parish schools would not provide this effect in their opinion.

Yet there were plenty of ways in which children would be aware of social differences within the classroom – dress, accent and manners for example. The argument that mixing reduces class consciousness replaces actual analysis with a set of more or less plausible assumptions which are left untested. Brotherly feelings originating in the school

---

[143] Parkinson (1845): 13; see also Somerville (1951): 22.   [144] Simon (1967): 17–19.
[145] SRO CH2/424/1: 12 September 1639; quoted in Law (1965): 53.
[146] Smout (1972): 443–4.   [147] Lewis (1834): 55.   [148] Smout (1972): 443.

may have been swamped by the many and powerful forces which created class consciousness. Indeed, there is evidence that social conflicts were played out at school in a way which would prepare children for a class-ridden world rather than protecting them from it. At the school which Alexander Somerville attended in south-east Scotland during the early nineteenth century the children played at radicals and soldiers. 'As the soldiers were the most respectable in the eyes of the better dressed sons of farmers and tradesmen, and as they took the lead in everything, they made themselves soldiers.'[149] The teacher at that school required the sons of gentry to be called 'master', again highlighting the reality of social distinctions. Class distinctions were reinforced in play, and the school may well have been important in forming class consciousness rather than fudging it. After all, class consciousness is formed in interactions between classes rather than when they are separated. The example we have just encountered is admittedly drawn from a period when class was becoming more developed, but it is not at all proven that the same was not true of the seventeenth and eighteenth centuries. Social classes might mix in schools but this did not necessarily blur social distinctions. Again, comfortable assumptions about the lack of social divisions in Scotland and especially in her parochial schools have displaced proper analysis of the role of education in hardening or softening differences between social groups.

Even when they were being taught in the same school, pupils from high- and low-status background received differing educations. The grammar school master at Dalkeith in Midlothian in 1712 'taught gentlemen Grotius *De veritate religionis* some time in Latin and sometime in Inglish'.[150] Schools like Dalkeith grammar existed not to create common perceptions across society as a whole, but to reproduce different social identities by raising children in environments which would help them acquire specialized adult identities. In 1728 Isaac Watts affirmed 'as the children of the rich in general ought to enjoy such an education as may fit them for the better businesses of life, so the children of the poor ... should not be generally educated in such a manner as may raise them above the services of a lower station'.[151] Especially at its higher levels, a classical education was designed primarily for the privileged classes who were trained to take up their places in the political elite. The schools helped to maintain the stability of the social order by creating a learned group with shared goals and understandings. This sort of institutional education was 'an attempt to

---

[149] Somerville (1951): 17.   [150] SRO CH2/424/10: fol. 11.
[151] Quoted in Flinn (1967): 16.

initiate students into the rituals of a dominant culture'.[152] Rosemary O'Day remarks on the sixteenth- and seventeenth-century development of the view that class and patronage determined the path in life which each youth would adopt. This was a commonplace of French educational theory at the time.[153] Children were to receive an education which would fit them for the station in life to which they were born. The fact that they all sat in the same classroom did not detract from the knowledge that different children had quite distinct backgrounds and were likely to have quite different social destinations. Social divisions were actually being reinforced in the curriculum as well as in the classroom.

One example of the socially divisive role of education was the cultural gulf created between those who used Latin as the language of culture and those who relied on the vernacular. However proficient they became in basic literacy, ordinary people could never aspire to becoming truly 'learned', since this depended on proficiency in Latin and Greek. For this reason, the potential of print as a way to disperse knowledge more widely through society may not have been realized. Diffusion of ideas was confined to specific groups. Education and literacy do not automatically act as a social and cultural leveller. An education in Latin helped distinguish the middle classes from the masses and by assimilating them more to a national culture helped reproduce or even harden social divisions. A gap between Latin and the vernacular could exist, but the problem of cultural differentiation would have been particularly pressing for Gaelic-speakers, who could be excluded by poverty and social class from access to, say, the subscription libraries of the eighteenth century. The libraries which did exist in areas like Easter Ross benefited mainly the English-speaking middle class. 'For the few Gaelic monoglots who could read, the material available' – 75% of which was religion or poetry – 'can only have forced them back to traditional ways of thinking and their ability to compete with the increasingly sophisticated outlook of English speakers grew ever less.'[154] We cannot automatically accept contemporary rhetoric that a classical education was necessarily the best education for individual or society. But we can state that literacy and education reinforced and perpetuated social distinctions.

In short, 'a democratic system in the sense of a system providing equality of opportunity did not exist'.[155] The educational system may have been egalitarian in its ethos, though even this is doubtful at all but

[152] I. Davies, 'Knowledge, education and power' (1973): 334.
[153] O'Day (1982): 64; Chartier (1976): 175–206.   [154] Mowat (1979): 9–10.
[155] Beale (1953): 338.

the most abstract level. Boys from lowly backgrounds could gain access to education, but there is no meaningful sense in which they competed on an equal footing with their middle- and upper-rank classmates. The workings of the educational system were palpably influenced by existing social, economic and political forces. We can see this even in the university education system of Scotland, which attained enormously high prestige in the nineteenth and twentieth centuries and formed the model, among others, for the Canadian university system. It is a keystone of the Scottish identity.

The first thing to note is that the number of students involved in higher education was very small. There were only 1,000 students at Scottish universities at the start of the eighteenth century and only 2,700 by its end.[156] Population rose from some one million to 1.6 millions over this period. It is unlikely that the percentage of the eligible population able to attend university in Scotland was particularly high by European standards.[157] During the eighteenth century, perhaps 1.5–2% of the relevant age group could have attended Scottish universities. This figure compares quite favourably with contemporary France's 0.9%, though the existence there of the colleges and the development by professional bodies of their own training procedures are not taken into account in this estimate.[158] However, it is very much in line with the 1–2% of the eligible population in eighteenth-century Germany, though whereas in Germany the percentage fell steadily over the eighteenth century, in Scotland it seems to have increased.[159] Of other countries, England had 1–1.5% of the eligible population attending institutions of higher education in the early eighteenth century; Castile 2.2% in the mid eighteenth century; more than 1.5% in the United Provinces during the eighteenth century. There were some 1,000 students at Uppsala University in Sweden in the 1630s out of a native population of just under one million people.[160] Assuming a similar age distribution this would make it an identical proportion to Scotland in 1700. In the 1860s the Scottish position was much better. There was one place per 1,000 of the population compared to 1:2,600 in Germany and 1:5,800 in England.[161] However there is nothing remarkable about the percentage of the eligible population attending university in eighteenth-century Scotland. Again, Scottish education may be more 'democratic' than English but the achievement is not outstanding in a wider European context.

Poor people probably did find it easier to get to university than in

[156] O'Day (1982): 277.   [157] Smout (1972): 449.   [158] Chartier (1976): 276.
[159] W. Frijhoff, 'Surplus ou déficit?' (1979): 211–12.   [160] Roberts (1953): 471.
[161] Anderson (1983): 157.

England, though many of the limited number of places which might have been available to the 1 or 2% of the eligible population who attended were taken by foreigners. In the 1740s, 25% of the 580 matriculated students at Glasgow University came from outside Scotland, a proportion which increased to 28% (of 1,070) in the period 1765–74 before falling to 17% of 1,062 in the 1790s.[162] The Lancashire schoolmaster and Nonconformist Adam Martindale sent a son to Glasgow University in 1670, for example.[163] Access to Scottish universities in the eighteenth century also appears to have been more open than in contemporary England, France or Germany where places were dominated by those from noble, professional and official backgrounds.[164] It was much cheaper to attend Glasgow University during the eighteenth century, and its intake was more socially representative than that of exclusive Cambridge. A university education was available at Glasgow for £5 a year – a tenth or less of the cost of attending Oxford or Cambridge.[165] Henry Simpson, a Durham gentleman who died in the early seventeenth century, left £50 to keep one of his sons at Cambridge for a year and £80 yearly to support another at the Inns of Court.[166] University education was expensive in England and even Ralph Josselin, the eldest son of a prosperous yeoman, was forced to come down from Jesus College, Cambridge, on a number of occasions 'for want of meanes'.[167]

Conceivably, Scottish universities were becoming less rather than more elitist over the eighteenth century compared to, say, Germany. On the other hand, opportunities for classes other than the nobility, gentry and professionals at the two English universities were contracting over the seventeenth and eighteenth centuries. Unfortunately, it is very difficult to assess whether the Scottish 'working class' was better represented over time as Mathews has argued, since occupational designations in matriculation registers may conceal the exact socioeconomic status of those artisans' and craftsmen's sons enrolled. The apparent decline in the percentage of Scottish landowners' sons attending Glasgow University may be accounted for partly by their greater propensity to attend English universities over the eighteenth century.[168] Only 12% of matriculands at St Andrews between 1750 and 1849 were from farming stock and 17% at Glasgow University in the years 1740 to 1839. Merchants and tradesmen together made up 19% of

---

[162] Smout (1972): 449; Mathew (1966): 75.   [163] Parkinson (1845): 190.
[164] Frijhoff (1979): 215; Chartier (1976): 277–8.
[165] Mathew (1966): 82–3; O'Day (1982): 276.   [166] *Wills*, pt IV (1929): 310.
[167] Hockliffe (1908): 3.   [168] O'Day (1982): 197, 280; Mathew (1966): 80–1.

St Andrews entrants, with the remaining 69% from the landowning and professional classes.[169] The imbalance is glaring. It is true that 44% of Glasgow matriculands came from 'industry and commerce', but whether these were master manufacturers or humble employees we do not know. Between 1780 and 1840 only eighteen of 661 entrants into the Faculty of Advocates can be described as coming from humble backgrounds. From 1660 to 1840 the landowning class were predominant among new entrants.[170] The lower echelons of society are still seriously under-represented among university matriculands, given their numbers among the population at large, and in any case the numbers involved were extremely small compared to the eligible population. Those attending Scottish universities in the eighteenth century did not form a representative cross-section of the social order.

It was very unlikely that more than a handful of persons from the lower classes would get to university, and even if they did, many failed to get a degree because of the initial disadvantages of poverty and poor preliminary training which mere application could not overcome. Formally at least more youths may have had the chance to reach university under the Scottish system, but there were also informal types of selection taking place, such as natural wastage within the university.[171] The success of entrants was closely tied to their social background. The lower-class lads who did make it to university in the nineteenth century tended to start later than their middle-class fellows and probably had to work between school and university both to earn a living and to reach adequate entrance standards in Latin and mathematics. These could not have reached the same polished standards as the middle-class entrants. It is no surprise to discover that a minister's son was one hundred times more likely to go to university in the 1860s than was a miner's son and that he was more likely to do well once there.[172] At the same time, those with the belief that they would succeed, born of confidence in their own social position, were likely to do much better. Recent studies of twentieth-century education and the way in which it perpetuates social inequality behind the rhetoric of independent criteria of worth have focused particularly on this aspect. In nineteenth-century Scotland we know that the working class did benefit from the relatively open-access university system. But they often entered that system as adults rather than through a career in the parish schools where access to secondary education was very difficult.

[169] R. N. Smart, 'The provinces of the Scottish universities' (1974): 104.
[170] N. T. Phillipson, 'The social structure of the faculty of advocates' (1980): 148, 156.
[171] A. McPherson, 'A sociology of the ancient Scottish universities' (1973): 165–6.
[172] Anderson (1983): 152, 155–6.

Only a minority of university students came from parish schools.[173] The parochial schools offered a foundation of basic literacy, but had little direct role to play in easing the path to higher education for the lower classes.

The further we go into the subject of Scottish education the more its much-vaunted achievements fade away into a range of mythology. Then we begin to wonder where this myth originated, why it stayed in being and what functions it served. Universal education was an aspiration of the Scottish Reformation, the *Book of discipline* feeding into national consciousness with an importance for education which lay mainly in a 'devout imagination' and in the hope for a national education system offering opportunities to all.[174] Just as myths exist that justify continuity, so they do that endorse change. For the hard-pressed Scottish Reformers, the notion of universal education may have been at least partly a way of winning over the population to their viewpoint. Used to facilitate change, the idea proved to be at the same time a conservative influence, since both in the 1560s and later it could be used to persuade the bulk of the population that they participated in a system from which they were as likely to benefit as the initiators. The emphasis of the Reformers was in fact on the needs of the church rather than the abstract rights of certain groups in society. The *Book of discipline*

reflected the belief that talent and suitability for the Church's or the State's service were not attributes of specific social classes, but it is questionable whether this attitude marked a sharp break from that of the pre-Reformation Catholic Church or whether it was any more than a parallel to the provision for limited social mobility present in the English endowed schools.[175]

Nevertheless, there was concern with the benefit to society which could be produced by fostering a wide catchment area for the professions. Elements of the ruling groups who created the Reformation for their own political reasons were in any case able to turn any potentially democratic elements to their own uses.[176] The aspirations of the *Book of discipline* became part of the Scottish identity.

The nature of Scottish society with its supposedly superior moral values was discussed more explicitly at the time of the debates on the Union in the 1700s. Advocates of and later apologists for the Union, such as Defoe, pointed to the superior Scottish education system. Observers sought to identify that which was peculiarly Scottish and to highlight the areas in which England could benefit from closer relations with Scotland. Ideas about education were used in this context as

---

[173] *Ibid.* 336.   [174] Scotland (1969): 47.   [175] O'Day (1982): 225.
[176] Smout (1972): 308–10.

political propaganda. And an aspiration which church and state had tried to implement in the seventeenth century was elevated to a concrete achievement to be envied and emulated.

A century later the supposedly democratic ideas surrounding education were revived as a means of justifying expenditure on an educational system which, as we have already seen, was in fact dominated by the middle classes. This revival may have been stimulated by the ruling groups in the late eighteenth century in response to the potentially unsettling effects of the French Revolution and the democratic ideas of Paine and others. Concern about the political impact of the French Revolution is clear in the school visitation records of the 1790s in Scotland, but alongside the more overt attacks on suspect popular education there seems to have developed a form of propaganda campaign. This was partly a response to developing lower-class ideas about education in both Scotland and England.

Tom Paine, for example, believed that the poor had much more awareness of the benefits of education than the ruling class gave them credit for. Further, he asserted that a proper government 'should permit none to remain uninstructed', since ignorance prevented the attainment of political rights and social justice.[177] Radical ideas of this sort were transmitted throughout the community in the 1790s, despite the tight control exercised by the government over the press. To such claims, Lord Braxfield retorted:

The Reformers talk of liberty and equality; this they hae in everything consistent wi' their happiness; and equality also. However low born a man may be, his abilities may raise him to the highest honours of the State ... If they hae ability, low birth is not against them.[178]

The aim seems to have been to convince people that playing along with the established system was ultimately in their best interest. The underlying message is that there is nothing wrong with the system *qua* system. Inequalities existed but capable individuals could overcome them. Those who did not manage to do so had only themselves to blame. A moral, individual interpretation of success or failure distracted attention from broader secular explanations of social inequality. Stories of social mobility through education, luck or a good marriage were common in chapbook literature of both the seventeenth and eighteenth centuries, as well as in Sunday schools.[179] These would help to preserve the existing fabric of society by drawing attention away from the more egregious injustices pointed out by the Radicals.

[177] Silver (1975): 10; West (1975): 113; Beale (1953):243–4.
[178] Quoted in T. Johnston, *The history of the working classes in Scotland* (1920): 223.
[179] Spufford (1981); Laqueur (1976c): 193–4.

It is here that the firmly political implications of education and literacy become clear. And there is a further angle on the politics of literacy. The view espoused by Spufford and Laqueur that the contents of chapbooks or the exercises taught in Sunday schools were not directly 'political' is based on a far too narrow definition of politics. There was, as Laqueur argues, 'widespread working-class adherence to the main outlines of the existing political order', but he does not examine how this consent was won.[180] There was little direct reference to Radicals, Chartists and other dissidents in the curricula and literature which Laqueur has studied, but literature which does not refer directly to politics cannot be automatically assumed to be apolitical. Literature such as English chapbooks reinforced the notion of social mobility in stories about clothiers and craftsmen who made good.[181] Much secular literature was deeply traditional and is unlikely to have stimulated thought. It is only when we see chapbooks in their correct social and ideological context that we can effectively question the notion that they were basically diversionary and did 'not serve any other ends polemic or political'. Secular-minded chapbooks went along with the myth of educational opportunity in 'forming the attitudes and sensibilities of generations of the uneducated'.[182]

George Orwell provided a more satisfactory definition of politics as a 'Desire to push the world in a certain direction, to alter other people's idea of the kind of society that they should strive after.'[183] The literature of chapbooks and the exercises of the Sunday schools were not directly propagandist in the main, because they would have been unsuccessful in this form. Nevertheless, both forms were conservative by default, or by claiming that the system ultimately worked well for everyone. This sort of propaganda was more effective because it was indirect. Claims about the educational system, many of which had little foundation in reality, were part of an attempt to use myth to buttress a social order which was under threat. Middle- and upper-class observers described a social and educational system which seemed to make sense of their own position and which served to reinforce what they saw as the acceptable social order. In some senses they were right, but as a description of the complexity of access to education and the opportunities which it offered it fell far short of being satisfactory.

Just as radical movements at this time developed their own educational ideas as part of political and economic programmes, so conservative forces may have clung closer to their own ethos of education and

---

[180] Laqueur (1976c): 201–2, 206. [181] Spufford (1981): 242, 249.
[182] *Ibid*. 249; Mitchison (1978): 34. [183] Orwell (1970): 26.

developed their own counter-ideology. There is no need to posit a conspiracy here, since the reproduction of social structures over long time-periods is not explicable solely in terms of individual intention. Consciousness of the function of a myth is not essential. Through the whole period from the sixteenth to the nineteenth centuries, the apparent altruism of philanthropical endowment of schools cannot be understood outside the context of a wish for order and continuity coupled with a deeply patronizing and pessimistic outlook on the moral state and unpleasant propensities of women, the young and the poor. During the late eighteenth and early nineteenth centuries, the full political implications of the myth of Scottish education were developed to cope with the radical ideas and unprecedented socio-economic change of the period.

All this pushes us closer to an understanding of the myth of equality of opportunity in and through education, and of the notion of Scotland's educational superiority. This last idea is dealt with in the concluding chapter, but some remarks on the former offer a con-clusion here. As seen by the middle and upper classes, education would make the masses think and act like their masters and thus keep them in their place. To maintain this broad and possibly unconscious aspiration, some measure of social mobility through education for all social classes was essential. This would be limited, however, in almost every case to positions of heavily circumscribed social and political power. The limit of social mobility for most 'working-class' students at Glasgow University was to become a minister of re-ligion.[184] Many arts graduates went into the ministry or into schoolteaching. For poor boys from humble backgrounds a university education was not really a path to wealth and status, but did offer, nevertheless, the comparative prestige and security of a clerical career. Ambivalence surrounding the moral implications of secular success was sublimated in the recruitment of successful 'lads o' pairts' to the ministry. However, stories of the lads of parts tended to ignore their typicality and by focusing on social mobility they obscure our understanding of the significance of education and literacy to social stability. Individual opportunity and structural inequality are not incompatible. Indeed, one writer in the *Aberdeen University Magazine* of 1836 explicitly recognized that the limited social mobility which did exist enhanced social stability, because people did not feel that they had been excluded from social mobility by anything other than their own failings.[185] Meanwhile, those who did make it were bound to the

---

[184] O'Day (1982): 276.   [185] McPherson (1983): 229.

system which had helped them. There had to be some social mobility but not too much.

In other words, a wide diffusion of educational opportunity was possible without equality of opportunity. The basic education provided for many working-class children did not necessarily provide them with useful literacy or the means to achieve the goals of their parents. But the notion that this education could provide a starting-point for social mobility was a powerful force in legitimating the existing social order. A mixture of philanthropy and self-interest was accepted as natural by the middle classes, but the apparently mutual benefits of education to high and low alike disguise the strong support being given to the status quo. A wholly open meritocracy was not accepted by the bulk of those advocating education for the masses in nineteenth-century England any more than in Scotland. But it was recognized that while education would not benefit most people, some would rise socially and would be bound to the system by ambition.[186]

What seems to have happened is this. The idea that Scotland had a superior education system originated in the early eighteenth century and was based on an existing tradition which drew on the aspirations of the Calvinist Reformation and the legislation of the seventeenth century. In the later eighteenth century a new myth of democratic education developed at a time of rapid social change and intellectual ferment. The idea that education was open to anyone of ability and that this made the society notionally meritocratic helped the middle classes to explain and to justify their hegemony in that society. Invented tradition was used to foster a corporate sense of identity in the middle and upper classes, to justify their position, attitudes and purposes, and to promote solidarity and self-confidence in the face of social change and an apparent threat to their dominance. Existing ideas about education supplied their preconceptions with an apparently solid historical reference point. The myth was presented as a long-established, original and distinctive tradition. Thus the response to a new situation was to draw on past traditions to sanction continuity. The older tradition of Scottish educational superiority through state action remained, however, and was a central feature of the debates of the 1830s.[187]

Firm studies of social mobility and literacy are all but lacking for Scotland before the mid nineteenth century. What evidence we have suggests that education for the working classes was strictly curtailed. Kirk Sessions might finance a promising poor child further than basic reading, but this was not at all usual.[188] Those who made it were very

---

[186] Kaestle (1976): 181.   [187] E. J. Hobsbawm, 'Inventing tradition' (1983).
[188] Beale (1953): 338.

lucky, and the fact that they did so reinforced the existing structures of inequality within the society by, rather than despite, making them fluid. There may have been more than lip-service to egalitarian ideals in late eighteenth- and early nineteenth-century Scotland, thanks to the long tradition of widespread access to education than was the case in contemporary England or even egalitarian America.[189] Nevertheless, emphasis was still heavily on the creation of a morally sound population. The tradition of acceptable mass education was inherited from specific events surrounding the Scottish Reformation rather than springing from any fundamentally egalitarian consensus. Social mobility was tolerated but there was no real commitment to equality of opportunity. In fact, stress on equality was largely a means of preserving inequality. Education is really very far from being ideologically neutral and indeed can be a powerful force in preserving and reproducing the structures of an unequal society. How exactly this happens forms the substance of our concluding remarks.

Historians have noted that alongside their usual stock-in-trade, change, there are a number of enduring structures in societies of the past. One persistent feature of European societies in the early modern period was the marked social and economic divisions between elements of the society. Identification of these structures and the elements of variance within them is relatively well advanced, but analysis of why and how societies tend to reproduce themselves in this way is still rudimentary. Traditions do not persist automatically, but since they are capable of experiencing decay or damage, they require continuous political and ideological effort to reproduce them. For most of the workers,

the larger outlines of power, station in life, political authority, appear to be as inevitable and irreversible as the earth and the sky. Cultural hegemony of this kind induces exactly such a state of mind in which the established structures of authority and even modes of exploitation appear to be in the very course of nature.[190]

The notion of open access to education was one way in which the lower classes were persuaded to acquiesce to the dominance of their superiors. Edward Thompson has drawn attention to the way in which 'real' resources such as land and money are preserved within a social class, although individual members of that group or families within it may rise or fall.

The inheritance grids . . . have often proved to be extremely effective as . . . the means by which a social group has extended its historical tenure of status and privilege . . . What is inherited is property itself, the claim on the resources of a

---

[189] Kaestle (1976): 182.   [190] Thompson (1974): 388.

future society; and the beneficiary may be, not any descendant of that particular family, but the historical descendant of the social class to which that
family once belonged.[191]

The implication for the study of literacy is that one can also transfer
'cultural' capital, and while individuals may gain or lose it, it is ultimately a social class which inherits this valuable commodity. Cultural
capital comprises both an attitude to success and education, and the
access to real and ideological resources which can help to preserve
social structures. In the case of Scotland, the middle and upper
classes were the inheritors of cultural capital and its powerful
ideological support for their position as the leaders of society.

The French sociologist Pierre Bourdieu has focused attention on the
role of education in inculcating the values of existing generations in
the coming one and in preserving the structures of social and
economic inequality.[192] His arguments are highly pertinent to the
early modern Scottish educational system. The chances of attaining
basic and post-elementary schooling are determined by both objective
economic circumstances (real and opportunity cost) and by a direct
and indirect selection process which is powerfully influenced by
social class. In other words, the son of a professional man, for
example, is many times more likely to go to university than is the son
of an agricultural labourer or miner. Once there, those from higher
social strata who have internalized the belief that they will succeed
tend to do better. In the process of socialization children acquire a
certain ethos which is 'a system of implicit and deeply interiorized
values which . . . helps to define attitudes towards the cultural capital
and educational institutions'.[193] This is a prime cause of unequal
achievement, since

the structure of the objective chances of social mobility and, more precisely,
of the chances of social mobility by means of education conditions attitudes to
school . . . through subjective hopes . . . which are no more than objective
chances intuitively perceived and gradually internalized.[194]

However, by espousing a formal equality of opportunity the school
provides an apparent justification for social inequalities. This formal
equality, epitomized in the Scots 'lads o' pairts' idea we have already
discussed, offers 'a cloak for and a justification of indifference to the
real inequalities' which were being perpetuated.[195]

---

[191] E. P. Thompson. 'The grid of inheritance' (1976): 360.
[192] P. Bourdieu and J. C. Passeron, *Reproduction in education, society and culture* (1977);
P. Bourdieu, 'The school as a conservative force' (1974).
[193] Bourdieu (1974): 32.   [194] *Ibid*. 34.   [195] *Ibid*. 38.

The exceptional success of those few individuals who escape the collective fate of their class apparently justify educational selection and give credence to the myth of the school as a liberating force among those who have been eliminated, by giving the impression that success is exclusively a matter of gifts and work.[196]

The fact that some people did make it against all the odds lends credence to the notion that the educational system helps to open up social ranks. A form of propaganda – a deliberate attempt to influence opinions and actions – which commands consent by having at least some measure of truth is a powerful instrument.

There is indeed some truth in the image of Scottish education – access to higher education seems to have been easier than in England, for example – but the picture is incomplete in that it deals not with what all people experienced, but only with the position of a retrospectively identified moral elect: 'lads o' pairts'. The myth of equality of opportunity in education which purports to describe the social system actually helps to reproduce it by guiding perceptions and actions. The myth is expressive but it is false.[197] Contradictory phenomena are simply discounted. The fact that aspects of the myth are demonstrably false need have little impact on its overall importance and acceptability, since other features, albeit exaggerated and over-simplified, are accepted. Individuals or social groups may share the values associated with one or more elements of the myth without necessarily subscribing to all of them, or for that matter being aware of their function.[198]

The educational system purports to redistribute people on the basis of an allegedly objective criterion of worth. 'Thus by its own logic the educational system can help to perpetuate cultural privileges without those who are privileged having to use it.'[199] There is then no need for direct supervision or intervention by the dominant classes as happened in nineteenth-century factory or mine or workhouse schools, or under the guise of inculcating allegedly value-free ideals such as religion or practical skills. Behind their apparent autonomy, other forms of school than these were apparently less effective in enforcing social or class-cultural control, but as *de facto* instruments of the existing ruling group they were crucial in preserving the cultural hegemony of certain received values. 'By giving cultural inequalities an endorsement which formally at least is in keeping with democratic ideals, it provides the best justification for these inequalities.'[200] Schools perpetrated what Bourdieu calls 'symbolic violence', imposing the culture of the ruling

---

[196] *Ibid*. 42.   [197] McPherson (1983): 218.   [198] Gray (1983): 44–5.
[199] Bourdieu (1974): 42.   [200] *Ibid*. 42.

classes on members of dominated groups such as the lower classes of
Scotland and England or the Scottish Highlanders. These were forced
to acknowledge the dominant culture as legitimate and their own as
illegitimate. Behind a façade of equality lay a powerful means of preserving inequality.

Literacy increased in the seventeenth and eighteenth centuries in
both Scotland and England. This much is plain. But it is hard to escape
the notion that early modern British society absorbed the impact of
increasing literacy in such a way as to limit change. This is indeed a far
cry from the 'lads o' pairts' fairy tale.

8

Literacy and the Scottish identity

We saw at the start of this study how Scotland's achievements in education and literacy have been elevated to the status of a legend. Scotland's state educational system, which began in the seventeenth century, is said to have produced an unusually literate population at a period when other countries were still struggling with ineffective voluntary systems. For some nineteenth-century educational reform lobbies and for many twentieth-century historians, this truly was 'a matter of history which cannot be denied'. The myth that Scotland enjoyed an unusually high level and wide social spread of literacy at an early date has been used to justify both educational change and the lack of it in Scotland and elsewhere since the eighteenth century. It forms part of the self-image of the Scots and of their image among other peoples.

In 1970 Tom Nairn went so far as to complain that 'Scotland is the land where ideal has never, even for an instant, coincided with fact'.[1] Notions about literacy and education in Scotland provide only some support for such a view. The picture is in actuality rather less black and white than this. The ideal of Scottish education and literacy is not always wholly divorced from reality, but some aspects of it do constitute an exaggeration and an over-simplification of the truth. Using both quantitative material and more traditional qualitative evidence, we have seen that the levels of literacy in seventeenth- and eighteenth-century Lowland Scotland were not greatly dissimilar from those in northern England. By the middle of the eighteenth century Scotland did have a lead over England as a whole, but the national average was influenced by the rather low literacy of south-east England compared to the northern counties. The hierarchical distribution of writing ability

---

[1] T. Nairn, 'The three dreams of Scottish nationalism' (1970): 35.

and the broader social meaning of illiteracy were much closer in areas of early modern Britain than has generally been assumed. The Highlands of Scotland remained highly illiterate far into the nineteenth century. What is more, the advantage enjoyed by Lowland Scotland was only true of men, since English women could boast higher literacy achievements than their Scottish counterparts. This was especially clear for the lower orders among women. We could say that the ideal of Scottish literacy was a long way from the practical experience of Scots men and women in the seventeenth and eighteenth centuries. Indeed, the traditional picture of Scottish education which we have analysed certainly exaggerates successes.

However, we cannot stop here for there are other implications which arise from this study. The northern counties of England and Lowland Scotland seem to have shared certain cultural patterns of which literacy was one. The systematic comparison of these supposedly quite distinct countries means that we can question the views of authorities who believe that 'it would be meaningless ... to speak of Scotland, or of Ireland for that matter, in the same breath as England'.[2] Of course we must be careful of over-simplification and avoid naive reductionism in analysing the two societies, but there is still a pressing need to see the countries in comparative perspective. When this approach is adopted, it becomes much harder to attribute a distinctive role to the sort of explanation of literacy usually adduced – Calvinism or Scotland's state educational system for example. Access to elementary education and to institutions of higher learning was probably slightly easier in Scotland, but the number of people involved was small and the impact on patterns of literacy and social mobility was probably slight. The contrast between Scotland and England may lie less in the institutional features of their societies than in less significant aspects of social customs.

In both countries, the abilities of men and women to sign their names were linked to definable secular influences, and cannot be understood properly outside the context of social attitudes towards women, children, the poor and linguistically distinct groups. Literacy was used not only for functional reasons associated with economic, political and religious developments but was also a powerful force helping to preserve the existing social, economic, political and mental world. In Scotland, every bit as much as in her allegedly more socially polarized neighbour, status, gender and residential divisions in society were manifested in and perhaps accentuated by a differing

[2] O'Day (1982): 217.

facility in reading and writing. Literacy helped to contribute to the rigidity of Scottish social structures remarked upon in recent work by L. M. Cullen.[3] For some men and women, literacy did liberate the mind and create new opportunities for thought and action, but this was relatively unusual and in any case the persistence of oral forms may have made literate skills rather less important than we assume from living in a universally literate society. The idea that Scotland was educationally well favoured is not wholly inaccurate. Her achievements were considerable given the poverty of many of Scotland's people and the geographical constraints on access to education. However, they were not as far ranging as we might expect given the rhetoric we find in much of the literature. Instead, the traditional image amounts to an 'idealization and distillation of a complex reality'.[4]

This study has adopted an explicitly comparative approach to the history of British society and has looked at similarities and contrasts between Britain and Europe. Comparisons of literacy need not be the end of the story, however. There are other aspects of Scottish and English society which could usefully be considered. Systematic comparison of Scotland and England could be taken into many fields other than those of witchcraft, poor relief and labour discipline which have been studied to date.[5] As far as literacy and education are concerned, we need more comparative studies of reading ability, difficult as it is to generate quantitative information on this. Comparing the content of Scottish, English and French chapbooks may help to reveal more about the comparative uses of literacy in Europe. Proper quantitative analysis of social mobility is needed if we are to be certain whether Scottish society really was more fluid and open than that of England. Devine suggests that while the merchant community was not a closed caste in the larger Scottish towns of the later seventeenth and early eighteenth centuries, most new merchant burgesses were petit bourgeois in origin.[6] Some systematic analysis of the chances of upward or downward social mobility for various social groups is needed and an assessment of the place of education in that mobility. Further comparison of literacy within areas of England would allow an assessment of the apparent homogeneity of society in that country already noted by historical demographers such as Wrigley and Schofield. We need to know more about why people wished to become literate.

---

[3] L. M. Cullen, 'Incomes, social classes and economic growth' (1983): 249.
[4] Anderson (1983): 1.   [5] Larner (1981); Mitchison (1974); Devine (1978).
[6] Devine (1983b): 170.

Used as a social indicator, the study of literacy can provide useful insights into some of the more general issues surrounding the comparative analysis of European societies, and in particular of *British* history as opposed to histories of England, Ireland, Scotland and Wales. It is plain, for example, that writing on the history of Scottish literacy and education cannot be understood properly outside the range of images which hold sway about Scottish society in both academic and non-academic circles. The Scottish historiographical tradition has to some extent been crippled by a set of romantic and anti-romantic, nationalistic and anti-nationalistic prejudices about her past. Conscious pursuit of Scotland's identity goes back to the invasions of Edward I, but was heightened by the experience of the Reformation and the Cromwellian occupation. At the time of the debate on a Union of Parliaments between England and Scotland commentators strove to identify what Scotland had to offer to a united Britain. They thus tried to exalt her particular values. Daniel Defoe, for example, was effusive about the moral superiority of Scotland's people. He affirmed that the 'Countrymen are worse Husbandmen and better Christians than ours, and they have both more Knowledge and more Practice of Religion among the Poor than we have'.[7] Scots opposed to the Union sought meanwhile to preserve their nation's identity. Most debate centred on trade and sovereignty, but religion and other ideological aspects also entered into consideration. Reaffirmation of a pre-existing stress on education was one way of preserving identity. During the eighteenth-century Enlightenment there came an efflorescence of introspection. Was Scotland 'a nation, a province, a lost kingdom; a culture, a history, a body of tradition; a bundle of sentiments, a state of mind; North Britain or Caledonia?'[8] Looking to the past to reaffirm present consciousness Scotland's virtues were expounded – independence and love of liberty, for example.

Both natives and outsiders credited the Scots with certain desirable features arising from their material backwardness. For Thomas Pennant in the 1760s, 'the devotion of the common people of *Scotland*, on the usual days of worship, is . . . much to be admired'.[9] Scots tried to balance out their loss of political independence by exaggerating their special characteristics – literature, education, religion and general 'moral fibre'.[10] Later eighteenth-century success in literature was

---

[7] Defoe (1708): 318; P. W. J. Riley, *The Union of England and Scotland* (1978): 221–45; I. Ross and S. Scobie, 'Patriotic publishing as a response to Union' (1974).
[8] J. A. Smith, 'Some eighteenth century ideas of Scotland' (1970): 107.
[9] Pennant (1774): 88.   [10] Smith (1970): 115; Gray (1983): 39; Nairn (1970): 38.

important to national morale, one reason perhaps why Bruce Lenman's recent volume on this period concentrates so much on these cultural aspects.[11]

Associated with this is the older and more durable concept that certain societies are not only different from but better than others. This is the sort of view propagated by Macaulay and others for England, but revived in a subtler form by Macfarlane in his recent book *The origins of English individualism*. It is also one which Kenneth Lockridge has tried to discredit with his work on the putatively 'modern' values of colonial Americans.[12] Romantic attitudes to Scotland plainly provide prime examples of this approach to social history. Scotland's educational system allegedly marked her out from England and added considerably to her moral superiority over England. It was therefore stressed by academics and non-academics alike.

One of the most important implications of Scotland's supposedly open access to education was that this could ease social frictions by persuading the lower classes that they were not being wholly discriminated against. We remember from chapter 1 the notion that harmony existed in peasant communities along with a 'democratic' outlook which only hardened during the nineteenth century into 'sardonic cynicism'.[13] The penetration of agricultural and industrial capitalism and the cash nexus are seen as crucial in breaking down this egalitarian and fundamentally content society – a society marked by a consensus which open access to education was vital in winning. An eighteenth-century Uist tacksman complained how 'The noblest virtues have been ruined, or driven into exile, since the love of money has crept in amongst us; and since deceit and hypocrisy have carried mercenary policy and slavish, sordid avarice into our land.'[14] But perhaps a divided society was already an established feature of Lowland Scotland in the seventeenth century or before, and is reflected in literacy patterns.

Images of Scotland derive from other sources too. The Highlands and rural Scotland in general were romanticized by middle- and upper-class observers of the eighteenth and nineteenth centuries. Indeed, the romanticism of the Enlightenment provided a focus of identity for urban middle-class Scots, though this was only achieved by selecting, exaggerating and distorting certain features of society. Under the

---

[11] Lenman (1981).   [12] Lockridge (1974).
[13] I. Carter, 'The changing image of the peasant in Scottish history and literature' (1981): 11.
[14] Quoted in Burke (1978): 250.

influence of Walter Scott they ultimately became chic, a development which has in the long run fed into the '"prince of the heather" school of sentimental historical obfuscation'.[15]

The prolongation of Scotch peculiarities, especially of our language and habits, I do earnestly desire ... Nothing can prevent the gradual disappearance of local manners under the absorption and assimilation of a far larger, richer and more powerful kindred adjoining kingdom. Burns and Scott have done more for the preservation of *proper Scotland* than could ever be accomplished by laws, statesmen, or associations.[16]

Seeking to illuminate 'the peculiar features' of the Scots, Sir Walter Scott was keen to glorify and romanticize the 'strange, precarious, and adventurous modes of life' of the Border people, by showing their tempestuous military and political history and by outlining 'some of their peculiar customs'.[17] What in fact emerged was a pot-pourri of prominent examples of folklore, specific aspects of which were interesting in themselves but which together did not add up to significant social or cultural differences except when seen out of context. For all the historical insight in his best works such as the *Heart of Midlothian*, in much of Scott's writing 'there is seldom a connection between scenery and livelihood; between the environment and the life and work of the rural population'.[18] At the same time, 'there is a basic contradiction between the all too real squalor of these Highlanders ... and the noble savages he persisted in creating from among them'.[19] Writers like Scott were instrumental in blurring the division between romance and reality which characterizes much of our understanding of Scottish history. Indeed, images of northern Britain form part of the cultural primitivism popular in nineteenth-century Europe, but which fed on a (misunderstood) literary tradition which originated in the sixteenth century.[20] Put simply, the belief was that life was rural in the past, therefore life was better in the past. Possessing a pastoral emphasis, this set of ideas stressed the supposedly superior moral qualities of a more backward people untainted by modern (urban) decadence. Thomas Pennant clearly had an axe to grind when claiming that

the common people of the north are disposed to be religious, having the example before them of a gentry untainted by luxury and dissipation, and the

---

[15] Carter (1981): 9–12.   [16] Quoted in Craig (1961): 151–2; my italics.
[17] Henderson (1902): 111, 116.
[18] J. H. Paterson 'The novelist and his region: Sir Walter Scott' (1965): 149.
[19] *Ibid*. 150–1.
[20] Burke (1978): 10; H. J. Hanham, *Scottish nationalism* (1969): 18; M. R. Weisser, *The peasants of the Montes* (1976): 16, 120–1; Nairn (1970).

advantage of being instructed by a clergy, who are active in their duty, and who preserve respect, amidst all the disadvantages of a narrow income.[21]

It is then hardly surprising that attempts to establish national identity by emphasizing the uniqueness of institutions and society have often tended to produce a narrow and parochial outlook on Scottish history. There has been a tendency to concentrate on identifying cultural and economic differences as a means of discovering particular attributes of Scottish and English society. This is all very well in so far as it highlights the discrepancies in the societies which mark the differences between diverse social organizations. But its impact for any attempts at proper comparative analysis of Scotland in its wider European context has been baneful. The sorts of problem created by this approach are ideally illustrated in traditional studies of education and literacy.

How exactly are we to identify the social characteristics which marked out Scottish society? There seem to have been a number of distinctively Scottish features, such as the strong desire for education we noticed above. Yet it is often hard to pin down the apparent differences, and in any case we keep encountering contemporary remarks about the ready intercourse between Scots and English Borderers and the 'similarity of their manners'.[22] There do indeed appear to have been resemblances in cultural patterns. One implication of Thomas Laqueur's work on lower-class demand for education in eighteenth-century England is that there may have been every bit as much desire for literacy there as in Scotland.[23] He argues that state intervention cannot explain the similarity of high literacy levels in northern England and Lowland Scotland, and points out that they 'were products of the same cultural constellation which worked to encourage education'.[24] West paraphrases this as a common 'national ethos' which emphasized education and which arose from 'national character' or religion rather than legislation.[25] In what did this 'cultural constellation' consist?

For Adam Ferguson, 'nationality is ... not just a matter of institutions, or of "high" culture, but of all the elements that make up the texture of life'.[26] We noticed in our introductory remarks that there was

---

[21] Pennant (1774): 219.   [22] Henderson (1902): 119.
[23] Laqueur (1976b): 193–4.   [24] Laqueur (1976a): 256–7.
[25] E. G. West, 'Resource allocation in education' (1973): 65.   [26] Smith (1970): 118.

a range of contacts between Lowland Scotland and the north of England. Similarities in social organization were also plain. Someone with experience of working in both areas claimed that 'the Scotch system of working and hiring on the one side [of the Tweed] and the English on the other are almost identical', while 'the style of working and many of the domestic customs and habits are as different as if the Merse and Lothian were separated by Mountains measuring hundreds of miles'. Husbandry and patterns of labour organisation were 'nearly alike' in this area.[27] This was effectively a mini cultural zone within a larger one which comprised Lowland Scotland and northern England. Brooke speculates that around AD 1,000 the English lands between Forth and Tweed became part of Scotland. These lands had anciently formed part of the northern-most English principality of Northumbria, and were quite distinct from the Celtic and Norse amalgams of northern Scotland.[28] In the sixteenth century, for example, Gaelic Scotland and Ireland 'formed a single culture-province'.[29] The geographical distribution of literacy may reflect a long-established cultural identity between Lowland Scotland and the north of England which had been overlaid in more recent times by political changes.

One prominent aspect of European historical development over the last few centuries has been the homogenization of culture over broad regions and the assimilation of peripheral cultures to the dominant national one. By editing Sir Walter Scott's collections of Border ballads, T. F. Henderson hoped to 'contribute somewhat to the history of my native country; the peculiar features of whose manners and character are daily melting and dissolving into those of her sister and ally'.[30]

This process had been going on for at least two centuries. Highland culture was becoming submerged in Lowland, which was in turn borrowing heavily from English urban and upper-class forms. In a sense the Welsh and Irish gentry as well as the Scottish were anglicized through a process of voluntary assimilation.[31] This same change happened relatively easily to the gentry of the Scottish Lowlands during the seventeenth and eighteenth centuries. The popularity of London periodicals in the bigger Scottish towns of the eighteenth century helped to foster the cultural integration.[32] The integration of the Highlands was much slower, since interaction seems to have

---

[27] Anon., 'On the hiring markets in the counties of Northumberland, Berwick and Roxburgh' (1834–5): 379; Somerville (1951): 105.
[28] C. Brooke, *From Alfred to Henry III* (1961): 198.   [29] Bannerman (1983): 214.
[30] Henderson (1902): 175.   [31] M. Hechter, *Internal colonialism* (1975): 80–1, 109–11.
[32] Devine (1983a): 12.

heightened the sense of a separate identity rather than fostering a common one.[33] There were more problems in creating a national culture which assimilated all regions of Scotland than were found in England during the seventeenth and eighteenth centuries. As we have seen, Scotland itself was not a homogeneous entity, the Highlands remaining highly illiterate into the late nineteenth century. Indeed, enduring tensions between Highlanders and Lowlanders gave rise to one form of ballad story. Hechter argues that to promote national development 'the core and peripheral cultures must ultimately merge into one all-encompassing cultural system to which all members of the society have primary identification and loyalty'.[34]

It is possible nevertheless that the continuation of literacy differentials in areas of Britain into the late nineteenth century implies persisting cultural divergences. The same phenomenon is observable in France, the high literacy of northern and eastern parts having a long historical lineage which cannot simply be related to economic advance or to the greater availability of schooling. The especially good performance of the Hautes Alpes, for example, has to be seen in relation to a spectrum of social, linguistic and religious factors. There were areas of Languedoc, often quite small, where education and the desire for literacy had a long and vigorous history, while in other parts people were apparently indifferent.[35] Perhaps the same is true of areas of early modern Britain. The divergences between levels of illiteracy in the Highlands and Lowlands of Scotland are much greater that those between areas of England, and indeed resembled the sorts of distinct region found in Continental Europe. Nevertheless, a sort of cultural zone is suggested comprising Lowland Scotland and the four northern counties of England. The importance of regions in understanding British social history may be greater than is usually allowed.

Similarity in literacy levels plus the range of comments on resemblances between work and leisure patterns in northern England and southern Scotland further suggest that the border was relatively unimportant for many people. Historians have tended to take a rather more truncated, compartmentalized view of social man. As Marc Bloch pointed out fifty years ago, there is no good reason why social developments should stop at national boundaries, since lines on the map are not a reflection of social and ethnic realities but of political,

[33] Hechter (1975): 10; I. Carter, 'Marriage patterns and social sectors in Scotland' (1973).
[34] Hechter (1975): 5; Buchan (1972): 33–4; T. C. Smout, 'Centre and periphery in history' (1980).
[35] See above ch. 4, pp. 159–61.

military and diplomatic adjustments. Assuming the existence of the sorts of 'outmoded topographical compartments within which we seek to confine social realities', too many historians tend to assume unity of experience within national boundaries due to shared legal and institutional structures.[36] It seems likely that cultural differences between areas of England were not nearly as marked as those between Highland and Lowland Scotland. However, in terms of cultural experience, northern England and Lowland Scotland may have formed a zone distinct from both southern England and Highland Scotland. An explicitly comparative approach has many possibilities for broadening our understanding of European societies.

A number of serious flaws have entered into historical writing on British history as a result both of compartmentalizing and of assuming that Scotland, Wales and Ireland are somehow peripheral to main developmental trends and can thus be treated as 'The Other Britain'.[37] Scottish Enlightenment thinkers such as Adam, Carlyle and Hume had a concept of Britain where Scotland was the northern part, albeit 'a narrow place', though more generally Scotland and England were perceived as separate entities.[38] Scotland and England are surely prime cases on which to use Marc Bloch's comparative method 'to make a parallel study of societies that are at once neighbouring and contemporary, exercising a constant mutual influence, exposed throughout their development to the action of the same broad causes just because they are close and contemporaneous, and owing their existence in part at least to a common origin'.[39] Such a project was suggested to the Lord Chancellor by Francis Bacon soon after the accession of James VI to the English throne. Calling to mind the 'unworthiness of the history of England ... and the partiality and obliquity of that of Scotland', he 'conceived it would be an honour for his Majesty, and a work very memorable, if this island of Great Britain, as it is now joined in Monarchy for the ages to come, so were joined in History for the times past; and that one just and complete History were compiled of both nations'.[40]

A number of benefits might be expected from simultaneous study of Scotland and England. Recently Macfarlane has shown that analysing only fairly short time-spans of a country's history in isolation can produce a spurious impression of change, especially when they are

---

[36] M. Bloch, *Land and work in medieval Europe* (1967): 70.
[37] E. J. Hobsbawm, *Industry and empire* (1969): 294–312.   [38] Smith (1970): 108.
[39] Bloch (1967): 47.   [40] J. Spedding, *The letters and life of Francis Bacon* (1868): 250.

compared with other periods for which the historian has to accept the accounts of other specialists. It is much harder to argue for a specific development occurring in a short space of time when we begin to look at a much longer period, and despite Macfarlane's more recent flights on England's distinctiveness, knowledge of parallel developments in other countries tends to make assertions about specific characteristics of limited geographical areas more difficult to maintain. Marc Bloch hoped that international comparisons would 'provide a means of confirming or rejecting explanations which might seem irrefutable if viewed in a single historical or geographical setting'.[41] It may be fruitless to dwell on differences when, beneath legal and institutional superstructures, society was basically similar in important respects.

Of course there were differences between Scotland and England, and we must beware of broad, possibly superficial similarities and of the tendency towards over-confident generalizations arising from enthusiasm for the new findings. As Peter Mathias has remarked, 'common features in .., cross-national comparisons stand out as prominently as so-called unique ones'.[42] At the same time, institutions and the law can be important influences on attitudes and values. We must analyse the complex interactions between a society and the legal, administrative and ecclesiastical structures associated with it. There may be subtle differences between, say, the uses of literacy in the two countries, but some of the more stark generalizations about fundamental divergences of experience do not stand up to testing. Further, when we identify differences or similarities it is vital to assess their importance as genuine indicators of divergent social organizations. Yet all this should not prevent us from trying to further the idea of *British* history. Indeed we should not be slow to follow Francis Bacon who nearly four centuries ago expressed the earnest hope that

the realme of Scotland is nowe an auncient and noble Realme of itself substantine, but when this Island shalbe made Brittaine then Scotland is no more to be considered as Scotland but as a parte of Brittaine, no more then England is to be considered England, but as parte likewise of Brittaine, and consequently neither of these are to be considered as thinges entier of themselves, but in the proportion they beare to the whole.[43]

[41] Quoted in T. M. Devine and D. Dickson, 'In pursuit of comparative aspects of Scottish and Irish development' (1983): 272.
[42] P. Mathias, *The transformation of England* (1979): 15.
[43] BM Add. MS 41613: fols. 42v, 43.

Appendix 1: Sources for the study of Scottish and English literacy

There were many occasions when the people of early modern Europe were called upon to authenticate a document with their personal subscription. Taxation documents, land or moveable property transfers (wills, dowry contracts or charters for instance), and the systematic questioning of military conscripts and prisoners during the nineteenth and twentieth centuries provide immediate examples. Let us look in detail at one of these sources in order to assess the usefulness of alternative sources to the court depositions used in the main body of our analysis. When we have assessed their value we will be in a better position to specify the type of source which will be most useful for comparing levels of literacy in Scotland and England in the early modern period.

As a source for the study of literacy, wills have been described as 'fundamentally unsatisfactory'. Local studies, such as Spufford's *Contrasting communities* on rural Cambridgeshire, have shown that they present a distorted and exaggerated picture of illiteracy. Other writers have gratefully eschewed wills as a source in favour of the much more tractable, representative and reliable church court depositions. In some countries, however, wills and deeds are the only available documents which provide information on literacy attainment, and a variety of techniques have been used to compensate for their acknowledged biases. Lockridge has argued for colonial New England that the acknowledged biases in wills – age and debility increase illiteracy while greater wealth and status of testators diminish it – cancel out, leaving signatures on wills a fair facsimile of signatures among the population. However, this is not conclusively proven, and the fact that will-making itself may have been literacy-specific creates serious interpretative problems.[1] It is unfortunate that for Scotland, only subscriptions to testaments offer

---

[1] Spufford (1974): 196–7; Cressy (1980): 105–8; Lockridge (1974).

much quantifiable information before the mid seventeenth century, since there are very few sets of surviving court depositions before this. Those which do exist only rarely have the subscription of witnesses or the accused. Some analysis of Scottish testaments is therefore necessary, if only to highlight the difficulties in their use.

Most Scottish wills are preserved in transcribed form in the large 'Register of Testament' volumes at General Register House in Edinburgh. These offer no indication of the testator's ability to sign. Only 'Warrants of Testaments' provide usable material. These are all 'testaments testamentar' – actual wills made by the deceased, and distinct from 'testaments dative', which are in fact only inventories compiled following the appointment of an executor by the Commissary Court to administer the estate of a person dying intestate. Warrants of Testaments from Edinburgh Commissary Court were used.[2] This Court had testamentary jurisdiction over the Lothians plus parts of Peebles and Stirlingshire, over those with property in more than one Commissariat's jurisdiction and over those dying outside Scotland who had moveable property in the realm.

In order to ensure proper disposal of moveable property after death, the testator had clearly to express his wishes in a document subscribed by him. If the whole document was written by him it had only to be subscribed at the end by himself, though if written for him it had to be witnessed by two males above fourteen years of age whose subscriptions, along with that of the testator plus the name and designation of the writer, had also to be appended. Thus it is usual to find at the end of the 'latter will and testament' either the holograph signature of the testator, or a formal attestation by the scribe or notary public to the authenticity of the will, plus a declaration that the testator could not write and had explicitly asked the notary to sign for him. Notarial subscriptions must be read carefully however, since prior to the late sixteenth century these often attest only to the accuracy with which the testator's wishes had been recorded or to the completeness of the inventory, giving no indication of his literacy.[3] At best, these documents provide information about a testator's wealth, occupation or social status and residence, and about his or her ability to sign their own name. A 50% random sample of boxes of wills was drawn, covering the century 1580–1680. Witnesses were almost invariably literate even at the earliest dates, and they are not analysed here. Their occupations are rarely given and it is strongly suspected that they were chosen for their literacy, and perhaps also for their social prestige.

---

[2] SRO CC8/10/1–15.   [3] W. Alexander, *Practice of the Commissary Courts* (1859): 63–4.

However, information was recovered about the literacy of 447 male will-makers and 143 female. This is presented in table A1.1.

There are a number of serious problems involved in the interpretation of the figures in this table. Scottish testators, like their English counterparts, were almost invariably 'seik in bodie' when they made their wills, and indeed most wills were made in the expectation of an imminent demise. This seems to have had a significant impact on ability to sign a will. Most wills analysed were written by professional scribes, and there must have been some temptation for possibly feeble testators simply to ask the notary to subscribe for them, rather than making the effort of signing or marking themselves. If the will-maker asked the notary to subscribe when he could have managed himself, then a further bias which would exaggerate illiteracy would be introduced. This would reinforce the effects of actual debility which might have produced only a mark when normally the testator could write for himself. There are frequent instances where the notary gives a reason for the person's failure to sign. James Speir, an Edinburgh merchant burgess, asked the notary to subscribe, 'because I may not writt myself throw the sevireness of my seikness'. The context makes it clear that these men were otherwise literate. Thomas Young, merchant in Edinburgh, stated he could not write himself 'in respect of the want of my perfite sight and of my sickness'. Andrew Bell, merchant burgess in Linlithgow, explicitly claimed he was no longer able to write. Testaments subscribed in this fashion are taken here to show illiteracy, since it is uncertain how often similar circumstances may have afflicted other will-makers, without being mentioned. George Douglas in Dalkeith could not write, 'in respect of the unstableness of my hand now in my sickness', and indeed many signed wills show a shaky and uncertain hand.[4]

This problem is not unique to testaments. In a society where disease and accidents combine with rudimentary medical facilities, a temporary or permanent disability may distort the profile of illiteracy. Alexander Fraser told the Justiciary Court that 'he cannot write because he is lame of a finger'. The nature of the circumstances where a will was made might also influence observed ability to sign, and the presence of plague or other contagious disease may have a distorting effect. Plague raged in Edinburgh during 1645–6, and Alexander Crombie, stabler there, was not allowed to sign himself, 'being under suspicioun of pestilence'. He was still alive five months later when another will was made in which it was specifically stated that he was

---

[4] SRO CC8/10/7 (1624); SRO CC8/10/10: 21 December 1638; SRO CC8/10/11: 25 June 1647.

able to write but could not touch the notary's pen for fear of contagion. Of course, this particular bias is not necessarily against under-estimation of literacy. Janet Alexander, the widow of Edinburgh vintner William Wyllie, was obliging enough to point out the two reasons why she was unable to subscribe her will, 'being unliterat and in respect of the contagious plague . . . may not tuche the notaris pen with my awin hand'. Overall, it seems likely that this factor would tend to lower the aggregate literacy levels.[5]

Though not invariably true, increased age may have decreased the ability to sign. One aspect of this would be lack of practise in writing. Except for professional purposes, writing seems rarely to have been used before the eighteenth century, and people might simply forget how to use a pen. Isabel Rowan, spouse to William Rowan (laird) of Dumbieck, concluded her deposition to the Justiciary Court by remarking that she 'hes altogither forgot her wreitting'. There was much more need for writing by the late seventeenth century, when Edinburgh tradesmen were turning increasingly to printed receipts.[6] Forgetting would be less likely over time for those exposed to such needs.

At the same time, Scottish wills are probably biased towards the better-off elements of society. Table A1.1 shows, for example, that the majority of male testators were lairds, professionals or tradesmen and craftsmen: 71% of all those whose occupation or social status is given. Only six were described as 'servant'. Most were Edinburgh-dwellers. In the case of women, outnumbered three to one by men in our sample, nearly all were widows to tradesmen who had taken over their husband's estate. Only exceptionally were married women able to make a will, and the surviving ones deal exclusively with paraphernalia (clothes and other personal adornments, such as jewellery). Deposition evidence shows widows to be more literate than other women, while there is also some indication that the daughters of high-status fathers, who are also represented among female will-makers at this court, were similarly more literate. We cannot properly analyse the connection between wealth and literacy, because in Scots law a full inventory was not required to inherit a deceased person's estate. Not all moveable goods (let alone land) would necessarily be included in the inventory, with the result that actual wealth would be under-estimated.

[5] SRO JC7/7; SRO CC8/10/11: 6 October 1645; 8 March 1646; SRO CC8/10/11: 18 August 1645.
[6] SRO JC10/6 (1699); SRO CC8/4/200–500 *passim:* receipts are often recorded with other papers in debt cases.

Table A1.1. *Occupational illiteracy of Edinburgh Commissary Court male testators, 1580–1680*

Occupation	N	% all testators	% illiterate	% Edinburgh
Laird	(49)	11	12	10
Professional	(26)	6	19	58
Craft & Trade	(162)	36	41	80
Farmer/Tenant	(38)	9	37	53
Others	(60)	13	52	35
Unknown	(112)	25	77	11
Total	(447)	100		

How then do figures on occupationally specific aspects of illiteracy compare? Occupations have been grouped to conform with the categories outlined in chapter 2. The first noteworthy aspect is the appreciably higher illiteracy of the groups 'laird' and 'professional' compared to deponents in this social category. We should obviously be suspicious when someone who made his living by writing is unable to sign his own will. The levels of 12% and 19% can be compared with the near-total literacy of deponents at the Justiciary Court during the mid seventeenth century. This is not simply due to the earlier start of this sample, since three-quarters of the testaments were made after 1620. Moving on to the larger craft and trade group, the level of 41% is far higher than that among deponents in table 2.1, and the predominance of Edinburgh men, 80% of all testators in this category, would lead us to expect that scores would, if anything, be lower than in the national sample. There are few tenant farmers, though it is clear from their legacies and inventories that many 'unknown' were in fact farmers of some kind. Only explicit descriptions of status have been used here, because of the problems of inferring occupation or status reliably from wills and inventories. None of the sets of court depositions has sufficient numbers for sound comparisons to be drawn with testamentary evidence on illiteracy among tenant farmers.

Overall, the results do confirm the picture in other sources though, given the problems outlined above, plus the fact that testators appear to have been among the wealthier and higher status members of society, the proportions of illiterate are suspiciously high. This is especially obvious for lairds and professionals. Yet in some cases illiteracy is suspiciously *low*. Aggregate illiteracy for males in the period from 1580 to 1680 is 47%: much lower than the 70% national average figure for the years of the Scottish Revolution. Female illiteracy runs at

73%, again a good deal lower than our estimate of roughly 95% for the mid seventeenth century. Debility may have been more than cancelled out by the effects of wealth, residence and social status. However, these influences could not erase the fundamental difference in levels of illiteracy based on gender. Variations in illiteracy between testaments and depositions are not the same for all social groups, suggesting that any universal compensating factor of the kind used by Lockridge to allow for biases in New England wills is open to serious doubt. The same lack of uniformity is shown below for northern England. Despite these problems, Scottish testaments do provide a valuable source, both because they survive earlier than depositions, and because of their close comparability with English wills.

Wills in the diocese of Durham are more plentiful, and more precise analysis of shorter time-periods has been possible. Testaments giving the signature or mark of the will-maker were sampled for the years 1590–1601, 1661–8, 1700–5 and 1750–7. There are few wills for the Interregnum period, and before this many surviving examples are copies which only infrequently give usable information on literacy. Nevertheless 2,243 were found to offer satisfactory material.[7] As in the case of Scottish testaments, the name, residence and occupation or social status of the testator is given (at best) and wills of the seventeenth and eighteenth centuries usually bear an autograph signature or mark. There is no equivalent to notarial subscription.

Analysis of literacy in these English wills is subject to the same problems of distortion through illness and old age outlined above for Scottish testaments. In medieval England there was a superstition against signing a will, with the result that subscription was left until the very last minute when a testator was more likely to make a mark even though he may normally have signed. The presence of a personal signature or mark on all the wills used here does however remove one possible source of bias. A personal subscription, usually beside the testator's seal, was needed to authenticate the document.[8] The literacy of the two or more witnesses generally required to authenticate wills was not considered, since only rarely are their occupations given and, as in the case of Scotland, they were probably chosen because of their reading and writing ability. One study of Worcestershire wills in the early eighteenth century has uncovered much lower levels of illiteracy among witnesses than among testators.[9] Only one husbandman in four could sign his own will, but husbandmen who acted as witnesses

[7] DPDD Durham probate records, wills and inventories.
[8] H. Swinburne, *A treatise of testaments and last wills* (1677): 293–301.
[9] Johnston (1978): 207.

Table A1.2. *Occupational illiteracy of Durham diocese male testators, 1590s, 1660s, 1700s, 1750s*

	Date			
	1590s	1660s	1700s	1750s
Occupation	N %	N %	N %	N %
Gentry	(27) 30	(66) 11	(110) 4	(95) 1
Professionals	(8) 13	(26) 4	(28) 4	(32) 0
Crafts & trades	(31) 52	(152) 44	(141) 27	(198) 16
Yeomen	(28) 86	(276) 74	(213) 58	(203) 36
Labourers	(9) 67	(4) 75	(3) 100	(3) 33
Total	(103)	(524)	(495)	(531)

were 66% literate. These divergences are too great to be explained simply by the debility of will-makers and must be due to the unrepresentative nature of those who acted as witnesses. For Durham diocese testators only, explicit occupational or status designations were employed, despite the fact that it is often possible to infer occupation from inventories. Finally, literacy was not analysed by wealth, though association between the factors is often assumed to be important. Inventories refer only to moveable property, and often only to household contents and farm goods, making no mention of the debt and credit which is known to have been a highly important aspect of local economies in early modern England. *Pre mortem* transfers may have lowered the apparent wealth of testators, while for tradesmen and the elderly (retired) farmers, omission of debt and credit is likely to produce significant distortion.[10] Wealth may have been converted into cash put out at interest, the retired person living on the proceeds. The simple analyses presented below do nevertheless offer interesting comparisons with figures on illiteracy derived from other sources.

The effects of age or illness are clear among gentry and professionals in the two earlier decades, and are still evident to a lesser extent in the 1700s. Table A1.2 shows this.[11]

However, if we compare the results of table A1.2 analyses with figures from Durham diocese Consistory Court deponents who were drawn from the same area, the levels of illiteracy are close for the key groups gentry, professionals, crafts and trades, and yeomen. In the 1590s deponents, whose average age would, it must be allowed, have been

[10] B. A. Holderness, 'Credit in a rural community' (1975).
[11] Categories conform to groupings in table 2.1.

younger than most will-makers, had the following levels of illiteracy:
gentry 36%, 'tradesmen' 57% and yeomen 71%.[12] Only for yeomen is
the testator figure appreciably higher. The performance of women will-
makers was better than that of female deponents, the effects of debility
having been counterbalanced by the generally higher socio-economic
status of the former. Twenty-one women made wills in the 1590s of
whom 86% could not sign their names. Again, this compares favourably
with the 97% illiteracy of female deponents. Comparison is also possible
with assize deponents in the seventeenth and eighteenth centuries. In
the 1660s, the levels among both will-makers and deponents in the craft
and trade category are close: 44% versus 37%. Taking the figure of 16%
illiterate for the 1750s from table A1.2 for craftsmen and tradesmen and
comparing it with the 31% among deponents which we saw in table 2.4
(chapter 2), we can see that ability to sign among craftsmen and tradesmen was much more resilient to the effects of age and debility. Indeed,
these mid eighteenth-century will-makers would seem to have been
selected from the most literate members of their social class. This was
doubtless associated with the greater frequency with which writing was
practised by the former. More practise, and also perhaps better medical
care or a change in the timing of will-making to a period before illness
had seriously influenced signing ability, may account for the more
robust signatures of the upper classes. Certainly, by the 1660s illiteracy
among gentry and professional deponents in other sources was less
than 1% whereas, in earlier decades, Cressy's work has shown that they
were unusually illiterate.

The numbers in some occupational groups are unacceptably low for
earlier decades. Members of the lower orders rarely made wills:
labourers and coalworkers form only 1% of all testators in the sample as
a whole. Husbandmen and gardeners have been grouped alongside
yeomen, since there were only thirty of the former and six of the latter in
all four decades sampled. Twenty-two of the wills made by husbandmen fall in the 1750s, at which time this occupational designation
made a reappearance after 150 years' absence from records relating to
Northumberland and Durham. The term 'farmer' also creeps into use at
this time, and it is impossible to assess whether all three are used inter-
changeably. For the 1750s, the 181 yeomen wills show illiteracy of 36%,
while for the 22 husbandmen it was 41%. Again, this reinforces arguments about the vague nature of this designation in northern England
that were put forward in the discussions on literacy and social structure
in chapter 2.

---

[12] Cressy (1978): 20.

Table A1.3. *Male and female illiteracy in different communities of residence,*
Durham diocese, 1590s, 1660s, 1700s, 1750s

	Sex			
	Male		Female	
Type of community	N	% illiterate	N	% illiterate
Village	(976)	44	(270)	75
Market town	(364)	39	(90)	69
City	(428)	19	(87)	50
Unknown	(15)	20	(13)	100
Total	(1,783)		(460)	

One final aspect which deserves attention is the distinction between the overall literacy levels of dwellers in the two major cities of the diocese, Newcastle and Durham, and those from elsewhere in the counties. This is shown in table A1.3; the categories are based on John Adams' *Index villaris* as in chapter 2.

Table A1.3 shows that the inhabitants of market towns were not significantly more literate than those in rural villages. It is likely that market towns formed only a part of the often large parishes in which they lay and that other townships were still highly rural and not subject to the occupational diversification and specialization which accounts for the higher literacy in the cities. Interestingly, this pattern is very similar to that recovered from assize depositions and documented in tables 2.8 and 2.9, chapter 2. Levels are lower, however, for testators as a whole.

Further work is needed on the problems of wealth as indicated in inventories since, despite the problems involved, the opportunity to relate literacy attainment to socio-economic status does offer interesting possibilities to determine whether literacy was indeed dependent on social position and economic utility in a similar way in both Scotland and England. Wills do provide a comparable source for analysing literacy in Scotland and England and they do cover a useful cross-section of early modern society. But they also contain biases, controlling for which is difficult, and this makes it hard to discover how representative the literacy figures we derive from them really are. This is a common problem with many potentially useful sources for the study of literacy before the nineteenth century.

What we need is a source where individuals do not select themselves, or where a particular section of the population is not selected either accidentally or consciously. It is essential to have documents where those who appear are a representative cross-section of the population, or where we can control for any bias caused by age, wealth, social status or residence. Another apparently promising instance would be witnesses to legal documents. However, the problems with this type of source become obvious when we consider the example of witnesses to the transfers of land registered in the Sasines Records of Scotland after 1617. They would scarcely be representative of the population at large and may, like witnesses to wills, have been selected expressly for their literate skills. Signed or marked marriage registers provide valuable information, since the majority of the population of early modern Europe married at some time in their lives. In other words, those who subscribed the record of their nuptials were representative of the society as a whole. In France, registers are available from 1686 and form the foundation of nearly all the many studies of illiteracy there prior to the Revolution. Marriage registers have been used for a number of English studies, and provide information from 1754. Unfortunately, signed or marked registers do not become available in Scotland until 1855, when civil registration of births, marriages and deaths began. Much interesting work has been done on English literacy between the mid sixteenth and late seventeenth centuries, notably by David Cressy, using depositions before the ecclesiastical courts. Depositions were statements of evidence taken by the court from those who had knowledge of a particular case. However, these are much less plentiful after the Restoration in England, leaving a gap in our knowledge about the late seventeenth and early eighteenth centuries.

There is then a pressing need to find a source which offers comparable information for Scotland and England in the period between the Restoration and the Industrial Revolution. Various possibilities have been considered to fill in the Scottish dimension.[13] Sets of depositions survive from the Scottish Commissary Courts, both ordinary Processes which were mainly for debt and Consistorial Processes which were principally concerned with moral and marital issues.[14] Testimonies can also be found interspersed with the minutes of Presbytery and Kirk Sessions, the agents of the Scottish kirk in the localities. However, these are comparatively rare because the church was anxious to prevent fraud by ensuring that only officials were allowed to write in its registers. Commissary Court depositions offer voluminous amounts of information, but suffer from the problem of attracting people who were

---

[13] Houston (1981): 133–271.   [14] SRO CC8/4; CC8/6.

probably not representative of the population at large. The sorts of people who used these courts may already have been particularly literate. Occupations are usually given in the depositions, but testimonies may be from elements of the craft and trade sector who were not typical of all its members: with only occupational information there is no way in which we can control for this bias. Criminal court depositions proved to be the most satisfactory source, for reasons we shall now examine.

Information on Scottish literacy between the 1650s and 1770s has been drawn exclusively from depositions before the High Court of Justiciary, Scotland's highest criminal court.[15] What functions did this court perform, and what were the court procedures which generated information on literacy? In addition to the High Court itself, which sat in Edinburgh, there were three circuit courts or 'Justice Ayres'. An Act of 1708 specified that the 'Lord Justice Clerk and Commissioners of Justiciary are appointed by two and two to go and keep the Circuit Court', according to the time and place.[16] These were the Northern Circuit, which included sittings at Perth, Aberdeen and Inverness, the South at Jedburgh, Dumfries and Ayr and the West at Inverary, Glasgow and Stirling. Cases before the Northern Circuit after 1708 were principally murder, infanticide and large-scale theft of livestock; at the early eighteenth-century western assizes, cases involving religious dissent and its consequences were prominent; in the south-west, cattle thefts and assaults associated with the droving routes were supplemented by customs violations and linked felonies.

An outline of the procedures adopted by the court in taking depositions will help to show the sorts of bias which might occur. Where a crime was not manifest and where the suspect was brought to trial, the Justiciary Court made provision for an enquiry into the circumstances surrounding the crime including, for example, the sorts of wounds suffered by a murdered man, or the taking of statements from those witnessing the act or events associated with it. Judges at the circuit courts were to 'cause to be summoned the haill witnesses contained in the said [Porteous] rolls to bear leall and suithfast witnessing in sua far as they know of the person's guiltiness'.[17]

Events might proceed as follows: 'the said persuer repeited the foresaid indictment and for proving thereof adduced severall famous witnesses who being all received were solemnly sworne examined and interrogat upon the points of the foresaid Indictment'.[18] A list of

[15] S. J. Davies, 'The courts and the Scottish legal system' (1980): 146–51.
[16] SRO JC7/2: 3 September 1708.
[17] SRO JC7/2: 6 September 1708; Larner (1981): 29–39; Logue (1979): 218–20.
[18] Cameron (1949): 170.

witnesses in any criminal libel was to be drawn up so that the parties might object to them. Arrangements were also made for a precognition or preparatory examination of the witnesses which might take place in a variety of acceptable contexts – before the actual judges in the case or before delegated officials in the localities, for example.[19] This step was designed to see whether there was a case to answer. There were then various levels of pre-trial and in-trial investigation. Where a case was in court, examination of prosecution witnesses look place before representatives of crown and panel. By 1661, and probably earlier, the accused could present his or her own witnesses for exculpation – proving their innocence. Statements made in the course of an inquisition were usually what was 'adduced to the trial either by production of that deposition alone, or by witnesses formally adhering to it'. Statements of witnesses and accused, variously described as precognitions or depositions, are the documents used here to provide evidence on literacy.

The survival of these statements is better in the case of the Scottish Justiciary Court than in that of English assizes, since the former was 'pre-eminently a court of record'.[20] It dealt with serious criminal offences, the pleas of the crown, over which most local courts were not allowed jurisdiction. However, this competence did not extend to all areas – specifically those under regalian jurisdiction – since some regality courts could hear all criminal cases except treason. They could also 'repledge' offenders from central courts – require their cases to be referred back to the jurisdiction of the local area where they lived or had committed an offence.[21] This was part of the jealous guarding of jurisdictional rights against encroachments by both subordinate and superior courts, which was a common feature of the Scottish legal scene before many of the former were swept away by the Heritable Jurisdictions Act of 1747. All courts could repledge offenders provided that their jurisdiction was competent in the case. Except for some cases, therefore, certain areas of Scotland are under-represented in these records. Local jurisdictions were usually keen to retain cases to be tried, but there were also instances where the regality would send cases to the High Court of Justiciary even where they were entitled to try them. After 1708–9 the reorganized High Court began to take over many of the regalities' functions, meaning that regional biases among the deponents were less pronounced.[22] This would tend to reduce any bias in literacy arising from the part of Scotland in which deponents lived. Lesser courts, such as local sheriff courts, handled less serious

[19] Imrie (1969): 269–72; Smith (1972): x–xiii, xxxi.
[20] S. A. Gillon, *Selected justiciary cases* (1953): 13.   [21] Imrie (1969): xiii.
[22] Davies (1980): 153; SRO JC6/12: Williamson (1688).

crimes. Despite these limitations the depositions used here do cover a wide geographical and social range.

This is not to suggest that they are altogether free of bias. There were certain criteria, explicit and implicit, which restrict the section of the population called upon to depone before the criminal courts. First, there was a wealth qualification, vaguely described as people 'not worth the King's unlaw', but specified by Mackenzie in the late seventeenth century as those worth less than £10 Scots: beggars. In practice, only manifest beggars were excluded, the aim being to prevent the witness being influenced by the hope for gain. Minors under fourteen years of age were also excluded, since their judgement was felt to be imperfect. Kin as far as cousin germane were debarred, as were accomplices, idiots, convicted adulterers, robbers, thieves and perjurers. Perhaps the most glaring legally induced bias was that against females. Only in special circumstances were women admissible as witnesses, and even then this was usually only when no men were available. Female judgement was felt to be easily swayed and thus fundamentally unreliable. Therefore, women rarely appear as either accused or witnesses except in connection with witchcraft, incest, adultery, infanticide and rebellion. *In criminibus domesticis* they were likely to be called 'because of the scantiness of probation'. Even here, women could not give evidence if their husband or father was involved. In short 'women *regulariter* are not witnesses' in Scotland but may be 'received witnesses, where women use only to be present'.[23]

The other main exclusion is of servants and others in an economically dependent position. Mr Andrew Borthwick, minister of Crighton in Midlothian, objected against Walter Steill 'becaus he is Martin Grinlaw's domestic servant and lykways brother sone to the wyfe' of Grinlaw, a kirk elder in dispute with Borthwick.[24] Domestic servants could not be witnesses for their masters, but could bear witness against them, though if they no longer worked for that master they might be admitted for him. Removable tenants were not allowed in cases involving the landowner, while cottars and sub-tenants were not formally admissible for the tenant from whom they held land in return for rent and labour services. However, there were legal doubts about this and in practice the objection might be overruled. Persons from excluded categories might be taken, but the assize was careful to assess possible partiality and was prepared to discount the testimony. In 'great crimes' even accomplices could be called as witnesses.[25]

[23] G. Mackenzie, *The laws and customes of Scotland in matters criminal* (1678): 527–43; quotations on 530.
[24] SRO CH2/424/3: 18 January 1649.   [25] SRO JC12/5: 10 May 1733; JC12/9: (1759).

Finally, there are certain glaring social biases. Higher status members of the community were clearly preferred as witnesses, the wording of some depositions implying that the testimony of a laird or minister was held to be weightier than that of a servant or tenant because of the formers' stronger 'social credit'. There were clearly difficulties getting witnesses to appear because of distance, weather, work, social pressures or even outright threats of violence; this in spite of heavy fines for non-appearance. Provisions could be made to take depositions in the localities or to reimburse witnesses for travel costs, but on the whole we can see why more substantial members of local society were less likely to be influenced by these hindrances.[26] The type of case similarly has a bearing on the sort of deponents appearing: surgeons frequently testify in murder cases to the nature of wounds sustained by the deceased. Nevertheless, we can allow for many biases in an analysis which controls for the effects of different factors. And despite the slants in the deponent sample it is surprising how many were thrown up in what appears to have been a far more random way than English church court witnesses.[27] Travellers through a village where a murder occurred, drinkers at an alehouse where treason was planned, chance passers-by happening upon a rape in progress – all find their way into the pages of the Justiciary Court minute books.

The time-span during which signed depositions are available is rather a short one. Evidence does not appear to have been reduced to writing before the mid seventeenth century and even when it was there is rarely any indication of literacy. The Justiciary Court Small Papers are rather better in this respect. Evidence 'disappeared with the utterance', witnesses being mentioned but testimonies not surviving.[28] By the time we reach the 1760s the names, occupations and residences of the witnesses for prosecution and defence are noted with a summary of procedural steps, but actual depositions are not included even when the case went to an assize. At Dumfries in September 1760 the list of witnesses in the case of Thomas Gibson is preceded by a note to the effect that they had been sworn and had deponed, but that the depositions 'in consequence of the late act of Parliament [21 Geo II] were not taken down in writing'.[29] Depositions peter out completely by 1790 among Justiciary Court documents. Written, attested depositions do survive, however, in considerable numbers for the intervening period *c*.1650–*c*.1770.

The most directly comparable English source which we have for the

[26] SRO JC6/12: 7 November 1688; Smith (1972): iii–v, ix; Davies (1980): 148.
[27] Cressy (1980): 104–17.   [28] Cameron (1949): xv–xvi.   [29] SRO JC12/10.

later seventeenth and eighteenth centuries is the assize court deposition. The assize was the highest non-central criminal court, trying serious felonies and sending prisoners to local gaols in all regions of England.[30] Murder, rape, theft, serious assault and what were termed 'treasons' – rebellion and coining, for instance – were dealt with. The Northern Circuit assize depositions which form the backbone of the English side of our analysis covered the six northernmost counties of Yorkshire, Northumberland, Cumberland and Westmorland, plus Durham and Lancashire, which were strictly subject to palatinate jurisdictions, but deponents from which still appear. Of 4,915 deponents whose residence is known, 70% came from Yorkshire and 28% from the four northern counties; the remainder came from elsewhere in Britain. Interspersed with recognizances, reports on the state of the highways, letters and other papers, depositions survive in relative abundance from the 1640s onwards. The next usable series for elsewhere in England begins in 1719.

As one might expect, the mix of cases dealt with and the survival of documents varies considerably over time and space. Unlike indictments and recognizances, however, there was no obligation on the clerk of assizes to preserve depositions, which were not strictly documents of record. They might be kept, for example, only if the accused had not been caught, and there were no explicit rules on the content or format of the statements of evidence.[31] In contrast with Continental (and Scottish) practice English legal procedure was predominantly oral. An Act of 1555 required all justices of the peace to take written testimony of the accused and of the prosecutor's accusations, and depositions seem to have been taken regularly in the localities.[32] JPs examined the offender largely on their own initiative before passing him on to gaol, and also taking: 'Information of such as bring him; viz. hee shall take their examination, and information of the fact, and circumstances thereof, and so much thereof, as shall be materiall to prove the felony, he shall put in writing.' If the accused confessed during the examination, 'it shall not bee amisse that the offender subscribes his name or marke under such confession'.[33] There were thus two types of deposition: the examination of an offender in response to the formal accusation and the information of accusers and witnesses 'that can

---

[30] PRO ASSI45; Macfarlane (1981): 30, 37.

[31] J. H. Langbein, *Prosecuting crime in the Renaissance* (1974): 87.

[32] J. S. Cockburn, *A history of English assizes* (1972): 15–22; 38–46; J. S. Cockburn, 'Early modern assize records as historical evidence' (1975): 216; Macfarlane (1981): 37; A. Macfarlane, 'Review essay' (1980).

[33] M. Dalton, *The country justice* (1618): 259–60.

speake to the matter'.[34] Informations were always taken under oath and were admissible as evidence in circumstances such as the death of the accuser or witness before trial. They had therefore to be signed. There was no question of an oath in examination and the need for a signature was less pressing. Besides ability to sign, depositions generally offer information on the occupation and residence of the witness. Examinations of prisoners give occupations much more rarely than informations of witnesses or accusers. Ages are given extremely rarely, and there is seldom any biographical information prefacing the statement of the sort found in church court depositions.[35]

Despite the apparently wide spread of deponents the legal background to the cases may again have introduced potential sources of bias. Surviving depositions cover both guilty and not-guilty cases. Accusers in property cases had to pay to bring the case, and informations from them are likely to exclude the poorer sections of society who would generally not have been able to prosecute. Recent research on the social composition of prosecutors before the Essex quarter sessions in the late eighteenth century shows that witnesses were close to being a cross-section of the Essex population, but that both assault and felony prosecutors were drawn disproportionately from the yeomen, and craftsmen and tradesmen. There is a definite bias towards the middling sort.[36] At the same time, offenders were characteristically drawn from the lower levels of society, notably in theft cases which formed the bulk of prosecuted crimes. They would be the poorer, more marginal elements of local communities.

During the seventeenth century many accused persons were itinerant, or at least not native to the parish where the offence occurred.[37] In a highly mobile society being a stranger did render prosecution and conviction a more likely sequel to apprehension after a crime than would be the case for persons well integrated into local communities. The place where felons were apprehended is often the only key to residence, since there is seldom any of the biographical information which often prefaces church court depositions. At the same time, less literate persons may have been more prone to steal and this might lower aggregate literacy levels. Yet nineteenth-century evidence shows that there is no difference between the literacy of guilty and not-guilty persons – strictly honest versus criminal – within delineated occupational groups. Crime was not literacy- but

[34] W. Lambard, *Eirenarcha* (1581): 432; Langbein (1974): 84–5.   [35] Clark (1979): 63–4.
[36] Houston (1982b): 202.   [37] M. J. Ingram, 'Communities and courts' (1977): 128–34.

social-group-specific: criminal literacy was low because mainly low-status people were prosecuted for crimes.[38] Examinants were definitely much less literate overall than informants, but their occupations are not given often enough before the late eighteenth century to allow analysis of occupation-specific literacy levels in the two groups. Finally, there are reasons for thinking that the social distribution of prosecution may have been widening over time. During the eighteenth century there was a systematic attempt to redefine traditionally acceptable practices, such as gleaning in agricultural communities or the taking of offcuts of cloth among employed weavers and tailors, which would have incorporated more of society into the category of criminals. The search by capitalists for rationalized production and accounting in the interest of maximizing profit meant that 'crime' came more than ever to encompass dependent artisans as well as labourers and servants.[39] Because of changes in the definition of crime and the willingness to prosecute, more people would have been brought within the aegis of the courts.

Given the church courts' preference for 'respectable' deponents, the criminal courts may actually provide a more representative sample of the lower levels of society, though only marginally so. Keelmen and pitmen were probably the largest occupational group in seventeenth-century Newcastle, but are almost unrepresented in church court depositions and are admittedly still few in number among assize testimonies. To a lesser extent the same is true of labourers, the proportion of whom, in the population of the north-west, was increasing from the late seventeenth century onwards.[40] Legal restrictions excluded wives (but not children) from giving evidence against a husband, and further debarred discredited persons such as forgers, conspirators and perjurers from being witnesses.[41] Depositions have escaped the damning (if probably unjustified) criticisms of the validity of occupational designations levelled against indictments.[42] Finally, other less obvious but probably also less important biases appear. In areas distant from a magistrate or court there may have been a disincentive to prosecute. Proximity to magistrates and to small, well-run towns may conversely have stimulated prosecutions. *If* more remote areas were less literate, we would have another bias which pushes up overall literacy levels. Market towns and cities are probably over-represented. Of all assize deponents whose residence is known for the period from 1640 to 1770,

---

[38] Campbell (1980): 139, 166.
[39] J. Rule, *The experience of labour in eighteenth century industry* (1981): 124–43.
[40] Hodgshon (1979): 90.   [41] Dalton (1618): 261.
[42] Cockburn (1975): 216; but see Macfarlane (1980).

17% came from Newcastle, Durham, York or Carlisle, 29% from market towns as defined by John Adams in his *Index villaris*, and 55% from rural villages. At Durham Consistory Court the proportions are 18, 33 and 49% respectively for 1716–1800. However, conventional breakdowns of the proportions living in towns are made on the basis of size rather than function (as we did in chapter 2), though the two are clearly related.[43] This makes it difficult to compare relative proportions of urban- and rural-dwellers appearing as deponents in the courts with those in the population at large. The impression is that deponents were drawn disproportionately from towns and cities.

Statistical analysis of early modern English literacy to date has been based largely on depositions before the diocesan Consistory Courts. These bodies dealt with a wide range of matters 'of ecclesiastical cognizance' and their procedures have been discussed at some length by Cressy.[44] Received opinion states that the church courts, highly active in the late sixteenth and early seventeenth centuries, became much less so after the Restoration, but in the west and north this does not seem to be the case. Durham Consistory Court records survive into the nineteenth century, and relate to all of Northumberland and Durham plus Berwick-on-Tweed and the area round Alston in Cumberland; the market town of Hexham and Hexhamshire were excluded. Depositions from this court have been analysed for the years 1716 to 1800 to provide some comparisons between levels of literacy found in different sorts of documents.

There is no point in pretending that deponents before the Consistory Court were a representative cross-section of the population. The age and sex distribution of the deponent sample is clearly biased, and probably more so than the assize sample in terms of age. Only 30% of deponents were women during the period 1716–1800. Virtually none of the 754 deponents of known age were less than fifteen years old. If we compare the age structure of eighteenth-century church court deponents in England with the national average age distribution of the population recovered by Wrigley and Schofield, the precise extent of under- or over-representation can be seen.[45] Those aged under fifteen are the most under-represented section of society. The servant group, aged from fifteen to twenty-four, are slightly less manifest than we should expect. Those in the prime of life are over-represented. Among the elderly too there is over-representation.

---

[43] R. A. P. Finlay, *Population and metropolis* (1981): 7; Patten (1972).
[44] Cressy (1980): 104–17.   [45] Wrigley and Schofield (1981): 528–9.

Table A1.4. *Age distribution of Durham Consistory Court deponents compared to the national average, 1716–1800*

Age Group	% deponents	% population	%+/−
0–14	2	32	−97
15–24	13	18	−28
25–59	68	40	+70
60+	17	10	+70

The figures in table A1.4 certainly do not confirm Cressy's odd contention that 'the witnesses who testified before the courts were of the same range of ages as the adult population at large'.[46] The extent of age, sex and status biases varies according to the type of case. Women are much better represented in defamation cases, while tithe and pew disputes drew deponents disproportionately from the older members of local communities who would have long memories about customary practices.[47] Pew-renters were probably regular churchgoers and of relatively high social status. Witnesses in testamentary cases may have been chosen to be present when a will was made precisely because of their literacy. Of 774 deponents of both sexes at the Durham Consistory Court between 1716 and 1800, 312 or 40% appeared in defamation cases, 23% in testamentary cases (175 deponents), 20% in pew disputes (155 deponents), 8% in tithe arbitration (61 deponents), and the remaining seventy-one or 9% in those cases dealing with incest, buggery, illegitimacy, adherence, church fabric and rating. Most of the analyses which we have conducted are based on depositions before criminal courts in Scotland and England, but the ecclesiastical court evidence can be usefully set alongside this as a means of testing or expanding the patterns.

For the late 1630s and early 1640s we can gather information on adult male illiteracy from the subscriptions to the great religious oaths associated with the 'Scottish Revolution' and Scotland's involvement in the English Civil War. These can be compared with English Protestation oaths of the early 1640s which cover a similar section of the population. Again, interpretation of these documents is not straightforward, as we shall now see.

Rather few Scottish Covenants are known to have survived. Besides the usual problems of accidental loss and damage, religious reaction in the later seventeenth century occasioned some systematic destruction

[46] Cressy (1980): 116.   [47] Chaytor (1980): 26.

of this bond.[48] Of the survivors, most are listed in Hewison, though more recent accessions have rendered this list partly obsolete. The 'Small Sources' repertory at the Scottish Record Office is helpful. With so few Covenants at our disposal, it is especially unfortunate that a large proportion are unusable for the study of Scottish literacy. Unlike with English Protestation oaths there seems to be a general lack of confidence in the reliability and inclusiveness of the Covenants as an indicator of adult male illiteracy in local areas. Some description of the available Covenants which were discarded, plus some justification of those analysed in chapter 3, is required.

Interest in the Covenants has traditionally been centred on the more aesthetically pleasing examples, and on those signed by the king or prominent Covenanting leaders, such as Montrose. One such example is the 'King's Confession' of 1582, which bears the signatures of a few nobles and clerics only, plus that of the king.[49] Like most of the Covenants described here, it refers only to the leaders of the nation, or to prominent local lairds. Often, as in the case of the around 800 subscriptions to the impressive 1638 bond preserved in the Presbytery Room of Free Church College, Edinburgh, the signatories are delegates to conventions. It is divided into sections: 'gentry of the shyre, subscribers', 'commissioners of the shyre, subscribers', 'ministers of the shyre', 'commissioners for burrows', 'remaining persons within the shyre', 'ministers not of the shyre, subscribers at the meeting in Edinburgh' on 15 June 1638. Most of the signatories – there is only one mark and one notarial subscription – are of men from Ayrshire, though burgh representatives are drawn from all over southern Scotland. There is nothing to be gained from analysing a group of men who were the leaders of society and almost totally literate. Other examples similarly cover only one or two atypical sections of the population. The bulk of signatories to the Newbattle Abbey Covenant are ministers, though the 166 names include 'nobles, lairds, burgesses'.[50] All the nobles' and some of the lairds' names can be found in other Covenants. A prominent example is Thomas Abernethie of Glencorse, 'sometime Jesuite', whose presence on the Covenant was especially useful, since he had once been an advocate of the religious system against which the bond was directed. This Covenant certainly does not describe a local area, having been subscribed at Glasgow around the time of the Assembly by representatives from all over Scotland. One signatory is Mr James Porteous, minister of Lasswade, summoned before the High Commission in 1620

---

[48] Edinburgh University Library LaIII 229 'Memorandum as to the copies of the Solemn League and Covenant' (eighteenth century).
[49] NLS Adv MS 20.6.12.   [50] SRO 'File T39'.

for not obeying the Articles of Perth, and noted in the *Fasti* as a member of that Assembly. Most usually, the section covered is 'lairds'. Local knowledge might help to identify whether these lairds were indeed all local dwellers, and whether they form the whole or a representative number of local landowners.

Even more promising documents, such as that for Peebles, are unusable. While signed by Jedburgh burgesses and others said to be 'provost, baillies and councillors of the burgh of Peebles', it is also attested by representatives from many other places, including ministers and lairds. There are around 200 signatures, all holograph. That signed at nearby Lauder includes only nobles, ministers, 'baillies and counsellors'.[51] The main problem is then to distinguish whether subscribers all lived in a defined local area, such as a parish or group of parishes, and whether they are an identifiable cross-section of that community. One example of the problems in determining the geographical origins of signatories is to be found in the 'Borders Covenant'.[52] The front of the document is covered in holograph signatures with little evidence of residence. On the back are a number of notarized blocks covering parishes such as Stobo, Athelstoun, Newlands, Peebles and Traquair. In the case of the impressive example in Huntly House Museum it is quite impossible to discover from which parishes in Edinburgh – if indeed all are Edinburgh-dwellers – the subscribers came.

In the case of the 1638 Covenant, it was usual for the bond to be signed in Edinburgh by the leaders prior to transmission to the localities for general subscription. It is often hard to determine who the local subscribers actually were, a serious problem with the Maybole Covenant.[53] This example includes eight women, a further problem making coverage difficult to assess. The problem of re-subscription or open-ended signing is also illustrated here. At the foot of the document, dated June 1642, is a list of persons, 'all strangeris from the kingdome of Ireland with our hands at the pen . . .': sixty-four parishioners, plus nineteen strangers of whom seven are women. Notarial subscriptions cover the majority of illiterates, all of whom are explicitly stated to be 'parochineris within the parochin' of Maybole. One subscriber described himself as a burgess of Ayr: he may still have lived in Maybole while enjoying trade privileges in the nearby royal burgh.

In some cases, subscription is completely open-ended. In 1650, Dalkeith presbytery ordered all its ministers to 'see to the subscribing of the Covenant by those that enter to the communion'. The example

---

[51] NLS Adv MS 20.6.16.   [52] BM Add Chrs 1380.   [53] SRO GD103/2/150.

preserved in this volume was subscribed by only a handful of people – mainly military officers and students of divinity – over a period of years. It is useless for the study of literacy.[54] The ninety-one ministers and graduates of Edinburgh University who signed a Covenant in April 1649 form a similar sub-section. Other Covenants rejected for this reason include the Dunblane bond, which was circulated and subscribed over the period March to July 1638. It appears that the Dunfermline Covenant (not found) 'bears the day moneth & place where every person subt. the same . . . for it seems they did not subscribe the said Covenant all at the same time'.[55] There are two surviving Covenants for St Andrews in the 1640s, one of 1643 which has 851 names (excluding students) and one of 1648, which offers only half that number. The former is almost certainly the most inclusive and the most representative of burgh society as a whole. The late 1640s example reveals much lower illiteracy and was probably restricted to the middling and upper levels of the town's population. Illiteracy in 1643 was 63%, but only 43% in 1648.

Problems such as wear and damp damage – many of the 1638 bonds are on sheepskin – are to be expected. From the point of view of purely interpretative difficulties, the assessment of the number of holograph signatures and of cases where a scribe has signed for someone presents obstacles. The printed booklet containing the Kilbarchan Solemn League and Covenant of 1648 has, apparently, a total lack of marks or notarial subscriptions.[56] There are similarities between groups of signatures, but also some individuality in the formation of particular letters, suggesting that some hands were led by a scribe. On the fifth folio of the list of subscribers there seem to be fifty-three notarized signatures, but there is no formal clause to alert us to this of the kind found in, say, the Newbattle example. The Kilbarchan document was therefore discarded.

Even among the seventeen Covenants analysed there are a number of interpretative problems. As noted above, the Covenant was circulated to some extent, and might be subscribed by those with landed interests in an area. Archibald Campbell of Caradale sent to Sir Colin Campbell of Glenorchy 'ane Covenante and all the nobillmens hands at quha are heire', urging Sir Colin to get more lairds to subscribe before returning it. This is particularly common for the 1638 Covenant.[57]

At the same time there are a variety of technical problems. Signatures,

[54] SRO CH2/424/3: 2 May 1650; SRO CH2/424/3: April 1649.
[55] Edinburgh University Library LaIII 229/2; SRO 'File T258'; Edinburgh University Library LaIII 229.
[56] Edinburgh University Library LaIII 229/3.
[57] SRO Breadalbane MS 763: 23 April 1639 – reference from SRO 'File T258'.

holograph and notarized, occupy only one folio of the Menmuir Solemn League and Covenant, and this has been trimmed after subscription, interfering with the names.[58] However, comparison with other examples of these printed booklets, which are the common form of the 1643 Covenant, suggest there would not have been space for any further names. These pages are headed 'The Subscribers of the League and Covenant' and appear to have been supplied with the printed oath. In the case of the Newbattle example of 1643, the last two folios have been damaged, but it is still possible to make an approximate assessment of the number of subscriptions which may have been lost.[59] Only notarial subscriptions are affected, the body of autograph signatures being at the front of the booklet. On the front side of the sixth folio of subscriptions there are nineteen notarially entered names plus four autographs, the right-hand column ending about one-third of the way down the page. The left hand of the two columns in which the names are conventionally arranged, however, is torn approximately half-way down. Given the practice in the rest of the booklet of filling the left-hand column first, it seems likely that there were a further sixteen to eighteen notarial subscriptions on the page. This is based on the calculation that the notary wrote nine names per $4\frac{1}{2}$ centimetres, and there would have been a further 9 centimetres on the page. The same problem affects six verso where seven names were added to make up the likely shortfall. On the seventh folio both columns are mutilated, though the right-hand column fortunately ends just above the tear. Again, sixteen were added. While it is likely that the figure for illiteracy of 76% is basically correct, it must be recognized that it may be up to 5% too high, since there may be fewer notarial subscriptions lost than estimated, or because there may be a few autographs among missing names.

A more serious problem than too few signatures in Covenants is that there may be too many. Re-subscription, often after the Glasgow Assembly, is the cause. The back of the Borgue Covenant has a body of re-subscriptions dated December 1638, after the Perth articles and Glasgow determination.[60] With the exception of the notary public, these are the same people who signed the original bond in April of the same year. However, this is not an insuperable problem. We are alerted to the fact, and can discard the repeated signatures. Nor does the fact of subscription on more than one occasion necessarily exclude a Covenant from consideration. Only when it occurs over a long or possibly indeterminate time can it vitiate analysis. Thus the Edzell

---

[58] NLS MS 3279.   [59] Museum of the Society of Antiquaries OA19.
[60] SRO SP13/160.

example has a group of notarized attestations appended to the minister's testimony 'that thair forsaid persons who could not subscribe themselfs hes sworne to the covenant'.[61] These additions are almost certainly attenders at the afternoon sermon who had not been present in the morning. Perhaps because of the pecuniary penalties attached to the Solemn League and Covenant, or through religious zeal, there was some attempt to maximize subscription. The same thing happened at North Leith, where the notary public subscribed on 7 and 15 April, and at Inveresk on 20, 23 and 25 March. In these coastal parishes, fishermen and sailors may well have been absent, and some attempt made to compensate. North Leith poll tax of the 1690s shows numbers of wives to seamen whose husbands were at sea when the assessment was made.[62]

The other side of the over-subscription problem is that the 1638 bonds were often subscribed by nobles and other Covenanting leaders, as well as by members of local communities. The Kinneil and Bo'ness example alone appears to have been subscribed only in the parish, having none of the usual names.[63] However, the top row of signatures on the Inveresk Covenant comprises seven prominent nobles.[64] There follows the signatures of fifty-two Covenanting lairds, many of whom signed other Covenants and petitions, such as that of 1637 against the Prayer Book. These people were excluded from the analysis of literacy which is based on 338 signatures, three marks and 366 notarized names following the fifty-nine leaders. The Ayr Covenant suffers from the same problem. Twenty prominent lairds and burgh representatives head the subscriptions.[65] There follows an inset gap and another group commencing with the dean of guild and two bailies, and including the minister, reader and schoolmaster at the burgh. In the case of North Leith, there is a 10 centimetre gap between nobles' signatures and the first parishioner, Mr John Hogg the minister.[66]

Even where we can be certain about who is included in the analysis, notarized signatures are not always clearly delineated. While this is specifically stated at Newbattle, there are other examples where it is suspected that one person subscribed for another without mentioning the fact. In the Newbattle document the small, neat and well-disciplined hand of the notary was easily detected among the holograph signatures with the help of palaeographical experts. The notary did indeed say that he had 'subscribit the names of thes underwritten and

---

[61] NCL.   [62] NCL; SRO E70/4/10.   [63] NCL.   [64] NLS Adv MS 20.6.18.
[65] NLS Adv MS 20.6.17b.   [66] NCL.

of some overwritten with thair own consent and desyr being such as could not wrytt thame selffis bot touchit the pen and expres thair desyr of this subscription on thair behalff'. This procedure augurs well for the accurate representation of illiteracy by notarial attestation, since people were given every opportunity to sign personally.

In ascertaining the actual residence of subscribers, essential if we are to be sure that Covenants deal only with defined local areas, blocks of notarial subscriptions are generally more useful than holographs. At Edzell and Dundonald, residence is given within the parish by 'ferm-toun' or hamlet.[67] The Kilmany example notes that all signatures were collected 'at Kilmany kirk 29 October 1643', while at Inveresk all illiterates were described as indwellers in the parish.[68] The Forfarshire Covenant is unusual, having been circulated in the county during October and November 1638, though luckily the places of subscription are included.[69] Nevertheless, it is not always possible to pin down the subscribers to limited spaces and short specific time periods, as would be preferred.

While Mitchison has used the Dundonald Kirk Session register to check on the inclusiveness of the Covenant for that parish, this is a time-consuming procedure not justified in a study such as the present one, which seeks to uncover broad patterns.[70] Detailed 'parish reconstruction' can however prove useful in such analyses: it has been used to good effect in examining the residence and socio-economic composition of subscribers to the Association Oath of 1696 for the Essex parish of Earls Colne.[71] Further reconstructions using other documents may qualify the picture of good overall inclusiveness presented here. Some simple tests of plausibility can be carried out.

For some of the Covenant parishes numbers of communicants in the mid seventeenth century have been discovered (Inveresk and Newbattle), while for the Tolbooth parish there is a 1678 household survey reproduced in the *Statistical account* of the 1790s.[72] In 1650 Inveresk had 2,629 communicants: 689 in the Fisherraw, 832 in Musselburgh, 1,108 elsewhere in the parish.[73] The age at which people were allowed to communicate varied from around twelve to sixteen, though some ministers favoured a younger start. If we assume that 25% of the population were under communicable age, a total parish size of about

---

[67] NCL. SRO CH2/104/1: fols. 146–50.   [68] SRO 'File T258'; NLS Adv MS 20.6.18.
[69] NLS Adv MS 34.5.15.   [70] Mitchison (1978): 43–6.
[71] Personal information from Alan Macfarlane.
[72] See *OSA*, vol. 6 (1793): 559–60. For a contemporary suggestion that 25% should be added to examinables to make up the total population see *ibid.*, 561. In 1722 there were 701 families and 2,418 examinables in the parish.
[73] SRO CH2/424/3: 31 May 1650.

3,300 can be estimated. Divided by 707, this produces a ratio of one male subscriber to 4.7 other parishioners: a close approximation to the sort of household size obtaining in this society. At Newbattle there were said to be 900 communicants in 1648, or perhaps 1,125 people. With 383 subscribers to the Covenant there was a ratio of 2.9.[74] To some extent the divergence between the ratios may be due to different ages of first communicating; alternatively masters may have signed more frequently for all dependents – adult children and servants – than at Newbattle, where virtually all males over the age of about eighteen must have had the opportunity to sign. At the same time, it is possible that changes in the parish boundary, apparently going on all the time, may produce different spatial areas on different occasions. In the case of Inveresk the subscribers may be biased towards a section of the parish – probably burgh-dwellers – while those outside the main settlements were under-represented. Parish boundaries were occasionally altered, as at Lasswade in the early seventeenth century, where population change had caused Pentland kirk to fall into decay and where the inhabitants of the area called Pentland were ordered by the ecclesiastical authorities to go to Lasswade kirk. Pentland was amalgamated with Lasswade, increasing the size of the parish by about 100 communicants. Of course people did not always go to their own parish church.[75]

A similar problem of only part of a parish being included may have occurred at Ayr: the small number of subscribers, plus the sort of people described, suggest that the subscribers may have been drawn from the burgh part, while the 'landward' part was ignored. As for the Tolbooth parish, the 513 houses in the 1678 survey suggest perhaps 2,500–3,000 people. Again, the ratio of subscribers to houses of around 4:1 seems plausible, though numbers in Edinburgh at any one time might vary according to the time of year, and urban households were usually smaller in any case. These figures cannot provide conclusive proof of the reliability of the Covenants, but they do suggest that they are not wildly unrepresentative.

What sections of the population are likely to have been excluded from the subscriptions analysed? Again, detailed parish reconstitution is necessary for any exact assessment, but some generalizations can be made, and the possible impact of any bias estimated. The time of year when the Covenants were signed may have some influence on the type of person excluded. We can pin down ten Covenants to particular

[74] SRO CH2/424/3: 2 November 1648.
[75] J. Kirk (ed.), *The records of the synod of Lothian and Tweeddale 1589–96, 1640–49* (1977): 200, 224.

months. Of these, two fall in April: North Leith and Borgue. This was
close to one of the main points of the year for population turnover.
Servants, cottars and tenants may then be under-represented. Of
course, servants and other transient elements of the population may
not have been felt to be worthy to sign this bond of community solidarity in any case. There are after all different levels of 'community',
recognized even by those living in limited geographical areas, depend-
ing on cultural experience and the extent of integration into a broad
range of social occasions. In Fife there is some indication that those
debarred from communion – the grossly ignorant plus those in dispute
with their neighbours – were not thought fit to subscribe the Covenant.[76] The Galston Covenant was signed in the depth of winter,
possibly causing more absence due to ill-health or bad weather:
excuses often used by those failing to appear when called upon to
present themselves before Kirk Session and presbytery hearings in
seventeenth-century Scotland.[77]

The other frequently proffered excuse was pressure of work. Sowing
would be going on in spring at Dundonald, Borgue and Inveresk,
when the Covenant was signed, while at Kilmany, Newbattle and in
Forfarshire in October seasonal workers would have gone, and the
remaining workforce would be clearing the land after harvest. The
Edinburgh Covenant, meanwhile, ends with a group of notarial subscriptions for men 'of the town of Edinburgh about our lawfull affaires
and business the tyme of the subscribing of the covenant by the rest of
our neighbours . . .'[78] On the assumption that people did move around
for work, Lasswade Kirk Session ordered that no child be baptized in
the father's absence unless he is sick or 'els on just and good occation to
be furth of the cuntry', providing two examples of possible reasons for
non-attendance.[79] Parishioners might be absent from the kirk for other
reasons, and it is quite clear that church attendance was not universal,
not even usual for many of the people of early modern Scotland.[80] One
of the duties of kirk elders was to go round the parish during service
time checking on non-attenders. In a Commissary Court process of
1700 James Rennie stated that 'it is well known that countrie men
sometimes may be necessarily withdrawn from their parish church
while they goe to the neighbouring paroch kirks which is nearer
[than] their own by three myles'. Patrick Young and Margaret Pringle

---

[76] Di Folco (1975): 10.
[77] In the Kirk Session register 1638–44, in the keeping of the minister. See e.g. SRO
CH2/424/1–15 *passim* and SRO CH2/471/1–5 *passim*.
[78] NLS Adv MS 23.3.16: fol. 7.   [79] SRO CH2/471/1: fol. 2.
[80] Brackenridge (1969).

his wife produced a testimonal at Haddington showing that they had lived in Belton (Dunbar parish) for three years 'and frequented the ordinances in the paroch of Stentoun and baptized their children there'.[81] In areas like Ayrshire and Fife, some compulsion may have been used to ensure maximum subscription, but it is clear that a number of factors could decrease the number of men signing.

What impact would these shortfalls have on aggregate levels of illiteracy? Anyone might be absent on business, though it seems that the poorer classes – servants, chapmen, fishermen for instance – were more likely to be away. Deposition evidence suggests that these would also be the less literate members of local communities. At the same time, religious needs meant that regular attenders at church were more literate, though even among kirk elders it is clear that universal literacy did not obtain. Offenders against church discipline were usually the poorer sections of society. They were also less regular church attenders. While some influences are not selective of any social group the overall bias is towards figures which would diminish the real level of illiteracy among adult males. The only possible counter-bias might be refusal by convinced religious objectors to subscribe. Catholics, however, were apparently rare in Lowland Scotland in the seventeenth century: in Dalkeith presbytery enquiries never produced more than a few dozen during this century, though problems in setting up Kirk Sessions in the late sixteenth century do suggest support for papacy from lairds at this time.

For these reasons the figures presented in table 3.2, chapter 3, must be regarded as minimum estates of illiteracy in mid seventeenth-century Scotland. Only more detailed work can positively confirm or disprove the reliance which has been placed on Covenants as a source.

One final comment is needed on the sources. Unfortunately, the use of sign-literacy is complicated by the fact that in Scotland personal subscription was not required to authenticate a will, bond, deposition or other document. English ecclesiastical court deponents were obliged to 'write their Names or Usual Mark to these their Depositions, with their own hand, lest the Register, or any other should afterwards vitiate this Deposition in any particular'.[82] Failure to provide some form of holograph authentication is recorded in the northern circuit assize papers, as when William Holmes of Clifford in Yorkshire 'pretended that he could neither write, nor set his mark to this confession'.[83] Even in the case of aged or infirm testators some sort of

---

[81] SRO CC8/6/4: Rennie v. Dobie; SRO CH2/799/2: fol. 41.
[82] H. Consett, *The practice of the spiritual or ecclesiastical courts* (1685): 116.
[83] PRO ASSI45: 18/5/46.

personal subscription was needed on the will. Cecily Ellison had her last will and testament written for her, then read out, 'she being then blind'. She asked one of the witnesses to guide her hand, using the pen 'which he guided or directed to the foot or bottom of the said will by taking hold of her hand and keeping hold thereof till she had wrote and subscribed her name to her said will'.[84]

Scottish testators and deponents had no need to do this, though it is clear that most preferred to sign if at all possible. Agnes Irving presented evidence to Dalkeith presbytery in 1702 and 'because she cannot write she touched the pen and then desired the Clerk to subscribe for her'.[85] Guiding of the hand was less usual in Scotland and was confined to situations where pride or effect were at stake. In 1751 Elizabeth Thompson appeared as a witness in an adherence case at Edinburgh Commissary Court against John Grinton in Lasswade. Wife of an Edinburgh merchant she had witnessed Grinton's marriage to Anne Grate, and the marriage lines bearing her signature were presented as evidence. The Commissaries noticed a discrepancy between her signature on the marriage lines and on her deposition before them. Elizabeth admitted that Anne Grate had led her hand on the marriage lines, and further mentioned that the lines had not been read to her before she signed, showing that she could not read.[86] A petition to Dalkeith presbytery from elders and household heads living in Fala, Midlothian, was queried, since 'several subscriptions appeared to have been written by one and the same hand', a well-meaning deception acknowledged by the framer of the petition who 'himself had led the hands of some few who could not write'.[87] The sources we are relying on here were compiled, however, under much stricter supervision and are unlikely to be subject to such difficulties. Depositions before the highest Scottish criminal court were taken with 'care and patience'.[88]

In the case of the main Scottish source used above, Justiciary Court depositions, personal subscription was rare. Instead, the clerk taking the testimony would write *sic subscribitur* plus the name of the deponent at the end of the evidence for those who could sign. A variety of other formulae were used to show illiteracy, most commonly 'with his hand touching the pen led by the clerk because he cannot write himself'. In the case of James Hume, town officer in Haddington, the clerk took the trouble to note that 'he cannot wreitt but by two initial letters', suggesting that the court's definition of illiteracy is the same as

[84] DPDD Durham diocese Consistory Court: Ellison (1760).
[85] SRO CH2/424/8: fol. 165.   [86] SRO CC8/6/19: (1751).
[87] SRO CH2/424/13: fol. 22.   [88] Smith (1972): x.

ours: inability to sign in full.[89] We can find instances in other sources where the same distinction has been drawn between ability to sign in full and initialling. A lease of some of the Priory Acres, small strips of land around the town of St Andrews, dated 1698, has the initials of the tenant alongside which is a *scribere nesciens* clause written for him by a notary.[90] Where it has been possible to compare the original, personally subscribed court papers with the transcribed court minute books the accuracy with which signatures or marks were recorded in the latter was complete. Finally, and as we have already noticed, notaries public could legally authenticate a document for illiterates. The National Covenant relating to the parish of Kinneil and Bo'ness has 161 names with the attestation 'with our hands toucheing the notar pen at our commandis (because) we cannot writ ourselves'.

The frequent lack of holograph signatures or marks raises the problem that unwillingness rather than inability was the reason for failure to sign. The notarial formulae do however show that every opportunity was given to would-be subscribers to write their names. Thus, the clerk would given the deponent the pen to sign his or her statement, but he might then 'putt the pen in my hand to subscribe for him'. The only time when the chance was denied was when plague was abroad. It is, however, unlikely that this factor was particularly important in distorting figures on signing ability. People were given every opportunity to subscribe and, given the pride which we find that many Scots took in being literate, it is likely that few would fail to avail themselves of the chance to display the skill.

Armed with these sources we have been able to discuss the profile of signing ability in early modern Britain, and to offer a more substantial and critical analysis of the supposed distinctiveness of Scottish literacy before the nineteenth century.

[89] SRO JC6/13.   [90] SAUL SA08/5.

Appendix 2: Bookownership in the Highlands and Islands

The following list of books found in inventories relating to the Northern and Western Isles provides an illustration of the sort of information which can be gleaned from this source. It is based largely on the work of Dr Frances Shaw of the Scottish Record Office, for whose help I am most grateful.

Orkney testaments (to 1700)

John Kirkness, cordiner in Kirkwall, d. 1636 (CC17/2/3: fols. 260–1) – a Bible

Mr James Wilson, minister at Deerness and St Andrews, d. 1632 (CC17/2/3: fols. 261–2) – his books (worth £100)

Mr Patrick Inglis, minister at Birsay and Harray, d. 1639 (CC17/2/4: fol. 40) – library (£200)

Beatrix Henryson, spouse to Mr Robert Pearson, minister of Firth and Stenness, d. 1640 (CC17/2/4: fols. 47–8) – husband's books (£48)

Euphame Halcro, spouse to same Robert Pearson, d. 1642 (CC17/2/4: fols. 48–9) – husband's books (£46)

Mr Daniel Callendar, minister at Birsay and Harray, d. 1641 (CC17/2/4: fols. 50–3) – books (£40)

James Nisbet, merchant in Kirkwall, d. 1641 (CC17/2/4: fols. 55–6) – an old Bible

William Craigie, merchant in Kirkwall, d. 1647 (CC17/2/4: fols. 97–9) – a great Bible

Thomas Hammer, tailor in Kirkwall, d. 1649 (CC17/2/4: fols. 131–2) – six proverbs and two psalm books (probably goods for sale)

Harry Prince, merchant in Kirkwall, d. 1649 (CC17/2/4: fol. 158) – bairns books (£2) (among goods in his booth)

Mr George Johnston, minister at Orphir, d. 1657 (CC17/2/4: fol. 211) – a press with books (£50)

Mr Henry Smith, minister at Shapinsay, d. 1658 (CC17/2/7: fols. 52–3) – books (£100)

Mr Walter Stewart, minister at South Ronaldsay and Burray, d. 1652 (CC17/2/8 pp. 168–9) – books (£30)

Hugh Halcro of that ilk, d. ante July 1666 (CC17/2/8 pp. 237–41) – 2 Bibles

Mr George Smith, minister at Shapinsay, d. 1665 (CC17/2/8 pp. 253–5) – books (£132)

Mr John Gray, student in divinity, d. 166– (CC17/2/10: fols. 68–9) – 17 books in Latin and English (£6)

Mr John Balvaird, minister at Hoy and Graemsay, d. 1668 (CC17/2/10: fol. 79) – books (£30)

James Boog, merchant in Edinburgh, d. 1669 (CC17/2/10: fols. 97–8) – a green Bible

James Georgeson, notary public in Kirkwall, d. ante 1669 (CC17/2/10: fol. 100) – books (£1)

David Beaton, bailie in Stromness, d. 1667 (CC17/2/10: fols. 115–16) – an old great Bible

Magnus Pottinger, skipper in Kirkwall, d. 1668 (CC17/2/10: fols. 131–2) – Blundweill's Works (in the custody of Robert Drummond clerk)

Mr John Innes, minister at Evie and Rendall, d. 1669 (CC17/2/10: fol. 133) – 'utencils, domicells, books and abulyiements' (£50)

Katherine Bothwell, spouse to David Beaton (above) d. 1660 (CC17/2/10: fols. 48–9) – an old great Bible

Isobel Murray, spouse to William Farquhar, glover in Kirkwall, d. 1676 (CC17/2/11: fols. 4–5) – a Bible with 3 old books

Mr Robert Honeyman, only son of the late Andrew, Bishop of Orkney and Shetland, d. 1679 (CC17/2/11: fols. 35–8) – books (£300)

Mr John Gibson, minister at Holm, d. *c.* 1681 (CC17/2/11: fols. 39–40) – books (£77)

William Laughten, merchant in Kirkwall, and Barbara Pottinger his spouse, d. 1681 (CC17/2/11: fols. 40–3) – 2 old Bibles with 2 little Bibles

Helen Louttit, spouse of George Mowat, deacon of the timbermen of Kirkwall, d. 1681 (CC17/2/11: fol. 51) – books in the house (£8)

Margaret Spence, servitrix to Bess Moncrieff, mistress of Tankerness, d. 1682 (CC17/2/11: fols. 68–9) – 1 Old Testament and 1 Psalm Book

John Baird, merchant in Kirkwall, d. ante 1682 (CC17/2/11: fol. 70) – a 'portuzane'; a large house Bible; a book of '?Shirunds Works'

John Baird, as above (CC17/2/11: fol. 85) – a small Bible

Thomas Dishington, precentor in Kirkwall, d. 1682 (CC17/2/11: fol. 96) – old books great and small (£12)

Mr Patrick Kindsay, physician in Kirkwall, d. 1682 (CC17/2/11: fol. 99) – physic books in Latin and Dutch (£9)

Hutcheon Cromartie, merchant in Kirkwall, d. 1682 (CC17/2/11: fol. 104) – an old Bible with 'the practice of pietie' and one other old book

Mr James Shanks, minister at Hoy and Graemsay, d. ante 1682 (CC17/2/11: fol. 122) – books (£20)

Elizabeth Chalmer, spouse of James Arbuthnot in Kirkwall, d. ante 1684 (CC17/2/11: fols. 132–5) – an old house Bible

Mr Thomas Baikie, minister in Rousay and Egilsay, d. 1665 (GD150/2249) – a kist of books (£30)

Andrew Honeyman, Bishop of Orkney and Shetland, d. 1676 (GD106/207) – plenishing with books (£400)

John Louttit, merchant in Kirkwall, d. ante 1700 (GD217/737) – 6 old little books

Shetland testaments (to 1700)

Patrick Hog, minister at Fetlar, d. 162– (CC17/2/1: fol. 122) – a Bible and other books

Mr James Pitcairn, minister at Northmavine, d. 1612 (CC17/2/2: fols. 3–5) – books (100 merks)

Argyll testaments

Mr John McLaurin, minister of Kilmoddan (CC2/3/5 [3/11/1698]) – books (£40)

Mr Alexander Campbell, advocate, Commissar of the Isles, d. 1713 (CC2/3/7) – 4 law books and a Hebrew Bible

John Davies, surgeon in Kilmichael, d. 1718 (CC2/3/8 p. 140) – books (£12)

Mr Dugald Campbell, minister of Lismore, d. 1722 (CC2/3/8: pp. 223–8) – itemized list of some 80 titles (c. £160)

Mr John McGilchrist, minister of north Knapdale, d. 1723 (CC2/3/8 p. 208) – books (£12)

Margaret McIlbride in Glasrie (formerly in Edinburgh), d. 1725 (CC2/3/8 p. 250) – a Bible; an *Essay on the Lord's Supper* by Mr John Warden minister of Gargunnock; a proverbs; *The Church Triumphant* by Mr Alpherd

William Duncanson, postmaster of Inverary, d. 1725 (CC2/3/8 p. 254) – 'ane old little pocket bible and psalm book' (45)

Mr Neil Campbell, minister at Dallarick, d. 1731 (CC2/3/8 p. 319) – books (£294 11s 4d)

John Campbell, surgeon in Inverary, d. 1731 (CC2/3/9) – 'old books' (£3 sterling)

Elizabeth, Dowager Duchess of Argyll, d. 1735 (CC2/3/9) – her books (£7 1s 1d sterling)

David Campbell, late baillie of Kintyre in Campbeltoun parish, d. 1737 (CC2/3/11 p. 46) – books (£24 14s 1d sterling)

Isobel Stewart, widow to Archibald McArthur of Milntoun, living in Dunoon, d. 1742 (CC2/3/11 p. 150) – 'a household Bible and three other books' (2s sterling)

Isles testaments

Mr John MacLeod, minister at Torsay and Pennygown, d. 1735 (CC12/3/2 pp. 99–101) – a chest with six itemized titles (abbreviated) (£12)

Lachlan Maclean the younger of Lochbuie, d. 1742 (CC12/3/2 pp. 141–7) – 15 volumes of Rapin's *History* (bad condition); some books sold by defunct's factor for £3 11s 8d sterling

William Campbell, tacksman of Kelsay, Islay, d. 1745 (CC12/3/4 [30/7/1746]) – *The History of the Kings of Scotland*; MacKenzie's *Institutions*; abridged Acts of Parliament; 2 little books; a book dealing with trade

Mr Aeneas MacLean, minister at Kilninian, Mull, d. 1675 (GD111/4/24) – library (£100)

Three accounts for books bought by John MacKenzie of Delvine for Sir Donald MacDonald dated 23 and 24 September 1707 (GD221/86) which includes titles from five Edinburgh booksellers: Thomas Cutler, Thomas Ruddiman, Mrs Margaret Mossman, Mr Henry Knox and Mr Robert Freebairn.

Appendix 3: List of active Scottish burghs, 1650–1750

The following list excludes Edinburgh and Glasgow but includes all settlements classified in the literacy analysis as towns. It follows the list of burghs given in Adams (1978): 278–82. I should like to thank Rosalind Mitchison, Christopher Smout and Ian Whyte for their help in compiling it. This is a provisional classification which tries to be inclusive rather than exclusive of possible active burghs. Much more research is needed on Scottish urban history.

Royal burghs

Aberdeen
Airth
Arbroath
Ayr
Banff
Berwick
Brechin
Cupar
Dingwall
Dumfries
Dundee
Dunfermline
Elgin
Forfar
Fyvie
Haddington
Hamilton
Inverary
Inverkeithing
Inverness
Irvine

Jedburgh
Kirkcaldy
Kirkcudbright
Kirkwall
Lanark
Lauder
Linlithgow
Montrose
Nairn
Peebles
Perth
Rothesay
St Andrews
Selkirk
Stirling
Wick

Burghs of barony and regality

Aberdeenshire
Aboyne
Ellon
Fraserburgh
Peterhead
Tarves
Turriff

Angus
Kirriemuir

Ayrshire
Kilmarnock
Maybole

Banff
Fordyce

Berwickshire
Coldingham
Duns
Eyemouth

Caithness
Thurso

Clackmannan
Alloa

Dumfrieshire
Langholm
Moffat
Sanquhar

East Lothian
Dunbar
Prestonpans
Tranent

Fife
Ceres
Dysart
Markinch
Wemyss

Invernesshire
Kingussie

Kincardine
Fettercairn
Fordoun

Lanarkshire
Carnwath
Lesmahagow
Strathhaven

Midlothian
Leith
Dalkeith
Musselburgh/Inveresk

Perthshire
Blairgowrie
Coupar Angus
Crieff
Dunblane
Dunkeld

Renfrewshire
Greenock
Paisley
Port Glasgow

Ross and Cromarty
Stornoway

Roxburghshire
Hawick
Kelso
Melrose

Shetland
Lerwick

Stirlingshire
Falkirk

West Lothian
Borrowstouness

Bibliography

MANUSCRIPT SOURCES

BRITISH MUSEUM
Add. Charters 1380
Add. MS 4851
Add. MS 33262
Add. MS 41613
Harleian MS 5191
Harleian MS 7042
Lansdowne MS 253

DEPARTMENT OF PALAEOGRAPHY AND DIPLOMATIC, DURHAM
Durham diocesan records – Consistory Court deposition books
  – uncatalogued loose Consistory Court depositions
  – wills and inventories

EDINBURGH UNIVERSITY LIBRARY
La III 229/1–3 Covenants
Dc.1.50 1638 Covenant

FREE CHURCH COLLEGE
Ayrshire Covenant, 1638

GENERAL REGISTER OFFICE
OPR 691/1–5 Lasswade old parochial register

MUSEUM OF THE SOCIETY OF ANTIQUARIES
OA19 Newbattle Covenant

NATIONAL LIBRARY OF SCOTLAND
Adv. MS 20.6.12 King's Confession 1582
Adv. MS 20.6.13 Fife Covenant 1638
Adv. MS 20.6.16 Peebles Covenant 1638
Adv. MS 20.6.17b Ayr Covenant 1638
Adv. MS 20.6.18 Inveresk Covenant 1638
Adv. MS 20.6.19 nobles Covenant 1638

Adv. MS 23.3.16 Tolbooth Covenant 1643
Adv. MS 72.1.37 Book of the Dean of Lismore
Adv. MS 34.5.15 Forfarshire Covenant 1643
Ch. 5329 Jedburgh Covenant 1638
Mf. 9 (18) Innerpefray library borrowing register, 1747–1962
MS 3279 Menmuir Covenant 1643

NEW COLLEGE LIBRARY
Edzell Covenant 1643
North Leith Covenant 1638
Confession of Faith of the Church of Scotland, 1637
Lauder Covenant 1638

NORTHUMBERLAND COUNTY RECORD OFFICE
1DE Delaval (Horsley) papers
2DE Delaval (Waterford) papers
ZAN M12–20 manuscript collections of Society of Antiquaries of Newcastle
    upon Tyne

PUBLIC RECORD OFFICE
ASSI45 Northern Circuit Assize Depositions

ST ANDREWS UNIVERSITY LIBRARY
B65/20/1 St Andrews taxation inventories, 1630–3
Cheap of Rossie papers 4/123–12/18
Covenants Abercorn (1643), St Andrews (1643, 1648)
Hay of Leys MS
MS DA890.S1.H2 Hammermen of St Andrews trade book
SA08/1–22
SL705/1–146
UY123/1,2

SCOTTISH RECORD OFFICE
CC2/3/5–11 Argyll Commissary Court, Register of Testaments
CC2/5/1–4 Argyll Commissary Court, Register of Inventories
CC8/4/2–500 Edinburgh Commissary Court, Processes
CC8/6/2–19 Edinburgh Commissary Court, Consistorial Processes
CC8/8/1–131 Edinburgh Commissary Court, Register of Testaments
CC8/10/1–15a Edinburgh Commissary Court, Warrants of Testaments
CC8/15/1–20 Edinburgh Commissary Court, Bonds of Caution
CC12/3/2–4 Commissary Court of the Isles, Register of Testaments
CC17/2/1–11 Orkney and Shetland Commissary Court, Register of
    Testaments

CH1/2 General Assembly of the Kirk of Scotland records
CH2/85/1 Dalmellington Kirk Session register
CH2/104/1 Dundonald Kirk Session register
CH2/264/1 Menmuir Kirk Session register
CH2/276/1–3 Newbattle Kirk Session register
CH2/424/1–30 Dalkeith presbytery register

CH2/471/1–10 Lasswade Kirk Session register
CH2/472/1 Kinghorn Kirk Session register
CH2/540/67 Kinneil & Bo'ness Kirk Session register
CH2/621/1 North Leith Kirk Session register
CH2/751/1–2 Ayr Kirk Session register

E69/16/1 Midlothian hearth tax, 1694
E70/4/6 Tolbooth poll tax
E70/4/10 North Leith poll tax
E70/8/1 Borthwick, Heriot, Crichton poll tax
E70/8/3 Carrington poll tax
E70/8/7 Cranston and Fala poll tax
E70/8/8 Dalkeith and Lasswade poll tax
E70/8/10 Inveresk poll tax
E70/8/15 Penicuik poll tax
E70/8/18 Temple poll tax
E70/13/3 Bo'Ness and Kinneil poll tax
E70/13/5 Dalmeny poll tax
E70/13/7 Livingston poll tax

GD18 Clerk of Penicuik papers
GD25/8/302 Carrick Covenant 1638
GD95/1/1–8 Minutes of the general meetings of the Society in Scotland for
    Propagating Christian Knowledge, 1709–1837
GD103/2/150 Maybole Covenant 1638

JC6/1–14 High Court of Justiciary, High Court minute books, 1577–1700
JC7/1–40 High Court of Justiciary, High Court minute books, 1701–70
JC10/2–6, 8 Justiciary Circuit Court minute books, 1655–1702
JC11/1–33 Northern circuit minute books, 1708–1770
JC12/1–22 Southern circuit minute books, 1708–1770
JC13/1–22 Western circuit minute books, 1708–1770
JC26/1–200 High Court of Justiciary, 'Small Papers' 1550–1770

RH1/2/608 nobles Covenant 1638
RH11/5/1 Baron Court book of Argatie, 1672–99

SC41/93/1 Burgh of Regality of Bo'ness, court book, 1669–92

SP13/159 Fife Covenant 1638
SP13/160 Borgue Covenant 1638
SP13/161 Gartly Covenant 1638

'File T39' transcript of Newbattle Abbey Covenant
'File T258' transcripts of Kilmany, Earlston, Duns, Dunblane Covenants

In private hands: Galston Covenant, 1640 in the Kirk Session register for
    1638–44, in the keeping of the minister.

PRINTED WORKS

Anon., 1834–5. 'On the hiring markets in the counties of Northumberland, Berwick, and Roxburgh'. *Quarterly Journal of Agriculture*, 5: 378–86.
Abrams, P., and Wrigley, E. A. (eds.), 1978. *Towns in societies*. Cambridge.
The Acts of the Parliaments of Scotland, vol. 5. 1870. London.
Adams, I. H., 1978. *The making of urban Scotland*. Montreal.
   1980. 'The agents of agricultural change'. In Parry and Slater (eds.), 1980.
Adams, J., 1690. *Index villaris*. London.
Aldis, H. G., 1904. *A list of books printed in Scotland before 1700*. Edinburgh.
Alexander, W., 1859. *The practice of the Commissary Courts in Scotland*. Edinburgh.
Anderson, C. A., and Bowman, M. J., 1973. 'Human capital and economic modernization in historical perspective'. In Lane, F. C. (ed.), *Fourth international conference of economic history, 1968*. Paris.
   1976. 'Education and economic modernization in historical perspective'. In Stone (ed.), 1976.
Anderson, R. D., 1983. *Education and opportunity in Victorian Scotland. Schools and universities*. Oxford.
Appleby, A. B., 1978. *Famine in Tudor and Stuart England*. Liverpool.
Armogathe, J. R., 1973. 'Les catéchismes et l'enseignement populaire au XVIIIe siècle'. In *Images du peuple au XVIIIe siècle*. Paris.
Arnot, H., 1816. *The history of Edinburgh*. Edinburgh.
Ashton, T. S., 1977. *The industrial revolution, 1760–1830*. Oxford.
Ashton, T. S., and Sykes, J., 1964. *The coal industry of the eighteenth century*. Manchester.
Aston, M., 1977. 'Lollardy and literacy'. *History*, 62: 347–71.
Bain, A., 1965. *Education in Stirlingshire from the Reformation to 1872*. London.
Bannerman, J., 1983. 'Literacy in the Highlands'. In Cowan and Shaw (eds.), 1983.
Barnes, R., 1850. *The injunctions and other ecclesiastical proceedings of Richard Barnes, Bishop of Durham, from 1575 to 1587*, ed. J. Raine. Durham.
Barrow, G. W. S. (ed.), 1974. *The Scottish tradition*. Edinburgh.
Barrowman, J., 1897–8. 'Slavery in the coal mines of Scotland'. *Transactions of the Federated Institute of Mining Engineers*, 14: 267–79.
Beale, J. M., 1953. 'A history of the burgh and parochial schools of Fife from the Reformation to 1872'. Unpublished Ph.D. thesis, Edinburgh University.
Beckett, J. V., 1981. *Coal and tobacco. The Lowthers and the economic development of west Cumberland, 1660–1760*. Cambridge.
Benedict, P., 1980. *Rouen during the wars of religion*. Cambridge.
Bennassar, B., 1967. *Valladolid au siècle d'or*. Paris.
Best, H., 1857. *Henry Best – rural economy in Yorkshire in 1641, being the farming and account books of Henry Best of Elmeswell in the East Riding*, ed. C. B. Robinson. Durham.
Bloch, M., 1967. *Land and work in mediaeval Europe*, ed. J. E. Anderson. London.
de Booy, E. P., 1977. *De weldaat der scholen*. Haarlem.
Borsay, P., 1977. 'The English urban renaissance: the development of provincial urban culture, c. 1680–c. 1760'. *Social History*, 5: 581–603.
Bouch, C. M. L., and Jones, G. P., 1961. *A short economic and social history of the lake counties, 1500–1800*. Manchester.
Bourdieu, P., 1974. 'The school as a conservative force: scholastic and cultural

inequalities'. In J. Eggleston (ed.), *Contemporary research in the sociology of education*. London.

Bourdieu, P., and Passeron, J.-C., 1977. *Reproduction in education, society and culture*. London.

Boyd, W., 1961. *Education in Ayrshire over seven centuries*. London.

Brackenridge, R. D., 1969. 'The enforcement of Sunday observance in post-Revolution Scotland, 1689–1733'. *Records of the Scottish Church History Society*, 17: 33–45.

Brodsky, V., 1981. 'Single women in the London marriage market: age, status and mobility, 1598–1619'. In Outhwaite (ed.), 1981.

Brooke, C. N. L., 1961. *From Alfred to Henry III, 871–1272*. New York.

Brougham, Lord, 1837. *Speeches and observations of Lord Brougham*. London.

Brown, P. H., 1891. *Early travellers in Scotland*. Edinburgh.

1893. *Scotland before 1700*. Edinburgh.

Brown, R. (ed.), 1973. *Knowledge, education and cultural change*. London.

Buchan, D., 1972. *The ballad and the folk*. London.

Burgess, R., 1838. *A letter addressed to J. C. Colquhon esq., M.P.* London.

Burke, P., 1978. *Popular culture in early modern Europe*. London.

Burns, T., and Saul, S. B. (eds.), 1967. *Social theory and economic change*. London.

Bush, M. L., 1975. *The government policy of Protector Somerset*. London.

Butel, P., 1976. 'L'instruction populaire en Aquitaine au XVIIIᵉ siècle: l'exemple de l'Agenais'. *Revue d'Histoire Economique et Sociale*, 54: 5–28.

Camden, W., 1695. *Britannia*. London.

Cameron, J. (ed.), 1949. *The justiciary records of Argyll and the Isles, 1664–1705*, vol. 1. Edinburgh.

Campbell, M. J., 1980. 'The development of literacy in Bristol and Gloucestershire, 1755–1870'. Unpublished Ph.D. thesis, Bath University.

Campbell, R. H., 1983. 'The influence of religion on economic growth in Scotland in the eighteenth century'. In Devine and Dickson (eds.), 1983.

Carnie, R. H., 1965. 'Scottish printers and booksellers, 1668–1775: a study of source-material'. *Bibliotheck*, 4: 213–27.

Carter, I., 1973. 'Marriage patterns and social sectors in Scotland before the eighteenth century'. *Scottish Studies*, 17: 51–60.

1981. 'The changing image of the peasant in Scottish history and literature, 1745–1979'. In Samuel (ed.), 1981.

Castan, Y., 1974. *Honnêteté et relations sociales en Languedoc, 1715–1780*. Paris.

Chalklin, C. W. and Havinden, M. (eds.), 1974. *Rural change and urban growth, 1500–1800*. New York.

Chartier, R., Julia, D., and Compère, M., 1976. *Education en France du XVIᵉ au XVIIIᵉ siècle*. Paris.

Chaytor, M., 1980. 'Household and kinship: Ryton in the late 16th and early 17th centuries'. *History Workshop Journal*, 10: 25–60.

Chevalier, M., 1976. *Lectura y lectores en España de los siglos XVI y XVII*. Madrid.

Chrisman, M. U., 1982. *Lay culture, learned culture. Books and social change in Strasbourg, 1480–1599*. New Haven.

Cipolla, C. M., 1969. *Literacy and development in the west*. Harmondsworth.

1972. 'The diffusion of innovations in early modern Europe'. *Comparative Studies in Society and History*, 14: 46–52.

Clanchy, M. T., 1979. *From memory to written record: England, 1066–1377*. London.

Clark, A., 1919. *The working life of women in the seventeenth century*. London.

Clark, G., 1972. *The seventeenth century*. Oxford.

Clark, P., 1976. 'The ownership of books in England, 1560–1640: the example of some Kentish townsfolk'. In Stone (ed.), 1976.

1979. 'Migration in England during the late seventeenth and early eighteenth centuries'. *Past & Present*, 83: 57–90.

(ed.), 1981. *Country towns in pre-industrial England.* Leicester.

Clark, P., and Slack, P., 1976. *English towns in transition, 1500–1700.* Oxford.

Clarkson, L. A., 1980. 'The writing of Irish economic and social history since 1968'. *Economic History Review*, 2nd series, 33: 100–11.

Clive, J., 1970. 'The social background of the Scottish Renaissance'. In Phillipson and Mitchison (eds.), 1970.

Cockburn, J. S., 1968. 'The northern assize circuit'. *Northern History*, 3: 118–30.

1972. *A history of English assizes, 1558–1714.* Cambridge.

1975. 'Early modern assize records as historical evidence'. *Journal of the Society of Archivists*, 5: 215–31.

(ed.), 1977. *Crime in England, 1550–1800.* London.

Collinson, P., 1982. *The religion of the protestants. The church in English society, 1559–1625.* Oxford.

Colls, R., 1976. '"Oh happy English children!"'. Coal, class and education in the north-east'. *Past & Present*, 73: 75–99.

Consett, H., 1685. *The practice of the spiritual or ecclesiastical courts.* London.

Cowan, I. B., 1978. *Regional aspects of the Scottish Reformation.* London.

Cowan, I. B., and Shaw, D. (eds.), 1983. *The Renaissance and Reformation in Scotland.* Edinburgh.

Craig, D., 1961. *Scottish literature and the Scottish people, 1680–1830.* London.

Crawford, P., 1981. 'Attitudes to menstruation in seventeenth-century England'. *Past & Present*, 91: 47–73.

Cressy, D., 1974. 'Literacy in pre-industrial England'. *Societas*, 4: 229–40.

1978. 'Social status and literacy in north-east England, 1560–1630'. *Local Population Studies*, 21: 19–23.

1980. *Literacy and the social order.* Cambridge.

Cullen, L. M., 1983. 'Incomes, social classes and economic growth in Ireland and Scotland, 1600–1900'. In Devine and Dickson (eds.), 1983.

Cullen, L. M., and Smout, T. C. (eds.), 1977. *Comparative aspects of Scottish and Irish economic and social history, 1600–1900.* Edinburgh.

Curtis, M. H., 1964. 'Education and apprenticeship'. *Shakespeare Survey*, 17: 53–72.

Dale, R., Esland, G., and Macdonald, M. (eds.), 1976. *Schooling and capitalism.* London.

Dalton, M., 1618. *The country justice.* London.

Davies, I., 1973. 'Knowledge, education and power'. In R. Brown (ed.), 1973.

Davies, J., 1979. 'Persecution and protestantism: Toulouse, 1562–1575'. *Historical Journal*, 22: 31–51.

Davies, S. J., 1980. 'The courts and the Scottish legal system, 1600–1747: the case of Stirlingshire'. In Gatrell, Lenman and Parker (eds.), 1980.

Davis, N. Z., 1975. *Society and culture in early modern France.* London.

Deane, P., 1965. *The first industrial revolution.* London.

Defoe, D., 1708. *Review of the state of the British nation*, vol. 5 (30 September 1708). London.

1978. *A tour through the whole island of Great Britain*, ed. P. Rogers. Harmondsworth.

Devine, T. M., 1975. *The tobacco lords.* Edinburgh.

1978. 'Social stability and agrarian change in the eastern Lowlands of Scotland, 1810–1840'. *Social History*, 3: 331–46.

(ed.), 1979. *Lairds and improvement in the Scotland of the Enlightenment.* Glasgow.

1983a. 'The English connection and Irish and Scottish development in the eighteenth century'. In Devine and Dickson (eds.), 1983.

1983b. 'The social composition of the business class in the larger Scottish towns, 1680–1740'. In Devine and Dickson (eds.), 1983.

Devine, T. M., and Dickson, D. (eds.), 1983. *Ireland and Scotland, 1600–1850. Parallels and contrasts in economic and social development.* Edinburgh.

Deyon, P., 1967. *Amiens: capitale provinciale.* Paris.

Dick, M., 1980. 'The myth of the working-class Sunday school'. *History of Education*, 9: 27–41.

Di Folco, J. A., 1975. 'Aspects of seventeenth-century social life in central and north Fife'. Unpublished Ph.D. thesis, St Andrews University.

1979. 'The Hopes of Craighall and land investment in the seventeenth century'. In Devine (ed.), 1979.

Dilworth, M., 1973. 'Literacy of pre-Reformation monks'. *Innes Review*, 24: 71–2.

Dodd, W., 1972. 'Ayr: a study of urban growth'. *Ayrshire Archaeological and Natural History Society Collections*, 10: 302–82.

Dodgshon, R. A., 1976. 'The economics of sheep farming in the Southern Uplands during the Age of Improvement, 1750–1833'. *Economic History Review*, 2nd series, 29: 551–69.

1981. *Land and society in early Scotland.* Oxford.

Dodgshon, R. A., and Butlin, R. A. (eds.), 1978. *An historical geography of England and Wales.* London.

Doe, V. S. (ed.), 1978. *The diary of James Clegg of Chapel en le Frith*, pt 1. Matlock.

Donaldson, G., 1974. *Scotland: the shaping of a nation.* Newton Abbot.

Drake, M., 1962. 'An elementary exercise in parish register demography'. *Economic History Review*, 2nd series, 14: 427–45.

Drake, M. (ed.), 1973. *Applied historical studies.* London.

Duckham, B. F., 1969. 'Serfdom in eighteenth-century Scotland'. *History*, 54: 178–97.

1970. *A history of the Scottish coal industry, 1700–1815.* Newton Abbot.

Duffy, B., 1981. 'Debate. Coal, class and education in the north-east'. *Past & Present*, 90: 142–51.

Duglio, M. R., 1971. 'Alfabetismo e societa' a Turino'. *Quaderni storici*, 17: 485–509.

Duncan, J. F., 1919. 'Scottish farm labour'. *Scottish Journal of Agriculture*, 2: 498–507.

Dunlop, O. J., and Denman, R. D., 1912. *English apprenticeship and child labour.* London.

Dunn, H., 1838. *National education, the question of questions; being an apology for the Bible in schools for the nation.* London.

Durkacz, V. E., 1978. 'The source of the language problem in Scottish education, 1688–1709'. *Scottish Historical Review*, 57: 28–39.

1983. *The decline of the Celtic languages.* Edinburgh.

Dutton, H. I., and King, J. E., 1982. 'The limits of paternalism: the cotton tyrants of north Lancashire, 1836–54'. *Social History*, 7: 59–74.

Eccles, A., 1982. *Obstetrics and gynaecology in Tudor and Stuart England.* London.

Ecclesiastical Records. Selections from the minutes of the presbyteries of St Andrews and Cupar, 1641–1698, 1837. Edinburgh.

Eisenstein, E., 1968. 'Some conjectures about the impact of printing on western society'. *Journal of Modern History*, 40: 1–56.

Everitt, A., 1967. 'Farm labourers'. In Thirsk (ed.), 1967.

Extracts from the records of the burgh of Edinburgh, AD 1403–1528, 1869. Edinburgh.

Eyre, A., 1877. *A Dyurnall, or catalogue of all my accions and expences*. Durham.

Fenton, A., 1974. 'Scottish agriculture and the union: an example of indigenous development'. In Rae (ed.), 1974.

1976. *Scottish country life*. Edinburgh.

Ferguson, C. M. F., 1981. 'Law and order on the Anglo-Scottish border, 1603–1707'. Unpublished Ph.D. thesis, St Andrews University.

Ferguson, J. A., 1982. 'A comparative study of urban society in Edinburgh, Dublin and London in the late seventeenth century'. Unpublished Ph.D. thesis, St Andrews University.

Ferguson, W., 1969. *Scotland, 1689 to the present*. Edinburgh.

Fewster, J. M., 1957–8. 'The keelmen of Tyneside in the eighteenth century'. *Durham University Journal*, 19: 24–33, 66–75, 111–23.

Finlay, R. A. P., 1981. *Population and metropolis: the demography of London, 1580–1680*. Cambridge.

Finnegan, R., 1973. 'Literacy versus non-literacy: the great divide'. In Horton and Finnegan (eds.), 1973.

Fleury, M., and Valmary, A., 1957. 'Les progrès de l'instruction élémentaire de Louis XIV à Napoleon III d'après l'enquête de Louis Maggiolo (1877–1879)'. *Population*, 12: 71–92.

Flinn, M. W., 1967. 'Social theory and the industrial revolution'. In Burns and Saul (eds.), 1967.

(ed.), 1977. *Scottish population history*. Cambridge.

1981. *The European demographic system, 1500–1820*. London.

Floud, R., and McCloskey, D. (eds.), 1981. *The economic history of Britain since 1700. Volume 1, 1700–1860*. London.

Fox, H. S. A., 1979. 'Local farmers' associations and the circulation of agricultural information in nineteenth-century England'. In Fox and Butlin (eds.), 1979.

Fox, H. S. A., and Butlin, R. A. (eds.), 1979. *Change in the countryside*. London.

Friedrichs, C. R., 1979. *Urban society in an age of war: Nördlingen, 1580–1720*. Princeton.

Frijhoff, W., 1979. 'Surplus ou déficit? Hypothèses sur le nombre réel des étudiants en Allemagne à l'époque moderne (1576–1815)'. *Francia*, 7: 173–218.

Fritz, P., and Morton, R. (eds.), 1976. *Women in the 18th century and other essays*. Toronto.

Furet, F., and Ozouf, J., 1982. *Reading and writing. Literacy in France from Calvin to Jules Ferry*. Cambridge.

Furet, F., and Sachs, W., 1974. 'La croissance de l'alphabétisation en France XVIIIe – XIXe siècle'. *Annales ESC*, 29: 714–37.

Fussell, G. E. (ed.), 1936. *Robert Loder's farm accounts, 1610–20*. Manchester.

1966. *The English dairy farmer, 1500–1900*. London.

Gatrell, V. A. C., Lenman, B., and Parker, G. (eds.), 1980. *Crime and the law. The social history of crime in western Europe since 1500*. London.

Gellner, E., 1983. *Nations and nationalism*. Oxford.

Gilboy, E., 1934. *Wages in eighteenth-century England*. London.

Gillespie, J. H., 1939. *Dundonald: a contribution to parochial history*, vol. 2. Glasgow.

Gillon, S. A. (ed.), 1953. *Selected justiciary cases, 1624–1650*, vol. 1. Edinburgh.

Gilly, W. S., 1842. *The peasantry of the Border*. Edinburgh.

Godolphin, J., 1678. *Repertorium canonicum or an abridgement of the ecclesiastical laws of this realm*. London.

Goldie, M. E., 1970. 'The standard of living of the Scottish farm labourer in selected areas at the time of the first two statistical accounts, 1790–1845'. Unpublished M.Sc. thesis, Edinburgh University.

Goody, J. (ed.), 1968. *Literacy in traditional societies*. Cambridge.

Goody, J., Thirsk, J., and Thompson, E. P. (eds.), 1976. *Family and inheritance. Rural society in western Europe, 1200–1800*. Cambridge.

Goubert, P., 1973. *The Ancien Régime. French society, 1600–1750*. London.

Graff, H. J., 1975. 'Literacy in history'. *History of Education Quarterly*, 15: 467–74.
1979. *The literacy myth*. New York.
(ed.), 1981. *Literacy and social development in the west: a reader*. Cambridge.

Grant, F. J., 1897–9. *The Commissariat records of Edinburgh: register of testaments, 1514–1800*, 3 vols. Edinburgh.

Grant, I. F., 1930. *The social and economic development of Scotland before 1603*. Edinburgh.

Grant, J., 1876. *History of the burgh and parochial schools of Scotland*. Vol. 1. *The burgh schools*. Glasgow.

Gray, J., McPherson, A. F., and Raffe, D., 1983. *Reconstructions of secondary education. Theory, myth and practice since the war*. London.

Gray, M., 1976. 'North-east agriculture and the labour force, 1790–1875'. In MacLaren (ed.), 1976.

Gray, W. F., 1944. *A short history of Haddington*. Edinburgh.

Gulvin, C., 1971. 'The Union and the Scottish woollen industry, 1707–1760'. *Scottish Historical Review*, 50: 121–57.

Haig, C., 1975. 'Slander and the church courts in the sixteenth century'. *Transactions of the Lancashire and Cheshire Antiquarian Society*, 78: 1–13.
1981. 'The continuity of catholicism in the English Reformation'. *Past & Present*, 93: 37–69.

Haldane, A. R. B., 1952. *The drove roads of Scotland*. London.
1961. 'Old Scottish fairs and markets'. *Transactions of the Royal Highland and Agricultural Society of Scotland*, 6th series, 6: 1–12.

Hanham, H. J., 1969. *Scottish nationalism*. London.

Hans, N., 1951. *New trends in education in the eighteenth century*. London.

Harding, A. (ed.), 1980. *Law-making and law-makers in British history*. London.

Hartwell, R. M., 1971. 'Education and economic growth in England during the industrial revolution'. *Annales Cisalpines d'Histoire Sociale*, 1: 75–93.

Hay, D., Linebaugh, P., and Thompson, E. P., 1975. *Albion's fatal tree*. Harmondsworth.

Hechter, M., 1975. *Internal colonialism: the Celtic fringe in British national development, 1536–1966*. London.

Henderson, J. B., 1898. *Borgue: its parish churches, pastors, and people*. Castle Douglas.

Henderson, T. F. (ed.), 1902. *Sir Walter Scott's minstrelsy of the Scottish border*, vol. 1. Edinburgh.

Hendrie, J., 1909. *History of Galston parish church*. Paisley.

Hewison, J. K., 1908. *The Covenanters*, vol. 2. Glasgow.

Hittle, J. M., 1979. *The service city. State and townsmen in Russia, 1600–1800*. London.

Hoare, Q., and Nowell-Smith, G. (eds.), 1971. *Selections from the prison notebooks of Antonio Gramsci*. London.

Hobsbawm, E., 1969. *Industry and empire*. Harmondsworth.

 1983. 'Introduction: inventing traditions'. In Hobsbawm and Ranger (eds.), 1983.

Hobsbawm, E., and Ranger, T. (eds.), 1983. *The invention of tradition*. Cambridge.

Hobsbawm, E., and Rudé, G., 1973. *Captain Swing*. Harmondsworth.

Hockliffe, E. (ed.), 1908. *The diary of the reverend Ralph Josselin, 1616–1683*. London.

Hodgshon, R. I., 1979. 'The progress of enclosure in county Durham, 1550–1870'. In Fox and Butlin (eds.), 1979.

Hogg, J., 1831–2. 'On the changes in the habits, amusements, and condition of the Scottish peasantry'. *Quarterly Journal of Agriculture*, 3: 256–63.

Holderness, B. A., 1975. 'Credit in a rural community, 1660–1800'. *Midland History*, 3: 94–116.

Horton, R., and Finnegan, R. (eds.), 1973. *Modes of thought*. London.

Hoskins, W. G., 1949. *Midland England*. London.

Houdaille, J., 1977. 'Les signatures au mariage de 1740 à 1829'. *Population*, 32: 65–90.

Houston, R. A., 1979. 'Parish listings and social structure: Penningham and Whithorn (Wigtownshire) in perspective'. *Local Population Studies*, 23: 24–32.

 1981. 'Aspects of society in Scotland and north-east England. *c.*1550–*c.*1750: social structure, literacy, and geographical mobility'. Unpublished Ph.D. thesis, Cambridge University.

 1982a. 'The literacy myth? Illiteracy in Scotland, 1630–1760'. *Past & Present*, 96: 81–102.

 1982b. 'The development of literacy: northern England, 1640–1750'. *Economic History Review*, 2nd series, 35: 199–216.

 1982c. 'Illiteracy in the diocese of Durham, 1663–89 and 1750–62: the evidence of marriage bonds'. *Northern History*, 18: 239–51.

 1982d. *Records of a Scottish village. Lasswade, 1650–1750*. Chadwyck-Healey Ltd., Cambridge.

 1982e. 'Illiteracy among Newcastle shoemakers, 1618–1740'. *Archaeologia Aeliana*, 5th series, 10: 143–7.

 1983a. 'Coal, class and culture: labour relations in a Scottish mining community, 1650–1750'. *Social History*, 8: 1–18.

 1983b. 'Literacy and society in the west, 1500–1850'. *Social History*, 8: 269–93.

 1985. 'Geographical mobility in Scotland, 1652–1811'. *Journal of Historical Geography*.

Hudson, P., 1981. 'Proto-industrialization: the case of the West Riding wool textile industry in the 18th and early 19th centuries'. *History Workshop Journal*, 12: 34–61.

Hughes, E., 1952. *North country life in the eighteenth century*. Vol. 1. *The north-east, 1700–1750*. London.

Hull, S. W., 1982. *Chaste, silent and obedient. English books for women, 1475–1640*. San Marino.

Humes, W. M., and Paterson, H. M. (eds.), 1983. *Scottish culture and Scottish education, 1800–1980*. Edinburgh.

Hunt, C. J., and Isaac, P. C. G., 1977. 'The regulation of the booktrade in Newcastle upon Tyne at the beginning of the nineteenth century'. *Archaeologia Aeliana*, 5th series, 5: 163–78.

Hunter, J. E., 1976. 'The 18th-century Englishwoman according to the *Gentleman's Magazine*'. In Fritz and Morton (eds.), 1976.

Imrie, J. (ed.), 1969. *The justiciary records of Argyll and the Isles*, vol. 2, 1705–1742. Edinburgh.

Ingram, M. J., 1977. 'Communities and courts: law and disorder in early seventeenth century Wiltshire'. In Cockburn (ed.), 1977.

James, M., 1974. *Family, lineage, and civil society*. Oxford.

Jessop, J. C., 1931. *Education in Angus*. London.

Jewell, H. M., 1982. '"The bringing up of children in good learning and manners": a survey of secular educational provision in the north of England, c.1350–1550'. *Northern History*, 18: 1–25.

Johansson, E., 1981. 'The history of literacy in Sweden'. In Graff (ed.), 1981.

Johnson, R., 1970. 'Educational policy and social control in early Victorian England'. *Past & Present*, 49: 96–119.

  1976. 'Notes on the schooling of the English working class, 1780–1850'. In Dale, Esland, and MacDonald (eds.), 1976.

Johnson, S., 1775. *A journey to the western islands of Scotland*. London.

Johnston, J. A., 1978. 'Worcestershire probate inventories, 1699–1716'. *Midland History*, 4: 191–211.

Johnston, T., 1920. *The history of the working classes in Scotland*. Glasgow.

Jones, R. E., 1979. 'Bookowners in eighteenth-century Scotland: a note on subscription lists in books edited by John Howie'. *Local Population Studies*, 23: 33–5.

Judt, T., 1981. 'The impact of the schools. Provence, 1871–1914'. In Graff (ed.), 1981.

Kaestle, C. F., 1976. '"Between the Scylla of brutal ignorance and the Charybdis of a literary education": elite attitudes towards mass schooling in early industrial England and America'. In Stone (ed.), 1976.

Kirk, J. (ed.), 1977. *The records of the synod of Lothian and Tweeddale, 1589–96, 1640–49*. Edinburgh.

Knox, H. M. 1953. *Two hundred and fifty years of Scottish education, 1696–1949*. Edinburgh.

Knox, J., 1905. *The history of the Reformation in Scotland with which are included Knox's Confession and the Book of Discipline*, ed. C. Lennox. London. .

Knox, J., 1784. *A view of the British empire, more especially Scotland; with some proposals for the improvement of that country, the extension of its fisheries, and the relief of the people*. London.

Kussmaul, A., 1981. *Servants in husbandry in early modern England*. Cambridge.

Kyd, J. G. (ed.), 1952. *Scottish population statistics*. Edinburgh.

Laget, M., 1971. 'Petites écoles en Languedoc au XVIIIe siècle'. *Annales ESC*, 26: 1398–1418.

Lambard, W., 1581. *Eirenarcha; or of the office of the justices of peace*. London.

Landes, D. S., 1969. *The unbound Prometheus*. Cambridge.

Langbein, J. H., 1974. *Prosecuting crime in the Renaissance*. Cambridge, Mass.

Langton, J., 1975. 'Residential patterns in pre-industrial cities: some case studies from seventeenth-century Britain'. *Transactions of the Institute of British Geographers*, 65: 1–27.

  1978. 'Industry and towns, 1500–1730'. In Dodgshon and Butlin (eds.), 1978.

1979. *Geographical change and industrial revolution*. Cambridge.

Lansdowne, 1839. *Substance of the Marquess of Lansdowne's speech ... on ... national education*. London.

Laqueur, T. W., 1976a. 'The cultural origins of popular literacy in England, 1500–1850'. *Oxford Review of Education*, 2: 255–75.

1976b. 'Working-class demand and the growth of English elementary education, 1750–1850'. In Stone (ed.), 1976.

1976c. *Religion and respectability. Sunday schools and working-class culture, 1780–1850*. London.

Larner, C., 1981. *Enemies of God. The witch-hunt in Scotland*. London.

Laslett, P., 1969. 'Scottish weavers, cobblers and miners who bought books in the 1750s'. *Local Population Studies*, 3: 7–15.

1971. *The world we have lost*. London.

Law, A., 1965. *Education in Edinburgh in the eighteenth century*. London.

Leinster-Mackay, D. P., 1976. 'Dame-schools: a need for review'. *British Journal of Educational Studies*, 24: 33–48.

Lenman, B. P., 1977a. *An economic history of modern Scotland, 1660–1976*. London.

1977b. 'Introduction' to Grant and Withrington (eds.), *The statistical account of Scotland, 1791–1799: north and west Perthshire*. Wakefield.

1981. *Integration, enlightenment, and industrialization: Scotland, 1746–1832*. London.

1982. 'Reinterpreting Scotland's last two centuries of independence'. *Historical Journal*, 25: 217–28.

Le Roy Ladurie, E., 1976. 'Family structures and inheritance customs in sixteenth-century France'. In Goody, Thirsk and Thompson (eds.), 1976.

Le Roy Ladurie, E., and Demonet, M., 1980. 'Alphabétisation et stature: un tableau comparé'. *Annales ESC*, 35: 1329–32.

Levine, D., 1979. 'Education and family life in early industrial England'. *Journal of Family History*, 4: 368–80.

Levitt, I., and Smout, T. C., 1979. *The state of the Scottish working class in 1843*. Edinburgh.

Lewis, G. R., 1834. *Scotland a half-educated nation*. Glasgow.

1838. *An address on the subject of education*. London.

Litak, S., 1973. 'The parochial school network in Poland prior to the establishment of the Commission of National Education'. *Acta Poloniae Historica*, 27: 45–65.

Loch, D., 1778. *A tour through most of the trading towns and villages of Scotland*. Edinburgh.

Lockhart, J. G., 1830. *The life of Robert Burns*. Edinburgh.

Lockridge, K. A., 1974. *Literacy in colonial New England*. New York.

1981. 'Literacy in early America, 1650–1800'. In Graff (ed.), 1981.

Logue, K. J., 1979. *Popular disturbances in Scotland, 1780–1815*. Edinburgh.

Longuet, Y., 1978. 'L'alphabétisation à Falaise de 1670 à 1789'. *Annales de Normandie*, 28: 207–23.

Lynch, M., 1981. *Edinburgh and the Reformation*. Edinburgh.

Macaulay, 1913. *The history of England from the accession of James II*, vol. 1, ed. C. Firth. London.

Macdonald, S., 1979. 'The diffusion of knowledge among Northumberland farmers, 1780–1815'. *Agricultural History Review*, 27: 30–9.

Macfarlane, A., 1970. *The family life of Ralph Josselin*. Cambridge.

1978. *The origins of English individualism*. Oxford.

1980. 'Review essay'. *American Journal of Legal History*, 24: 171–7.

1981. *The justice and the mare's ale*. Oxford.

Macfarlane, W., 1906–8. *Geographical collections relating to Scotland*, 3 vols., ed. A. Mitchell. Edinburgh.

Mackenzie, G., 1678. *The laws and customes of Scotland in matters criminal*. Edinburgh.

Mackenzie, W. M., 1949. *The Scottish burghs*. Edinburgh.

McKerral, A., 1948. *Kintyre in the seventeenth century*. Edinburgh.

Mackie, J. D., 1978. *A history of Scotland*. Harmondsworth.

Mackinnon, K. M., 1972. 'Education and social control: the case of Gaelic'. *Scottish Educational Studies*, 4: 125–37.

MacLaren, A. A. (ed.), 1976. *Social class in Scotland past and present*. Edinburgh.

McMullen, N., 1977. 'The education of English gentlewomen, 1540–1640'. *History of Education*, 6: 87–101.

McPherson, A., 1973. 'Selections and survivals: a sociology of the ancient Scottish universities'. In Brown (ed.), 1973.

1983. 'An angle on the geist: persistence and change in the Scottish educational tradition'. In Humes and Paterson (eds.), 1983.

Markussen, I., and Skovgaard Petersen, V., 1981. 'Læseindlærning of læsebehov i Danmark, *ca*.1550–*ca*.1850'. *Ur Nordisk Kulturhistoria. Studia Historica Jyväskyläensiä*, 22.

Marshall, G., 1980. *Presbyteries and profits: Calvinism and the development of capitalism in Scotland, 1560–1707*. Oxford.

Marshall, J. D. (ed.), 1967. *The autobiography of William Stout of Lancaster, 1665–1752*. Manchester.

Marshall, J. S., 1969. 'A social and economic history of Leith in the eighteenth century'. Unpublished Ph.D. thesis, Edinburgh University.

Martin, H.-J., 1978. 'The *bibliothèque bleue*'. *Publishing History*, 3: 70–103.

Marwick, J. D., 1909. *The river Clyde and the Clyde burghs*. Glasgow.

Mathew, W. M., 1966. 'The origins and occupations of Glasgow students, 1740–1839'. *Past & Present*, 33: 74–94.

Mathias, P., 1979. *The transformation of England*. London.

Meyer, J., 1974. 'Alphabétisation, lecture et écriture. Essai sur l'instruction populaire en Bretagne du XVIᵉ au XIXᵉ siècle'. In *Actes du 95ᵉ Congrès National des Sociétés Savantes*, vol. 1. Paris.

Miller, K. (ed.), 1970. *Memoirs of modern Scotland*. London.

Mitchell, J., 1939. *Memories of Ayrshire about 1780*. Edinburgh.

Mitchison, R., 1974. 'The making of the old Scottish poor law'. *Past & Present*, 63: 58–93.

1978. *Life in Scotland*. London.

1983. *Lordship to patronage. Scotland, 1603–1745*. London.

Moral statistics of the Highlands and Islands of Scotland, compiled from returns received by the Inverness society for the education of the poor in the Highlands. 1826. Inverness.

Mowat, I. R. M., 1979. 'Literacy, libraries and literature in 18th and 19th century Easter Ross'. *Library History*, 5: 1–10.

Nairn, T., 1970. 'The three dreams of Scottish nationalism'. In Miller (ed.), 1970.

Neuburg, V. E., 1971. *Popular education in eighteenth-century England*. London.

New Statistical Account of Scotland. 1845.

O'Day, R., 1982. *Education and society, 1500–1800*. London.

Ollard, S. L., and Walker, P. C. (eds.), 1928, 1929. *Archbishop Herring's visitation returns, 1743*, 5 vols. Wakefield.

Ong, W. J., 1982. *Orality and literacy*. London.

Orwell, S., and Angus, I. (eds.), 1970. *The collected essays, journalism and letters of George Orwell*. Vol. 1. *An age like this, 1920–1940*. Harmondsworth.

Outhwaite, R. B. (ed.), 1981. *Marriage and society*. London.

Overton, M., 1980. 'Agricultural change in Norfolk and Suffolk, 1580–1740'. Unpublished Ph.D. thesis, Cambridge University.

Pagan, J. H., 1897. *Annals of Ayr in the olden time, 1560–1692*. Ayr.

Parker, D., 1983. *The making of French absolutism*. London.

Parker, G., 1980. 'An educational revolution? The growth of literacy and schooling in early modern Europe'. *Tijdschrift voor Geschiedenis*, 93: 210–20.

Parker, W. N., and Jones, E. L. (eds.), 1975. *European peasants and their markets*. Princeton.

Parkinson, R. (ed.), 1845. *The life of Adam Martindale, written by himself*. Manchester.

(ed.), 1852. *The autobiography of Henry Newcome, M.A.*, vol. 1. Manchester.

Parry, M. L., and Slater, T. R. (eds.), 1980. *The making of the Scottish countryside*. London.

Paterson, J., 1857. *History of the regality of Musselburgh*. Musselburgh.

Paterson, J. H., 1965. 'The novelist and his region: Scotland through the eyes of Sir Walter Scott'. *Scottish Geographical Magazine*, 8: 146–52.

Paton, H. (ed.), 1936. *The session book of Dundonald, 1602–1731*. Privately printed.

Patten, J., 1972. 'Village and town: an occupational study'. *Agricultural History Review*, 20: 1–16.

1978. *English towns, 1500–1700*. Folkestone.

Payne, P. L. (ed.), 1967. *Studies in Scottish business history*. London.

Pearl, V., 1979. 'Change and stability in seventeenth-century London'. *London Journal*, 5: 3–34.

Pennant, T., 1774. *A tour in Scotland, 1769*. Warrington.

Phillipson, N. T., 1980. 'The social structure of the faculty of advocates in Scotland, 1661–1840'. In Harding (ed.), 1980.

Phillipson, N. T., and Mitchison, R. (eds.), 1970. *Scotland in the age of improvement*. Edinburgh.

Pocock, D. C. D., 1979. 'The novelist's image of the north'. *Transactions of the Institute of British Geographers*, 4: 62–76.

Pocock, J. G. A., 1974. 'British history: a plea for a new subject'. *The New Zealand Journal of History*, 8: 3–21.

Potkowski, E., 1979. 'Écriture et société en Pologne du bas moyen age (XIVe – XVe siècles)'. *Acta Poloniae Historica*, 39: 47–100.

Pryde, G. S., 1965. *The burghs of Scotland*. Oxford.

Rae, T. I. (ed.), 1974. *The union of 1707: its impact on Scotland*. Glasgow.

Recent measures for the promotion of education in England. 17th edn, 1840. London.

Redfield, R., 1960. *The little community*. Chicago.

Reeder, D. (ed.), 1977. *Urban education in the 19th century*. London.

Register containing the state and condition of every burgh within the kingdom of Scotland, in the year 1692. 1881. Edinburgh.

Reports on the state of certain parishes in Scotland [1627] made to his majesty's commissioners for plantation of kirks. 1835. Edinburgh.

Reports from commissioners. Vol. 18. *First detailed annual report of the Registrar-General of births, deaths, and marriages in Scotland*. 1861. Edinburgh.

18th annual report of the Registrar-General of births, deaths, and marriages in England [1855]. 1857. London.

Riley, P. W. J., 1978. *The union of England and Scotland*. Manchester.

Roberts, M., 1953. *Gustavus Adolphus. A history of Sweden, 1611–1632*, vol. 1. London.

Robertson, G., 1793. *General view of the agriculture of the county of Midlothian*. Edinburgh.

1829. *Rural recollections*. Irvine.

Rodriguez, M.-C., and Bennassar, B., 1978. 'Signatures et niveau culturel des témoins et accusés dans les procès d'inquisition du ressort du tribunal de Tolède (1525–1817), et du ressort du tribunal de Cordoue (1595–1632)'. *Cahiers du Monde Hispanique et Luso-Brésilien*, 31: 17–46.

Rogers, K., 1976. 'The feminism of Daniel Defoe'. In Fritz and Morton (eds.), 1976.

Romanes, C. S. (ed.), 1914–17. *Selections from the records of the regality of Melrose, 1605–1706*. 3 vols. Edinburgh.

Ross, I., and Scobie, S., 1974. 'Patriotic publishing as a response to the union'. In Rae (ed.), 1974.

Rostow, W. W., 1971. *The stages of economic growth*. Cambridge.

Rule, J. G., 1981. *The experience of labour in eighteenth-century industry*. London.

Russell, J. A., 1971. *Education in the stewartry of Kirkcudbright, 1560–1970*. Newton Stewart.

Sachse, W. L. (ed.), 1938. *The diary of Roger Lowe, 1663–74*. London.

Salmon, T. J., 1913. *Borrowstouness and district*. Edinburgh.

Samuel, R. (ed.), 1981. *People's history and socialist theory*. London.

Sanderson, M., 1967. 'Education and the factory in industrial Lancashire, 1780–1840'. *Economic History Review*, 2nd series, 20: 266–79.

1968. 'Social change and elementary education in industrial Lancashire, 1780–1840'. *Northern History*, 3: 131–54.

1972. 'Literacy and social mobility in the Industrial Revolution'. *Past & Present*, 56: 75–104.

Sanderson, M. H. B., 1982. *Scottish rural society in the 16th century*. Edinburgh.

1983. 'The Edinburgh merchants in society, 1570–1603: the evidence of their testaments'. In Cowan and Shaw (eds.), 1983.

Saunders, L. J., 1950. *Scottish democracy, 1815–1840*. Edinburgh.

Schofield, R. S., 1968. 'The measurement of literacy in pre-industrial England'. In Goody (ed.), 1968.

1981. 'Dimensions of illiteracy, 1750–1850'. In Graff (ed.), 1981.

Scotland, J., 1969. *The history of Scottish education*, vol. 1. London.

Scott, H. (ed.), 1883. *Fasti ecclesiae Scoticanae*. Edinburgh.

Scott, W. (ed.), 1916. *The parish lists of Wigtownshire and Minnigaff*. Edinburgh.

Scribner, R. W., 1981. *For the sake of simple folk. Popular propaganda for the German Reformation*. Cambridge.

Shakespeare, J., and Dowling, M., 1982. 'Religion and politics in mid-Tudor England through the eyes of an English Protestant woman: the recollections of Rose Hickman'. *Bulletin of the Institute of Historical Research*, 55: 94–102.

Shaw, F. J., 1981. *The northern and western islands of Scotland: their economy and society in the seventeenth century*. Edinburgh.

Silver, H., 1975. *English education and the radicals, 1780–1850*. London.

Simon, B. (ed.), 1968. *Education in Leicestershire, 1540–1940*. Leicester.

Simon, J., 1967. *Education and society in Tudor England*. Cambridge.

1968a. 'Post-Restoration developments: schools in the county [Leicestershire], 1660–1700'. In B. Simon (ed.), 1968.

1968b. 'Town estates and schools in the sixteenth and early seventeenth centuries'. In B. Simon (ed.), 1968.

1968c. 'Was there a charity school movement? The Leicestershire evidence'. In B. Simon (ed.), 1968.

Simpson, G. G., 1973. *Scottish handwriting, 1150–1650*. Edinburgh.

Simpson, I. J., 1947. *Education in Aberdeenshire before 1872*. London.

Sinclair, J., 1826. *Analysis of the statistical account of Scotland*, pt 2. London.

Skipp, V., 1978. *Crisis and development*. Cambridge.

Smart, R. N., 1974. 'Some observations on the provinces of the Scottish universities, 1560–1850'. In Barrow (ed.), 1974.

Smith, A., 1977. *The wealth of nations*, ed. A. Skinner. Harmondsworth.

Smith, J. A., 1970. 'Some eighteenth-century ideas of Scotland'. In Phillipson and Mitchison (eds.), 1970.

Smith, J. I. (ed.), 1972. *Selected justiciary cases, 1624–50*, vol. 2. Edinburgh.

Smith, R. M., 1983. 'Some thoughts on hereditary and proprietary rights in land under customary law in thirteenth- and early fourteenth-century England'. *Law and History Review*, 1: 95–128.

Smollett, T., 1981. *The adventures of Roderick Random*. Oxford. First published 1748.

Smout, T. C., 1958–9. 'The foreign trade of Dumfries and Kircudbrightshire, 1672–1696'. *Transactions of the Dumfries and Galloway Natural History and Antiquarian Society*, 3rd series, 37: 36–47.

1963. 'The trade of East Lothian at the end of the seventeenth century'. *Transactions of the East Lothian Antiquarian and Field Naturalists Society*, 9: 67–78.

1967. 'Lead mining in Scotland, 1650–1850'. In Payne (ed.), 1967.

1970. 'Problems of modernisation in multi-sectoral economies: the role of non-economic factors in Scottish growth in the eighteenth century'. *Fifth International Congress of Economic History, Leningrad*. Moscow.

1972. *A history of the Scottish people, 1560–1830*. 2nd edn, Glasgow.

1980. 'Centre and periphery in history, with some thoughts on Scotland as a case study'. *Journal of Common Market Studies*, 18: 256–71.

1982. 'Born again at Cambuslang: new evidence on popular religion and literacy in eighteenth-century Scotland'. *Past & Present*, 97: 114–27.

Smout, T. C., and Fenton, A., 1965. 'Scottish agriculture before the improvers – an exploration'. *Agricultural History Review*, 13: 73–93.

Snell, K. D. M., 1981. 'Agricultural seasonal unemployment, the standard of living, and women's work in the south and east, 1690–1860'. *Economic History Review*, 2nd series, 34: 407–37.

Solé, J., 1973. 'Lecture et classes populaires à Grenoble au XVIIIᵉ siècle. Le témoinage des inventaires après décès'. In *Images du peuple au dix-huitième siècle*. Paris.

Somerville, A., 1951. *Autobiography of a working man*. Edinburgh.

Spedding, J. (ed.), 1868. *The letters and the life of Francis Bacon*, vol. 3. London.

Spufford, M., 1974. *Contrasting communities*. Cambridge.

1981. *Small books and pleasant histories. Popular fiction and its readership in seventeenth-century England*. London.

Statistical account of Scotland, 21 vols., ed. J. Sinclair. Edinburgh.

Stephens, W. B., 1977. 'Illiteracy in the provincial towns, 1640–1870'. In Reeder (ed.), 1977.

Stone, L., 1964. 'The educational revolution in England, 1560–1640'. *Past & Present*, 28: 41–80.

1969. 'Literacy and education in England, 1640–1900'. *Past & Present*, 42: 69–139.

(ed.), 1976. *Schooling and society*. Baltimore.

Strauss, G., 1976. 'The state of pedagogical theory *c.*1530: what Protestant reformers knew about education'. In Stone (ed.), 1976.

1978. *Luther's house of learning. Indoctrination of the young in the German Reformation*. London.

Stuart, M. C., 1976. 'The capital of the stewartry of Fife'. *The Stewarts*, 15: 24–6.

Supple, B. E., 1959. *Commercial crisis and change in England, 1600–1642*. Cambridge.

Swinburne, H., 1677. *A treatise of testaments and last wills*. London.

Thirsk, J. (ed.), 1967. *The agrarian history of England and Wales*. Vol. 4, 1500–1640. Cambridge.

1970. 'Seventeenth-century agriculture and social change'. *Agricultural History Review*, 18 (supplement): 148–77.

1974. 'New crops and their diffusion: tobacco growing in seventeenth-century England'. In Chalklin and Havinden (eds.), 1974.

Thirsk, J., and Cooper, J. P. (eds.), 1972. *Seventeenth-century economic documents*. Oxford.

Thomas, D. M., 1979. 'Printing privileges in Spain'. *Publishing History*, 5: 105–26.

Thomas, K., 1973. *Religion and the decline of magic*. Harmondsworth.

Thompson, E. P., 1967. 'Time, work-discipline, and industrial capitalism'. *Past & Present*, 38: 56–97.

1971. 'The moral economy of the English crowd in the eighteenth century'. *Past & Present*, 50: 76–136.

1974. 'Patrician society, plebeian culture'. *Journal of Social History*, 7: 382–405.

1976. 'The grid of inheritance: a comment'. In Goody, Thirsk and Thompson (eds.), 1976.

1977. *Whigs and hunters*. Harmondsworth.

1978. 'Eighteenth-century English society: class struggle without class?' *Social History*, 3: 133–65.

Thompson, F. G., 1972–4. 'Technical education in the Highlands and Islands'. *Transactions of the Gaelic Society of Inverness*, 48: 244–338.

Tilly, C., 1973. 'Population and pedagogy in France'. *History of Education Quarterly*, 13: 113–28.

Tilly, L. A., 1979. 'Individual lives and family strategies in the French rural proletariat'. *Journal of Family History*, 4: 137–52.

Tolstoy, L., 1978. *Anna Karenina*. Harmondsworth.

Tranter, N. L., 1974. 'The Reverend Andrew Urquhart and the social structure of Portpatrick in 1832'. *Scottish Studies*, 18: 39–62.

1981. 'The labour supply, 1780–1860'. In Floud and McCloskey (eds.), 1981.

Trenard, L., 1977. 'Histoire des sciences de l'éducation (période moderne)'. *Revue Historique*, 257: 429–72.

Urban, W., 1977. 'La connaissance de l'écriture en Petite Pologne dans la seconde moitié du XVIe siècle'. *Przeglad Historyczny*, 68: 257. [French summary of an article in Polish]

Van Roey, J., 1968. 'De correlate tussen het sociale-beroepsmilieu en de god-sdienstkeuze te Antwerpen op het einde der XVIe eeuw'. In *Sources de l'Histoire Religieuse de la Belgique*. 1968. Louvain.

Van Uytven, R., 1968. 'Invloeden van het sociale en professionele milieu op de godsdienstheuze: Leuven en Edingen'. In *Sources de l'Histoire Religieuse de la Belgique*. 1968. Louvain.

Van der Woude, A. M., 1980. 'De alfabetisering'. In *Algemene Geschiedenis der Nederlanden*, vol. 7. Haarlem.

Vigo, G., 1972–3. 'Istruzione e societa' nel regno Italico. Il caso di Vigevano (1806–1814)'. *Bolletino della Societa' Pavese di Storia Patria*, 22–3: 125–39.

Vogler, B., 1975. 'La politique scolaire entre Rhin et Moselle: l'exemple du duché de Deux Ponts (1556–1619)'. *Francia*, 3: 236–320.

 1976. 'La politique scolaire entre Rhin et Moselle: l'example du duché de Deux Ponts (1556–1619)'. *Francia*, 4: 287–364.

Vovelle, M., 1975. 'Y a-t-il eu une révolution culturelle au XVIIIe siècle? A propos de l'éducation populaire en Provence'. *Revue d'Histoire Moderne et Contemporaine*, 22: 89–141.

Vries, J. de, 1975. 'Peasant demand patterns and economic development: Friesland, 1550–1750'. In Parker and Jones (eds.), 1975.

Walter, J., and Wrightson, K., 1976. 'Dearth and the social order in early modern England'. *Past & Present*, 71: 22–42.

Warden, A. J., 1880–5. *Angus or Forfarshire. The land and people, descriptive and historical*, 5 vols. Dundee.

Webb, R. K., 1954. 'Literacy among the working classes in nineteenth-century Scotland'. *Scottish Historical Review*, 33: 100–14.

 1955. *The British working class reader, 1790–1848*. London.

Weisser, M. R., 1976. *The peasants of the Montes: the roots of rural rebellion in Spain*. London.

West, E. G., 1973. 'Resource allocation and growth in early nineteenth century British education'. In Drake (ed.), 1973.

 1975. *Education and the industrial revolution*. London.

 1978. 'Literacy and the industrial revolution'. *Economic History Review*, 2nd series, 31: 369–83.

Westminster Review, vol. 7. 1827.

Whyte, I. D., 1978. 'Scottish historical geography – a review'. *Scottish Geographical Magazine*, 94: 4–23.

 1979a. *Agriculture and society in seventeenth-century Scotland*. Edinburgh.

 1979b. 'Written leases and their impact on Scottish agriculture in the seventeenth century'. *Agricultural History Review*, 27: 1–9.

Whyte, I. D., and Whyte, K. A., 1981. 'Sources for Scottish historical geography. An introductory guide'. *Historical Geography Research Series*, 6.

 1983. 'Some aspects of the structure of rural society in seventeenth-century lowland Scotland'. In Devine and Dickson (eds.), 1983.

Wilkie, J., 1919. *Historic Musselburgh*. Edinburgh.

Willan, T. S., 1938. *The English coasting trade, 1600–1750*. Manchester.

Williams, P., 1978. *The Tudor regime*. London.

Willis, A. J., 1968. *A calendar of Southampton apprenticeship registers, 1609–1740*. Southampton.

Wills and inventories from the registry at Durham, pt III. 1906. Durham.

Wills and inventories from the registry at Durham, pt IV. 1929. Durham.

Wisniowski, E., 1973. 'The parochial school system in Poland towards the close of the middle ages'. *Acta Poloniae Historica,* 27: 29–43.

Wisniowski, E., and Litak, S., 1974. 'L'enseignement paroissial en Pologne jusqu'au XVIIIe siècle à la lumière des plus récentes recherches'. *Miscellanea Historiae Ecclesiasticae,* 5: 320–3.

Withers, C., 1982. 'Education and anglicization: the policy of the SSPCK towards Gaelic in education, 1709–1825'. *Scottish Studies,* 26: 37–56.

Withrington, D. J., 1963. 'Schools in the presbytery of Haddington in the 17th century'. *Transactions of the East Lothian Antiquarian and Field Naturalists Society,* 9: 90–111.

  1965. 'Lists of schoolmasters teaching Latin, 1690'. *Miscellany of the Scottish History Society,* 10:121–42.

  1970. 'Education and society in the eighteenth century'. In Phillipson and Mitchison (eds.), 1970.

Withrington, D. J., and Grant, I. R. (eds.), 1975–9. *Statistical account of Scotland.* Wakefield.

Wollstonecraft, M., 1975. *Vindication of the rights of woman,* ed. M. B. Kramick. Harmondsworth.

Wormald, J., 1981. *Court, kirk, and community. Scotland, 1470–1625.* London.

Wrightson, K., 1982. *English society, 1580–1680.* London.

Wrigley, E. A., 1978. 'Parasite or stimulus: the town in a pre-industrial economy'. In Abrams and Wrigley (eds.), 1978.

Wrigley, E. A., and Schofield, R. S., 1981. *The population history of England, 1541–1871: a reconstruction.* London.

Wyczanski, A., 1974. 'L'alphabétisation et structure sociale en Pologne au XVIe siècle'. *Annales ESC,* 29: 705–13.

Yasumoto, M., 1973. 'Urbanization and population in an English town: Leeds during the industrial revolution'. *Keio Economic Studies,* 10: 61–94.

Young, A., 1770. *A six-months tour through the north of England,* vol. 3. London.

Young, R. T., 1931–3. 'A Borgue covenant, 1638'. *Transactions of the Dumfries and Galloway Natural History and Antiquarian Society,* 3rd series, 18: 402–5.

Index

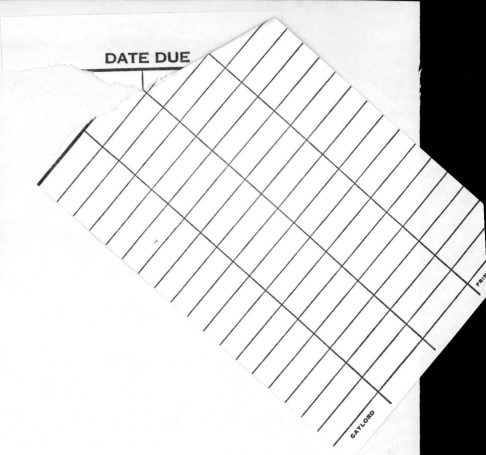